WORKERS AND INCENTIVES

CONTRIBUTIONS TO ECONOMIC ANALYSIS

140

NORTH-HOLLAND PUBLISHING COMPANY
AMSTERDAM · NEW YORK · OXFORD

WORKERS AND INCENTIVES

MURAT R. SERTEL
Boğaziçi University, Istanbul

with the collaboration of

TAMER BAŞAR
CARL CHIARELLA
YVO M.I. DIRICKX
PAUL R. KLEINDORFER
HASAN SELBUZ

1982

NORTH-HOLLAND PUBLISHING COMPANY
AMSTERDAM · NEW YORK · OXFORD

ISBN: 0 444 86360 5

Publishers:

NORTH-HOLLAND PUBLISHING COMPANY
AMSTERDAM · NEW YORK · OXFORD

Sole distributors for the U.S.A. and Canada:

ELSEVIER SCIENCE PUBLISHING COMPANY, INC.
52 VANDERBILT AVENUE
NEW YORK, N.Y. 10017

Library of Congress Cataloging in Publication Data

Sertel, Murat R.
Workers and incentives.

(Contributions to economic analysis ; 140)
Includes index.
1. Producer cooperatives--Addresses, essays, lectures. 2. Employees' representation in management--Addresses, essays, lectures. 3. Incentives in industry--Addresses, essays, lectures. I. Title. II. Series.
HD3121.S45 338.6 81-22515
ISBN 0-444-86360-5 AACR2

PRINTED IN THE NETHERLANDS

Introduction to the series

This series consists of a number of hitherto unpublished studies, which are introduced by the editors in the belief that they represent fresh contributions to economic science.

The term "economic analysis" as used in the title of the series has been adopted because it covers both the activities of the theoretical economist and the research worker.

Although the analytical methods used by the various contributors are not the same, they are nevertheless conditioned by the common origin of their studies, namely theoretical problems encountered in practical research. Since for this reason, business cycle research and national accounting, research work on behalf of economic policy, and problems of planning are the main sources of the subjects dealt with, they necessarily determine the manner of approach adopted by the authors. Their methods tend to be "practical" in the sense of not being too far remote from application to actual economic conditions. In addition they are quantitative rather than qualitative.

It is the hope of the editors that the publication of these studies will help to stimulate the exchange of scientific information and to reinforce international cooperation in the field of economics.

The Editors

Contents

Preface

This book collects some of the work which – to put it in the utter vernacular – "me and my buddies" have been doing during the past few years in the neighboring areas of Economic Design and Comparative Political Economy, from which we have derived a growing interest in workers' self-management.

In a preface, if anywhere, one might indulge in a bit of intellectual history. This whole thing started when Paul Kleindorfer and I met at the end of the Sixties as the latest intake of junior faculty members at the Sloan School, M.I.T. We were both finishing our dissertations then, and Paul took kind interest in mine, where I made incentives and informational imperfections explicit in what was otherwise a thesis (Sertel, 1971) extending normal equilibrium existence results.[1] Little did I then know that the interaction of incentives and information was so dear to the heart of Paul Kleindorfer, and for how long I was to have the pleasure of his intellectual comradery in pursuing principles of economic design through incentives under various informational circumstances. Some of our joint work in this area appears as Chapters 4, 6, 9 and the Appendix of this book. (See also Kleindorfer and Sertel, 1980.)

Meanwhile, in 1974 I had the good fortune of coming across the interest of Yvo Dirickx in Comparative Political Economy, which we first approached in Dirickx and Sertel (1979) and then in a series of papers with the sound of "comparative political economy in a *nutshell*". Of these the "nutshell" most befitting of the present context appears here as Chapter 3. (See also the "nutshells" of Dirickx and Sertel, 1978a, 1978b.)

It is through the exercise of these nutshells that the idea of a worker–partnership market and how it would bring economic common sense to an otherwise somewhat strangely behaving labor-managed firm occurred to me in 1977, while I was a guest of the Technion (Haifa, Israel). The "rehabilitation" of the labor-managed firm through the operation of this market was

[1] The extensions were enabled by fortified fixed point theorems of Prakash and Sertel (1974a) in topological semivector spaces. For some similar extensions see Prakash (1971), and for further applications see Prakash and Sertel (1974b) and an account of the latter in Ichiischi (1982). For more on topological semivector spaces see Prakash and Sertel (1976).

explained many times to many audiences since. I should have thought it to be old hat by now, but my coauthors in this book tell me that I ought to record it here, and the work of many of my other colleagues writing on labor-managed firms or economies seems to corroborate the need to do so. Hence, Chapter 2.

Enter Politicus. At the turn of the year from 1977 into 1978, the government in Turkey changed hands from the pact of the Right to a mild Left led by Prime Minister Bülent Ecevit. A Professor of Economics, our colleague Kenan Bulutoğlu, became Minister of Enterprises – meaning state enterprises, which comprised close to half of Turkey's industry. Ecevit and Bulutoğlu were all for serious workers' participation in this sector, and we all burnt quite a bit of midnight oil, separately and together, to design legislation to advance effective workers' participation at a healthy pace in the public sector.[2] It was in this period that I approached the teacher – student team of Tamer Başar and Hasan Selbuz, who were easily convinced that the theory of workers' enterprises, while far from electrical engineering, was interesting from a game-theoretic viewpoint, and we wrote such a theory (Başar, Selbuz and Sertel, 1978) as a study commissioned by Bulutoğlu's ministry. Written up as papers in English, part of this study appears here as Chapters 7 and 8.

All of the work mentioned up to here was static and essentially built in a world of certainty. With Işık İnselbağ and then with Alfred Steinherr, we tackled the finance of workers' enterprises under uncertainty (see İnselbağ and Sertel, 1979, and Sertel and Steinherr, 1979, the latter of which was extended by Onanç, 1979). While none of this work appears here, Chapter 10 presents one of a series of studies by Carl Chiarella and myself investigating the dynamic behavior of variously designed political economies (see also Chiarella and Sertel, 1979, 1980) offering a dynamic "nutshell" extending Chapter 3.

So much for intellectual history. Now I have many thanks to express. First, to all my coauthors for the immense fun of working with them and for their kindness in accepting my strange hours and places of work (i.e. fun).

[2] Bulutoğlu appointed an International Council of Advisers consisting of Branko Horvat, Paul Kleindorfer, Jaroslav Vanek and myself and soon Gerard Kester and Henk Thomas joined, with Mehmet Uca helping us all along. Then, during the final stages when Ecevit himself got directly involved and the midnight oil burned most, my advisory role became addressed to the Prime Minister.

The legislation we designed was virtually vetoed in September 1979, by a minority of "independent" ministers, despite the overwhelming support of the rest of the cabinet. The designing activity and the political career of the bill have nevertheless left behind a valuable experience from which a next try is bound to benefit.

Also, my thanks to Birol Akmeriç for his painstaking work in preparing the index. Secondly, to Jenny, who loves to keep the workshop going despite its pronounced spatio-temporal irregularities. Thirdly, to the institutions which kindly allowed me to carry on: the Sloan School at M.I.T. (special thanks to Zenon Zannetos); the International Institute of Management in West Berlin (special thanks to the late Gerd Brandt and to Walter Goldberg); the Technion in Haifa (special thanks to Giora Teltsch, Uri BenZion and Abraham Subotnik); the Mathematics Department of the Middle East Technical University in Ankara (special thanks to my teacher Cahit Arf and Mehmet Orhon); the Applied Mathematics Division of the Marmara Research Institute (special thanks to Erdoğan Şuhubi and Tamer Başar); l'Université Catholique de Louvain (special thanks to Alfred Steinherr and Jacques Drèze). Finally, thanks to the wise and sincere example of three institutions of self-management: Branko Horvat, my teacher Evsey Domar, and my parents.

M.R.S.

Istanbul
August 1980

References

Başar, T., H. Selbuz and M.R. Sertel (1978) "Özyönetilen İşletme Kuramı", T.B.T.A.K. Tatbiki Matematik Ünitesi, Teknik Rapor No. 43.

Chiarella, C. and M.R. Sertel (1979) "The Dynamic Inefficiency of Competitive Capitalism", Working Paper No. 7901, Institut des Sciences Economiques, Université Catholique de Louvain.

Chiarella, C. and M.R. Sertel (1980) "Some Dynamic Comparisons of Competitive Capitalism and Co-operative Labor-Management", paper presented at the Second International Conference on the Economics of Workers' Self-Management, Istanbul, 1980.

Dirickx, Y.M.I. and M.R. Sertel (1978a) "Capitalism, Communism and Labor-Management Under Constant Returns to Scale", Working Paper 78-1, European Institute for Advanced Studies in Management, Brussels.

Dirickx, Y.M.I. and M.R. Sertel (1978b) "Comparative Political Economy of Capitalism, Communism, Slavery, and Colonialism in a Nutshell", *Recherches Economiques de Louvain*, 44, no. 3.

Dirickx, Y.M.I. and M.R. Sertel (1979) "Class Conflict and Fairness in Democratic Capitalism", *Public Choice*, 34, no. 1.

Ichiishi, T. (1980) "Non-cooperation and Cooperation", in: M. Deistler *et al.*, eds., *Games, Economic Dynamics, and Time Series Analysis* – A Symposium In Memorium Oskar Morgenstern (Physica-Verlag, Wien).

İnselbağ, I. and M.R. Sertel (1979) "The Workers' Enterprise Under Uncertainty in a Mixed Economy", *Economic Analysis and Workers' Management*, 13.

Kleindorfer, P.R. and M.R. Sertel (1980) "Labor-Management and Codetermination in Regulated Monopolies", in: P.R. Kleindorfer and B.M. Mitchel, eds., *Regulated Industries and Public Enterprise* (Lexington Books, Lexington, Mass.).

Onanç, H. (1979) "Incentives and Design of Efficient Institutions in an Uncertain Environment", unpublished MA thesis, Faculty of Administrative Sciences, Boğaziçi University.

Prakash, P. (1971) "Foundations of Systems for Decision, Planning, Control and Social/Economic Analysis", unpublished Ph.D. thesis, M.I.T.

Prakash, P. and M.R. Sertel (1974a) "Topological Semivector Spaces: Convexity and Fixed Point Theory", *Semigroup Forum*, 9, no. 2 (MR 51, no. 11063).

Prakash, P. and M.R. Sertel (1974b) "On the Existence of Noncooperative Equilibria in Social Systems", Preprint I/74-27, International Institute of Management, West Berlin.

Prakash, P. and M.R. Sertel (1976) "Hyperspaces of Topological Vector Spaces: Their Embedding in Topological Vector Spaces," *Proceedings of the American Mathematical Society*, 61, no. 1.

Sertel, M.R. (1971) "Elements of Equilibrium Methods for Social Analysis", unpublished Ph.D. thesis, M.I.T.

Sertel, M.R. and A. Steinherr (1979) "Information, Incentives, and the Design of Efficient Institutions", Working Paper, Institut des Sciences Economiques, Université Catholique de Louvain.

CHAPTER 1

Introduction

MURAT R. SERTEL

The essays which form this book only briefly introduce themselves, and there is nothing more fitting for the book itself than to follow suit. This introduction will do two things. The second of these is to give a preview of the coming chapters. The first is to present their common notions, framework, and method in approaching Economic Design and Comparative Political Economy.

In approaching an economic design problem we start by spelling out the *basic data* given to us. In the traditional fashion of economic theory, these include a *technology* (represented by a production function) and the *preferences* (represented by utility functions) of the participating agents commanding the supply of various productive factors. So much specifies what might be regarded as an *economic presystem*, lacking as yet the rules governing how the agents are to be remunerated for their respective contributions to production, and hence missing the motivating element which sets the presystem into motion as a system. By adjoining to it the man-made element of an *incentive scheme*, we pass from an economic presystem to an *economic system*. In economic design problems we focus on the incentive scheme as the key element.

Now, having started with one or another set of basic data, the design of an economic system may be gauged to serve various alternative purposes. A typical purpose would be to flatter the interests of some subset of the participating agents, e.g. the coalition of all participants, or the subcoalition of those contributing a particular productive input (say labor), or the complement of the latter coalition. As a technician, the economist may very well set out to design incentive schemes to best suit the interests of one or another client, and everybody is free to commission their own economic designer.

But not everyone commissioning an economic design gets to institute it. Some coalitions may enjoy the authority to institute their chosen designs while others are left with the fate of having to live with them. This brings us to the genuinely political question of wherein the *authority* resides to install the rules and regulations simultaneously defining the incentives governing economic behavior and the distribution of the consequent output. A technically competent economist who can figure out best designs for various interest groups may now turn to Comparative Political Economy and inquire as a scientist into the foundations of alternative political economies and their relative performance from the viewpoint of the interests in question. To understand Political Economy, though, fathoming the "technical" subject of Economic Design is likely to be useful if not requisite.

Two types of constraint, noteworthy at our present stage, impose themselves in designing an incentive scheme. One of these applies directly to the incentive schemes which may be chosen for implementation, limiting them to one or another subspace of the theoretically conceivable space of incentive schemes. The other is dictated by what one might regard as the laws of Economics to which the designer has to bow in computing the economic behavior and consequent performance in terms of output and distribution which are to result from instituting a given incentive scheme. It is worth examining the nature of these two types of constraint in some more detail, as we turn to do right away.

Abstractly specified, an *incentive scheme* is nothing but a family of *incentive functions* indexed by the agents given in an economic presystem, each incentive function (addressed to a particular agent) determining the economic consequences of the agents' behavior, considered all together, for the agent indexing that function. So if A is the set of agents whose preferences are given among the basic data describing the economic presystem from which we set out, and if X describes the set of theoretically possible joint behaviors $x=\{x_\alpha | \alpha \in A\}$ of the agents with x_α denoting the behavior of a generic agent $\alpha \in A$, an incentive scheme would be any family $r=\{r_\alpha | \alpha \in A\}$ of incentive functions $r_\alpha: X \to Y_\alpha$, for suitable reward spaces $Y_\alpha (\alpha \in A)$. In our case the rewards to each agent are real-valued and, in fact, expressed in units of the output $y=f(x)$ achieved, through a production function $f: X \to R$ representing the technology of our economic presystem, when the agents exhibit the behavior $x \in X$. Now if in fact the rewards r_α are to be paid out as promised by an incentive scheme r, then the incentive scheme has to obey the *feasibility* constraint, expressed as the functional inequality of $\int_A r_\alpha \leqslant y$, to the effect that the sum total of rewards to be distributed by the incentive scheme not exceed that which is made available for distribution by the economic behavior incited. So the Napoleons cannot distribute to their generals estates in both Russia and Italy if either of these remains beyond the frontiers they are to extend. This feasibility constraint is perhaps the economically most obvious limitation on the space of otherwise possible incentive schemes.

But speaking of the military, or for that matter the clerical or other orders whose exhibiting the mundane aspirations of the ordinary mortal might belie their adherence to the very purpose for which they are supposed to be present, offers us a good example of the *legitimacy* constraint on the space of incentive schemes which may be employed in an economic design. After all, one may be hard put to pay in gold to generals per enemy casualty – foreign or domestic – or to priests, per converted infidel, at least overtly. To get less touchy, one may be unable to pay sexual or racial or other minorities lower wages, not because they are difficult to distinguish from the rest of the population, but because of legitimacy considerations, whether or not these are legally binding.

A third type of restriction on the incentive schemes one is able to implement derives from *informational* considerations. If the abstractly specified "economic behavior" x_α of an agent is sufficiently costly to observe and measure, as when it amounts to the contribution of productive "effort" or "managerial wisdom", one will have to remunerate some of the agents on the basis of outputs rather than inputs. If the outputs are joint and economically indecipherable into individually gained results, the economic designer is led to incentive schemes based on sharing a jointly produced output which is easy to observe, measure and legally contest within regular commercial law.

Like feasibility, the informational constraint on the space of implementable incentive schemes is an inherent one indigenous to the design of incentives and economic systems. The legitimacy constraint on how people may be rewarded also presents a very real, if not inherent, boundary to economic design. So much runs through all but one of the direct limitations on incentive schemes which circumscribe the economic designs one may wish to implement. Inasmuch as we get to design only a small part of a large economy at a time, we also have to worry about the *external opportunities* offered to the agents we started out counting as available in the presystem on which our designs were based. In the long run, if not also within economically pressing time horizons, people are mobile from one economic system to another in the pursuit of greater personal advantage. The individual costs of mobility and the timespans beyond which they cease to be binding describe the limits beyond which a fallback "reserve utility" cannot be ignored by an economic designer who may otherwise wish to defy members of his economy compensation for foregone opportunities of membership elsewhere.

Whatever the direct restraints on the implementable incentive schemes, the economic designer proposing an incentive scheme within his given boundaries to serve a certain purpose will have to see (and maybe even show) just how it is that this purpose will in fact be served by instituting his proposed scheme. This requires an analysis of what sort of economic behavior the proposed incentives will impart to the agents they address. For whatever behavior they settle at in response to these incentives, it is this behavior which will determine the output and its distribution. Here the economic designer faces, not direct constraints limiting the space from which implementable incentive schemes may be chosen, but the very constraint of the laws of Economics, which are to tell him what economic behavior will characterize an equilibrium response of the populus of economic agents at hand to any of his proposed designs. This may be likened to the bridge-designer facing the laws of Physics, except that we know less about *workers and incentives* than, say, about billiard balls and inclined planes. What may a collectivity of economic agents be expected to do when subjected to various incentives?

The way we approach this question in the coming chapters is by imagining a game to be defined among the agents in question when an incentive scheme is imposed on them. Given their preferences, the agents may settle on one or another solution as accords to one or another game-theoretic solution concept. We have taken three such solution concepts as elementary: the noncooperative Nash and Stackelberg, and the cooperative. By derivation from these we have also constructed further solution concepts and applied them in the analysis of how the agents may respond to an incentive scheme. Often we have analyzed this response in terms of more than one type of solution to the game defined by the incentives. This seems especially advisable in the absence of empirically tested laws of Economics in this key domain as to which solution concept is most realistic under which circumstances. Should the types of solution we have used prove to be unrealistic, our method might nevertheless withstand the winds of much-needed progress to indicate which game-theoretic solution concepts can be used most fruitfully in the analysis of the various relevant categories of economic game.[1]

Our method here amounts to comparing economic designs for a given presystem in terms of the equilibrium behavior and consequent systemic performance under their respective incentive schemes. The equilibrium behavior of the agents under an incentive scheme is interpreted as a game-theoretic solution of the sorts mentioned above. With which type of solution the economic designs are compared again also reflects the analyst's perception of a political aspect of economic systems. For the agents in command of a certain factor of production may or may not enjoy the authority of leadership in the sense of a von Stackelberg solution, and the comparisons of economic designs are quite sensitive to this politically telling aspect of economic interaction. So, in these solutions either a group of agents act as von Stackelberg leader, or no one is given a leadership role. In the latter case the agents either behave noncooperatively, or they cooperate. And, when they cooperate, side-payments may or may not be used. In each case the equilibrium behavior of the agents gives rise to equilibrium values of a whole array of economic magnitudes, such as input and output levels, factor productivities, relative prices, and income and welfare distribution. These are tabulated in various ways to give clear rankings between the economic systems compared. The ranking in terms of some of these economically relevant magnitudes is sensitive to the particularities of the economic presystem with which one is dealing, and such dependencies of our comparisons on critical parameters of the presystem are clearly displayed.

[1]A problem with empirical research in Economics has been its almost total preoccupation with the past, analyzing historical data of economic systems already seen. The comparative analysis of even such systems has been hampered by the expectable problems posed by the practical difficulties in commensurateness of data pertaining to distant points in space–time. To take stock, we know very little as economists about systems yet to be designed, and will have to make do with our ignorance in this respect as long as we insist that Economics is not an experimental science.

Luckily, the trickiness of experimentation in Economics has failed to completely terrorize and pacify all economists. Charles S. Plott and Vernon L. Smith have led some research in this area which may soon offer extremely pertinent results for use in Economic Design. In this research many game-theoretic solution concepts (including some which we do not use in this book) were tested in experiments designed to reveal which of them best approximated the real outcomes of variously designed economic games (see, for example, Smith 1979 and Plott, 1981). This book, it might be hoped, could further encourage such activity by suggesting and emphasizing just how much it matters which type of solution may be most trusted to characterize the outcome of an economic design.

In the process of our comparisons we run through many versions of capitalistic and many versions of workers' enterprises, and we let these coexist and compete in a mixed economy. Sometimes the capital inputs are decided by a central authority, e.g. the state representing communal interests, sometimes by a capitalist, and sometimes by a workers' council. Throughout, the analysis looks essentially at a world of certainty, although sometimes far-reaching extensions of our results to a world with uncertainty are made quite clear, and all the way up to the final chapter the analysis is static.

I take the blame (or credit?) for the static certainty flavor of the studies that follow. For my coauthors in the coming chapters are all known for their interest and competence in dealing with either dynamic phenomena or the lack of certainty, or both. My attitude has been to work as follows until one sees where and how a dynamic or uncertain world would make a genuine difference. After all, what often looks like a dynamic analysis under uncertainty turns out to be easily reduced to a static analysis applied to a world of certainty. At this point, after all the work that follows, and some more, I believe that we all have finer conjectures about the genuine effects of either uncertainty or a dynamic setting on the results obtained so far.

We have begun to drift into a preview of the rest of the book. The chapters which form the rest of the book are each quite self-contained. So the reader would lose little by reading them in some other order than that in which they are presented. They have, nevertheless, been arranged in an order which I feel is best pursued, although I should like to share with the reader my remaining suspicion that an ordering placing the present Chapter 4 right after this Introduction might have worked just as well.

Chapter 2 is where it is for a number of reasons. First, workers' enterprises (and/or labor-managed firms) summon our continual interest in this book, and the subsequent chapters were extremely brief in their definition of these firms. Chapter 2 tries to make up for this by juxtaposing the forming rules of a workers' enterprise with those of a capitalistic firm and elaborating on these. But, further, it spells out the idea of a worker–partnership market in its role as a "stock market" for workers' enterprises. This market rids the "labor-managed firm" of Ward and Vanek of its two well-known but otherwise nonexistent maladies indicated by Ward himself and by Furubotn and Pejovich, namely the backward-bending short-run supply curve and the chronic underinvestment syndrome, respectively. The adjustments of firm size determining the long-run equilibrium relative sizes of capitalistic and workers' enterprises, worked out further and used in subsequent chapters, rests on an understanding of the "Rehabilitation of the

Labor-Managed Firm", accomplished through the workers' enterprises of Chapter 2 as equipped with their worker–partnership market.

As an extension of Dirickx and Sertel (1978a, b), Chapter 3 places the rest of the book within a broad perspective of a "nutshell" of feasible economic designs. It identifies and fully compares three kinds of capitalistic and five kinds of workers' enterprise within a long-run "nutshell" of feasible economic systems. Apart from its concentration on workers' enterprises, at the expense of ignoring various sorts of communism, slavery, and colonialism examined in Dirickx and Sertel (1978b), it compares economic systems at their indigenous levels of utilization of capital goods rather than at a given uniform level. Chapter 3 forms a framework for what comes after Chapter 4.

Chapter 4 is the first chapter in which the various direct limitations on the space of economic designs were explicitly taken as constraints and an optimal design found by explicit use of a game-theoretic solution. In particular, the study considers the case where observing effort input may be too costly and shares in output present a form of incentives which a profit-maximizing designer may be wise to assign to the workers. If the supervising or monitoring of labor is cheap, workers may instead be paid a price (wage) per unit of their respective inputs. In either sort of informational setting (supporting sharecropping or waging) the profit-maximizing incentive scheme is computed and consequent economic behavior and performance are comparatively displayed, appealing to noncooperative behavior among the workers and von Stackelberg leadership of the agent providing capital goods and commissioning the economic designer. When the workers behave cooperatively among themselves, the analysis holds *mutatis mutandis*, and similarly for a broad class of cases where uncertainty affects output.

Chapter 5 is merely a note which pursues further a question answered in part by Alkan and Sertel (1981). The question asks what one might do in sharecropping if the individual characteristics (regarding preferences and effectiveness in production) of the workers of Chapter 4 are private to the workers themselves, although they may also be known to the "landlord" designing incentives. It indicates the advantages to all which may be reaped by allowing the workers to pretend to be other than themselves subject to a commitment to perform according to their declared characteristics.

Now sharecropping is a form of economic organization often resorted to, in agriculture for millenia, in partnerships such as law firms or consulting enterprises or research ventures, where output is clearly seen but individual contributions are difficult to observe and purchase per well-defined unit.

The value added by labor, i.e. sales minus the cost of all factors of production other than labor, is also a kind of net output, and it forms the total income of the worker–partners gained from a workers' enterprise. So, in such an enterprise too the workers share a type of output. In Economics we have a well-developed equilibrium theory of economies which function through prices, but we lack an equilibrium analysis for economies where incentives have to be specified as shares in one or another jointly produced output. Chapter 6 provides some fundamental mathematical results of partial equilibrium analysis which one can hardly avoid using in studying economies where certain inputs are genuine unobservables but their joint outputs are easily seen. It studies equilibrium behavior and performance in sharecropping, establishing the continuity and monotonicity of various economically interesting functions for the requisite equilibrium analysis here. This chapter is far from necessary for an understanding of what follows it in this book, but the researcher who wishes to go beyond may very well benefit from it.

The next two chapters, Chapters 7 and 8, examine various workers' enterprises in a mixed economy where they compete with capitalistic firms. Building upon Chapters 2, 3 and 4, they each use the worker–partnership market to establish the long-run relative sizes of various types of enterprises, they explicitly pay attention to feasibility constraints in the design of incentive schemes, and they make a clear separation between the case where workers' contributions are economically observable from a center and where they are not. Chapter 7 deals with the case where these contributions are costlessly observable and analyzes workers' enterprises which institute differential wages for worker–partners of different characteristics. It obtains equilibrium outcomes for both capitalistic enterprises and for two types of workers' enterprise where internal wages may be applied, one of the latter imposing ceilings on effort contributed. Chapter 8 looks at the same picture with a filter which makes workers' efforts unobservable. The various sorts of worker are allowed either to cooperate within their groups or not, while the groups themselves either cooperate among themselves or not, and in each case the outcome is compared with that in the rival capitalistic firm. In either case the game-theoretic solution concepts used are explicit and the worker–partners in a workers' enterprise always share the value added by labor.

The sharing of the value added by labor is the principle of economic design studied in Chapter 9. Here, especially, solution concepts are juxtaposed, with a distinction throughout between contributors of various sorts of labor and capital goods, each partly allowed in turn to play the role of von Stackelberg leader. The results are tabulated and compared under von Stackelberg, noncooperative and cooperative solutions. A nutshell of less simple geometry – which takes a while to establish – affords itself in this extension of earlier chapters allowing many kinds of labor to be effective in production. Political and informational aspects of economic design reach a full-blown picture in this chapter where workers' enterprises continue to come up as efficient but now also find a new identification in a spectrum of designs for political economies.

The efficiency property of workers' enterprises pervades throughout this book in rivalry with their capitalistic counterparts. Lest this should be thought to be due to the essentially static analysis up to the final chapter, Chapter 10 returns to the "nutshell" of Chapter 3 and re-establishes much of it, including efficiency comparisons, in a dynamic setting with savings and investment explicitly modeled, albeit with constant returns to scale in production. The dynamic nutshell of Chapter 10 handles three types of capitalism and two types of workers' management (one of which is called "communism") in the form of differential games, contrasting their solutions and consequent outcomes with those of an extended "neoclassical" growth model. It corroborates much of what holds in the static nutshell of Chapter 3, and so suitably caps this book.

The Appendix contains a result characterizing efficient solutions of economic games based on the economic presystems used in this book. This result will be used frequently but sometimes without proper mention, and so it may be useful for the reader to consult it upon first confrontation with questions of efficiency in the following chapters.

References

Alcan, A. and M.R. Sertel (1981) "The Pretend-But-Perform Mechanism in Sharecropping", Discussion Paper, International Institute of Management, West Berlin.

Dirickx, Y.M.I. and M.R. Sertel (1978a) "Capitalism, Communism and Labor-Management Under Constant Returns to Scale", Working Paper 78-1, European Institute for Advanced Studies in Management, Brussels.

Dirickx, Y.M.I. and M.R. Sertel (1978b) "Comparative Political Economy of Capitalism, Communism, Slavery, and Colonialism in a Nutshell", *Recherches Economiques de Louvain*, 44, no. 3.

Plott, C. R. (1981) "Industrial Organization Theory and Experimental Economics", Social Science Working Paper 405, Caltech.

Smith, V.L. (ed.) (1979) *Research in Experimental Economics* (JAI Press, Greenwich, Conn.).

CHAPTER 2

A rehabilitation of the labor-managed firm*

MURAT R. SERTEL

1. Introduction

The "labor-managed firm" has been ascribed two major illnesses in the economic theory dealing with it. One of these, diagnosed in Ward's (1958) very early account of "the firm in Illyria", may be summarily expressed as *pathological short-run behavior*. Accordingly, when complimented by an increase in the price of its output, the Wardian firm (construed then to model the new Yugoslavian form of enterprise) is supposed to tend in the short run to curtail rather than expand employment, output and its supply to the market. The other malady, popularized by the writings of Furubotn and Pejovich (1970a, 1970b, 1975), is one which the labor-managed firm (fashioned again to portray Yugoslavian enterprises) is claimed to have to suffer beyond the realm of a mere short run, for this ailment is one of chronic *underinvestment*.

There is a common artificial cause of both of these (and probably many more) perversities to be found built into all the customary models of a "labor-managed firm", dooming an otherwise rather promising form of economic organization to an early – if not prenatal – and unnatural death. Namely, these models effectively commit the labor-managed firm to a total isolation from every sort of institution which so much as emulates a *partnership market*. Now even the very formation and liquidation of firms is

*My special thanks to Paul Kleindorfer and Jan Aaftink, discussions with whom led to this chapter in its form presented here. Of course, the remaining imperfections are mine, but on this occasion I feel the need to reiterate this.

difficult to imagine in the absence of such a market, and it turns out to be in vain to expect firms deprived of it to exhibit much economic sense in their behavior. Thus, it is no wonder that a Wardian firm, immune as it is to the doings of a partnership market, is willing – whether able or not – to dismiss members when times improve and become all the better to share among the fewer. For a member dismissed from a Wardian firm is able to claim no compensation for lost partnership rights. And neither is it at all surprising that members of Furubotn and Pejovich's labor-managed firm become less and less bent on ploughing back earnings the closer they feel to retirement. For retirement in their context is to occur void of the protection of sensible contractual clauses, commonly found in partnership deeds, guaranteeing retirement compensation commensurate with a member's accumulated contributions or with the value of his or her membership position to other parties interested in filling it.

In consequence, the "labor-managed firm" is construed here, in the presence of an effective partnership market, as a *workers' enterprise*. The analysis of workers' enterprises shows that they behave, in both the long and the short run, just like capitalistic firms in everything but the distribution of welfare, displaying none of the two pathologies indicated above. For facility in exposition, we consider a mixed economy allowing both capitalistic and workers' enterprises, although the vindication of the latter from the usual perversions attributed to "labor-managed firms" does not depend on the presence of a capitalistic sector.

To start with, section 2 spells out our understanding of workers' enterprises along with their natural partnership market, contrasting them with capitalistic firms. Then section 3 presents a comparative analysis of the behavior of these two types of firms operating in the same industry, facing identical tastes and utilizing the same technology – all with the simple tools of comparative statics and void of uncertainty throughout. So much suffices to discard the pathological short-run behavior of a workers' enterprise as imaginary. In section 4 we briefly dismiss the chronic underinvestment syndrome for such an enterprise. Finally, section 5 ends the chapter with some closing remarks.

2. Workers' enterprises and capitalistic enterprises

By an *enterprise* or *firm* we mean, first of all, a partnership. We presume that a partnership is formed and run for the benefit of its partners. We understand that partnership or a partner to a firm is gained through voluntary negotiation, between potential and existent partners, of a legally contestable contract specifying rights and duties of partners and covered by sanctions sufficient to guarantee fulfillment of such contract. We refer to such a contract as a *partnership deed*. Just as it is necessary to purchase a partnership deed in order to become a partner in a firm, the retirement of an existing partner may be achieved only by purchasing that partner's partnership deed.

The defining characteristic of a *workers' enterprise* is the coincidence of its partners with its workers. That is to say, a firm is a workers' firm if and only if its partners are all workers in the firm and its workers are all partners in the firm. As a direct consequence, the employers and the employees in a workers' enterprise constitute not distinct groups but the very same coalition of worker–partners.

In contrast, by a *capitalistic enterprise* we mean a firm whose list of partners is disjoint from its list of workers, so that no partner of such a firm is a worker (and no worker is a partner) in the firm. It follows, of course, that the employers and the employees in a capitalistic enterprise form disjoint groups – and, incidentally, it is this disjunction which fosters the usual collective employment bargaining institutions of modern capitalism.

Evidently, the above pure dichotomy between workers' and capitalistic enterprises is meant only to offer two extreme paradigms from which aberrations are not to be denied. Sometimes workers may own partnership shares in an essentially capitalistic enterprise where they work, and what is nearly enough a workers' enterprise may actually hire workers, either for reasons of seasonality in business or as managers in the fashion of managerial capitalism. In any case, here we wish to stick to clearly idealized paradigms so as to communicate our main points.

The nature of a partnership deed and of a partnership market in the capitalistic context, being all too familiar, scarcely require elaboration here. Essentially, partnership in a capitalistic firm is a financial matter, the deeds in question spelling out partners' various rights to the firm's profitability and, in case of bankruptcy or liquidation, rights to assets and duties to creditors, all in accordance with a partner's financial contribution. For the largest part, deeds of partnership in capitalistic firms may be bought and sold without the approval of other partners: the sole interesting characteristic of a partner here is the financial commitment he or she makes to the firm, and one fellow's money is just as good as another's.

In contrast, the most important characteristics of a partner in a workers' enterprise are personal productive attributes and how these – typically involving much in the nature of "human capital" – fit in with the firm's productive processes. A deed of partnership in a workers' enterprise being one of *worker*-partnership, its transferability from person to person must naturally be limited and subject to the approval of the remaining members. Thus, in effect, a plumber may not be able to sell his worker–partnership deed to an electrician.

Yet, for the proper functioning of the worker–partnership market – and, to no less extent, of a sector of workers' enterprises – the transferability of partnership deeds cannot be entirely prohibited. Here we have to imagine the presence of generally established operative rules or guidelines specifying acceptable regions of substitutability at work between working people, closely safeguarding the transferability of deeds within the boundaries of these regions. Otherwise, i.e. if worker–partnership deeds are completely nontransferable, members of a workers' enterprise will have little arm's length objective evidence on the basis of which to claim retirement rights with the force of legal contestability, a simple fact which would lead in quite transparent fashion to a number of interrelated economically unhealthy consequences: it would hamper members' interests in the long-run value of their firm as an ongoing concern, validating the core argument of Furubotn and Pejovich (even in a very general sense of "investment"); it would enhance the kind of majoritarian tyranny whereby members could be cheaply dismissed in times of relative prosperity, the better to share among the fewer, giving strength to the tendency underlying the claimed perversity of labor-managed firms in their short-run behavior; it would thus depress the initial willingness of potential worker–partners to join a workers' enterprise. In summary, the lack of an arms' length market value for worker–partnership deeds, such as would be established by safeguarding the utmost transferability of deeds within regions of productive substitutability, would foster a host of factors detrimental to the economic success of workers' enterprises.

In effect, the need for the protection of transferability in the worker–partnership market must be viewed as a special instance of the general need for the protection of competitive markets. It will undoubtedly require legislation of a certain intricacy, which may succeed in leaving explicit antitrust activity unnecessary if contracts could be designed wisely enough and find practical enforceability in ordinary courts. Whatever the requisite legislation for an age of self-management, man's proven ingenuity in designing commercial and labor law to make capitalism and collective bargaining workable leaves little room to despair that our legal minds would flounder at this novel challenge.

3. The common sense of the worker–partnership market

The purpose of this section is to spell out, in a simple way, the workings of the market for worker–partnership deeds and the effect of this market in imparting common-sensical behavior to workers' enterprises, both in the long and in the short run, dispelling finally with the Wardian (1958) diagnosis of pathological short-run behavior on the part of "labor-managed firms".

We consider a competitive economy in which both capitalistic and workers' enterprises may operate, and we look at a small industry of (yet much smaller) price-taking firms all faced with the same technology and tastes. The output of a typical firm in this industry is given as a positive and quasi-concave, increasing function

$$Y = F(K, L)$$

of K and L, where K stands for the input of capital goods and

$$L = \sum_{i=1}^{m} x_i$$

for the total labor input of the workers, $i = 1,\dots,m$, in the firm, the ith worker contributing $x_i \geqslant 0$ of effort or labor. For the marginal product F_K of K and F_L of L we assume that each is positive, with F_K decreasing in K and F_L decreasing in L. People in this economy all have the same preferences between income y, measured in the units of Y, and effort (or labor) x, as represented by an immediately tractable utility

$$u = y - E(x),$$

where E is a positive and strictly convex, increasing real-valued function representing the disutility of effort with $E'(0) = E(0) = 0$. The *price* of output is denoted by π, the *rental* on capital goods by ρ, and the *wage* on L by ω.

The typical capitalistic firm in this industry is, of course, interested in maximizing the firm's profit

$$P = \pi Y - \rho K - \omega L,$$

the first-order conditions for which, in the "long-run" where K is adjustable to will, subject to the prices π, ρ and ω, are the usual

$$\pi F_K = \rho \tag{1}$$

and

$$\pi F_L = \omega. \tag{2}$$

Meanwhile, the typical worker in the capitalistic sector, receiving an income

$$y=\omega x$$

as a wage-taker, maximizes u by setting the marginal disutility of effort at

$$E'=\omega. \tag{$\underline{3}$}$$

Of these, ($\underline{3}$) determines x equal to some positive $\underline{x}$, and thus u as some positive $\underline{u}=\omega\underline{x}-E(\underline{x})$. Equations ($\underline{1}$) and ($\underline{2}$) determine the long-run profit-maximizing levels $\underline{K}$ and $\underline{L}$ of K and L, respectively, facing the prices π, ρ, and ω. Thus, the long-run *size* $\underline{m}$ of the typical capitalistic enterprise in this industry facing the prices mentioned, as measured in terms of workers employed, is determined as

$$\underline{m}=\underline{L}/\underline{x}.$$

Turning now to the typical workers' enterprise in the industry, we assume that its m (identical) members share and share alike in both the toils and fruits of their labor. Thus,

$$x=L/m$$

is the typical worker–partner's contribution of effort, and

$$y=V/m$$

is the income of such a member from the enterprise, where

$$V=\pi Y-\rho K$$

stands for the value added by labor in the firm. The typical worker–partner's utility then becomes

$$u=V/m-E(L/m),$$

and the typical workers' enterprise of size m maximizes this function. In the "long run", where K is variable, the first-order conditions for this maximization give

$$\pi F_K=\rho \tag{$\bar{1}$}$$

and

$$\pi F_L=E'. \tag{$\bar{2}$}$$

We see immediately that ($\bar{1}$) duplicates ($\underline{1}$) above and that if the workers' enterprise were the same size $\bar{m}=\underline{m}$ as the typical capitalistic enterprise its members would then be contributing the same effort $\bar{x}=\underline{x}$, thus using the same inputs $\bar{K}=\underline{K}$ and $\bar{L}=\underline{L}$ and producing the same output $\bar{Y}=\bar{F}=F(\bar{K},\bar{L})$, but that the incomes of the members of the workers' enterprises would be augmented, in comparison with their working colleagues in the capitalistic sector, by one-$\underline{m}$th of the non-negative profit earned by the typical capitalistic firm, leaving the worker–partners just so much better off than their colleagues in the other sector. The question is, then, what the long-run equilibrium size of the typical workers' enterprise would be, and this is where the worker–partnership (deed) market plays a determinative role.

To see how this market operates, we look at the demand for worker–partnership deeds and the supply of these. Denoting the utility of a typical member in a workers' enterprise of size m by $\bar{u}(m)$, a worker in the capitalistic sector is willing to pay a *demand price* of up to

$$D(m)=\bar{u}(m)-\underline{u}$$

of his income to quit his present job and join the workers' enterprise. On the other hand, his joining the workers' enterprise would cause each current member a loss of $-\mathrm{d}u/\mathrm{d}m$, so the workers' enterprise would admit the marginal applicant to worker–partnership only as long as he is willing to forego at least the *supply price* of

$$S(m)=-m\frac{\mathrm{d}\bar{u}}{\mathrm{d}m}$$

in units of his income upon joining. The workers' enterprise achieves its long-run equilibrium size only when the market for its worker–partnership deeds is equilibrated, i.e. only when $D(m)=S(m)$. This equilibrium condition amounts to

$$\frac{\pi\bar{F}-\rho\bar{K}}{m}-E(\bar{x})-\underline{u}=-m\frac{\mathrm{d}\bar{u}}{\mathrm{d}m}, \tag{4}$$

the right-hand (supply price) side of which expands to

$$-m\left(\frac{\partial\bar{u}}{\partial\bar{K}}\frac{\mathrm{d}\bar{K}}{\mathrm{d}m}+\frac{\partial\bar{u}}{\partial\bar{L}}\frac{\mathrm{d}\bar{L}}{\mathrm{d}m}+\frac{\partial\bar{u}}{\partial m}\right),$$

where, at a long-run equilibrium, $\partial\bar{u}/\partial\bar{K}$ vanishes on account of ($\bar{1}$) and $\partial\bar{u}/\partial\bar{L}$ vanishes on account of ($\bar{2}$), to leave

$$\begin{aligned}-m\frac{\partial\bar{u}}{\partial m}&=-m\left(\frac{\pi\bar{F}_L\bar{x}}{m}-\frac{\pi\bar{F}-\rho\bar{K}}{m^2}\right)\\&=\frac{\pi\bar{F}-\rho\bar{K}}{m}-\pi\bar{F}_Lx.\end{aligned}$$

Thus, (4) becomes

$$\pi\bar{F}_Lx-E(\bar{x})=\underline{u}.$$

Recalling ($\underline{1}$)–($\underline{3}$) we see that this is satisfied precisely when the workers' enterprise is of size

$$\overline{m} = \underline{m},$$

in which case its worker–partners each contribute the same effort input $\overline{x} = \underline{x}$ as their colleagues in the capitalistic sector, employing the same level $\overline{K} = \underline{K}$ of capital goods and producing the same output as the capitalistic homologue of their enterprise. In this long-run equilibrium position, of course, the members of the typical workers' enterprise enjoy an average utility

$$\bar{u} = \underline{u} + \underline{P}/\underline{m},$$

exceeding that of their working colleagues in the capitalistic sector by an amount just equal to the long-run profit per worker in the capitalistic sector.

So much fits the long-run equilibrium conclusions of many competent economists, including Drèze (1976), and applications of this analysis have been presented in a number of other studies (see, for example, Chapters 3, 7 and 8 below).

Now we turn explicitly to the matter of the Wardian hypothesis claiming perverse short-run behavior on the part of ("Illyrian") labor-managed firms, with which we have to disagree for workers' enterprises. For now we allow the long-run equilibrium position of the firms in our exemplary industry to be perturbed by a change – say an increase – in the price of output to some $\tilde{\pi}$. Since we already know what would happen in the long run, and since the hypothesis concerns the short run where K is fixed for each firm, having just computed that the capitalistic and the workers' firms settle in the long run at identical capital goods utilization levels $\underline{K}$, at identical sizes $\underline{m}$ and identical labor employment levels $\underline{L}$, we apply our perturbation against this background.

In both types of firm, K is now fixed at the level $\underline{K}$ and we must now concern ourselves with the values $\underline{Y}$, $\underline{F}$, and $\underline{V}$ of Y, F, and V as evaluated at $\underline{K}$. Now the profit maximization of the typical capitalistic firm in our industry gives the first-order conditions

$$\pi \underline{F}_L = \omega \qquad (\tilde{\underline{2}})$$

and

$$E' = \omega. \qquad (\tilde{\underline{3}})$$

of course, ($\tilde{\underline{3}}$) yields the same effort supply by the typical worker in the capitalistic sector as does ($\underline{3}$), but ($\tilde{\underline{2}}$) requires $\underline{F}_L$ to decrease, i.e. L to increase. Thus, the typical capitalistic firm responds (in the short run) to the perturbation of increasing π to $\tilde{\pi}$ by hiring $\underline{\tilde{m}} > \underline{m}$ workers, each of whom works the same and earns the same as before, achieving the same utility $\underline{\tilde{u}} = \underline{u}$.

The short-run response of the typical workers' enterprise is just as unsurprising. Such a firm now maximizing

$$\underline{\tilde{u}}(m) = \underline{\tilde{V}}/m - E(L/m),$$

where $\underline{\tilde{V}} = \tilde{\pi}\underline{F} - \rho\underline{K}$, behaves so as to satisfy the first-order condition

$$\tilde{\pi}\underline{F}_L = E' \tag{$\tilde{\bar{2}}$}$$

subject to the equilibration condition

$$\underline{\tilde{D}}(m) = \underline{\tilde{S}}(m) \tag{$\tilde{4}$}$$

in the worker–partnership (deed) market, where now

$$\underline{\tilde{D}}(m) = \underline{\tilde{u}}(m) - \underline{\tilde{u}} = \underline{\tilde{u}}(m) - \underline{u}$$

and

$$\underline{\tilde{S}}(m) = -m\frac{\partial \underline{\tilde{u}}}{\partial m}.$$

Now ($\tilde{4}$) is simply

$$\frac{\pi\underline{\underline{F}} - \rho\underline{\underline{K}}}{m} - E(x) - \underline{u} = -m\frac{\mathrm{d}\underline{\tilde{u}}}{\mathrm{d}m},$$

the right-hand (supply price) side of which expands to

$$-m\left(\frac{\partial \underline{\tilde{u}}}{\partial K}\frac{\mathrm{d}K}{\mathrm{d}m} + \frac{\partial \underline{\tilde{u}}}{\partial L}\frac{\mathrm{d}L}{\mathrm{d}m} + \frac{\partial \underline{\tilde{u}}}{\partial m}\right),$$

where $\mathrm{d}K/\mathrm{d}m$ vanishes on account of K being fixed in the "short run" and $\partial\underline{\tilde{u}}/\partial L$ vanishes on account of ($\tilde{\bar{2}}$), leaving

$$-m\frac{\partial \underline{\tilde{u}}}{\partial m} = -m\left(\frac{\tilde{\pi}\underline{F}_L x}{m} - \frac{\tilde{\pi}\underline{F} - \rho\underline{K}}{m^2}\right)$$

$$= \frac{\tilde{\pi}\underline{F} - \rho\underline{K}}{m} - \tilde{\pi}\underline{F}_L x.$$

Thus, ($\tilde{4}$) becomes

$$\tilde{\pi}\underline{F}_L x - E(x) = \underline{u}$$

and, in similar fashion to what we obtained in the long run, this is satisfied precisely when the typical workers' enterprise adjusts its size to $\bar{\tilde{m}} = \underline{\tilde{m}}$, duplicating the short-run response of its typical capitalistic homologue in size as well as in the effort input of its typical member. The workers' enterprise therefore increases its size, its labor input, its output and its supply of output to the market, in its "short-run" response to an increase in the relative price of its output, all in perfectly standard and economically sensible fashion.

So much should suffice to toss out, once and for all, the age-old accusation that labor-managed firms will exhibit pathological short-run behavior, an accusation which turns out to be based on a lack of economic analysis – at least in so far as the worker–partnership deed market is allowed to function and as far as workers' enterprises are concerned.

4. Worker–partners' stakes in their firm

The purpose of this section is to re-examine the concern, as expressed by Furubotn and Pejovich (1970a, 1970b, 1975), that labor-managed firms are doomed by their very design to a chronic shortage of investment funds. At the risk of being unfair to these authors, who have painstakingly and eloquently repeated their misgivings in this regard with "labor-managed firms" as they have modeled them, in posing the problem here we must unavoidably suffice by summarizing the economic scenario which has caused them distress.

There are two main features of this genuinely aweful scenario. One of these is that the labor-managed firm is virtually cut off from external sources of credit and investment, so that investment in the firm is restricted to retained earnings. Such a strict unaccessibility of capital markets is, of course, a severe handicap for any kind of firm. The question is why labor-managed firms need be particularly prone to being boycotted by financiers.

To be sure, by definition a labor-managed firm self-imposes a sovereignty constraint on the means it can utilize to secure external finance. It cannot issue voting stock to nonworkers since this would mean extending the roster of voters affecting management beyond that of workers, thus violating the principle of total sovereignty of the workers in the running of the enterprise. This leaves open to the workers' enterprise, however, all sorts of nonvoting stock and bonds as means of obtaining external finance. But this observation invokes two further questions. One concerns the relative importance of the taboo for a workers' enterprise on voting stock issued to nonworkers. The other question asks whether outsiders are going to be willing to finance the operations of a workers' enterprise in whose management they will have no say.

The first question really involves difficult comparisons. Who is to say whether a taboo leaving external financiers out of management will be more or less helpful to the finance or any other aspect of a firm than taboos preventing the firm's workers from playing a role in the venture's management? While many of my colleagues may be willing to voice a strong opinion one way or the other on this issue, I am all for tabling this item for further investigation, advocating our holding back scientific commentary until it can be based on its usually acceptable grounds of theory and data. (One could add that healthy skepticism might prepare one for ambiguous answers in this domain, favoring one or the other inequality as the setting varies.)

The second question invoked, however, is one which promises the profundity of an iceberg. In a way the matter is simple: perhaps the typical investor and even the typical dollar or pound or franc, or whatever invested, is invested with no intention of ever interfering with business, except through switching to and from other bonds and nonvoting stock at one's brokers. In that case, there seems to be little to worry about from the viewpoint of self-management or workers' enterprises. For then firms of this economic design may offer just as reputable and attractive returns to the typical nonvoting investor as firms of some other design.

Yet the analytic submarine who fathoms well the seas of uncertainty, as does Drèze (1976), catches a glimpse of the otherwise unapparent depth of the problem here. For there is something of a "moral hazard problem" in an outsider financing a workers' enterprise when certain forms of uncertainty prevail. If business is sufficiently bad in a particular year, the firm may prefer to go bankrupt than to undertake heroic measures in order to satisfy creditors. And, what is more, a risk premium which the creditors may wish to exact for this reason, may tend to worsen things, effectively triggering the bankruptcy declaration of their debtor in years which are even not so lean as before.

Nevertheless, these are somewhat deeper issues than those which have allowed the Furubotn and Pejovich concern to become so popular in discrediting labor-managed firms. The practical solution to such problems seems to lie in designing forms of contract which can cope with the intricacies of the situation at hand. A key element in the design of such contracts is the priority ranking of various creditors at bankruptcy of the debtor workers' enterprise. Just as labor may usefully occupy first priority for a defaulting capitalistic firm, "capital" (external financiers) may do the same for a defaulting workers' enterprise. (See İnselbağ and Sertel, 1979, for some relevant analysis under alternative priority schemes.) Actually, for the case where the uncertainty applying to the value of output is independently observable in the form of, say, the price of output, Sertel and Steinherr (1979) have presented a simple form of contract, between a workers' enterprise and its creditors, which efficiently solves the resource allocation problem by what mocks a parity guarantee, i.e. a guarantee on relative prices. This has been partially extended by Onanç (1979). The generally wise idea of farming out risk to proper insurance markets continues to demand further research and creative contract design to find practical solutions to the problems encountered by Drèze (1976).

Even in addressing the first pillar of the chronic underinvestment syndrome attributed to labor-managed firms, namely the restriction of their investment funds to their retained earnings, we have evidently reached beyond the analytic horizon of the Furubotn and Pejovich (1970a, 1970b, 1975) scenario. On an entirely different platform, of course, one can hardly ignore the practical sense of a large group of firms' securing their own finance through their own banks and financial intermediaries. A very profitable avenue which holding companies may gainfully pursue in face of restrictive capital markets, this also has its legendary counterpart in the self-managed world of Mondragon (see the *Caja Laboral Popolar* in Oakeshot, 1978, and in Thomas and Logan, 1980).

In any case, we are brought through the above to perhaps the critical feature of the scenario of financially deprived workers' enterprises. This manifests itself in the general unwillingness of a labor-managed firm's very workers–managers to increase retained earnings very far. Furthermore, the closer a member of such a firm feels to retirement, the more pronounced is the member's unwillingness to invest in the firm supposed to become.

Now such utter alienation of people from their staple economic activities, while hardly unencountered in history, is certainly strange to find built right into economic institutions by design and at the obvious loss of all concerned. If worker–managers have such lack of interest in the ongoing success of their firm, this is here quite clearly because their stakes in the firm are not ongoing, but coterminate with their membership as workers, void of severance or retirement rights. The income-generating potential of the firm, which is increased by accumulated investment of toil, managerial effort and resources, matters to the typical worker–manager only to the extent of income generated during the member's association with the firm, thus only up to retirement. The economic potential of the firm to generate income for its remaining members and for newcomers who may join after this member's retirement is robbed of its relevance to the latter by a design which prohibits his benefiting from it. And this demotivation is achieved, of course, by no means other than the outright denial to worker–managers of what ought to be their regular partnership rights in their firm. (It may be instructive to imagine the likely catastrophe that one could cause in the capitalistic world by a prohibition on stock exchange activities. Let alone shutting down the stock market, which would prevent the conversion of shares into consumers' goods to be enjoyed by current shareholders, even a halving of inheritance rights in capitalistic economies should dampen their propensity to invest significantly enough to illustrate the present point.)

Once we accept workers' enterprises with full worker–partnership rights for their members as the natural form of organization for worker-managed economies and allow these to operate in full rapport with a properly functioning worker–partnership market, we should no longer be able to observe the alienated attitude of workers which supports the claimed tendency of labor-managed firms to shy away from autofinancement. If we add to this the fact that ploughed-back earnings simply are not the only source of investment funds for workers' enterprises, we have scarce little left of the chronic underinvestment syndrome attributed to labor-managed firms.

5. Closing remarks

The design of economic systems and of their supporting forms of contract, contestable in legal courts, is an extremely intricate matter. As architecture, it is an art, but not immune to technical advice. A small piece of technical advice to economic designers may be derived from the well-known efficiency theorems for competitive free trade. These are theorems which hold under limited circumstances and have counterexamples beyond these (see Chiarella and Sertel, 1979), but are intuitively suggestive that economic life might suffer from artificial constraints. Although this type of intuition may be carried too far with only a superficial understanding of the efficiency of competitive *laissez-faire*, within bounds it probably offers a good starting point for an economic designer.

So, one may ask, why ever think of a type of firm where the workers are required to be identical with the partners, i.e. of a workers' enterprise? There are, of course, many reasons why some should like to do so, on ethical or ideological or other grounds, and for these reasons they may be willing to participate in such firms even at a material loss to themselves or to the rest of society. For us, however, the primary question might be whether any loss at all in efficiency would be caused by the operation of a workers' enterprise. In other words, we might ask whether the constraint that the list of partners coincide with that of workers in an enterprise would be binding from the viewpoint of achieving the "utility frontier". It turns out that in itself the defining form of a workers' enterprise poses no binding constraint against the achievement of an efficient allocation of resources.

But one may rightly expect a loss of efficiency when certain markets are closed. The simplest example of such a loss would manifest itself in a standard Edgeworth box where trade is prohibited. And when worker–partnership rights and duties cannot be exchanged for normal commodities, not only may the same phenomenon of lost efficiency be expected, but one may further be deprived of a competitive equilibrium, or at least the stability of one, in the remaining markets: witness an economy of Wardian firms. We have seen that opening a competitive worker–partnership market eliminates these problems and rehabilitates the "labor-managed firm" to a well-behaved workers' enterprise.

On the other hand, certain markets have often been closed for considerations beyond the realm of a naive efficiency. Slave markets are a prime example of these. Although it may be "efficient" relative to many other systems which have persisted, slavery, along with its slave markets, has more or less been universally eradicated. (See Dirickx and Sertel, 1978, for positive and normative comparisons involving a dozen political economies, including slavery.) There appears to be a strain of Marxist thought which argues that the kind of individual property rights requisite for a worker–partnership deed market should be abolished. Without subscribing to, or even quite understanding, the argument, its followership has to be noted in many socialist political economies, especially where self-management is not intended to be practiced.

Turning back to regular economic theory, there has been a recent development in equilibrium analysis treating the very formation of firms as endogenous, and Ichiishi (1977) has successfully advanced this analysis to include labor-managed economies. From these we know sufficient conditions for the existence of a more general type of equilibrium where not only all the usual markets are in equilibrium, but so also is the formation of productive coalitions (firms) at a rest point. The present study can be seen as a modest contribution of some of the "nuts and bolts" of an extended general equilibrium theory in that the extended type of equilibrium may be viewed as one where all the usual markets and the partnership markets, including the *worker–partnership market*, are at equilibrium.

As to the specific issue of the "short-run" behavior of a labor-managed firm, since the various versions of the present chapter were exposed (beginning with lectures at the Technion, Haifa, Israel, in December 1977), there have appeared a number of partial disclaimers of perversity in this regard. These include, notably, Steinherr and Thisse (1979), Miyazaki and Neary (1979) and Bonin (1980). All three consider the risk from a member's viewpoint, of being dropped, without due compensation, from membership in a labor-managed firm. Typically, risk-averse members in these studies prefer the firm to adopt a no-drop policy in those circumstances where a Wardian firm would curtail membership. This, of course, takes care of at most half of the problem, for the firm then still fails to admit new members while efficient resource allocation demands that new members indeed be admitted. A competitive worker–partnership market, on the other hand, is a simpler mechanism whose operation imparts efficient behavior in these "short-run" circumstances (as well as in the long run).

References

Bonin, J.P. (1980) "Optimal Membership and Contractual Employment in a Cooperative with Implications for Output Supply in an Uncertain Environment", paper presented at the Workshop on the Economics of Internal Organization, International Institute of Management, West Berlin, July 1980.

Chiarella, C. and M.R. Sertel (1979) "The Dynamic Inefficiency of Competitive Capitalism", Working Paper 7901, Institut des Sciences Economiques, Université Catholoque de Louvain.

Dirickx, Y.M.I. and M.R. Sertel (1978) "Comparative Political Economy of Capitalism, Communism, Slavery and Colonialism in a Nutshell", *Recherches Economiques de Louvain*, 44, no. 3.

Drèze, J.H. (1976) "Some Theory of Labor Management and Participation", *Econometrica*, 44, no. 6.

Furubotn, E.C. and S. Pejovich (1970a) "Tax Policy and Investment Decisions of the Yugoslav Firm", *National Tax Journal*.

Furubotn, E.C. and S. Pejovich (1970b) "Property Rights and the Behavior of the Firm in a Socialist State: The Example of Yugoslavia", *Zeitschrift für Nationalökonomie*, 30.

Furubotn, E.C. and S. Pejovich (1975) "Property Rights, Economic Decentralization and the Evolution of the Yugoslav Firm, 1965–1972", *Journal of Law and Economics*, 89.

Ichiishi, T. (1977) "Coalition Structure in a Labor Managed Market Economy", *Econometrica*, 45, no. 2.

İnselbağ, I. and M.R. Sertel (1979) "The Workers' Enterprise under Uncertainty in a Mixed Economy", *Economic Analysis*, 13, nos. 1–2.

Miyazaki, M. and H.M. Neary (1979) "The Illyrian Firm Revisited", Discussion Paper 25, Stanford Workshop on the Microeconomics of Inflation.

Oakeshot, R. (1978) *The Case for Workers' Co-ops* (Routledge and Kegan Paul, London).

Onanç, H. (1979) "Incentives and Design of Efficient Institutions in an Uncertain Environment", unpublished MA thesis, Faculty of Administrative Sciences, Boğaziçi Üniversitesi.

Sertel, M.R. and A. Steinherr (1979) "Information, Incentives, and the Design of Efficient Institutions", Working Paper 7904, Institut des Sciences Economiques, Université Catholique de Louvain.

Steinherr, A. and J.F. Thisse (1979) "Is there a Negatively Sloped Supply Curve in the Labour-Managed Firm?", *Economic Analysis*, 43, nos. 1–2.

Thomas, H. and C. Logan (1980) *Mondragon Producer Cooperatives* (Institute of Social Studies, The Hague).

Ward, B. (1958) "The Firm in Illyria: Market Syndication", *American Economic Review*, 48, September.

CHAPTER 3

The comparative political economy of workers' management and capitalism in a nutshell*

YVO M.I. DIRICKX and MURAT R. SERTEL

1. Introduction

This chapter extends two of our earlier "nutshell" analyses (Dirickx and Sertel, 1978a, 1978b). In Dirickx and Sertel (1978a) we compared a dozen political economies, not only equipped with the same technology and involving the same participants, but also endowed with the same stock of capital goods. In Dirickx and Sertel (1978b) we allowed each politico-economic system to settle at its indigenous utilization level of capital goods, whose cost of utilization was common to all the systems that could be instituted, but we assumed constant returns to scale and restricted our analysis to only some of the dozen systems compared in Dirickx and Sertel (1978a). Here we study and compare three types of capitalism and five types of worker-managed economy, allowing each to adjust in its own way to its indigenous utilization of capital goods, continuing to keep our intersystemic comparisons "fair", in the sense of considering the participants and the technology at their disposal to be the same in each case, but we work with decreasing returns to scale. Our conclusions, however, yield the constant-returns-to-scale conclusions in the limit as the degree of homogeneity of the production function is allowed to converge to unity. The political economies of two types of slavery, three types of colonialism and two cases of democratic capitalism considered in Dirickx and Sertel (1978a) are left

*This chapter is based on the authors' study, with the same title, appearing as European Institute for Advanced Studies in Management Working Paper 79-2, Brussels, February 1979.

Workers and Incentives, by M.R. Sertel

unsaid here, but the reader will easily be able to obtain and compare them for himself in the present setting by minimal consultation of the earlier work, once the present chapter is understood.

Thus, the purpose is once again to compare institutions which a community with given tastes (regarding income and leisure) and technology can adopt, employing the simple and summary methods of the "nutshell" of political economy. The same type of analysis has lent itself quite well to extensions (Basar *et al.*, 1978b; Kleindorfer and Sertel, 1978; Sertel *et al.*, 1978), where many kinds and groups of participating agents are allowed, and our final tabulation (table 3.1) of relevant economic magnitudes for the systems we compare here forms a point of departure for a refutation (Sertel, 1978) of the famous Wardian (Ward, 1958) backward-bending supply of a labor-managed firm (see also Conte, 1978, and Steinherr, 1978, for a modern understanding and evaluation) by setting up a market for (worker-) partnership in such firms. (See, also, Basar *et al.*, 1978a, 1978b; İnselbağ and Sertel, 1979; Kleindorfer and Sertel, 1978; and Sertel *et al.*, 1978.)

We see that some workers' enterprises duplicate competitive capitalistic enterprises in all physical aspects, distributing utility differently, while some do not (cf. Drèze, 1974, where only one kind of workers' enterprise is considered), the internal incentive structure in the enterprise being the critical determinant. Apart from competitive capitalism, we consider also capitalism where the capitalists enjoy monopsony or the workers enjoy monopoly position in the labor market, and apart from the Ward (1958)–Domar (1966)–Vanek (1970) type of labor-managed enterprise (maximizing labor's average value added), we consider four types of workers' enterprise which are all superior.

First we specify the participants and the technology as basic data (section 2). Then we construct our "nutshell" (fig. 3.1), next identifying our eight systems in this figure, computing their indigenous position regarding 13 economic magnitudes in table 3.1. Finally, we carry out a complete intersystemic comparison along each of these magnitudes, and we close the study by indicating certain extensions of the present analysis with similar methods to treat uncertainty (İnselbağ and Sertel, 1979) and dynamic effects as well (Chiarella and Sertel, 1978).

2. Basic facts and notions

In analyzing and comparing our eight forms of economic institution we accept certain basic data as given, namely a production function with decreasing returns to scale and a collection of workers whose labor contributions are indistinguishable from the productive viewpoint and whose preferences between income and leisure are identical. In particular, on the productive side output is given as

$$Y = K^{\alpha} L^{\beta}, \tag{1}$$

where K stands for the capital goods input and

$$L = \sum_{i=1}^{a} x_i \tag{2}$$

measures the total labor inputs of a workers to production, the input of the ith worker ($i = 1, \ldots, a$) being denoted by x_i. With K and L both unambiguously productive, and dealing with the case of decreasing returns to scale, in summary we have

$$0 < \alpha, \beta, \qquad \alpha + \beta < 1. \tag{3}$$

As to the preference of a typical worker i ($i = 1, \ldots, a$) between the income y_i received and the labor x_i contributed by that worker, it is represented by means of the utility

$$u_i = y_i - x_i^{\gamma}, \tag{4}$$

with $\gamma > 1$.

In all the eight forms of economic institution, whether they pertain to capitalism or to workers' management, the enterprises we analyze will all be price-takers, both in the market where they sell their produce and in that from which they procure capital goods. In fact, we will always take the output, Y, of the enterprise as numéraire, so that its price is unity, and ρ ($0 < \rho$) will express the market rental for capital goods in units of the output. Thus, the value added by labor, i.e. the residual output after paying off factors of production other than labor, will always be the quantity

$$V = Y - \rho K. \tag{5}$$

So much for the givens. Turning toward the man-made institutions characterizing the types of political economy or the types of enterprise we are about to consider, perhaps the most important feature common to these is that a worker's labor is the private property of that worker, to be done with only as wished by its owner – facing, as he may be, one or another incentive scheme or agreement of collegial cooperation – a distinguishing feature, indeed, *vis-à-vis* the political economies of slavery, as analyzed in Barzel (1977) or Dirickx and Sertel (1978a), for example.

As to the essential feature distinguishing the two modes of political economy we study in their respective varieties here, it is centered in the question of to what extent employees are separated in identity from employers. In fact, we study two extremes. A *workers' enterprise* is characterized by the condition that the workers of the enterprise coincide with the partners, so that there is no distinction between employees and employers. In contrast, the *capitalistic enterprise* makes a perfect distinction in this regard: here no partner (employer) is a worker (employee), and no worker is a partner. While in either case it is the partners who run the enterprise, the consequences differ as the partners' interests vary with their identities from one enterprise type to another. In particular, the interest of a partner in a capitalistic enterprise resides entirely in the residual output after all the inputs utilized in production are paid their market prices, i.e. in the profit of the enterprise. For, although a partner has in principle the same preference regarding income and work, in a capitalistic enterprise where partners do not work, utility reduces to income. What guides the management of a capitalistic enterprise is thus the maximization of the partners' total income from the enterprise, and at any market wage ω this is given as the profit

$$P = V - \omega L. \tag{6}$$

In a workers' enterprise the interest of a partner is somewhat more complex, for the partner here is actually a worker–partner. The utility derived by a worker–partner will depend not only on the income received but also on the labor contributed. The labor contributed and the consequent income of a worker–partner will depend in general not only on the internal incentive scheme instituted by the workers' council, i.e. the general assembly of worker–partners, but also on the game-theoretic solution concept which the worker–partners choose to approximate in contributing individual efforts to their collective output. A clear discussion of these matters must await the relevant section of this chapter.

In fact, to proceed any further we must immediately turn attention to putting together the "nutshell" within which all the political economies of present interest will be identified as points summarily representing solutions which we will finally juxtapose and compare from various viewpoints.

3. Assembling the nutshell

Our present task consists of constructing a geometric montage (fig. 3.1) of four economically significant curves into an aesthetically pleasing form, our

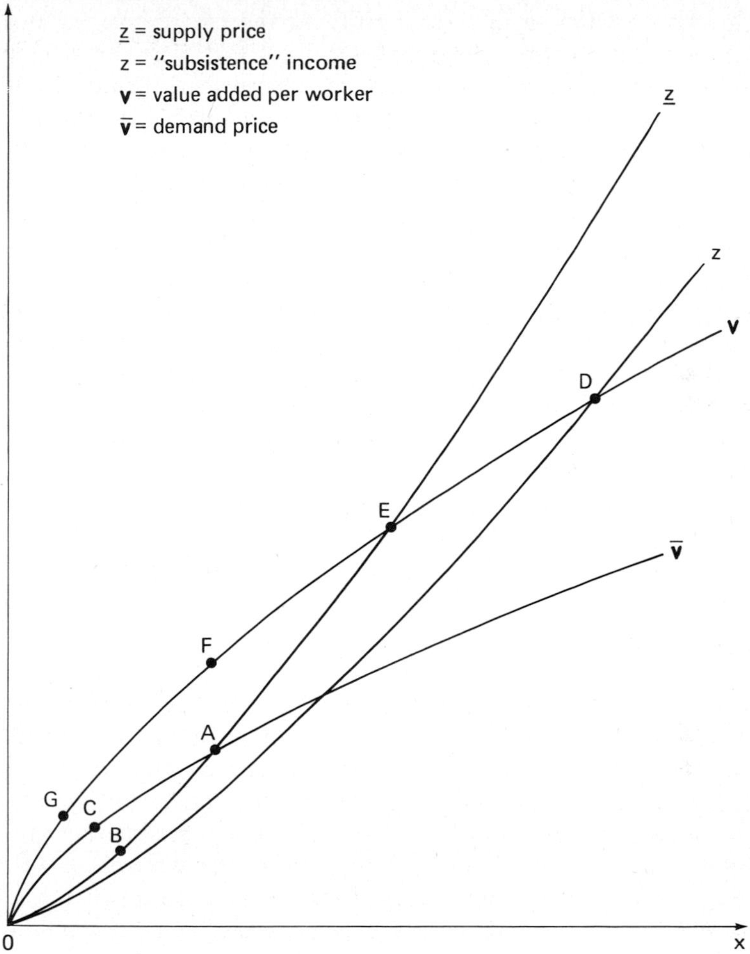

Figure 3.1a. Summary of outcomes under eight political economies: The case $1-\alpha>\gamma\beta$.

nutshell (see also Dirickx and Sertel, 1978a, 1978b and Kleindorfer and Sertel, 1978), with the help of which we will be able to express at least some of our analysis *en comprimé*.

First we note that the maximization of profit in face of any given wage ω, or the maximization of value added at any given level of labor input, is a matter of adjusting K so that its marginal product just balances its price ρ, i.e.

$$\boldsymbol{K}=\left(\frac{\alpha}{\rho}L^{\beta}\right)^{1/(1-\alpha)}. \tag{7}$$

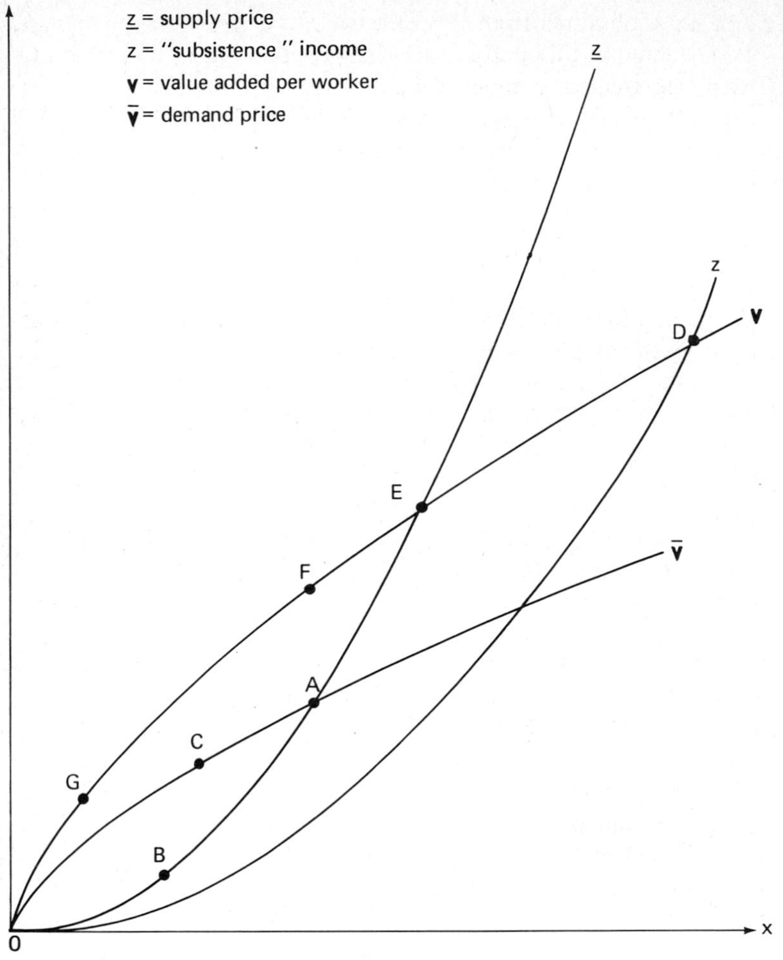

Figure 3.1b. Summary of outcomes under eight political economies: The case $1-\alpha<\gamma\beta$.

Substituting $\boldsymbol{K}$ for K in eqs. (1), (5) and (6) which defined Y, V and P, respectively, we obtain $\boldsymbol{Y}$, $\boldsymbol{V}$, and $\boldsymbol{P}$, respectively. In particular,

$$\boldsymbol{V}=(1-\alpha)\boldsymbol{Y}=(1-\alpha)\left[\left(\frac{\alpha}{\rho}\right)^{\alpha}L^{\beta}\right]^{1/(1-\alpha)}. \tag{8}$$

Thus, so long as the input of capital goods is chosen according to (7), $\boldsymbol{V}$ in (8) will give the value added generated by the enterprise as a function of the labor input L obtained from the workers. Now, in every type of enterprise to be considered in this study, the workers will all face the same wage or, in any case, be treated symmetrically by any incentive scheme directed at them. Consequently, it will turn out that the workers will all contribute the same amount, say x, of labor. Denoting the per-worker quantity V/a of value added by $\boldsymbol{v}$, we therefore have

$$\boldsymbol{v}=\frac{1}{a}(1-\alpha)\left[\left(\frac{\alpha}{\rho}\right)^{\alpha}(ax)^{\beta}\right]^{1/(1-\alpha)}. \tag{9}$$

We are now able to plot the value added $\boldsymbol{v}$ per worker as a function of the typical worker's employment level x; this forms the upper part of the outer shell depicted in fig. 3.1.

To complete the outer shell of fig. 3.1 we simply plot the indifference curve of a typical worker enjoying zero utility, regarding

$$z=x^{\gamma} \tag{10}$$

as the worker's "subsistence" income, since it shows the income in units of the output Y just enough to balance the worker's disutility of work.

The economic interpretation of the outer shell we have so far constructed in fig. 3.1 is quite simple. It circumscribes the set of feasible outcomes (x, q) of political economies under which our a workers may be organized, subject to the technology at hand, by use of our incentive schemes treating the workers symmetrically. For a point (x, q) falling within the nutshell corresponds to a typical worker's contributing the quantity x of his labor, receiving a payment of income q sufficient for subsistence and not beyond the means of the productive economy operating at the typical worker's mentioned level of labor input and the associated efficient level of capital goods input displayed by (7). While each outcome represented as a point lying within our outer nutshell is feasible in this sense, the realizability of such an outcome invokes the demonstrability of institutions describing a political economy bringing about the outcome in question. Turning to the realizability issue and the associated questions of institutional design, we proceed with the construction of the remaining elements of fig. 3.1.

Since the workers will remain free proprietors of their respective potential labor contributions in all the economic systems we are about to consider, it will be essential to have a description of their behavior as suppliers of a factor of production. Now, facing any positive wage ω, a typical worker will decide to contribute

$$\underline{x}=\left(\frac{\omega}{\gamma}\right)^{1/(\gamma-1)}. \tag{11}$$

This records the supply of labor by a typical worker in reaction to a positive wage ω, so the minimal income in return for which the wage-incentivized sovereign worker is willing to contribute $\underline{x}$ of his labor will be the income $\underline{z} = \omega \underline{x}$, i.e.

$$\underline{z} = \gamma z. \tag{12}$$

We refer to $\underline{z}$, as the supply price of labor, with the same slight misusage of language committed in Dirickx and Sertel (1978a, 1978b).

The natural counterpart of the supply price of labor is – carrying on with our slight misusage of language as in Dirickx and Sertel (1978a, 1978b) – the demand price of labor, by which we mean the maximal expenditure which will be incurred by a profit-maximizing employer in procuring labor from the market. Facing any positive wage ω, the quantity of labor input demanded per worker by a profit-maximizing employer will be

$$\bar{x} = \frac{1}{a}\left[\left(\frac{\alpha}{\rho}\right)^{\alpha}\left(\frac{\beta}{\omega}\right)^{1-\alpha}\right]^{1/\varepsilon}, \tag{13}$$

where

$$\varepsilon = 1 - \alpha - \beta, \tag{14}$$

so the demand price $\bar{v} = \omega \bar{x}$ will be simply

$$\bar{v} = \frac{\beta}{1-\alpha} v. \tag{15}$$

4. Three types of capitalism

Characterized by the perfect distinction between employers and employees which it embodies, capitalism stages a politico-economic scenario in which profit-maximizing capitalists, i.e. nonworking partners of an enterprise, interact through a wage mechanism with utility-maximizing sovereign workers supplying productive labor, at the expense of personal disutility incurred by working, in exchange for income.

The profit generated by a capitalistic enterprise is the residual value added after paying for the labor utilized; and, since the workers are free agents, payments to labor must cover the supply price of labor. Thus, the maximal profit per worker achievable at any level x of the typical worker's employment is the quantity $\boldsymbol{p}$ defined as the difference

$$\boldsymbol{p}=\boldsymbol{v}-\underline{z}, \tag{16}$$

visible in fig. 3.1 as the vertical distance between the curves $\boldsymbol{v}$ and $\underline{z}$.

The three types of capitalism which we identify and include in our comparative study here arise according to which, if any, of the two classes, capitalists' and workers', is given a leadership role in the game-theoretic sense of von Stackelberg. They can also be seen as arising from three distinct forms of institutional mechanism by which the wage is determined.

4.1. *Competitive capitalism*

In competitive capitalism the wage is determined through the market mechanism in the absence of any collusion of economic agents, i.e. by equating the supply (11) of labor with the demand (13) for labor. This culminates in the outcome summarized in fig. 3.1 by the point A and detailed in the first column of table 3.1 in terms of the thirteen variables whose mechanically computable values are displayed there. The last variable tabulated in table 3.1, namely communal surplus s per worker, is of special interest at our present juncture. What we mean by communal surplus (see also Basar *et al.*, 1978a, 1978b; Dirickx and Sertel, 1978a, 1978b; Kleindorfer and Sertel, 1978; and Sertel *et al.*, 1978) is value added net of the output equivalent of the total disutility caused to the workers by their work, i.e. the difference

$$S=V-ax^{\gamma}. \tag{17}$$

In accordance with our general notational convention, we write $s=S/a$ and $\boldsymbol{s}=\boldsymbol{v}-x^{\gamma}$. Now $\boldsymbol{s}$ has a clear efficiency connotation in that it shows, independent of its distribution to recipients, the utility per worker that is generated. It is strictly concave as a function of x and easily checked to be maximized uniquely at the competitive capitalistic employment level $\bar{\underline{x}}$. This speaks clearly for the efficiency – in the current sense – of competitive capitalism and of other political economies matching it in its level of employment but possibly distributing communal surplus in a different manner. (See the Appendix at the end of this volume.)

We note that the column in table 3.1 corresponding to competitive capitalism reproduces much of the conventional wisdom about the political economy in question. Its outcome corresponds to the Nash solution for the game set up in capitalism between capitalists and workers.

Table 3.1

Summary of outcomes under eight political economies.

	Competitive capitalism (A)	Capitalism with monopsony capital (B)
x	$\underline{\bar{x}}=\left[\left(\frac{\alpha}{\rho}\right)^{\alpha}\left(\frac{\beta}{\gamma}\right)^{1-\alpha}\left(\frac{1}{a}\right)^{\varepsilon}\right]^{1/\delta}$	$\underline{x}_*=\left(\frac{1}{\gamma}\right)^{(1-\alpha)/\delta}\underline{\bar{x}}$
k	$\underline{\bar{k}}=\frac{\alpha\gamma}{\beta\rho}\underline{\bar{x}}^{\gamma}$	$\underline{k}_*=\left(\frac{1}{\gamma}\right)^{\beta/\delta}\underline{\bar{k}}$
y	$\underline{\bar{y}}=\frac{\gamma}{\beta}\underline{\bar{x}}^{\gamma}$	$\underline{y}_*=\left(\frac{1}{\gamma}\right)^{\beta/\delta}\underline{\bar{y}}$
v	$\underline{\bar{v}}=\frac{1-\alpha}{\beta}\gamma\underline{\bar{x}}^{\gamma}$	$\underline{v}_*=\left(\frac{1}{\gamma}\right)^{\beta/\delta}\underline{\bar{v}}$
p	$\underline{\bar{p}}=\frac{\varepsilon}{\beta}\gamma\underline{\bar{x}}^{\gamma}$	$\underline{p}_*=\delta\left(\frac{1}{\beta}\right)^{\gamma(1-\alpha)/\delta}\underline{\bar{x}}^{\gamma}$
q	$\underline{\bar{q}}=\gamma\underline{\bar{x}}^{\gamma}$	$\underline{q}_*=\left(\frac{1}{\gamma}\right)^{\gamma(1-\alpha)/\delta}\underline{\bar{q}}$
u	$\underline{\bar{u}}=(\gamma-1)\underline{\bar{x}}^{\gamma}$	$\underline{u}_*=(\gamma-1)\left(\frac{1}{\gamma}\right)^{\gamma(1-\alpha)/\delta}\underline{\bar{x}}^{\gamma}$
s	$\underline{\bar{s}}=\frac{\delta}{\beta}\underline{\bar{x}}^{\gamma}$	$\underline{s}_*=\left(\gamma\frac{\gamma(1-\alpha)}{\beta}-1\right)\left(\frac{1}{\gamma}\right)^{\gamma(1-\alpha)/\delta}\underline{\bar{x}}^{\gamma}$
ω	$\underline{\bar{\omega}}=\gamma\underline{\bar{x}}^{\gamma-1}$	$\underline{\omega}_*=\left(\frac{1}{\gamma}\right)^{(\gamma-1)(1-\alpha)/\delta}\underline{\bar{\omega}}$
λ	$\underline{\bar{\lambda}}=\beta$	$\underline{\lambda}_*=\frac{\beta}{\gamma}$
μ	$\underline{\bar{\mu}}=\frac{\beta}{1-\alpha}$	$\underline{\mu}_*=\frac{\beta}{(1-\alpha)\gamma}$
Y/L	$\underline{\bar{y}}/\underline{\bar{x}}=\frac{\gamma}{\beta}\underline{\bar{x}}$	$\underline{y}_*/\underline{x}_*=\gamma^{\varepsilon/\delta}(\underline{\bar{y}}/\underline{\bar{x}})$
Y/K	$\underline{\bar{y}}/\underline{\bar{k}}=\frac{\rho}{\alpha}$	$\underline{y}_*/\underline{k}_*=\rho/\alpha$

4.2. Capitalism with monopsony capital

If the capitalists form a monopsony and dictate the wage, profit maximization subject to the supply (11) of labor clearly calls for the choice of ω so as to engender that supply $\underline{x}_*$ of labor per worker which maximizes the strictly concave $\underline{p}$ (see (16)) as a function of x. We mechanically fill out the entries

Table 3.1 (*continued*)

	Capitalism with monopoly labor (C)	The Ward–Domar–Vanek enterprise (D)
x	$\bar{x}^* = \left(\frac{\beta}{1-\alpha}\right)^{(1-\alpha)/\delta} \underline{\bar{x}}$	$x_0 = \left(\frac{1-\alpha}{\beta}\gamma\right)^{(1-\alpha)/\delta} \underline{\bar{x}}$
k	$\bar{k}^* = \left(\frac{\beta}{1-\alpha}\right)^{\beta/\delta} \underline{\bar{k}}$	$k_0 = \left(\frac{1-\alpha}{\beta}\gamma\right)^{\beta/\delta} \underline{\bar{k}}$
y	$\bar{y}^* = \left(\frac{\beta}{1-\alpha}\right)^{\beta/\delta} \underline{\bar{y}}$	$y_0 = \left(\frac{1-\alpha}{\beta}\gamma\right)^{\beta/\delta} \underline{\bar{y}}$
v	$\bar{v}^* = \left(\frac{\beta}{1-\alpha}\right)^{\beta/\delta} \underline{\bar{v}}$	$v_0 = \left(\frac{1-\alpha}{\beta}\gamma\right)^{\beta/\delta} \underline{\bar{v}}$
p	$\bar{p}^* = \frac{\varepsilon}{\beta}\gamma\left(\frac{\beta}{1-\alpha}\right)^{\beta/\delta} \underline{\bar{x}}^{\gamma}$	$p_0 = 0$
q	$\bar{q}^* = \left(\frac{\beta}{1-\alpha}\right)^{\beta/\delta} \underline{\bar{q}}$	$q_0 = \left(\frac{1-\alpha}{\beta}\right)^{\gamma(1-\alpha)/\delta} \gamma^{\beta/\delta}\underline{\bar{q}}$
u	$\bar{u}^* = \frac{\delta}{1-\alpha}\left(\frac{\beta}{1-\alpha}\right)^{\beta/\delta} \underline{\bar{x}}^{\gamma}$	$u_0 = 0$
s	$\bar{s}^* = \left[\gamma\left(\frac{1-\alpha}{\beta}\right)^2 - 1\right]\left(\frac{\beta}{1-\alpha}\right)^{\gamma(1-\alpha)/\delta} \underline{\bar{x}}^{\gamma}$	$s_0 = 0$
ω	$\bar{\omega}^* = \left(\frac{1-\alpha}{\beta}\right)^{\varepsilon/\delta} \underline{\bar{\omega}}$	$\omega_0 = \left(\frac{1-\alpha}{\beta}\right)^{(\gamma-1)(1-\alpha)/\delta}\left(\frac{1}{\gamma}\right)^{\varepsilon/\delta} \underline{\bar{\omega}}$
λ	$\bar{\lambda}^* = \beta$	$\lambda_0 = 1-\alpha$
μ	$\bar{\mu}^* = \frac{\beta}{1-\alpha}$	$\mu_0 = 1$
Y/L	$\frac{\bar{y}^*}{\bar{x}^*} = \left(\frac{1-\alpha}{\beta}\right)^{\varepsilon/\delta} \frac{\underline{\bar{y}}}{\underline{\bar{x}}}$	$\frac{y_0}{x_0} = \left(\frac{\beta}{\gamma(1-\alpha)}\right)^{\varepsilon/\delta} \frac{\underline{\bar{y}}}{\underline{\bar{x}}}$
Y/K	$\bar{y}^*/\bar{k}^* = \rho/\alpha$	$y_0/k_0 = \rho/\alpha$

of the second column of table 3.1 for the outcome of the political economy at hand. This outcome is summarily depicted as the point B in fig. 3.1.

We see that the employment level $\underline{x}_*$ of capitalism with monopsony capital is strictly less than the employment level $\underline{\bar{x}}$ of competitive capitalism. So, in view of (7), the capital goods input k per worker and, therefore, y and v are now also smaller. Of course, not so with p, which is now at its unique maximum. Unsurprisingly, the typical worker's income q and utility u, as well as the communal surplus s per worker, are here inferior to their respective competitive capitalistic magnitudes, as is the wage ω. Of course,

Table 3.1 (*continued*)

	Workers' enterprise with internal wages (E)	Workers' enterprise with internal wages and quotas (F)
x	$\underline{x}^* = \left(\frac{1-\alpha}{\beta}\right)^{(1-\alpha)/\delta} \underline{\bar{x}}$	$x^* = \underline{\bar{x}}$
k	$\underline{k}^* = \left(\frac{1-\alpha}{\beta}\right)^{\beta/\delta} \underline{\bar{k}}$	$k^* = \underline{\bar{k}}$
y	$\underline{y}^* = \left(\frac{1-\alpha}{\beta}\right)^{\beta/\delta} \underline{\bar{y}}$	$y^* = \underline{\bar{y}}$
v	$\underline{v}^* = \left(\frac{1-\alpha}{\beta}\right)^{\beta/\delta} \underline{\bar{v}}$	$v^* = \underline{\bar{v}}$
p	$\underline{p}^* = 0$	$p^* = 0$
q	$\underline{q}^* = \left(\frac{1-\alpha}{\beta}\right)^{\gamma(1-\alpha)/\delta} \underline{\bar{q}}$	$q^* = \frac{1-\alpha}{\beta} \underline{\bar{q}}$
u	$\underline{u}^* = (\gamma-1)\left(\frac{1-\alpha}{\beta}\right)^{\gamma(1-\alpha)/\delta} \underline{\bar{x}}^\gamma$	$u^* = \frac{\delta}{\beta} \underline{\bar{x}}^\gamma$
s	$\underline{s}^* = (\gamma-1)\left(\frac{1-\alpha}{\beta}\right)^{\gamma(1-\alpha)/\delta} \underline{\bar{x}}^\gamma$	$s^* = \frac{\delta}{\beta} \underline{\bar{x}}^\gamma$
ω	$\underline{\omega}^* = \left(\frac{1-\alpha}{\beta}\right)^{(\gamma-1)(1-\alpha)/\delta} \underline{\bar{\omega}}$	$\omega^* = \frac{1-\alpha}{\beta} \underline{\bar{\omega}}$
λ	$\lambda^* = 1-\alpha$	$\lambda^* = 1-\alpha$
μ	$\underline{\mu}^* = 1$	$\mu^* = 1$
Y/L	$\frac{\underline{y}^*}{\underline{x}^*} = \left(\frac{\beta}{1-\alpha}\right)^{\varepsilon/\delta} \frac{\underline{\bar{y}}}{\underline{\bar{x}}}$	$y^*/x^* = \underline{\bar{y}}/\underline{\bar{x}}$
Y/K	$\underline{y}^*/\underline{k}^* = \rho/\alpha$	$y^*/x^* = \rho/\alpha$

the shares λ and μ of labor income in output and value added, respectively, also fall below their competitive capitalistic values.

It will have been noted that the present solution to the capitalistic game corresponds to the von Stackelberg solution with the capitalists' class leading and wage incentives operative. (cf. Kleindorfer and Sertel, 1978, for the corresponding analysis where the capitalists' class leads but shares in value added constitute the operative incentive scheme.)

Table 3.1 (*continued*)

	Workers' noncooperative enterprise (G)	Workers' cooperative enterprise (F)
x	$\tilde{x}=\left(\frac{1}{a}\right)^{(1-\alpha)/\delta}\underline{x}$	$x^0=x^*$
k	$\tilde{k}=\left(\frac{1}{a}\right)^{\beta/\delta}\underline{k}$	$k^0=k^*$
y	$\tilde{y}=\left(\frac{1}{a}\right)^{\beta/\delta}\underline{y}$	$y^0=y^*$
v	$\tilde{v}=\left(\frac{1}{a}\right)^{\beta/\delta}\underline{v}$	$v^0=v^*$
p	$\tilde{p}=0$	$p^0=p^*$
q	$\tilde{q}=\left(\frac{1}{a}\right)^{\beta/\delta}\frac{1-\alpha}{\beta}$	$q^0=q^*$
u	$\tilde{u}=\left(\frac{1}{a}\right)^{\gamma(1-\alpha)/\delta}\left(a\frac{\gamma(1-\alpha)}{\beta}-1\right)\underline{x}^{\gamma}$	$u^0=u^*$
s	$\tilde{s}=\left(\frac{1}{a}\right)^{\gamma(1-\alpha)/\beta}\left(a\frac{\gamma(1-\alpha)}{\beta}-1\right)\underline{x}^{\gamma}$	$s^0=s^*$
ω	$\tilde{\omega}=a^{\varepsilon/\delta}\frac{1-\alpha}{\beta}\underline{\omega}$	$\omega^0=\omega^*$
λ	$\tilde{\lambda}=1-\alpha$	$\lambda^0=\lambda^*$
μ	$\tilde{\mu}=1$	$\mu^0=\mu^*$
Y/L	$\tilde{y}/\tilde{x}=a^{\varepsilon/\delta}\underline{y}/\underline{x}$	$y^0/x^0=y^*/x^*$
Y/K	$\tilde{y}/\tilde{k}=\rho/\alpha$	$y^0/x^0=\rho/\alpha$

4.3. *Capitalism with monopoly labor*

In the present variant of capitalism we suppose that the workers unite and dictate the wage to the capitalists. The guiding principle is now the maximization of a typical worker's utility, but the workers must reckon with the capitalists' demand for labor in face of any wage they contemplate dictating, since the capitalists are still the employers. The workers' problem, then, is to maximize, as a monopoly on labor, the typical worker's utility facing a wage ω, but subject to the demand (13) for labor, all of which amounts to maximizing the utility

$$\bar{u}=\omega\bar{x}-\bar{x}^{\gamma} \tag{18}$$

as a function of ω. Corresponding to the outcome of the present sort of capitalism, we compute the entries of the third column in table 3.1, summarizing the outcome in question as the point C in fig. 3.1.

The comparison of the present capitalism with competitive capitalism in table 3.1 is entirely straightforward. The comparison against capitalism with monopsony capital is again plain, except possibly as concerns the variables $\boldsymbol{k}$, $\boldsymbol{y}$, $\boldsymbol{v}$ and $\boldsymbol{s}$, all of which will be greater under whichever of the two systems leads to a higher employment level $\boldsymbol{x}$. In this regard, the reader may check that the employment levels $\underline{\boldsymbol{x}}_*$ and $\bar{\boldsymbol{x}}^*$ of capitalism with monopsony capital and capitalism with monopoly labor, respectively, compare as follows:

$$\underline{\boldsymbol{x}}_* \leqslant \bar{\boldsymbol{x}}^*, \quad \text{iff } \frac{1-\alpha}{\beta} \leqslant \gamma. \tag{19}$$

Thus, the comparisons in question will depend on the parameters constituting our basic data. (Certainly as β converges to $1-\alpha$, i.e. the technology converges toward constant returns to scale, we obtain the limiting comparison of Dirickx and Sertel, 1978b, and, for instance, capitalism with monopoly labor coincides in the limit with the $\boldsymbol{s}$-efficient competitive capitalism while capitalism with monopsony capital employs less than the $\boldsymbol{s}$-efficient amount of labor.)

Again it will be noticed that we have just dealt with another von Stackelberg solution to the capitalistic game with wage incentives – in contrast to the solution of the last section, this time with the working class leading. (Cf. Kleinberger and Sertel, 1978, for the corresponding case with shares in value added serving as incentives.)

5. Five types of workers' management

In a workers' enterprise it is the worker–partners who are responsible for management and so it is also they who decide on the capital goods utilization. Furthermore, however, the worker–partners are free to select an internal organization for their enterprise, and to institute and implement their chosen internal incentive scheme or collegial agreements regarding their division of labor. As a rule, workers' enterprises behave just like capitalistic enterprises in their choice of capital goods inputs as a function of the labor input, in so far as they accord to (7). Their differences arise from the internal incentives they set up and the game-theoretic solution concept they approximate in their behavior as individual contributors of labor *vis-à-vis* the payoffs determined by any incentive scheme which they install. The worker–partners are obliged to forgo no portion of their value added as profits, so the entirety of their output remaining after settling their capital goods account may be channeled into their individual coffers. The main constraint to be obeyed in the incentives design of a workers' enterprise is that the total payments promised to the worker–partners be covered by the value added generated through the total labor input which the incentive scheme incites in conjunction with whatever solution concept the worker–partners end up resolving their game according to.

In the fashion of Kleindorfer and Sertel (1979) we will consider two salient types of incentive, one based on sharing a collectively produced good – in the present case, value added (see also Basar *et al.*, 1978a; and Kleindorfer and Sertel, 1976, 1978) – and the other based on remunerating individual inputs through wages. It will already have been noticed that there is no problem in matching the worker–partners' total income to their value added, so long as individual shares, according to which value added is to be divided up, sum to unity. With incentives of this type, however, it makes a great difference to the outcome which solution concept the worker–partners adopt, and we focus here on two extremes, namely the cooperative solution and the noncooperative. When, instead, internal wages are used as incentives, the outcome depends not only on the wages operative, but also on whether or not certain auxiliary mechanisms – employing, for example, "quotas" – may be brought to assistance.

With all these considerations we really analyze not five, but four types of workers' enterprise. The fifth which we count in our title is actually a different sort of creature encountered as the "labor-managed firm" in the standard literature. It occupies a curious position in our nutshell of fig. 3.1 and in table 3.1, and we deal with it first.

5.1. The Ward–Domar–Vanek enterprise

The standard literature on what has come to be known as "labor-managed firms" has benefited from many contributions, but certainly from those of Ward (1958), Domar (1966), and Vanek (1970). Differences as there may be between authors in this literature on certain issues, it is fair to say that there has arisen a common understanding in the associated theory that a labor-managed firm may be characterized as a firm, in fact a workers' enterprise in our present sense, which maximizes value added per worker. It is often useful to characterize firms by ascribing a maximand to them and then analyzing the consequences. A case in point is the capitalistic enterprise recognized through its profit maximization, and there may be insights to be gained from analyzing firms which maximize sales. Against this background it might be understandable that economists interested in workers' enterprises should adopt the maximand of value added per worker to analytically identify the object of their interest, especially because this would amount, in a workers' enterprise, to the maximization of the average worker–partners' income. After all, when capitalists run an enterprise and their income as capitalists amounts to profits, profit maximization functions quite well as a working hypothesis for economists – even empirically. When the firm of interest turns into a workers' enterprise, why should not the maximization of average workers' income serve with an explanatory power commensurate to that of profit maximization in the ordinary economics of capitalism? Before we discuss why not, let us first see how not.

For the workers' enterprise maximizing V/a is easily checked to obey (7) and to end up maximizing $\boldsymbol{v}$, subject to the constraint, of course, of meeting its members' subsistence requirements and thus remaining within the feasible area of our nutshell. Obviously, this leads to the outcome identified as point D in fig. 3.1 and detailed in the fourth column of table 3.1. Now this is a rather bizarre outcome for workers running their own enterprise since they end up working themselves to the brink of their possible tolerance and receive no more utility from the whole exercise than if they had not worked at all – certainly ending up worse off than they would have been as simple workers in an ordinary capitalistic enterprise. So much should suffice to demonstrate how, i.e. in what sense, the present enterprise was falsely construed in its objective function.

Now to see why it does not make sense for a workers' enterprise to be maximizing value added per worker, it is enough to recognize that the partners of such an enterprise, in contrast to the partners of a capitalistic enterprise, contribute labor to the venture, and so the utility they derive from it cannot simply be seen as income earned but has to be reckoned by discounting this income so as to properly account for the disutility suffered as a result of the labor which had to be provided in order to make possible the income in question. To illustrate this, one need only consider the simplest of workers' enterprises, namely the common one-man shop of, say, a cobbler. If workers' enterprises maximized value added per worker–partner, we ought to be very surprised that the cobbler should ever lock up and go home at the end of a day's work.

Ascribing value added per capita as maximand to the labor-managed firm, coupled with an analysis lacking in a certain critical way, has managed to create a theoretical creature whose economic behavior was pathological.

(See Steinherr, 1978, for an account of this. For an analysis which allows us to dismiss diagnoses of pathological behavior on the part of workers' enterprises see Sertel, 1978, and its application in Basar *et al.*, 1978b; Kleindorfer and Sertel, 1978, and Sertel *et al.*, 1978.)

We have to admit that even Joan Robinson's (1967) critique of Domar (1966) for having his firm maximize short-run rather than long-run worker income, really misses the point. But what is regretable is that a bad name has been spread for workers' enterprises, inviting – though still not deserving – lamentations as elaborated by Jensen and Mecklin (1979). We must refer the reader to Sertel (1978) for a continuation of this discussion and push on to study what we regard to be workers' enterprises.

5.2. The workers' enterprise with internal wages

In the present subsection we study a workers' enterprise whose worker–partners' council decides to rely entirely on wages in their internal incentive design. In fact, being egalitarian, the worker–partners decide that they will all be given the same wage, ω. The worker–partners see right away that, at any wage $\omega > 0$, they will each be supplying labor according to (11), each reaping a utility $\underline{u} = (\gamma - 1)\underline{x}^{\gamma}$, which, by virtue of (11), is increasing in ω. Thus, they unanimously see that the best wage they can institute is the highest feasible one, i.e. the highest wage at which the labor supplied generates enough value added to pay the supply of labor at that wage. Wanting, therefore, to maximize V at any level $\underline{L} = a\underline{x}$ of their aggregate labor supply, the worker–partners adopt the policy of adjusting K according to (7), whereupon they find themselves facing $\boldsymbol{v}$ as the ceiling to their typical member's income. Finding themselves back in the nutshell of fig. 3.1, they see that their best feasible wage is the tangent of the angle formed between the straight line joining the intersection E of $\underline{z}$ with $\boldsymbol{v}$ to the origin O and the line Ox (summarily tan EOx). Instituting this wage, $\underline{\omega}^*$, the worker–partners obtain for themselves the outcome summarized in our nutshell by point E and detailed in table 3.1 as its fifth column.

The comparison of this outcome with those we have encountered so far is obvious, except possibly as involves the magnitudes of a typical worker's income, wage and utility, and communal surplus per worker. Looking at the typical worker's income, which is obviously higher (maximized) in the Ward–Domar–Vanek labor-managed firm, one easily sees that it is inferior in each of the capitalistic outcomes seen so far. For all of these outcomes employ less labor than the present, hence generating less value added per worker, and give less of that value added to the worker. As to wage comparisons with outcomes, so far we have seen it is clear that the present wage, $\underline{\omega}^*$, exceeds that in every outcome except possibly the wage $\bar{\omega}^*$ in capitalism with monopoly labor. In this regard, it is easy to check that

$$\bar{\omega}^* \left\{ \begin{matrix} > \\ = \\ < \end{matrix} \right\} \underline{\omega}^*, \quad \text{iff } 2\varepsilon \left\{ \begin{matrix} > \\ = \\ < \end{matrix} \right\} \delta, \tag{20}$$

where

$$\delta = \gamma(1-\alpha) - \beta \tag{21}$$

and ε is as in (14). The typical worker's utility and communal surplus per worker are certainly greater in the present outcome than their values of zero in the outcome of the Ward–Domar–Vanek enterprise. In fact, typical worker utility in the present outcome clearly exceeds that under competitive capitalism, hence that under capitalism with capitalists' monopsony. Its comparison with a typical worker's utility obtaining under capitalism with workers' monopoly will be delayed until section 6, as will the comparison of communal surplus per worker under the present system with its magnitudes under capitalism with capitalists' monopsony or workers' monopoly.

Perhaps the main point to recall at the moment is that communal surplus in a workers' enterprise, unlike in capitalism where certain decisions and profit are left to capitalists, may be reaped in its entirety by the workers, who would therefore be wise to achieve and share the highest feasible value of communal surplus. For, although the workers are in full charge, when they design and operate their enterprise as the workers' enterprise with internal wages whose outcome we have just seen, they fail to maximize the communal surplus which is theirs to make and to take. The reason is that the internal incentives with which they operate lead them to *over*work themselves. As communal surplus is maximized uniquely at the competitive capitalistic employment level $\underline{\bar{x}}$ of the typical worker, in the next subsection we examine one way in which the worker–partners might be able to set up their enterprise and its operation so that each worker ends up contributing $\underline{\bar{x}}$ of his labor and receiving the whole of the value added $\underline{\bar{v}}$ per worker thus generated.

5.3. The workers' enterprise with internal wages and quotas

The obvious thing to correct the inefficiency in producing communal surplus seen in the last type of workers' enterprise would seem to be the enforcement of a ceiling, a one-sided *quota*, on the typical worker's labor input, restricting it to be no greater than the efficient $\underline{x}$, whilst implementing an internal wage sufficient to bring about a supply of labor no less than $\underline{x}$. By a workers' enterprise with internal wages and quotas we mean a workers' enterprise which does just this. Now it is clear that any wage above the competitive capitalistic $\bar{\omega}$, e.g. the wage $\underline{\omega}^*$ of the last section, would incite a sufficient supply of labor for this purpose. Even $\underline{\omega}^*$, however, would be too low to exhaust $\underline{\bar{v}}$ in payments to the workers. To exhaust $\underline{\bar{v}}$ in distributing it to its owners, one would have to institute the wage $\omega^* = \underline{\bar{v}}/\underline{x}$. The workers' enterprise implementing this wage in conjunction with the competitive capitalistic employment level as a ceiling on the typical worker's employment level ends up producing the outcome shown in column six of table 3.1 and summarized by the point F in our nutshell (fig. 3.1).

The comparison of this outcome with those we have seen so far is quite simple. A workers' enterprise with internal wages and quotas completely duplicates the physical outcome in the competitive capitalistic enterprise; for the rest, i.e. the distribution of income and utility, the workers achieve their feasible best, leaving nil to the capitalists. Also, ω^* exceeds all the wages we have encountered so far.

Perhaps the "realizability" of the outcome deserves some attention. The actual enforcement of a ceiling on labor expended by the workers can be achieved by shutting down the factory early during the day, taking long Summer vacations or respecting the holidays of as many religions as possible. Technically it is essential to be able to measure labor inputs in order to be able to cut them off at the right level. But this very observability is necessary for the implementability of any incentive scheme remunerating inputs, e.g. any of the wage-based incentive designs we have looked at so far. If labor inputs are readily observable, it is clear that the outcome of a workers' enterprise with internal wages and quotas should be realizable just as well through an internal incentive scheme remunerating individual labor inputs up to the level $\underline{x}$ by the wage ω^*, and beyond $\underline{x}$ by a wage of nil. When input observation is impossible or sufficiently costly, incentives based on output rather than inputs suggest themselves. (See, for example, Kleindorfer and Sertel, 1979.) The next and last two types of workers' enterprise we consider employ precisely this idea in their incentives design.

5.4. The workers' noncooperative enterprise

Instead of instituting internal wages and remunerating themselves according to their respective labor inputs, the worker–partners of a workers' enterprise may resort to the simple incentive scheme defined by sharing the value added which they collectively generate. This is not unlike sharecropping (see, for example, Kleindorfer and Sertel, 1979) in its incentive effects, except that what is shared here is value added (see also Kleindorfer and Sertel, 1978) rather than output, the workers share only among themselves and not with capitalists or landlords, and the (*ex ante*) stipulation of the worker–partners' individual shares is entirely up to the workers' council. We study the case where these shares are equal, so that a typical worker–partner's income is simply $\boldsymbol{v}$. It is easy to see that the worker–partners will then agree perfectly regarding how much K to rent at any given rental $\rho>0$, adopting the familiar rule (7), whereby the income of a typical worker i becomes

$$\boldsymbol{v}_i=\frac{1}{a}(1-\alpha)\left[\left(\frac{\alpha}{\rho}\right)^{\alpha}\left(\sum_{j=1}^{a}x_j\right)^{\beta}\right]^{1/(1-\alpha)}. \tag{22}$$

As to the effective utility determined by $\boldsymbol{v}$ for this worker–partner, it is

$$\boldsymbol{u}_i=\boldsymbol{v}_i-x_i^{\gamma}. \tag{23}$$

What we have, then, is an a-person game between the worker–partners $i=1,\dots,a$ with their respective effective utilities $\boldsymbol{u}_i$. It is clear that so long as the solution of this game results in all the worker–partners contributing the same amount of labor, the outcome of this solution for a typical worker–partner will be a point, e.g. G, on the curve $\boldsymbol{v}$ in fig. 3.1.

We analyze this game by applying two solution concepts: the noncooperative in this subsection and the cooperative in the next subsection.

The noncooperative (Nash) solution to the game in hand is obtained by first setting $\partial\boldsymbol{u}_i/\partial x_i=0$ for each $i\in\{1,\dots,a\}$ to obtain a equations

$$x_i=\left[\frac{\beta}{a\gamma}\left(\frac{\alpha}{\rho}\right)^{\alpha/(1-\alpha)}L^{-\varepsilon/(1-\alpha)}\right]^{1/(\gamma-1)},$$

which obviously yield the same labor input, say x, for each worker–partner, whereby we see that our a equations boil down to just a single equation whose solution $\tilde{x}$ we tabulate in column 7 of table 3.1. The rest of this column is now computed in straightforward fashion.

Since all the worker–partners in the noncooperative workers' enterprise end up working the same amount, it is clear that the outcome is a point G on the curve $\boldsymbol{v}$, but the exact position of this point depends on the parameters of our system. Certainly, so long as $a>1$, $\tilde{x}$ can exceed only $\underline{\boldsymbol{x}}_*$ and $\bar{\boldsymbol{x}}^*$ among the employment levels we have seen so far; if a exceeds both $(1-\alpha)/\beta$ and γ, $\tilde{x}$ will fall even below $\underline{\boldsymbol{x}}_*$ and $\bar{\boldsymbol{x}}^*$. It is easily seen that the imputed wage $\tilde{\omega}$ defined as $\tilde{v}/\tilde{x}$ exceeds all the wages we have seen so far, except that $\tilde{\omega} = \omega^*$ when $a = 1$. Communal surplus per worker coincides in this outcome with the typical worker–partner's utility $\tilde{\boldsymbol{u}}$. Evidently this fails to be maximized here except trivially when $a = 1$. In fact, this inefficiency of noncooperation becomes ever more exaggerated as a grows; and, for sufficiently large a, workers' noncooperative enterprises will be inferior in both communal surplus per worker and typical worker utility to all the enterprises so far seen. As we will see in the next subsection, all these troublesome aspects are fully ameliorated when the worker–partners approximate a cooperative solution in their behavior.

5.5. *The workers' cooperative enterprise*

Given the game set up in the last subsection, each worker–partner would obviously prefer a solution where they all worked the efficient amount $\underline{\bar{x}}$ and thus appropriated the maximal feasible communal surplus per worker, $\underline{\bar{s}}$. To achieve this, all they have to do is to accept and enforce an agreement whereby each worker–partner will be insured that his fellow worker–partners will on the average work as much as himself. For, so long as each worker–partner can trust that $L = ax$ for any level x of labor contribution he himself undertakes, maximizing $\boldsymbol{u}$ he will choose the efficient employment level $\underline{\bar{x}}$, as will all his fellow worker–partners. This employment level is precisely the one which maximizes worker–partners' communal utility $\sum \boldsymbol{u}_i$, and it represents the cooperative solution to the game we have been examining. Of course, the outcome of the workers' cooperative enterprise, using this solution concept, exactly copies that of the workers' enterprise with internal wages and quotas. Thus, the outcome of the workers' cooperative enterprise in the nutshell occupies the point F again, and column 8 of table 3.1 repeats column 6.

6. Comparisons

This section essentially concludes our study by making comparisons along each row of table 3.1. For the purposes of summary, we repeat some of the comparisons we have already made as we fill in the incompletes.

Our first quantity in table 3.1 is $\boldsymbol{x}$. Now, clearly,

$$\max\{\tilde{x}, \underline{x}_*, \bar{x}^*\} < \underline{\bar{x}} = x^* = x^0 < \underline{x}^* < x_0,$$

so long as $a > 1$, and the first three $\boldsymbol{x}$-values are ordered among themselves according to the values of the parameters α, β, γ and a, in a fashion which the reader may discern for himself. The quantities $\boldsymbol{k}$, $\boldsymbol{y}$ and $\boldsymbol{v}$ will, of course, be ordered across columns in precisely the same manner as $\boldsymbol{x}$-values are ordered.

Profit per worker, $\boldsymbol{p}$, vanishes after the first three columns. In the first three columns, evidently $\underline{\boldsymbol{p}}_* > \bar{\boldsymbol{p}} > \bar{\boldsymbol{p}}^*$. For the typical worker's income $\boldsymbol{q}$, we have $\boldsymbol{q}_0 > \underline{\boldsymbol{q}}^* > \boldsymbol{q}^* = \boldsymbol{q}^0 > \bar{\boldsymbol{q}} > \max\{\underline{\boldsymbol{q}}_*, \bar{\boldsymbol{q}}^*\}$. The comparison between $\underline{\boldsymbol{q}}_*$ and $\bar{\boldsymbol{q}}^*$ is a matter of $1-\alpha/\beta$ or of γ: as $\beta/(1-\alpha)$ (respectively, $1/\gamma$) tends to 0 (respectively, 1) we have $\underline{\boldsymbol{q}}_* > \bar{\boldsymbol{q}}^*$; and as $1-\alpha/\beta$ (respectively, $1/\gamma$) tends to 1 (respectively, 0), we have $\underline{\boldsymbol{q}}_* < \bar{\boldsymbol{q}}^*$. Of course, $\underline{\boldsymbol{q}}_* = \bar{\boldsymbol{q}}^*$ when $\gamma^{\gamma(1-\alpha)} = ((1-\alpha)/\beta)^{\alpha}$. As to $\bar{\boldsymbol{q}}$, so long as $a > 1$, we have $\bar{\boldsymbol{q}} < \boldsymbol{q}^* = \boldsymbol{q}^0$; and for a sufficiently large we even have $\bar{\boldsymbol{q}} < \min\{\underline{\boldsymbol{q}}_*, \bar{\boldsymbol{q}}^*\}$. Less interesting comparisons are left unsaid.

The typical worker's utility $\boldsymbol{u}$ obeys the following intersystemic inequalities: $\boldsymbol{u}^* = \boldsymbol{u}^0 > \max\{\underline{\boldsymbol{u}}^*, \bar{\boldsymbol{u}}^*\} \geqslant \min\{\underline{\boldsymbol{u}}^*, \bar{\boldsymbol{u}}^*\} > \bar{\underline{\boldsymbol{u}}} > \underline{\boldsymbol{u}}_* > \boldsymbol{u}_0 = 0$. These are clear by comparison of entries in table 3.1 or from the geometry of the nutshell. Furthermore,

$$\underline{\boldsymbol{u}}^* \left\{ \begin{matrix} > \\ = \\ < \end{matrix} \right\} \bar{\boldsymbol{u}}^*, \quad \text{iff } \frac{(\gamma-1)(1-\alpha)}{\delta} \left\{ \begin{matrix} > \\ = \\ < \end{matrix} \right\} \left(\frac{\beta}{1-\alpha} \right)^{[\gamma(1-\alpha)+\beta]/\delta}$$

so that $\underline{\boldsymbol{u}}^* > \bar{\boldsymbol{u}}^*$ holds for $\beta/(1-\alpha)$ or $1/\gamma$ sufficiently small, $\underline{\boldsymbol{u}}^* \to \bar{\boldsymbol{u}}^*$ as $\beta/(1-\alpha) \to 1$, and $\underline{\boldsymbol{u}}^* < \bar{\boldsymbol{u}}^*$ for γ sufficiently small ($\gamma > 1$). As to $\tilde{\boldsymbol{u}}$, of course when $a = 1$ this matches even $\boldsymbol{u}^*$, but its ratio to any of the $\boldsymbol{u}$ levels excluding $\boldsymbol{u}_0$ becomes arbitrarily small by choice of a sufficiently large.

Comparisons of $\boldsymbol{s}$, communal surplus per worker, are quite straightforward up to a point. Clearly, $\boldsymbol{s}$ attains its highest value in the case of $\boldsymbol{s}^* = \boldsymbol{s}^0 = \bar{\underline{\boldsymbol{s}}}$ and its lowest value in the case of $\boldsymbol{s}_0$. As for $\bar{\boldsymbol{s}}$, when $a = 1$ it matches $\boldsymbol{s}^*$, but its ratio to any of the $\boldsymbol{s}$-values excluding $\boldsymbol{s}_0$ becomes arbitrarily small by choice of a sufficiently large. The rest of the comparisons of $\boldsymbol{s}$ are somewhat more involved. We take them up one by one below.

First we establish that $\bar{\boldsymbol{s}}^* > \underline{\boldsymbol{s}}^*$. Define $\theta = (1-\alpha)/\beta$ and

$$r(\theta) = \left(\frac{\gamma\theta^2 - 1}{\gamma - 1} \right) \left(\frac{1}{\theta} \right)^{2\gamma\theta/(\gamma\theta - 1)}$$

and note that $r = \bar{\boldsymbol{s}}^* / \underline{\boldsymbol{s}}^*$. Observing that $r(1) = 1$ and that $r' = \mathrm{d}r/\mathrm{d}\theta$ is continuous on $[1, \infty)$ with $r'(1) = 1$, it remains to show only that $r' > 0$ on $(1, \infty)$. Toward this we first check that $\operatorname{sgn} r' = \operatorname{sgn}(\gamma\theta(1-\theta+\theta\ln\theta) - (1-\theta+\ln\theta))$. For $\theta > 1$, we have $\theta - 1 > \ln\theta$, so if $\theta(1-\ln\theta) < 1$, then $r' > 0$. But, in fact, defining the function $t(\theta)=\theta(1-\ln\theta)$, we see that $t(1)=1$ and $dt/d\theta=-\ln\theta$ which is negative on $(1,\infty)$. So, $\bar{s}^*>\underline{s}^*$.

Since s is increasing in x for $x<\bar{x}$, recalling (19) it is evident that $\underline{s}_*\leqslant\bar{s}^*$ iff $(1-\alpha)/\beta\leqslant\gamma$. Thus, whenever $(1-\alpha)/\beta\geqslant\gamma$, we certainly have $\underline{s}_*>\underline{s}^*$. From table 3.1 we see that, in fact,

$$\underline{s}^*\left\{\begin{matrix}>\\=\\<\end{matrix}\right\}\underline{s}_*,\quad \text{iff } T(\gamma,\theta)\left\{\begin{matrix}>\\=\\<\end{matrix}\right\}1,$$

where

$$T(\gamma,\theta)=\frac{\gamma-1}{\gamma^{2\theta-1}}\gamma^{\gamma\theta/(\gamma\theta-1)},$$

and again $\theta=(1-\alpha)/\beta$. Now

$$\lim_{\theta\to\infty}T(\gamma,\theta)=(\gamma-1)/\gamma<1,$$

so $\underline{s}^*<\underline{s}_*$ for θ sufficiently large (independent of γ). On the other hand,

$$T(\gamma,1)=\frac{1}{\gamma+1}\gamma^{\gamma/(\gamma-1)}$$

and the reader may check that this strictly exceeds unity, so that $\underline{s}^*>\underline{s}_*$ for β sufficiently close to $1-\alpha$. ($T(\gamma,1)$ is decreasing in γ, $\lim_{\gamma\to\infty}T(\gamma,1)=1$.)

Turning to the wage ω – whether it operates as an incentive, or is imputed, or is a "wage" in a wage–quota system – it is clear from the geometry of our nutshell that $\omega^*=\omega^0>\underline{\omega}^*>\bar{\omega}>\underline{\omega}_*$ and that $\omega^0>\bar{\omega}^*>\underline{\bar{\omega}}$. For the rest, first note that $\tilde{\omega}\geqslant\omega^0$ and, in fact, $\tilde{\omega}$ grows beyond bound as a increases. It can be checked from table 3.1 that

$$\underline{\omega}^*\left\{\begin{matrix}>\\=\\<\end{matrix}\right\}\bar{\omega}^*,\quad \text{iff } 2\left\{\begin{matrix}>\\=\\<\end{matrix}\right\}\gamma+\frac{1}{\theta}.$$

Finally, we look at ω_0. It is clear that $\omega^0>\omega_0$. Also, defining $H^{\beta/\gamma}(\theta)=\omega_0/\underline{\bar{\omega}}$, we have $H(\theta)=\theta^{(\gamma-1)\theta}(1/\gamma)^{\theta-1}$, and $H(\theta)\to1$ as $\theta\to1$, while $\ln H(\theta)=(\gamma-1)\theta\ln\theta-(\theta-1)\ln\gamma$. Now, as long as $\theta>1$, $\theta\ln\theta/(\theta-1)>1$ and $\ln\gamma/(\gamma-1)<1$, so $\ln H(\theta)>0$. Thus, we see that $\omega_0>\underline{\bar{\omega}}$. But ω_0 can exceed $\bar{\omega}^*$, as we see by considering, for example, the case where $\gamma\geqslant3$.

The intersystemic comparisons of $\boldsymbol{\lambda}$, the workers' share in output, are quite obvious from table 3.1: $\boldsymbol{\lambda}_0=\underline{\boldsymbol{\lambda}}^*=\boldsymbol{\lambda}^*=\tilde{\boldsymbol{\lambda}}=\boldsymbol{\lambda}^0>\underline{\bar{\boldsymbol{\lambda}}}=\bar{\boldsymbol{\lambda}}^*>\underline{\boldsymbol{\lambda}}_*$. The intersystemic comparisons of $\boldsymbol{\mu}$, the workers' share in value-added, are the same: $\boldsymbol{\mu}_0=\underline{\boldsymbol{\mu}}^*=\boldsymbol{\mu}^*=\tilde{\boldsymbol{\mu}}=\boldsymbol{\mu}^0>\underline{\bar{\boldsymbol{\mu}}}=\bar{\boldsymbol{\mu}}^*>\underline{\boldsymbol{\mu}}_*$. Of course, $\boldsymbol{Y/L}$ accords inversely to $\boldsymbol{x}$, so that a system exhibits a labor productivity higher than that of another system equipped with the same production function (1) and obeying the same adjustment (7) of capital goods input to labor input precisely when it inputs less labor. (Now consult the intersystemic comparisons of $\boldsymbol{x}$ above.)

Finally, $\boldsymbol{Y}/\boldsymbol{K}$, the productivity of capital equipment, poses for us the easiest intersystemic comparisons, though not necessarily the least interesting. In that all our systems settle at the same output/capital ratio $\boldsymbol{Y}/\boldsymbol{K}$, from a macro-economic viewpoint of growth potential they can differ only in so far as they diverge from one another in their savings rates, a matter which needs to be studied elsewhere in a dynamic model. (But see Chiarella and Sertel, 1978, and Chapter 10 below for the beginnings of the required analysis.)

7. Extensions of the analysis

There are a number of extensions of our present analysis which are worth mentioning here.

Regarding the position of workers' enterprises, in Sertel (1978) some of the results here have been used in refuting a certain "pathological" behavior ascribed to such enterprises as a result of work by Domar (1966), Vanek (1970) and Ward (1958). In particular, it is possible to show that workers' enterprises of various sorts in a mixed economy with capitalistic firms will behave just or quite like their capitalistic counterparts in the factor and output markets in response to economic fluctuations, i.e. certainly not pathologically (see Sertel, 1978). In fact, the combined analyses of this study and Sertel (1978) have been used to extend our comparisons of capitalism with worker–management in the case of many types of labor (see Basar *et al.*, 1978 and Sertel *et al.*, 1978). The idea of our nutshell has also been used to study enterprises where value added is shared between workers and a capitalist (see Kleindorfer and Sertel, 1978).

But there are further directions in which the comparative political economy here could be fruitfully extended. One of these would involve a dynamic setting and explicit consideration of savings, investment and accumulation paths indigenous to the systems in question, comparing then the time paths of economic quantities worthy of attention, weighing out the relative benefits accruing to participating agents in the various systems, and the efficiency of these systems. For beginnings of such an analysis, see Chiarella and Sertel (1978) and Chapter 10 below.

Another extension of interest would involve letting each system settle at its indigenous technology in a common set of possible technologies from which each system can pick its choice. The simplicity of the present nutshell might be lost to some extent in such an analysis, but only the analysis itself will show to what extent.

Finally, the assumption of decreasing returns to scale which we have adhered to is actually to be taken less seriously than it might demand on first sight. In fact, the limiting case where $\alpha+\beta \to 1$ is easy to compute, e.g. as in Dirickx and Sertel (1978b). Also, for many purposes, a certain degree of increasing returns to scale is permissible: namely, it turns out to be feasible to work with α, β and γ satisfying $\gamma(1-\alpha)-\beta>0$.

References

Barzel, Y. (1977) "An Economic Analysis of Slavery", *The Journal of Law and Economics*, 20, no. 1, 87–110.

Başar T., H. Selbuz and M.R. Sertel (1978a) "Özyönetilen İşletme Kuramı", Technical Report No. 43, Applied Mathematics Division, Marmara Research Institute, Gebze-Kocaeli, Turkey.

Başar T., H. Selbuz and M.R. Sertel (1978b) "Workers' Cooperatives and Semi-Cooperatives Facing Competitive Capitalism", Technical Report no. 45, Applied Mathematics Division, Marmara Research Institute, Gebze-Kocaeli, Turkey. (See Chapter 8 of this book.)

Chiarella, C. and M.R. Sertel (1978) "The Dynamic Inefficiency of Competitive Capitalism", IRES Discussion Paper Series, Université Catholique de Louvain.

Conte, M. (1978) "The Theory of the Labor Managed Firm in the Short Run", paper prepared for the Second International Conference on Economics of Workers' Self-Management, Dubrovnik.

Dirickx, Y.M.I. and M.R. Sertel (1978a) "Comparative Political Economy of Capitalism, Communism, Slavery and Colonialism in a Nutshell", *Recherches Economiques de Louvain*, 44, no. 3.

Dirickx, Y.M.I. and M.R. Sertel (1978b) "Capitalism, Communism, and Labor Management under Constant Returns to Scale", EIASM Working Paper No. 78-01.

Domar, E. (1966) "The Soviet Collective Farm as a Producer Cooperative", *American Economic Review*, 56, 734–757.

Drèze, J. (1974) "The Pure Theory of Labor-Managed and Participatory Economies – Part I: Certainty", CORE Discussion Paper No. 7422.

İnselbağ, I. and M.R. Sertel (1979) "The Workers' Enterprise in a Mixed Economy under Uncertainty", *Economic Analysis and Workers' Management*, 13, 1979.

Jensen, M.C. and Meckling, W.H., "Rights and Production Functions: An Application to Labor-Managed Firms and Codetermination", *Journal of Business*, 52, no. 4, 469–506.

Kleindorfer, P.R. and M.R. Sertel (1978) "Value-Added Sharing Enterprises", Discussion Paper, International Institute of Management, West Berlin. (See Chapter 9 of this book.)

Kleindorfer, P.R. and M.R. Sertel (1976) "Equilibrium Analysis of Sharecropping", IIM-Preprint Series, I/76-33, International Institute of Management, West Berlin. (See Chapter 6 of this book.)

Kleindorfer, P.R. and M.R. Sertel (1979) "Profit-Maximizing Design of Enterprises through Incentives", *Journal of Economic Theory*, 20, no. 3, 318–339.

Robinson, J. (1967) "The Soviet Collective Farm as a Producer Cooperative: Comment", *American Economic Review*, 57, 222–223.

Sertel, M.R. (1978) "Relative Size and Share Price of a Workers' Enterprise Facing Competitive Capitalism", paper presented at the Second Bosphorus Workshop on Industrial Democracy, Istanbul. (See Chapter 2 of this book.)

Sertel, M.R., T. Başar and H. Selbuz (1978) "Workers' Enterprises Facing Competitive Capitalism", Technical Report No. 44, Applied Mathematics Division, Marmara Research Institute, Gebze-Kocaeli, Turkey. (See Chapter 7 of this book.)

Steinherr, A. (1978) "The Labor-Managed Economy: A Survey of the Economics Literature", *Annals of Public and Co-Operative Economy*, 49, no. 2, 129–148.

Vanek, J. (1970) *The General Theory of Labor Managed Economies* (Cornell University Press).

Ward, B.N. (1958) "The Firm in Illyria: Market Syndicalism", *American Economic Review*, 48, 566–589.

CHAPTER 4

Profit-maximizing design of enterprises through incentives*

PAUL R. KLEINDORFER and MURAT R. SERTEL

1. Introduction

This chapter presents a comparative study of incentives within productive enterprises set up and designed for the purpose of profit. We envision a collection of economic agents, each of whom has "signed on" to take part in a certain productive process, contributing, for example, work or effort or some other privately owned factor. By making monetary reward paid to these agents dependent on their individual or collective input or output, one obtains an incentive scheme. After defining an appropriate class of such incentive schemes, one may then adopt the viewpoint of one or another group of enterprise participants and strive for an optimal incentive scheme in the given class.

We consider two types of incentive scheme, one based on *input-pricing* and the other on *output-sharing*. Of these the first type amounts to declaring wages according to which each unit of an input will be remunerated. The implementation of such an incentive scheme requires, of course, that the

*This chapter is reprinted from the *Journal of Economic Theory*, Vol. 20, No. 3, June 1979, with permission of Academic Press.

This work was supported by the International Institute of Management, West Berlin. Partial support of this research by the Office of Naval Research under Contract N0014-77-C-0171 is also acknowledged. Helpful comments on an earlier draft by the editors of J.E.T. and an anonymous referee, as well as by Yvo Dirickx, Felix Fitzroy, and by participants at the Economics Workshop at Wesleyan University, are gratefully acknowledged.

Workers and Incentives, by M.R. Sertel

magnitudes of inputs contributed by the participants in the enterprise be accurately measurable. The implementation of the second type of incentive scheme, where each participant is promised a certain share of the enterprise output, requires no observation of participants' input contribution but, instead, an accurate measurement of the resulting output. Thus, assuming inputs are more costly to measure than output, the information base required to implement a pricing incentive scheme will generally be more costly than that required for the implementation of an output-sharing incentive scheme. On the other hand, we will see that a profit-maximizing designer will be able to reap a greater profit, gross of information costs, by instituting input-pricing rather than output-sharing. In the end, the profit performance differential of the two incentive types would therefore have to be compared against the information costs required for their implementation. So, it is of interest to assess the profit differential lying between input-pricing and output-sharing. This chapter provides such an assessment for a reasonable description of production technology, preferences of participating agents and their behavioral adjustment to incentives. In addition, the study also provides a comparison of the profit-maximizing input-pricing and output-sharing schemes in terms of output and participants' inputs, incomes and utilities.

One can also interpret the approach and the results here in a more general setting. Just as above, the general enterprise incentives design problem is determined, given the production technology and the preferences of the agents involved, by a specification of what class of incentives and monitoring information may be used and which interests will govern the choice of enterprise design, specifically who will have the authority to select and implement a particular incentive scheme from the given class. Regarding the class of feasible incentives, two issues are involved. First, such incentives must abide with institutional and cultural constraints, as well as with the provision of the contracts under which agents join the enterprise. These latter provisions might typically be understood to be the result of market forces equilibrating the opportunities available to various potential entrants to the enterprise. Secondly, such incentives must be compatible with supervisory and informational resources available for their implementation. Thus, the first of the above feasibility requirements is concerned with range-of-acceptance considerations of incentives, both in terms of their structure as well as the remuneration they entail, and the second is an important technical restriction on the class of feasible incentives open to an enterprise designer. This study illustrates how these requirements may be incorporated and evaluated in enterprise design.

The structuring of economic activity through incentives is, of course, not a new topic and it enjoys an extensive literature.[1] Recent research in the incentives area has taken two alternative approaches to the joint problems of optimal information gathering (or monitoring) and incentives design. One approach, exemplified by Hurwicz (1973), Groves (1973) and Bonin (1976), is concerned with cases where the information used in the design or implementation of an incentive scheme is provided by the very agents to whom the incentives are addressed, with the consequence that these agents may find it in their interest to misrepresent the information provided to the incentives designer. In contrast, our approach, following Spence and Zeckhauser (1971) and Harris and Raviv (1978), will focus on incentive problems where the information used in the design and implementation of an incentive scheme is not subject to misrepresentation by the agents at which the scheme is directed. In our model all information is in principle available at the incentives design stage, although its procurement may carry a cost. The question of interest in this matter is then to weigh the costs of collecting and using such information against the increased profits which may ensue through more effective incentives whose implementation this information makes possible. To this point, the share–price gap theorems derived below precisely assess the value of information which is critical in a profit-maximizer's choice between output-sharing and input-pricing incentives.

The plan of the chapter is as follows. In section 2 we define the class of enterprises of concern. These exhibit Cobb–Douglas production technology with preferences of enterprise participants having constant marginal utility for income. The enterprise designer, denoted agent 0, is assumed to both choose the incentive scheme to remunerate other enterprise participants, denoted $i \in N = \{1, \ldots, n\}$, as well as to contribute capital inputs to the production process. The two design problems of interest are then to find the profit-maximizing input-pricing and output-sharing incentive schemes. Whichever incentive scheme is implemented, we assume that enterprise participants adjust to one another in a noncooperative fashion, and we derive the associated internal (Nash) equilibrium. It is at this equilibrium that we evaluate the consequences of each incentive scheme in terms of output, profit, incomes and participants' welfare.

In section 3 we derive the equilibrium behavior of enterprise participants in response to any fixed output-sharing scheme. We then determine the

[1]See, for example, Bonin (1976), Groves (1973), Harris and Raviv (1978), Hurwicz and Shapiro (1978), Kleindorfer and Sertel (1976a), Mirrlees (1974, 1976) and Stiglitz (1974, 1975).

shares which, at equilibrium, lead to maximum profits. We complete the solution to the output-sharing enterprise design problem by solving for the optimal capital input corresponding to the profit-maximizing shares. Section 4 is the analogue of section 2 for the input-pricing incentives design problem.

In section 5 we compare the profit-maximizing pricing enterprise and the profit-maximizing sharing enterprise. First we show that, for each fixed level of capital input, profits are strictly greater under the profit-maximizing pricing scheme than under the corresponding optimal sharing scheme, although agents $i \in N$ may prefer the latter scheme to the former, depending on the particular production function and preferences in question. A further interesting feature exhibited by this comparison is that the ratio of earned income under the two profit-maximizing schemes is the same for all enterprise participants. Continuing our comparison of sharing and pricing, we show that the share–price gap reported for the case where capital input was fixed persists and, in fact, increases when the optimal pricing and sharing enterprises are evaluated at their respective optimal capital input levels. We conclude the chapter with a discussion of some extensions, variations and open problems suggested by these results.

0. Notation and conventions. For the set of natural numbers, we denote $\mathcal{N} = \{1, 2, \ldots\}$. Given $n \in \mathcal{N}$, we denote $N = \{1, \ldots, n\}$ and $\bar{N} = \{0, \ldots, n\}$. For the reals (with the usual topology), we denote $\mathcal{R}$. Cartesian products of topological spaces are understood to carry the product topology. For any family $\{X_i \mid i \in \bar{N}\}$ of nonempty sets, X_i, and given $n \in \mathcal{N}$, we use the following conventions:

$$\bar{\prod} X_i = \prod_{\bar{N}} X_i; \quad \prod X_i = \prod_{N} X_i; \quad \bar{\prod}^i X_j = \prod_{\bar{N}\setminus\{i\}} X_j; \quad \prod^i X_j = \prod_{N\setminus\{i\}} X_j,$$

generic elements being in lower case (e.g. $\bar{x} \in \bar{\prod} X_i$). In a similar way, we suppress indices in sums and products, so that if $x \in \mathcal{R}^n$, $\bar{x} \in \mathcal{R}^{n+1}$, we denote

$$\bar{\sum} x_i = \sum_{\bar{N}} x_i; \qquad \bar{\prod} x_i = \prod_{\bar{N}} x_i; \qquad \sum x_i = \sum_{N} x_i;$$

$$\prod x_i = \prod_{N} x_i; \qquad \prod^i x_j = \prod_{N\setminus\{i\}} x_j.$$

Projection is denoted by π [e.g. for $x \in X = \prod X_i$, $x_i = \pi_{X_i}(x)$].

When a function $g: \mathcal{R} \to \mathcal{R}$ is differentiable from the left (as, for example, in the case when g is concave), we denote its left-hand derivative by g'.

2. Log-linear pre-enterprises and enterprises

What we have in mind generally as a "pre-enterprise" is, roughly, a collection of economic agents whose joint contribution to a productive process yields a certain output which each of them considers a "good", but whose individual contributions may be increased only in return for increasingly greater individual remuneration in terms of this good. For the sake of concreteness and some amount of technical simplicity, from here on we fix attention to a "log-linear" pre-enterprise Ω, as defined in 1, below.

1. Definition. By a *log-linear pre-enterprise* we mean an ordered quadruplet

0. $\Omega = \langle \overline{N}, \overline{X}, u, f \rangle$,

where, using the notation of the previous section,

1. $\overline{N} = \{0, \ldots, n\}$, with $n \in \mathfrak{N}$, is the *personnel*;
2. $\overline{X}$ is the product $\overline{\prod} X_i$ of a family $\{X_i \mid i \in \overline{N}\}$ of *behavior spaces* $X_i = \mathfrak{R}_+$, whereupon we define $X = \prod X_i$, $\overline{X}^i = \overline{\prod}^i X_j$, and $X^i = \prod^i X_j$ $(i \in N)$;
3. $u = \{u_i\colon X_i \times \mathfrak{R} \to \mathfrak{R} \mid i \in \overline{N}\}$ is a family of *utility functions* of the form $u_i(x_i, r_i) = -b_i x_i^{\beta_i} + r_i$ $(x_i \in X_i, r_i \in \mathfrak{R})$ with $b_i > 0$ $(i \in \overline{N})$, $\beta_0 \geqslant 1$, and $\beta_i > 1$ $(i \in N)$;
4. $f\colon \overline{X} \to \mathfrak{R}$ is a *production function* of the form $f(\bar{x}) = \overline{\prod} x_i^{\eta_i}$ with $\overline{\Sigma} \eta_i \leqslant 1$ and $\eta_i > 0$ $(i \in \overline{N})$.

Agent 0 here may be regarded as contributing land or the services of capital goods (x_0) to the productive process at a cost of $b_0 x_0^{\beta_0}$ to himself. Whether this agent is a landlord or a central planning agency, we nickname him "capitalist" and his utility, u_0, "profit". The agents $i \in N$ are nicknamed "workers." Besides determining the level of contribution, x_0, the capitalist will have the additional role, in the enterprise design problems studied here, of instituting an incentive scheme.

By an *incentive scheme* we generally mean any continuous function $r\colon \overline{X} \to \mathfrak{R}^n$, its ith coordinate function $r_i\colon \overline{X} \to \mathfrak{R}$ serving as an *incentive* for the ith worker. In particular, every *price system* $p = (p_1, \ldots, p_n) \in \mathfrak{R}_+^n$ defines a *pricing scheme* $\dot{p}\colon \overline{X} \to \mathfrak{R}^n$ through $\dot{p}_i(\bar{x}) = p_i x_i$, and every *share system*, i.e. every point belonging to $\Lambda = \{\lambda \in \mathfrak{R}_+^n \mid \Sigma \lambda_i \leqslant 1\}$, defines a *sharecropping* (i.e. *output-sharing*) *scheme* $\tilde{\lambda}\colon \overline{X} \to \mathfrak{R}^n$ through $\tilde{\lambda}_i(\bar{x}) = \lambda_i f(\bar{x})$ $(\bar{x} \in \overline{X};\ i \in N)$. A *pricing* (resp. *sharecropping*) *enterprise design* is any ordered pair $\delta = (r, x_0)$ with r a pricing (resp. sharecropping) scheme and $x_0 \in X_0$, and we denote the space of pricing (resp. sharecropping) enterprise designs by $\dot{\Delta}$ (resp. $\tilde{\Delta}$). We often identify $\dot{\Delta}$ and $\tilde{\Delta}$ with their iseomorphs $\mathfrak{R}_+^n \times X_0$ and

$\Lambda \times X_0$, respectively. Every pricing (resp. sharecropping) enterprise design $\dot{\delta} = (\dot{p}, x_0)$ (resp. $\tilde{\delta} = (\tilde{\lambda}, x_0)$) determines a *pricing* (resp. *sharecropping*) *enterprise* $\underline{\Omega}(\dot{\delta})$ (resp. $\underline{\Omega}(\tilde{\delta})$), i.e. an *n*-worker noncooperative game with *effective utilities* ("payoffs") $u[\dot{\delta}]_i(\bar{x}) = u_i(x_i, p_i x_i)$ (resp. $u[\tilde{\delta}]_i(\bar{x}) = u_i(x_i, \lambda_i f(x_0, x_i, x^i))$). Furthermore, it is easy to see that each pricing (resp. sharecropping) enterprise has an associated noncooperative *pricing* (resp. *sharecropping*) *adjustment process* $\alpha[\delta]: X \to X$ with $\delta \in \dot{\Delta}$ (resp. $\delta \in \tilde{\Delta}$), defined through $\alpha[\delta](x) = \{\alpha_i[\delta](x^i)\}_N$, where $\alpha_i[\delta](x^i)$ solves the problem[2]

$$\underset{X_i}{\text{maximize}}\, u[\delta]_i(x_i, \bar{x}^i), \tag{1}$$

as the reaction of the ith worker to the behavior x^i of the others, given the enterprise design ($i \in N$; $\bar{x} = (x_0, x)$, $x \in X$). A *pricing* (resp. *sharecropping*) *equilibrium* of an enterprise $\underline{\Omega}(\dot{\delta})$ (resp. $\underline{\Omega}(\tilde{\delta})$) or of Ω is any fixed point $x = \alpha[\delta](x)$ of $\alpha[\delta]$ with $\delta = \dot{\delta} \in \dot{\Delta}$ ($\delta = \tilde{\delta} \in \tilde{\Delta}$, respectively).

Our analysis of enterprises will be based on their performance at certain of their equilibria which, in a sense suitable for present purposes, may be taken as representative. Patently unrepresentative of an enterprise $\underline{\Omega}(\delta)$ for these purposes would be a point which is *irregular*[3] w.r.t.δ, by which we mean a point $x \in X$ such that every worker strictly prefers the adjustment $\alpha[\delta](y)$ at any $y \in X$ differing from x in every coordinate ($y_j \neq x_j$ for every $j \in N$) over every point $z \in X$ agreeing with x in some coordinate, i.e. formally,

$$\dagger(x) <_i \alpha[\delta](X \setminus \dagger(x)) \qquad (i \in N), \tag{2}$$

[2] Thus, a noncooperative game is assumed "played" among the workers once δ is set, with utility functions $u[\delta]_i$ and strategy spaces X_i ($i \in N$). Of special interest here is the implicit assumption in the adjustment process determined through (1) that $\bar{x}^i$ is observed perfectly (or at least in a fashion unfalsified at equilibrium) and, given the definition of $u[\delta]_i$, that the technology f is also known (i.e. understood) with certainty by each of the workers when $\delta \in \tilde{\Delta}$. Extensions of the present analysis to cooperative adjustment processes and to adjustment processes explicitly allowing misperceptions of f and $\bar{x}^i$ are pursued in Kleindorfer and Sertel (1976a, 1976b, 1978) and Kleindorfer (1978), respectively.

[3] A possible misinterpretation of excluding irregular equilibria from being representative, to be dispelled from the outset, is that prisoners' dilemma situations are therefore also excluded, defining away as "unrepresentative" a paradigm that so often captures indeed the very essence of a multitude of issues central to public economics. If we generally understand by a "prisoner's dilemma situation" one admitting a locally stable equilibrium which is strictly inferior in the view of all participating agents to some other point $x \in X$, then the reader may be assured that we will not discard such situations from consideration by eliminating the inferior equilibrium in question as irregular. This whole matter is discussed at some length in Kleindorfer and Sertel (1976b).

where

$$\dagger(x)=\{z\in X \mid z_k=x_k \text{ for some } k\in N\}. \tag{3}$$

By a *regular* point w.r.t. an enterprise design δ we mean a point in X which is not irregular. We define $\underline{\dot{\Delta}}$ (resp. $\underline{\tilde{\Delta}}$) to be the set of pricing (resp. sharecropping) enterprise design $\dot{\delta}$ (resp. $\tilde{\delta}$) determining an enterprise $\underline{\Omega}(\dot{\delta})$ (resp. $\underline{\Omega}(\tilde{\delta})$) with a *unique* regular equilibrium $\underline{x}(\dot{\delta})$ (resp. $\underline{x}(\tilde{\delta})$), an equilibrium which we say *represents* the enterprise in question. We say that the pre-enterprise Ω is *pricing* (resp. *sharecropping*) *representable* at any design belonging to $\underline{\dot{\Delta}}$ (resp. $\underline{\tilde{\Delta}}$) or on any subset of $\underline{\dot{\Delta}}$ (resp. $\underline{\tilde{\Delta}}$).

Now writing $\underline{\Delta}=\underline{\dot{\Delta}}\cup\underline{\tilde{\Delta}}$, we are able to define the equilibrium map $\underline{x}:\underline{\Delta}\to X$ through

$$\underline{x}(\delta)=\alpha[\delta](\underline{x}(\delta)) \qquad (\delta\in\underline{\Delta}). \tag{4}$$

The restriction $\dot{\underline{x}}$ (resp. $\tilde{\underline{x}}$) of $\underline{x}$ to $\underline{\dot{\Delta}}$ (resp. $\underline{\tilde{\Delta}}$) will be called the *pricing* (resp. *sharecropping*) *equilibrium map*. We will be interested in the evaluation of all the functions f, r_i $(i\in N)$, $r_0=f-\Sigma r_i$, and u_i $(i\in \bar{N})$ at equilibria $\underline{x}(\delta)$ with $\delta=(r,x_0)\in\underline{\Delta}$, and so we write $\underline{f}(\delta)=f(x_0,\underline{x}(\delta))$, $\underline{r}_i(\delta)=r_i(x_0,\underline{x}(\delta))$ $(i\in N)$, $\underline{r}_0(\delta)=\underline{f}(\delta)-\Sigma\underline{r}_i(\delta)$, and $\underline{u}_i(\delta)=u_i(\underline{x}_i(\delta),\underline{r}_i(\delta))$ $(i\in\bar{N})$, thereby defining also the *equilibrium product* $\underline{f}$, the *workers' equilibrium incomes* $\underline{r}_i$ $(i\in N)$, the *capitalist's equilibrium income* $\underline{r}_0$, the *workers' equilibrium utilities* $\underline{u}_i$ $(i\in N)$ and the *capitalist's equilibrium profit* $\underline{u}_0$, all as functions on $\underline{\Delta}$. To indicate the evaluation of these functions at a pricing (resp. sharecropping) equilibrium, we write $\dot{\underline{f}}$, $\dot{\underline{r}}_i$ and $\dot{\underline{u}}_i$ (resp. $\tilde{\underline{f}}$, $\tilde{\underline{r}}_i$ and $\tilde{\underline{u}}_i$).

Our main task in the rest of this study will be to find and compare the solutions to the problems defined in definition 2, below.

2. Definition. The *pricing* (resp. *sharecropping*) *enterprise design problem* for agent 0 is that of maximizing $\underline{u}_0$ over $\underline{\dot{\Delta}}$ (resp. $\underline{\tilde{\Delta}}$) subject to the constraint that $\underline{u}_i\geqslant 0$ for every $i\in N$.

Maximizing the vector $\{\underline{u}_i\}_M$ over $\underline{\dot{\Delta}}$ or $\underline{\tilde{\Delta}}$ for some subset $M\subset\bar{N}$ of agents subject to the same non-negativity constraints for the equilibrium utilities poses other enterprise design problems, of which a most notable case is encountered in designing labor-managed enterprises (see Vanek, 1970), the case where $M=N$. This case is studied in Kleindorfer and Sertel (1976b), where its strikingly different outcomes are compared with those obtained here.

The non-negativity constraint for the equilibrium utilities in the design problems of definition 2 are minimal feasibility requirements for a firm in isolation from an external labor market. Viability of a designed enterprise in face of such a market would naturally require tighter constraints, since the workers would then have to be guaranteed equilibrium utilities not exceeded by what they could achieve by quitting the enterprise and joining the external economy.[4] We will return to this topic in section 6 after we obtain (sections 3 and 4) and compare (section 5) solutions to definition 2.

2. Profit-maximizing design of sharecropping enterprises

In this section our first theorem, theorem 3, determines the sharecropping equilibrium map for a log-linear pre-enterprise. Then, in theorem 4, for each $x_0 \in X_0$ we solve for the profit-maximizing sharecropping scheme $\lambda^*[x_0]$. Finally, assuming a constant per unit cost of capital $b_0 > 0$, i.e. that capital is rentable in a perfect capital market, we obtain, in theorem 5, the profit-maximizing capital input x_0^*, thus solving (with the design $(\lambda^*[x_0^*], x_0^*)$) the sharecropping design problem for agent 0.

3. Theorem. Ω is sharecropping representable on $\underline{\tilde{\Delta}} = \Lambda \times X_0$. In fact, the sharecropping equilibrium map $\underline{\tilde{x}}: \Lambda \times X_0 \to X$ has the form

$$\underline{\tilde{x}}_i(\lambda, x_0) = \left[(C_i\lambda_i)^{\gamma_0} x_0^{\eta_0} \prod (C_j\lambda_j)^{\eta_j/\beta_j}\right]^{1/\gamma_i} \qquad (i \in N), \tag{5}$$

where

$$C_j = \frac{\eta_j}{b_j\beta_j}; \qquad \gamma_j = \beta_j\gamma_0 \qquad (j \in N) \quad \text{with } \gamma_0 = 1 - \sum \eta_j/\beta_j \tag{6}$$

(and so is continuous, continuously differentiable on the interior of $\Lambda \times X_0$, and monotonically increasing). The equilibrium product $\underline{\tilde{f}}: \Lambda \times X_0 \to \mathcal{R}_+$ has the form

$$\tilde{f}(\lambda, x_0) = K\left(x_0^{\eta_0} \prod \lambda_i^{\eta_i/\beta_i}\right)^{1/\gamma_0} \tag{7}$$

where, using the notation of (6) above,

$$K = \prod C_i^{\eta_i/\gamma_i}. \tag{8}$$

For every $\tilde{\delta} \in \text{bdry}\,\underline{\tilde{\Delta}}$, $\underline{\tilde{x}}(\tilde{\delta})$ $(=0)$ is a global attractor, and, for every $\tilde{\delta} \in \text{int}\,\underline{\tilde{\Delta}}$, $\underline{x}(\tilde{\delta})$ is asymptotically stable with region of attraction[5] int X.

[4]See, for example, Mirrlees (1976), Sertel (1978), and Sertel, Başar and Selbuz (1978) for a discussion of such range-of-acceptance constraints and their use in analyzing market equilibrium.

Proof. Take any $\tilde{\delta}=(\lambda, x_0)\in\Lambda\times X_0$. By definition, any equilibrium $\tilde{x}$ of $\underline{\Omega}(\tilde{\delta})$ is determined through

$$-b_i\tilde{x}_i^{\beta_i}+\lambda_i x_0^{\eta_0}\prod\tilde{x}_j^{\eta_j}=\max_{X_i}\left[-b_i x_i^{\beta_i}+\lambda_i x_0^{\eta_0}x_i^{\eta_i}\prod{}^{i}\tilde{x}_j^{\eta_j}\right]\qquad(i\in N). \tag{9}$$

From (3) it is clear that $\alpha[\tilde{\delta}]\,(\dagger(\underline{0}))=\{\underline{0}\}$, so an equilibrium $\tilde{x}$ of $\underline{\Omega}(\tilde{\delta})$ has all coordinates zero or all coordinates nonzero. If $x_0=0$ or $\lambda_i=0$ for some $i\in N$, then the equilibrium $\underline{0}$ is the unique equilibrium of $\underline{\Omega}(\tilde{\delta})$ and is regular. So, until the end of this paragraph, assume $x_0>0$ and $\lambda_i>0$ for every $i\in N$. Now, from (2) and (3), we see that the equilibrium $\underline{0}$ is irregular. We show that $\underline{\Omega}(\tilde{\delta})$ actually has a positive equilibrium, indeed a unique such point $\underline{\tilde{x}}(\tilde{\delta})$ which is given by (5), and that this point is regular. As $u[\tilde{\delta}]_i$ is concave and continuously differentiable in x_i on int X, the necessary and sufficient conditions characterizing the strictly positive solutions x to the maximization problems (1) are the following first-order conditions:

$$\beta_i b_i\tilde{x}_i^{\beta_i-1}=\eta_i\lambda_i x_0^{\eta_0}\tilde{x}_i^{\eta_i-1}\prod{}^{i}\tilde{x}_j^{\eta_j}\qquad(i\in N), \tag{10}$$

i.e.

$$\beta_i b_i\tilde{x}_i^{\beta_i}=\eta_i\lambda_i x_0^{\eta_0}\prod\tilde{x}_j^{\eta_j}=\eta_i\lambda_i f(x_0,\tilde{x})\qquad(i\in N). \tag{11}$$

From (6) and (11) we have

$$\tilde{x}_i^{\beta_i}=C_i\lambda_i f(x_0,\tilde{x})\qquad(i\in N). \tag{12}$$

Writing $c_i=\log C_i\lambda_i$, $y_0=\log x_0$ and $y_i=\log\tilde{x}_i$ $(i\in N)$, and taking logarithms of both sides of (12) yields the following system of n linear equations:

$$\beta_i y_i=c_i+\overline{\sum}\eta_j y_j\qquad(i\in N). \tag{13}$$

This system is solved uniquely by

$$y_i=\frac{1}{\gamma_i}\left(\gamma_0 c_i+\eta_0 y_0+\sum\frac{\eta_j}{\beta_j}c_j\right)\qquad(i\in N), \tag{14}$$

[5] We follow Bhatia and Szegö (1970) in our definition of terms related to stability. In particular, for a pre-enterprise Ω and any $\delta\in\underline{\Delta}(\Omega)$, we say that the enterprise equilibrium $\underline{x}(\delta)$ is *stable* iff, for every nbd $V\subset X$ of $\underline{x}(\delta)$, there exists a nbd $U\subset V$ of $\underline{x}(\delta)$ with $\alpha[\delta](U)\subset U$, and $\underline{x}(\delta)$ is said to be an *attractor* iff there exists a nbd $V\subset X$ of $\underline{x}(\delta)$ such that $\lim_{\kappa\to\infty}\alpha[\delta]^{\kappa}(x)=\underline{x}(\delta)$ whenever $x\in V$, where $\alpha[\delta]^{\kappa}\colon X\to X$ is the κ-fold composition of $\alpha[\delta]$ with itself. The notions of *local* and *global attraction* are defined relative to the domain of attraction V. Finally, $\underline{x}(\delta)$ is said to be (*globally*) *asymptotically stable* iff it is both stable and an attractor (a global attractor).

with γ_i as in (6), and taking antilogarithms in (14) yields $\tilde{x} = \underline{\tilde{x}}(\tilde{\delta})$ as given by (5), showing that $\underline{\tilde{x}}(\tilde{\delta})$ is the unique positive equilibrium of $\underline{\Omega}(\tilde{\delta})$. To see that $\underline{\tilde{x}}(\tilde{\delta})$ is regular, simply note that $\underline{0} = \alpha[\tilde{\delta}]\,(\underline{0}) \in X \setminus \dagger(\underline{\tilde{x}}(\tilde{\delta}))$ and $u[\tilde{\delta}]_i(\underline{0}) < u[\tilde{\delta}]_i(\underline{\tilde{x}}(\tilde{\delta}))$ for some (in fact all) $i \in N$. So much shows that $\underline{\tilde{\Delta}} = \Lambda \times X_0$, on which (5) describes the equilibrium map $\underline{\tilde{x}}$.

To see (7), use (13) to write

$$\log f\left(x_0, \underline{\tilde{x}}(\tilde{\delta})\right) = \bar{\sum} \eta_j y_j = \beta_i y_i - c_i \qquad (i \in N), \tag{15}$$

substitute (14), and take antilogarithms. For this describes $\tilde{f}(\tilde{\delta})$ for $\tilde{\delta} = (\lambda, x_0)$ with $x_0 > 0$ and $\lambda_i > 0$ for each $i \in N$, and $\underline{\tilde{f}}(\tilde{\delta}) = 0$ otherwise (as in (7)). □

[Proof of the claimed attraction and stability properties of the values assumed by the equilibrium map $\underline{\tilde{x}}$ is technical and lengthy, and therefore is omitted.]

4. Theorem (profit-maximizing sharecropping scheme). For each $x_0 \in X_0$, the profit-maximizing sharecropping enterprise design problem (restricted to $\Lambda \times \{x_0\}$) is solved by the design $\tilde{\delta}^* = (\tilde{\lambda}^*, x_0)$ with shares[6] $\lambda_i^* = \eta_i / \beta_i$ (independent of x_0) ($i \in N$).

Proof. Take any $x_0 \in X_0$. We wish to find the (profit-maximizing[7]) designs $\tilde{\delta}^* \in \Lambda \times \{x_0\}$ which solve the problem:

$$\underset{\Lambda \times \{x_0\}}{\text{maximize}}\, \underline{\tilde{r}}_0(\lambda, x_0) = \left(1 - \sum \lambda_i\right) f(x_0, \underline{\tilde{x}}(\lambda, x_0)). \tag{16}$$

First note that, since Λ is compact and f and $\underline{\tilde{x}}$ are continuous, a solution to (16) exists. If $x_0 = 0$, then $\tilde{r}_0(\lambda, x_0) = 0$ for all $\lambda \in \Lambda$, so the asserted design $\tilde{\delta}^* = (\lambda^*, x_0)$ is optimal. Now assume $x_0 > 0$. If $\lambda_i = 0$ for any $i \in N$, then, from (7) and (16), $\tilde{f}(\lambda, x_0) = 0$. Also, if $\lambda_i > 0$ ($i \in N$) and $1 - \Sigma\lambda_i > 0$ (i.e. if $\lambda \in \text{int}\,\Lambda$), then (7) and (16) imply $\underline{\tilde{r}}_0(\lambda, x_0) > 0$. We may therefore restrict attention to the design set $\text{int}\,\Lambda \times \{x_0\}$. Taking first-order conditions yields from (7)

$$\left(1 - \sum \lambda_j\right) \frac{\eta_i}{\gamma_i \lambda_i} f(x_0, \underline{\tilde{x}}(\lambda, x_0)) - f(x_0, \underline{\tilde{x}}(\lambda, x_0)) = 0 \quad (i \in N), \tag{17}$$

[6] From definition 1 it may be noted that λ_i^* is the ratio of the elasticity of output with respect to x_i to the elasticity of agent i's opportunity costs ($b_i x_i^{\beta_i}$) of contributing x_i. In this sense the more productive a worker is and the lower the opportunity costs (or disutility) of his contributing x_i, the higher will be his share in the profit-maximizing sharecropping enterprise.

[7] When x_0 is fixed, as assumed here, maximizing profit U_0 is equivalent to maximizing $r_0 = u_0 + b_0 x_0^{\beta_0}$.

or, cancelling f,

$$1-\sum \lambda_j = \gamma_i \lambda_i / \eta_i \qquad (i \in N). \tag{18}$$

The unique solution to (18) is the asserted profit-maximizing sharing-scheme λ^*. □

Note that although we had fixed x_0 above, λ^* is actually independent of x_0. To fully determine the profit-maximizing sharecropping design $\tilde{\delta}^* = (\lambda^*, x_0^*)$ we need to determine x_0^*. When x_0 is capital input, this is essentially a matter of the cost of capital. Assuming a constant per unit cost of capital, i.e. that $\beta_0 = 1$, we solve for $\tilde{\delta}^*$ in the following.

5. Theorem (profit-maximizing sharecropping design). Assuming $\beta_0 = 1$, the profit-maximizing level $\tilde{x}_0^*$ of capital investment under the profit-maximizing sharing scheme λ^* (see theorem 4) is

$$\tilde{x}_0^* = \left(\frac{\eta_0 \tilde{G}}{b_0} \right)^{\gamma_0/(\gamma_0 - \eta_0)}, \tag{19}$$

where

$$\tilde{G} = \prod \left(\frac{\eta_i^2}{\beta_i^2 b_i} \right)^{\eta_i/\gamma_i}, \tag{20}$$

with γ_i as given in (6) $(i \in N)$. [Thus, the sharecropping enterprise design problem for agent 0 is solved by $\tilde{\delta}^* = (\lambda^*, \tilde{x}_0^*)$ with $\lambda_i^* = \eta_i / \beta_i$ $(i \in N)$ and $\tilde{x}_0^*$ as given in (19).]

Proof. From the optimality of λ^*, as shown in theorem 4, all that we need show here is that $\tilde{x}_0^*$ in (19) is the optimal capital input. [*Note*: The reader may check that $\tilde{\delta}^*$ satisfies the constraint $\{u[\delta]_i\}_{\bar{N}} \geqslant 0$ in definition 2 so that the indicated profit-maximizing design is feasible.] The optimal $\tilde{x}_0^*$ is found by maximizing $\underline{\tilde{u}}_0^*[x_0] = -b_0 x_0 + \underline{\tilde{r}}_0^*[x_0]$. Now $\gamma_0 = 1 - \Sigma(\eta_i/\beta_i) > 1 - \Sigma\eta_i \geqslant \eta_0$ since $\beta_i > 1$ for every $i \in N$ and $\bar{\Sigma}\eta_i \leqslant 1$. From (7), the function

$$\underline{\tilde{r}}_0^* = \left(1 - \sum \lambda_i^*\right) \underline{\tilde{f}}(\lambda^*, \cdot) \tag{21}$$

is concave and, hence, so is $-b_0 x_0 + \underline{\tilde{r}}_0^*$, allowing us to use first-order conditions in maximizing it. Using (7) and (21) with $\lambda_i^* = \eta_i/\beta_i$, these conditions give us

$$\eta_0 \tilde{G} x_0^{(\eta_0 - \gamma_0)/\gamma_0} = b_0, \tag{22}$$

which solves to give (19). □

As $\gamma_0 \geqslant \gamma_0 - \eta_0 > 0$ in the above, (19) implies the intuitively pleasing fact that $\tilde{x}_0^*$ is nonincreasing in b_0.

3. Profit-maximizing design of pricing enterprises

In a development paralleling that of the last section, we derive, in theorem 6 below, the pricing equilibrium map and then in theorem 7, the profit-maximizing pricing scheme $p^*[x_0]$ $(x_0 \in X_0)$, and finally, in theorem 9, the pricing-design $\dot{\delta}^* = (p^*[\dot{x}_0^*], \dot{x}_0^*)$.

6. Theorem. Ω is pricing representable on $\dot{\underline{\Delta}} = \mathfrak{R}_+^n \times X_0$. In fact, the pricing equilibrium $\dot{x} : \mathfrak{R}_+^n \times X_0 \to X$ has the form[8]

$$\underline{\dot{x}}_i(\dot{\delta}) = \left(\frac{p_i}{\beta_i b_i}\right)^{1/(\beta_i - 1)} \quad (\dot{\delta} = (p, x_0) \in \mathfrak{R}_+^n \times X_0;\ i \in N) \tag{23}$$

(and so is continuous, continuously differentiable on the interior of $\dot{\underline{\Delta}}$, and monotonically increasing in p, with each equilibrium $\dot{x}(\dot{\delta})$ globally asymptotically stable $(\dot{\delta} \in \dot{\underline{\Delta}}(\Omega))$). The equilibrium product $\underline{\dot{f}} : \mathfrak{R}_+^n \times X_0 \to \mathfrak{R}$ has the form

$$\underline{\dot{f}}(p, x_0) = f(x_0, \underline{\dot{x}}(p, x_0)) = x_0^{\eta_0} \prod \left(\frac{p_i}{\beta_i b_i}\right)^{\eta_i/(\beta_i - 1)}. \tag{24}$$

Proof. Taking any $\dot{\delta} = (p, x_0) \in \mathfrak{R}_+^n \times X_0$, the effective utility of i is

$$u[\dot{\delta}]_i = -b_i x_i^{\beta_i} + p_i x_i \qquad (i \in N) \tag{25}$$

[8]The equations of (23) display the individual supplies of individually owned inputs as a function of prices, given an enterprise design. Profit-maximizing prices are to be chosen subject to these supply constraints. This corresponds to "monopsonistic capitalism" in Dirickx and Sertel (1977). When the choice of prices is not constrained so but rather by agent's subsistence requirements, one obtains "slavery" (Dirickx and Sertel, 1977), a case where individuals' inputs are effectively not their own property. In the literature (e.g. Spence and Zeckhauser, 1971, and Harris and Raviv, 1978) authors have proposed also "threat" or "forcing" systems, paying agents only when their inputs exceed a certain input level. This is similar to the (Pareto-optimal) political economies of "slavery with prices *and quotas*" or "communism with prices *and* quotas" in Dirickx and Sertel (1977), where not only price incentives but also a further typical instrument, quotas, may be utilized. In our present system not only are such extra instruments not at the disposal of the system designer but, furthermore, individuals' inputs are assumed to be individuals' own property, and their disposal or use is fully at their command so that supply constraints such as (23) must be respected.

and the first-order conditions of maximizing each $u[\dot{\delta}]_i$ on X_i yield the equilibrium map $\underline{\dot{x}}$ described by (23). From this all is clear. □

7. Theorem (profit-maximizing pricing scheme). For any $x_0 \in X_0$, the pricing-enterprise design problem for agent 0 (restricted to $\mathfrak{R}^n_+ \times \{x_0\}$) is solved uniquely by the design $\dot{\delta}^* = (p^*, x_0)$ with prices

$$p_i^*[x_0] = \left[\beta_i b_i \left(\frac{\eta_i}{\beta_i} \left\{ \prod \left(\frac{\eta_j}{\beta_j^2 b_j} \right)^{\eta_j/\gamma_j} \right\} x_0^{\eta_0/\gamma_0} \right)^{(\beta_i - 1)} \right]^{1/\beta_i} \qquad (i \in N). \tag{26}$$

Proof. When $x_0 = 0$ the optimal pricing scheme is clearly $p_i^* = 0$ $(i \in N)$ as asserted in (26). Now take any $x_0 \in \text{int}\, X_0$, recall that

$$\underline{\dot{r}}_0(p, x_0) = f(x_0, \underline{\dot{x}}(p, x_0)) - \sum p_i \underline{\dot{x}}_i(p, x_0) \qquad (p \in \mathfrak{R}^n_+, x_0 \in X_0) \tag{27}$$

and consider the problem

$$\underset{\mathfrak{R}^n_+ \times \{x_0\}}{\text{maximize}}\, \underline{\dot{r}}_0(p, x_0). \tag{28}$$

We may rewrite the maximand in (28), using (23)–(24), as

$$\underline{\dot{r}}_0(p, x_0) = x_0^{\eta_0} \prod \left(\frac{p_i}{\beta_i b_i} \right)^{\eta_i/(\beta_i - 1)} - \sum p_i \left(\frac{p_i}{\beta_i b_i} \right)^{1/(\beta_i - 1)}. \tag{29}$$

Now denote

$$h_0 = x_0^{\eta_0} \prod \left(\frac{1}{\beta_i b_i} \right)^{\eta_i/(\beta_i - 1)}; \qquad h_i = \left(\frac{1}{\beta_i b_i} \right)^{1/(\beta_i - 1)} \qquad (i \in N), \tag{30}$$

noting that these are all positive, and write

$$\underline{y}_i(p) = p_i^{1/(\beta_i - 1)}; \qquad \underline{y}(p) = \{\underline{y}_i(p)\}_N \qquad (p \in \mathfrak{R}^n_+, i \in N) \tag{31}$$

and

$$\rho(y) = h_0 \prod y_i^{\eta_i} - \sum h_i y_i^{\beta_i} \qquad (y = \{y_i\}_N). \tag{32}$$

Now $\underline{\dot{r}}_0(p, x_0) = \rho(\underline{y}(p))$ $(p \in \mathfrak{R}^n_+)$ and $\underline{y}: \mathfrak{R}^n_+ \to \mathfrak{R}^n_+$ in (31) is one-to-one onto. Therefore, (28) has a solution $p^* = \bar{p}^*[x_0]$ iff $\max\{\rho(y) \mid y \in \mathfrak{R}^n_+\}$ has a solution $y^* = \underline{y}(p^*)$ (where, then, $p^* = \underline{y}^{-1}(y^*)$). We may therefore concentrate our attention on maximizing ρ. In order not to distract from the main argument here, we summarize its solution in lemma 8 below. From lemma 8 we see that ρ achieves a unique maximum at the point y^* given in (35). Substituting for h_i $(i \in \bar{N})$ in (35) the expressions in (30), we see that

$$y_i^* = \left[(\beta_i b_i)^{1/(\beta_i - 1)} \frac{\eta_i}{\beta_i} \left\{ \prod \left(\frac{\eta_j}{\beta_j^2 b_j} \right)^{\eta_j/\gamma_j} \right\} x_0^{\eta_0/\gamma_0} \right]^{1/\beta_i} \qquad (i \in N). \qquad (33)$$

From (31), the optimal solution to (28) is $p_i^* = y_i^{*(\beta_i - 1)}$ $(i \in N)$, which is none other than (26). □

8. Lemma. Let η_i, β_i, h_i $(i \in \bar{N})$ be positive constants, satisfying (as do the parameters of any log-linear pre-enterprise) $\Sigma \eta_i \leq 1$ and $\beta_i > 1$ $(i \in N)$. Define the function $\rho : \mathfrak{R}_+^n \to \mathfrak{R}$ through

$$\rho(y) = h_0 \prod y_i^{\eta_i} - \sum h_i y_i^{\beta_i} \qquad (y \in \mathfrak{R}_+^n). \qquad (34)$$

Then $\max\{\rho(y) \mid y \in \mathfrak{R}_+^n\}$ exists and is attained at the unique point $y^* = \{y_i^*\}_N$ given by

$$y_i^* = \left(\frac{\eta_i}{\beta_i h_i} \right)^{1/\beta_i} \left[h_0 \prod \left(\frac{\eta_j}{\beta_j h_j} \right)^{\eta_j/\beta_j} \right]^{1/\gamma_i} \qquad (i \in N), \qquad (35)$$

$$\rho(y^*) = \max\{\rho(y) \mid y \in \mathfrak{R}_+^n\} = \gamma_0 h_0^{1/\gamma_0} \prod \left(\frac{\eta_i}{\beta_i h_i} \right)^{\eta_i/\gamma_i}. \qquad (36)$$

Proof. Straightforward. □

9. Theorem (profit-maximizing pricing design). Assuming $\beta_0 = 1$, the profit-maximizing level $\dot{x}_0^*$ of capital investment under the profit-maximizing pricing scheme $p^*[x_0]$ $(x_0 \in X_0)$ of theorem 7 is

$$\dot{x}_0^* = \frac{\eta_0 \dot{G}}{b_0}^{\gamma_0/(\gamma_0 - \eta_0)}, \qquad (37)$$

where

$$\dot{G} = \prod \left(\frac{\eta_i}{\beta_i^2 b_i} \right)^{\eta_i/\gamma_i}, \qquad (38)$$

with γ_i as given in (6) $(i \in N)$. Thus, the pricing enterprise design problem for agent 0 is solved by $\dot{\delta}^*=(p^*[\dot{x}_0^*], \dot{x}_0^*)$ with

$$p_i^*[x_0^*]=\left[(\beta_i b_i)\left(\frac{\eta_i \dot{G}}{\beta_i}\left(\frac{\eta_0 \dot{G}}{b_0}\right)^{\eta_0/(\gamma_0-\eta_0)}\right)^{\beta_i-1}\right]^{1/\beta_i} \qquad (i\in N) \qquad (39)$$

and $\dot{x}_0^*$ as given in (37).

Proof. From the optimality of $p^*[x_0]$ $(x_0\in X_0)$, as shown in theorem 7, the optimal $\dot{\underline{x}}^*$ is found by maximizing $\dot{\underline{u}}_0^*[x_0]=-b_0x_0+\dot{\underline{r}}_0^*[x_0]$, where

$$\dot{\underline{r}}_0^*[x_0]=\dot{f}^*[x_0]-\sum p_i^*[x_0]\dot{\underline{x}}_i(p_i^*[x_0], x_0) \qquad (x_0\in X_0). \qquad (40)$$

Using (24) and (26) we have

$$\dot{\underline{u}}_0^*[x_0]=-b_0x_0+\gamma_0\left[\frac{\eta_0}{b_0}\dot{G}^{\gamma_0/\eta_0}\right]^{\eta_0/(\gamma_0-\eta_0)}. \qquad (41)$$

Duplicating the proof of theorem 5, we see that $\dot{\underline{u}}_0^*$ is concave with first-order conditions yielding (37). Finally, substituting (37) in (26) yields (39). Thus, $\dot{\delta}^*$ is the profit-maximizing pricing design. Clearly, $\dot{\delta}^*$ satisfies the constraint $\{\underline{u}[\delta]_i\}_{\bar{N}}\geqslant 0$ of definition 2. □

4. Sharing versus pricing

In this section we first compare the optimal sharecropping and pricing schemes at any common level x_0 of capital input. Then, adopting a constant per unit cost b_0 for the factor x_0, we compare the output, income, profit, and welfare consequences of the profit-maximizing sharecropping and pricing enterprise designs, allowing x_0 to adjust to its indigenous (profit-maximizing) level under each of the two modes of enterprise design. Our first result, theorem 10, summarizes parts of theorems 3–7, lemma 8 and theorem 9.

10. Theorem (small share price gap). Writing

$$\tilde{G}=\prod\left(\frac{\eta_i^2}{\beta_i^2 b_i}\right)^{\eta_i/\gamma_i} \quad \text{and} \quad \dot{G}=\prod\left(\frac{\eta_i}{\beta_i^2 b_i}\right)^{\eta_i/\gamma_i}, \qquad (42)$$

for every $x_0\in X_0$, table 4.1 compares the outcome of instituting the profit-maximizing sharecropping scheme (see theorem 4) with that of instituting the profit-maximizing pricing scheme (see theorem 7). Denoting the ratio $\tilde{G}/\dot{G}$ by G, we have

$$G=\frac{\tilde{G}}{\dot{G}}=\left(\prod\left(\eta_i^{\eta_i/\beta_i}\right)\right)^{1/\gamma_0}<1; \tag{43}$$

so, we see from table 4.1 that

$$\frac{\underline{\tilde{f}}^*[x_0]}{\underline{\dot{f}}^*[x_0]}=\frac{\underline{\tilde{r}}_i^*[x_0]}{\underline{\dot{r}}_i^*[x_0]}=\frac{\tilde{p}_0^*[x_0]}{\dot{p}_0^*[x_0]}=G<1 \qquad (i\in\bar{N}), \tag{44}$$

$$\frac{\underline{\tilde{x}}_i^*[x_0]}{\underline{\dot{x}}_i^*[x_0]}=(\eta_i G)^{1/\beta_i}<1 \qquad (i\in N), \tag{45}$$

$$\frac{\tilde{p}_i^*[x_0]}{\dot{p}_i^*[x_0]}=\left(\frac{G^{\beta_i-1}}{\eta_i}\right)^{1/\beta_i} \qquad (i\in N), \tag{46}$$

$$\frac{\underline{\tilde{u}}_i^*[x_0]}{\underline{\dot{u}}_i[x_0]}=\frac{\beta_i-\eta_i}{\beta_i-1}G \qquad (i\in N). \tag{47}$$

By (44) the income of each agent $i\in N$ is uniformly and proportionately higher under the profit-maximizing pricing scheme as compared with the profit-maximizing sharing scheme. In particular, for each $x_0\in X_0$, $\underline{\dot{r}}_0^*[x_0]>\underline{\tilde{r}}_0^*[x_0]$ so that, gross of information costs, the pricing enterprise design $(\dot{p}^*[x_0], x_0)$ is strictly more profitable than the sharecropping enterprise

Table 4.1
Comparing profit-maximizing sharecropping and pricing schemes ($i\in N$).

Sharecropping	Pricing
$\underline{\tilde{f}}^*[x_0]=\tilde{G}x_0^{\eta_0/\gamma_0}$	$\underline{\dot{f}}^*[x_0]=\dot{G}x_0^{\eta_0/\gamma_0}$
$\lambda_i^*=\frac{\eta_i}{\beta_i}$	$\dot{\lambda}_i^*=\frac{\underline{\dot{r}}_i^*[x_0]}{\underline{\dot{f}}^*[x_0]}=\frac{\eta_i}{\beta_i}$
$\tilde{p}_0^*[x_0]=\frac{\underline{\tilde{r}}_0^*[x_0]}{x_0}=\gamma_0\underline{\tilde{f}}^*[x_0]$	$\dot{p}_0^*[x_0]=\frac{\underline{\dot{r}}_0^*[x_0]}{x_0}=\gamma_0\underline{\dot{f}}^*[x_0]$
$\tilde{p}_i^*[x_0]=\frac{\underline{\tilde{r}}_i^*[x_0]}{\underline{\tilde{x}}_i^*[x_0]}=\left[\left(\frac{\beta_i b_i}{\eta_i}\right)\left(\frac{\eta_i}{\beta_i}\underline{\tilde{f}}^*[x_0]\right)^{(\beta_i-1)}\right]^{1/\beta_i}$	$\dot{p}_i^*[x_0]=\left[(\beta_i b_i)\left(\frac{\eta_i}{\beta_i}\underline{\dot{f}}^*[x_0]\right)^{(\beta_i-1)}\right]^{1/\beta_i}$
$\underline{\tilde{x}}_i^*[x_0]=\left[\frac{\eta_i^2\underline{\tilde{f}}^*[x_0]}{\beta_i^2 b_i}\right]^{1/\beta_i}$	$\underline{\dot{x}}_i^*[x_0]=\left[\frac{\eta_i\underline{\dot{f}}^*[x_0]}{\beta_i^2 b_i}\right]^{1/\beta_i}$
$\underline{\tilde{r}}_0^*[x_0]=\gamma_0\underline{\tilde{f}}^*[x_0]$	$\underline{\dot{r}}_0^*[x_0]=\gamma_0\underline{\dot{f}}^*[x_0]$
$\underline{\tilde{r}}_i^*[x_0]=\frac{\eta_i}{\beta_i}\underline{\tilde{f}}^*[x_0]$	$\underline{\dot{r}}_i^*[x_0]=\frac{\eta_i}{\beta_i}\underline{\dot{f}}^*[x_0]$
$\underline{\tilde{u}}_i^*[x_0]=\left(1-\frac{\eta_i}{\beta_i}\right)\frac{\eta_i}{\beta_i}\underline{\tilde{f}}^*[x_0]$	$\dot{u}_i^*[x_0]=\left(1-\frac{1}{\beta_i}\right)\frac{\eta_i}{\beta_i}\underline{\dot{f}}^*[x_0]$

design $(\tilde{\lambda}^*, x_0)$. Thus, we see that if the cost of measuring inputs does not exceed that of measuring output by more than the gap, $\dot{r}_{\underline{0}}^*[x_0]-\tilde{r}_{\underline{0}}^*[x_0]$, reported in (44), then agent 0 will prefer pricing to sharecropping for whatever level $x_0 \in X_0$ of capital input he considers contributing, so long as he is able to institute the profit-maximizing prices and shares.[9] It should be noted, however, that some or all of the agents $i \in N$ may prefer the profit-maximizing sharecropping scheme $\tilde{\lambda}^*$ to the profit-maximizing pricing scheme $\dot{p}^*[x_0]$. According to (47) agent $i \in N$ prefers $\tilde{\lambda}^*[x_0]$ to $\dot{p}^*[x_0]$ when $(\beta_i - \eta_i)G$ exceeds $(\beta_i - 1)$. [Note, from (47), that this preference will again be independent of the particular $x_0 \in X_0$ at which the comparison is made.] That this is possible (e.g. for η_i and β_i sufficiently small) can be verified from (43) and (47), but we delay the detailed discussion of this matter until the end of this section.

Turning to the information requirements of incentives design, we may first note that profit-maximizing prices embody knowledge of b_i, β_i and η_i, whereas the profit-maximizing shares depend only on the ratios η_i/β_i. Thus, pricing and sharing require different information (measurement of inputs versus output) not only in their implementation, but also in their optimal design. Now, an incentives designer able to implement a pricing scheme, i.e. able to observe inputs, can in principle ascertain the parameters b_i and β_i by experimentally estimating these through the reaction function (23), assuming, of course, that agents do not engage in information concealment or other strategic behavior to foil such experimentation.[10] If, in addition, this incentives designer could observe output, then he could estimate the remaining parameters η_i required to compute profit-maximizing prices. In contrast,

[9]We feel the need to express our difficulties with a number of assertions which Stiglitz (1975) makes at the outset of his study. A case in point is his contention that "The greater the responsiveness of individuals to monetary incentives, the greater the reliance on piece rates" (Stiglitz, 1975, p. 558). The context of this assertion is a one employer/one employee relation and Stiglitz's comparison refers to piece rates versus times rates. Interpreting Stiglitz in the present context, a time rate is a wage p_1, and a piece rate is a share λ_1 in output on a one-worker farm: "responsiveness to monetary incentives" is presumably meant to be understood as being some quantity which is higher when the elasticity ε (resp. ε') of the worker's equilibrium contribution $\underset{\cdot}{x}(p)$ (resp. $\underline{x}(\lambda)$) with respect to p (resp. λ) is higher. Now $\varepsilon = 1/(\beta_1 - 1)$ and $\varepsilon' = 1/(\beta_1 - \eta_1)$, so that the higher the responsiveness in question, the lower must be β_1. But we know that the higher the advantage of (profit-maximizing) pricing over sharing, the higher is G (see (44)), and $\partial G/\partial \beta_1 > 0$, in evident contradiction of Stiglitz's conjecture. (We would have reached the same conclusion, had the employer's contribution been allowed to adjust, this time reasoning with (48) below.)

[10]As announced in the introduction, this chapter does not consider such special problems arising when incentives must be designed, using information (messages) provided by the very agents whom the incentives are to address. For a discussion and analysis of this issue see Hurwicz (1973), Groves (1973) and Bonin (1976).

in order to estimate the profit-maximizing sharecropping design only output needs to be observed. For, using (7) and recalling from (6) that $\gamma_0 = 1 - \Sigma\eta_j/\beta_j$, the behavior of equilibrium output in response to changes in λ will reveal the parameters η_i/β_i. Thus, the informational requirements for computing profit-maximizing designs also appear stronger than for the profit-maximizing sharecropping design.[11]

Our next theorem summarizes the outcomes of profit-maximizing sharing and pricing at the respective optimal capital input levels $\tilde{x}_0^*$ and $\dot{x}_0^*$. We use the *notational convention* here that quantities evaluated at their respective optimal capital input levels carry a simple superscript *, e.g. $\tilde{p}_0^* \triangleq \tilde{p}_0^*[\tilde{x}_1^*]$, $\underline{\dot{f}}^* \triangleq \underline{\dot{f}}^*[\tilde{x}_0^*]$.

11. Theorem (large share–price gap). Assume $\beta_0 = 1$. Then comparing the outcome of instituting (the profit-maximizing sharecropping enterprise design) $\tilde{\delta}^*$ (see theorem 4) with that of instituting the profit-maximizing pricing enterprise design) $\dot{\delta}^*$ (see theorem 9) leads to the conclusions that $\tilde{p}_0^* = \dot{p}_0^*$,

$$\frac{\tilde{x}_0^*}{\dot{x}_0^*} = \frac{\tilde{f}^*}{\underline{\dot{f}}^*} = \frac{\underline{\tilde{r}}_i^*}{\underline{\dot{r}}_i} = \frac{\underline{\tilde{u}}_0^*}{\underline{\dot{u}}_0^*} = G^{\gamma_0/(\gamma_0 - \eta_0)} < G < 1 \qquad (i \in \bar{N}), \tag{48}$$

$$\frac{\underline{\tilde{x}}_i^*}{\underline{\dot{x}}_i} = \left(\eta_i G^{\gamma_0/(\gamma_0 - \eta_0)}\right)^{1/\beta_i} \leqslant (\eta_i G)^{1/\beta_i} < 1 \qquad (i \in N), \tag{49}$$

$$\frac{\tilde{p}_i^*}{\dot{p}_i^*} = \left[\frac{G^{\gamma_0(\beta_i - 1)/(\gamma_0 - \eta_0)}}{\eta_i}\right]^{1/\beta_i} \qquad (i \in N), \tag{50}$$

$$\frac{\underline{\tilde{u}}_i^*}{\underline{\dot{u}}_i^*} = \frac{\beta_i - \eta_i}{\beta_i - 1} G^{\gamma_0/(\gamma_0 - \eta_0)} < \frac{\beta_i - \eta_i}{\beta_i - 1} G \qquad (i \in N). \tag{51}$$

In particular, the equilibrium product, profit, net profit and the income of each agent $i \in N$ are higher by the same proportion ($G^{\gamma_0/(\eta_0 - \gamma_0)}$) in the profit-maximizing pricing enterprise $\underline{\Omega}(\dot{\delta}^*)$ than in the profit-maximizing sharecropping enterprise $\underline{\Omega}(\tilde{\delta}^*)$ (see (48)).

Proof. By substituting (19) and (37) for $\tilde{x}_0$ and $\dot{x}_0$, respectively, in table 4.1, a "table" is obtained from which all the equations in (48)–(51) are directly computed. Given that $G < 1$ from (43), the remaining part of (48)

[11] The reader can check, however, that both sharecropping and pricing equilibrium profit are sufficiently regular (differentiable and strictly quasi-concave) to admit hill-climbing techniques in successively approximating profit-maximizing prices and shares.

left to see that $G^{\gamma_0/(\gamma_0-\eta_0)}<G$, which follows from the fact that $\gamma_0>\eta_0\geqslant 0$, as seen in theorem 5. This also explains the remaining inequalities. □

Comparing (48)–(51) with (44)–(47) we see that the share–price gap reported in the former set of inequalities is, if anything, greater than that reported in the latter. It is for this reason that we distinguish between theorems 10 and 11 as, respectively, the small share–price gap theorem and the large share–price gap theorem. We had already seen from theorem 10 that a profit-maximizing pricing scheme imparts a strictly greater affluence to all participants – "capitalist" (agent 0) and "workers" (agents $i\in N$) alike – than does a profit-maximizing sharecropping scheme (see (42)). Now we know that the affluence gap between sharecropping and pricing is only widened when we compare incomes under the profit-maximizing sharecropping and pricing designs (see (48)).

On the other hand, as a matter of interest especially from a central planner's viewpoint of development or growth, one may examine the capital/output ratio. From table 4.1 it is clear that, since equilibrium output is greater under the profit-maximizing pricing scheme $\dot{p}_0^*[x_0]$ than under the profit-maximizing sharecropping scheme $\tilde{\lambda}^*[x_0]$ when the comparison is made at a common level x_0 of capital input, the capital/output ratio at such a level of x_0 is higher under $\tilde{\lambda}^*[x_0]$ than under $\dot{p}^*[x_0]$. Allowing x_0 to adjust to its respective indigenous (profit-maximizing) levels under the two modes of design, however, one readily computes that this form of "gap" then disappears, as $\tilde{x}_0^*/\tilde{f}^*=\dot{x}_0^*/\dot{f}^*$.

We now compare wages and then utilities under profit-maximizing sharecropping and pricing enterprise designs. We find that, in terms of wages, more importantly, in terms of utilities, neither sort of enterprise design is unambiguously Pareto-superior to the other.

First we look at wages. From (44) we see that, compared at any given level x_0 of capital input, the capitalist's "wage" (i.e. gross income per unit of capital input) $\dot{p}_0^*[x_0]$ under the profit-maximizing pricing scheme is greater than $\tilde{p}_0^*[x_0]$, his wage under the corresponding profit-maximizing sharing scheme. However, from theorem 11 his wage $\tilde{p}_0^*=\tilde{p}_0^*[\tilde{x}_0^*]$ under the profit-maximizing sharecropping enterprise design is identical to his wage $\dot{p}_0^*=\dot{p}_0^*[\dot{x}_0^*]$ under the profit-maximizing pricing enterprise design.

For a typical worker $i\in N$ the wage comparison under the profit-maximizing sharecropping and pricing schemes at any fixed $x_0\in X_0$ is given in (46), which may be rewritten, using (43), as

$$\frac{\tilde{p}_i^*[x_0]}{\dot{p}_i^*[x_0]}=\left(\frac{G^{\beta_i-1}}{\eta_i}\right)^{1/\beta_i}=\left[\frac{1}{\eta_i}\left(\prod\eta_j^{\eta_j/\beta_j}\right)^{(\beta_i-1)/\gamma_0}\right]^{1/\beta_i}. \tag{52}$$

The reader may check that this ratio will be less than unity for sufficiently large β_i, and will exceed unity for sufficiently small η_i or β_i. Precisely the same applies to the ratio (50) comparing a worker's wage under the profit-maximizing sharecropping and pricing enterprise designs. Thus, whether a worker receives a higher wage under pricing than under sharecropping cannot be answered unambiguously, i.e. independently of the parameters describing preferences and production relations in the pre-enterprise in question.

Turning now to utilities of enterprise participants, we see that the capitalist always prefers profit-maximizing pricing whether compared at the same capital input (theorem 10) or at the respective profit-maximizing capital inputs (theorem 11), over profit-maximizing sharecropping. For agents $i \in N$ utility comparisons are provided by (47) and (51) for these two cases. In the former case, where the comparison is made at the same capital input x_0, we see that the ratio $\underline{\tilde{u}}_i^*[x_0]/\underline{\dot{u}}_i^*[x_0]$ of the utility of any agent $i \in N$ at the respective profit-maximizing incentive schemes is

$$\frac{\underline{\tilde{u}}_i^*[x_0]}{\underline{\dot{u}}_i^*[x_0]} = \frac{\beta_i - \eta_i}{\beta_i - 1} G = \frac{\beta_i - \eta_i}{\beta_i - 1} \left(\prod \eta_i^{\eta_i/\beta_i}\right)^{1/\gamma_0} \qquad (i \in N). \tag{53}$$

The reader may check from (53) that this ratio increases beyond bound as β_i approaches unity (from above). [Note that $\eta_i^{\eta_i}$ always exceeds $(1/e)^{1/e} \cong 0.69$ $(e \cong 2.7128)$, as can be verified considering the function $\log \eta_i^{\eta_i} = \eta_i \log \eta_i$.] To get an idea of the nature of the dependence of this ratio on η_i, assume for the moment that $\beta_i = \beta$ and $\eta_i = \eta$ for all $i \in N$. Then (53) implies

$$\frac{\underline{\tilde{u}}_i^*[x_0]}{\underline{\dot{u}}_i^*[x_0]} = \frac{\beta - \eta}{\beta - 1} G = \frac{\beta - \eta}{\beta - 1} \left(\eta^{n\eta/\beta}\right)^{1/(1 - n\eta/\beta)} \qquad (i \in N), \tag{54}$$

from which we see that the ratio approaches $\beta/(\beta - 1) > 1$ as η approaches zero. In general, from the viewpoint of agents $i \in N$, low values of β or η would tend to lead to a preference for the profit-maximizing sharecropping scheme over the profit-maximizing pricing scheme. In particular, neither the profit-maximizing pricing scheme nor the profit-maximizing sharecropping scheme, at a common level of capital input x_0, need be uniformly preferred by all agents $i \in N$, although, as noted above, incomes and output are uniformly higher under the former incentive scheme than under the latter. A similar analysis applies to the ratio (51), so that the preferences of an agent $i \in N$ may favor either the profit-maximizing sharecropping enterprise design or the profit-maximizing pricing enterprise design.

5. Closing remarks

We have until this point confined our attention to firms isolated from an external labor market. Perhaps the first point to recognize in this regard is that such enterprises may be less unrealistic than the standard assumption of perfect labor mobility in a perfectly competitive economy. After all, it is usually only subject to passports, work permits and much regulation that a worker can seek employment abroad, or, in cases where the state regulates internal mobility, even elsewhere at home. Barriers of entry into unions, effective discrimination on the basis of be it sex, race, or other attributes, not to mention factors of natural inertia on the part of individual workers, may all count against free mobility of labor, even when this mobility is not intentionally restricted by state agencies. Furthermore, when the state itself is the employer designing enterprises and setting prices and shares, it is not necessarily subject to an external labor market. In that case, a rule of thumb may be to design enterprises so as to maximize net proceeds of the state – proceeds which may then be distributed through public services or in lump-sum (nonincentivizing) fashion. Our results would certainly have something to say in this case about how to design enterprises.

All this might be somewhat foreign to standard contemporary Western economics, and in any case the degree to which our results would have to be modified in face of an external labor market deserves attention. So, let us briefly consider at least two extreme cases of an external labor market. First, suppose that the enterprise designer is a price-taker from such a market in equilibrium with it. In this case, the pricing enterprise design problem effectively vanishes, leaving the alternative of sharecropping. The sharecropping enterprise design problem, however, must now be solved subject to tighter constraints $\{\underline{u}[\tilde{\delta}]_i \geqslant \bar{u}_i\}_{\bar{N}}$ with $\bar{u}_i$ a likely positive utility level achievable in the external labor market by the workers $i \in N$. The designer–capitalist is then in the position of offering the workers (not necessarily positive) lump-sum compensations to the amount $c_i = \underline{\tilde{u}}_i^* - \bar{u}_i$ in order to contract with them, as sharecroppers, and the total compensation $c = \Sigma c_i$ required to sign on such workers may leave[12] $\underline{\tilde{u}}_0 - c \geqslant 0$, so that the design $\tilde{\delta}$ remains viable in combination with the side-payment scheme $\{c_i\}_N$. The second case we may consider is that of an external labor market where capitalists are in a monopsonistic position, dictating wages, so that $\dot{p}^*[\dot{x}_0]$

[12]A full analysis of the process of enterprise formation and of which firms may coexist viably when this process is at a rest point requires an extended general equilibrium approach, as introduced by Ichiishi (1977) and Sertel (1978) and applied in Başar, Selbuz and Sertel (1978).

obtains.[13] So long as external pre-enterprises duplicate the ones we studied, our results apply directly here. In either of these two cases sharecropping enterprises may be expected to employ workers tending to prefer sharecropping to pricing (*vis-à-vis* the relevant prices) and to operate in sectors where output is significantly less costly to observe with sufficient precision than workers' inputs.

Our model here has a number of extensions worth briefly reporting on. To mention, first, the constancy of marginal utility of income assumed in our specification of log-linear pre-enterprises may be relaxed to one of constant elasticity ξ_i of utility of income w.r.t. income, so long as $0<\xi_i<\beta_i$, and our whole analysis applies here in the sense that there is a simple way of rescaling the parameters b_i and β_i so as to obtain pre-enterprises of the sort studied whose analysis answers questions asked in the context of the new sort of pre-enterprise. (The profit-maximizing shares, for example, are now $\xi_i(\eta_i/\beta_i)$.) Thanks to this rescaling technique, it is also possible to apply our results here even in dealing with the case[14] where each x_i is multiplicatively perturbed by a non-negative real random variable θ_i with positive β_ith moment $E[\theta_i^{\beta_i}]$, and where each worker has a positive *ex ante* impression $\zeta_i f$ of enterprise production and ζ_i has a positive ξ_ith moment $E[\zeta_i^{\xi_i}]$. (See also Hurwicz, 1973, Kleindorfer, 1978, and Mirrlees, 1976). Elsewhere (Kleindorfer and Sertel, 1976a) we have also studied enterprise design problems for pre-enterprises with more general production technology and preference specifications than those here, as well as other solution concepts describing enterprise equilibrium (e.g. cooperative solutions) and interactions between workers and capitalist (e.g. von Stackelberg and Nash solutions).

Finally, turning toward what might form an interesting research area, we might note that the two typical modes of information which we have made available to the incentive designer correspond to the finest partition $\{\{x\}\mid x \in X\}$ of the input space (input-observability) on the one hand, and to the partition $\{\{x\in X\mid f(x)=y\}\mid y\in R_+\}$ consisting of the isoquants of the production function (output-observability) on the other hand. These two partitions constitute a sublattice of the lattice L of all partitions of X. The coarsest partition $\{X\}$ of X allows, of course, no incentives. Having seen that finer information (being equipped with a finer partition of X) allows greater profitability, one might wish to investigate the value of refinements

[13] Cf. "democratic capitalism" in Dirickx and Sertel (1976) and see especially monopsonistic capitalism" in the later study (Dirickx and Sertel, 1978).

[14] Wilson (1968) treats the related problem of determining a Pareto-optimal sharing scheme under conditions of uncertainty.

within L from the viewpoint of optimal incentives which such would permit. Again, the incentivized agents may be equipped with various partitions of their colleagues' joint behavior spaces, and consequences of refining these partitions (information structures) under any given game-theoretic solution concept are also of theoretical interest.

References

Bhatia, N.P. and G.P. Szegö (1970) *Stability Theory of Dynamical Systems* (Springer-Verlag, New York).

Bonin, J.P. (1976) "On the Design of Managerial Incentive Structures in a Decentralized Planning Environment", *The American Economic Review*, 66, no. 4 682–687.

Dirickx, Y.M.I. and M.R. Sertel (1976) "Class conflict and fairness in 'Democratic Capitalism'", Preprint Series No. I/75-26, International Institute of Management, West Berlin; forthcoming in *Public Choice*.

Dirickx, Y.M.I. and M.R. Sertel (1978), "Comparative Political Economy of Capitalism, Communism, Slavery and Colonialism in a Nutshell", *Recherches Economiques de Louvain*, 44, no. 3.

Groves, T. (1973) "Incentives in Teams", *Econometrica*, 41, no. 4, 617–631.

Harris, M. and A. Raviv (1978) "Some Results on Incentive Contracts, *The American Economic Review*, 68, no. 1, 20–30.

Hurwicz, L. (1973) "The Design of Mechanisms for Resource Allocation, *The American Economic Review*, 63, no. 2, 1–30.

Hurwicz, L. and L. Shapiro (1978) "Incentive Structures Maximizing Residual Gain under Incomplete Information, *The Bell Journal of Economics*, 9, no. 1, 180–191.

Ichiishi, T. (1977) "Management Versus Ownership", G.S.I.A. Working Paper 46-76-77, Carnegie-Mellon University.

Kleindorfer, P.R. (1978) "Informational Aspects of the Design of Enterprises through Incentives, in: K. Krippendorff, ed., *Communication and Control in Social Systems* (Gordon Breech Science Publishers, London).

Kleindorfer, P.R. and M.R. Sertel (1976a) "Equilibrium Analysis of Sharecropping". (See Chapter 6 of this book.)

Kleindorfer, P.R. and M.R. Sertel (1976b) "Optimal Design of Labor-managed Enterprises", Preprint Series No. I/76-77, International Institute of Management, West Berlin.

Kleindorfer, P.R. and M.R. Sertel (1978) "Value-added Sharing Enterprises". (See Chapter 9 of this book.)

Mirrlees, J.A. (1974) "Notes on Welfare Economics, Information and Uncertainty, in: M. Balch, D. McFadden and S. Wu, eds., *Essays in the Economics of Uncertainty* (North-Holland, Amsterdam), ch. 9.

Mirrlees, J.A. (1976) "The Optimal Structure of Incentives and Authority Within an Organization", *Bell Journal of Economics*, 7, no. 1, 105–131.

Sertel, M.R. (1978) "The Relative Size and Share-price of a Workers' Cooperative Facing Competitive Capitalism", paper presented at the Second Bosphorus Workshop on Industrial Democracy, Bosphorus University, Istanbul, July 1978. (See Chapter 2 of this book.)

Sertel, M., T. Başar and H. Selbuz (1978), "Workers' Enterprises Facing Competitive Capitalism", Technical Report No. 44, Marmara Scientific and Industrial Research Institute, Applied Mathematics Division, Gebze, Turkey. (See Chapter 7 of this book.)

Spence, M. and R. Zeckhauser, (1971) "Insurance, Information and Individual Action", *The American Economic Review*, 61, no. 2, 380–387.

Stiglitz, J.E. (1974) "Incentives and Risk Sharing in Sharecropping", *Review of Economic Studies*, 61, 219–256.

Stiglitz, J.E. (1975) "Incentives, Risk and Information: Notes Towards a Theory of Hierarchy, *Bell Journal of Economics*, 6, no. 2, 552–579.

Vanek, J. (1970) *The General Theory of Labor Managed Market Economics* (Cornell University Press, Ithaca).

Wilson, R. (1968), "The Theory of Syndicates", *Econometrica*, 36, no. 1, 119–132.

CHAPTER 5

Note on pretend-but-perform mechanisms*

MURAT R. SERTEL

The optimal economic design rules of Chapter 4 were found for a profit-maximizing designer, say "landlord", who knew the relevant characteristics of the other agents, say "workers", contributing to production. These relevant characteristics pertained to both the tastes of the workers regarding their respective incomes and input intensities as well as the response of output to these input intensities. In possession of all this information, the designer set the rules of remuneration and his own input so as to maximize his profit. Depending on his facility in observing the workers' contributions to production, the designer either purchased their inputs at a price or, when their inputs were sufficiently costly to observe, gave them each a share in output, depending on their respective characteristics.

Now these characteristics forming a workers' identity are essentially data private to the agent they describe, hence inherently open to mispresentation by that agent. In particular, considering a sharecropping enterprise with a single landlord and single worker, and granted that the enterprise will be designed in the profit-maximizing fashion of the previous chapter but according to the worker's self-declared identity, the worker may have an incentive to *pretend* to be other than himself, even though he gets to receive his share in output only if he also *performs* in accordance with his claimed identity.

It is such a hunch which led to a study (Alkan and Sertel, 1981) by Ahmet Alkan and myself into the "pretend-but-perform mechanism" (PPM) in

*My thanks to Ahmet Alkan for allowing me to announce the flavor of some of our results here prior to their publication in detail.

sharecropping. Actually, there are many types of PPM, depending on which regions of their space of theoretically possible identities the agents are constrained to pretend-but-perform within. But a number of things are striking even in the case of the PPMs studied for sharecropping with the basic data of Kleindorfer and Sertel in the preceding chapter. First, all but the workers on a knife-edge line in a plane of true identities have an incentive to pretend and perform as if their identity were different. Secondly, they will always understate their utility for leisure when their other relevant characteristics are publicly known and to be abided by, whereas when their relative weight attached to disutility of effort is to be abided by, they may either under- or overstate the ratio which will identify their share in output, namely the ratio of elasticity of output to effort and the elasticity of disutility of effort to effort. Thirdly, and possibly most interesting, for a majority of possible tenants distributed uniformly, various PPMs not only improve the welfare of the worker but also that of the landlord directly. And when the worker is allowed to compensate the landlord for a fall in profit relative to that when the worker does not pretend, even more workers can compensate the landlord and still be better off under a PPM. In consequence, with or without such compensations, for a majority of workers even a landlord who knows his worker's true identity does better by turning an eye yonder and allowing the worker to pretend (and perform) otherwise.

This roughly summarizes the results obtained in the first exploration we made with Alkan into pretend-but-perform mechanisms. The idea of PPMs clearly has a wider appeal, however. To illustrate, it is useful to consider a 2×2 bimatrix game. Players $\underline{\alpha}$ and $\underline{\beta}$ have behavior spaces $A = \{a_1, a_2\}$ and $B = \{b_1, b_2\}$, respectively. The following table of double entries shows the payoffs $(p_\alpha(a_i, b_j), p_\beta(a_i, b_j))$ of $\underline{\alpha}$ as first and $\underline{\beta}$ as second coordinate $(i, j \in \{1,2\})$:

b_2	(2,3)	(3,1)
b_1	(1,2)	(0,0)
	a_1	a_2

The reaction of $\underline{\beta}$ to the behavior of $\underline{\alpha}$ is the constant function with $\underline{\beta}(a_1) = \underline{\beta}(a_2) = b_2$, and the point (a_2, b_2) offers (both the unique Nash solution and) the unique von Stackelberg solution with $\underline{\alpha}$ leading. Now suppose that $\underline{\alpha}$ is totally transparent to $\underline{\beta}$ and that $\underline{\beta}$ gets to declare his "identity" accordingly. The space of theoretically possible identities for the latter player may be regarded as nothing but the space B^A of all reaction functions $\beta: A \to B$. While the follower with true identity $\underline{\beta}$ is simply the constant function just indicated, this player nevertheless does best by pretending to be $\beta^* \in B^A$ with $\beta^*(a_1)=b_2$ and $\beta^*(a_2)=b_1$. For now the von Stackelberg solution with $\underline{\alpha}$ leading moves to (a_1, b_2) when $\underline{\beta}$ pretends and performs as β^*. This decreases $\underline{\alpha}$'s payoff from 3 to 2, but increases the pretending player's payoff from 1 to 3. With side-payments operative, $\underline{\alpha}$ could be made better off than before the PPM while the payoff of the other player could be improved as well, reaching the solution with highest communal payoff – a solution which is Pareto-efficient with suitable side-payments.

Even with no appeal to side-payments, an unambiguous improvement in welfare may be reaped by all participants from adopting the PPM. Change the payoff table above to the following:

b_2	(0,3)	(1,1)
b_1	(2,2)	(3,0)
	a_1	a_2

The true identity β of the player choosing strategies in B^A is again represented by the reaction function with $\beta(a_1)=\beta(a_2)=b_2$, as before. The von Stackelberg solution with $\underline{\alpha}$ leading and the Nash solution are again the point (a_2, b_2). With the PPM operative, however, the player with true identity $\underline{\beta}$ now pretends and performs as one with identity β^* represented by the reaction function β^* with $\beta^*(a_1)=b_1, \beta^*(a_2)=b_2$. In consequence, $\underline{\alpha}$ chooses a_1 as von Stackelberg leader, and the outcome corresponding to (a_1, b_1) is achieved, with a uniform improvement for both players from the dominated payoffs (1, 1) to the Pareto-efficient payoffs (2, 2).

For those who believe that "solving" the prisoners' dilemma is the prime item on the agenda of Public Finance or Economic Design, it is worth noting that what the PPM has just corrected is the waste incurred in what started out as a typical prisoners' dilemma situation.

There is a further wrinkle in the PPMs studied by Alkan and Sertel (1981) which is missing in the PPMs of the bimatrix games above. Here we have carried on as if both players' actual behaviors were publicly visible, whereas in sharecropping the worker's behavior is typically unobservable to others, and so it is in the PPMs of Alkan and Sertel (1981). Once the worker pretends in the latter study, he has only to perform in production, although his *actual* effort is known only to himself. This adds an extra aspect to the idea of a PPM, which will unfortunately have to remain unexplored here. In fact, there is much more to pretend-but-perform mechanisms which should prove fruitful to investigate further. For example, one might suggest studying what happens when all the players operate as pretender-but-performers in a world where the characteristics of each agent are private or at least unfalsifiable without resort to inconsistency between pretension and performance.

Of course, the Game Theory here is easier than the Economics. For as an economist one has to ask what sorts of basic data (preferences and technology) will present payoffs such as those above, and with which basic data and under what informational settings what sorts of authority structures will lend themselves to improvements by a PPM. When an economic system achieves efficiency, it is not unwise to seek strategy-proofness, i.e. faithful declarations of true private data. But when not, it should be wise to understand where and when and how a PPM might yield everyone involved better off. Clearly, much broader exploration will have to be ventured to chart for us the economic designer's topography of information and incentives here.

Reference

Alkan, A. and M.R. Sertel (1981) "The Pretend-But-Perform Mechanism in Sharecropping", Discussion Paper, International Institute of Management, West Berlin.

CHAPTER 6

Equilibrium analysis of sharecropping*

PAUL R. KLEINDORFER and MURAT R. SERTEL

1. Introduction

Sharing the gains and losses of collective activity is a central feature of economic reality. Typically, the manner in which the spoils of such activities are to be shared amongst participants is understood before and during the activity in question. Indeed, this *ex ante* understanding is often critical in explaining why and how the activity takes place. Distribution, in other words, is generally not without its incentive effects. In this chapter we investigate such incentive effects, studying the manner in which economic activity is brought about by organizational designs using sharing schemes.

We envision a group of economic agents, each contributing some privately owned factor to a productive process whose output is to be shared by the agents. The institution of a sharing scheme determines a productive "enterprise", a certain game in which the mutual adjustments of agents to each other's contribution levels admits of the notion of equilibrium. We study the existence, uniqueness, stability, continuity and smoothness of noncooperative equilibrium as a function of the sharing scheme when the output to be shared is smooth and the agents have utilities additively separable into the amount of output received and a smooth function of the agent's contribution level.

The paradigm of sharing has been studied, unsurprisingly, in many contexts. First, of course, is the agricultural context, which inspired the title

*This chapter is a revision of Discussion Paper I/76-33 of the International Institute of Management, Berlin.

Workers and Incentives, by *M.R. Sertel*

of the present study. Sharecropping, as it is most properly called in agriculture, is an age-old phenomenon and has been of natural interest to economists.[1]

A common feature of the usual treatment of sharecropping is that the sharecropping arrangement is typically construed as one between a "landlord" and a *single* "tenant". The equilibrium contribution of effort by a single tenant on a plot of land as a function of the sharing scheme is, of course, relatively simple to analyze. Thus, the incentive effects of a sharing scheme, as construed, are rather transparent, although their explicit investigation had to await Mirrlees (1974) and Stiglitz (1974).

The last two works together with Diamond (1967), Ross (1973), Newberry (1976) and Bell and Zusman (1976) also investigate the basic theory of *risk*-sharing in contracts between *two* agents,[2] which has applications in the theory of "screening"[3] and in explaining certain forms of integration of firms,[4] and offers building blocks of a theory of hierarchy.[5]

A natural extension of all this is to consider sharing schemes between, say, a "landlord" and many factor-contributing agents whose individually optimal levels of contribution, so incentivized, may be sensitive to one another. Such "enterprises" are exemplified by the labor-managed firm (farm) renting capital (land), where output or value-added-sharing is the paradigm incentive scheme.[6] Allowing shares in output to exceed unity in their sum, as when each agent enjoys the entire output, one obtains also the paradigm of a public good produced by the contributions of a community.[7]

An analysis of such situations seems to demand a reasonably general underlying equilibrium theory of the sort we pursue in this chapter. Such a theory also provides the main tools in posing and solving optimal enterprise design problems, characterizing sharing schemes which best address the interests of one or another group of participating agents, as presented in Kleindorfer and Sertel (1978, 1979a, 1979b). This, in turn, apart from its normative interest, offers the basis for a theory of the firm with explicit

[1]The sharecropping literature is accessible through Cheung (1969), Bardham and Srinivasan (1971), Rao (1971), Stiglitz (1974), and Hsiao (1975), especially the first. Georgescu-Roegen (1960) is also enlightening on related economic thought.

[2]The related area of "incentives contracting" is accessible through Canes (1975).

[3]See Stiglitz (1975).

[4]See Arrow (1975).

[5]See Stiglitz (1975) and Mirrlees (1976).

[6]See Vanek (1970) and Kleindorfer and Sertel (1979a, 1979b).

[7]See Tulkens (1979) for a method of curtailing the production of a public bad with differential (shares of) incidence on participants. Regarding effects of sharing gains of cooperation see Gately (1974).

recognition of internal organization. General equilibrium in an economy whose firms possess internal organization would involve an equilibration of the very contractual arrangements forming the internal design of enterprises, determining endogenously the formation of firms.[8]

2. Pre-enterprises and enterprises

In this section we introduce the formal and intuitive notions of certain basic objects which we will be dealing with, e.g. "pre-enterprises", "incentive schemes", "adjustment maps and processes", "enterprise designs", "enterprises" and "equilibrium maps". To do so we require the following:

0. Notation. For the set of natural numbers we denote $\eta=\{1,2,\ldots\}$. For the reals (with usual topology) we denote $\mathfrak{R}$. Let $\bar{N}=\{0,1,\ldots,n\}$ and $N=\bar{N}\setminus\{0\}$, where $n\in\eta$. For any family $\{X_i\,|\,i\in\bar{N}\}$ of nonempty sets we use the following conventions when a fixed n is understood:

$$\bar{\prod} X_i=\prod_{\bar{N}} X_i; \qquad \prod X_i=\prod_{N} X_i;$$

$$\bar{\prod}^{i\prime} X_j=\prod_{\bar{N}\setminus\{i\}} X_j; \qquad \prod^{i\prime} X_j=\prod_{N\setminus\{i\}} X_j;$$

and, if $\{x_i\,|\,i\in N\}\subset\mathfrak{R}$,

$$\bar{\sum} x_i=\sum_{\bar{N}} x_i; \qquad \sum x_i=\sum_{N} x_i;$$

$$\sum^{i\prime} x_j=\sum_{\bar{N}\setminus\{i\}} x_j; \qquad \sum^{i\prime} x_j=\sum_{\bar{N}\setminus\{i\}} x_j.$$

Projection into a space S will be denoted by π_S.

When a function $g:\mathfrak{R}\to\mathfrak{R}$ is differentiable from the left (as, for example, is the case when g is concave), we denote its left-hand derivative by g'. For a real-valued function h of several real variables we denote the left-hand derivative of h with respect to the ith argument by h'_i and abbreviate $(h'_j)'_j$ to h''_{ij}.

[8]It is pleasant to observe developments toward such a general equilibrium theory, as in Sondermann (1974) and Ichiishi (1977). In the modeling so far, however, matters of internal structure (authority, information, incentives and behavior) of firms have been largely ignored. It is to these structural issues to which the present analysis gives weight.

What we have in mind as a "pre-enterprise" is, roughly, a collection of economic agents whose joint contribution to a productive process yields a certain output which each of them considers as a "good", but whose individual contributions, at least beyond a certain level, may be increased only in return for increasingly greater compensations in terms of this good.

1. Definition. By a pre-enterprise we mean an ordered quadruplet
0. $\Omega = \langle \bar{N}, \bar{X}, u, f \rangle$,
where, using the notation above,
1. $\bar{N} = \{0, \ldots, n\}$ with $n \in \eta$;
2. $\bar{X}$ is the product $\bar{\Pi} X_i$ of a family $\{X_i \mid i \in \bar{N}\}$ with each $X_i \subset \mathfrak{R}$ nonempty, closed and convex, and from which we define $X = \Pi X_i$, $X^i = \Pi^i X_j$; and $X^i = \Pi^i X_j$;
3. $u = \{u_i \colon X_i \times \mathfrak{R} \to \mathfrak{R} \mid i \in \bar{N}\}$ is a family of continuous real-valued functions u_i, each of which is additively separable in the form $u_i(x_i, r_i) = w_i(x_i) + r_i (x_i \in X_i, r_i \in \mathfrak{R})$ with $w_i \colon X_i \to \mathfrak{R}$ strictly concave and bounded from above by a $\sup w_i \in \mathfrak{R}$ $(i \in N)$;
4. $f \colon \bar{X} \to \mathfrak{R}$ is continuous and, for each $x_0 \in X_0$, concave on $\{x_0\} \times X$.

To interpret the elements of Ω, one may regard $\bar{N}$ as the *personnel* of a potential enterprise (which we begin to structure immediately below), with each member i of which is associated an abstract *behavior space* X_i and preferences represented by u_i, the map f serving as a production function. For example, $x_i \in X_i$ may be regarded as the contribution of agent i to the productive process, $f(\bar{x})$ as the monetary value of the product created by the collective behavior $\bar{x} = (x_0, \ldots, x_n)$; and, turning to the preferences of the agents $i \in N$, w_i may be regarded as the utility of (e.g. work, effort) contribution, r_i indicating a monetary compensation accruing to agent i – a compensation which will be the essential instrument through which incentives are to be specified.

Agent 0 may be regarded as contributing land or the services of capital goods (x_0) to the productive process at a cost $-w_0(x_0)$ to himself. Whether this agent is a landlord or a capitalist in the usual sense or headquarters in a centrally planned economy, we nickname him "capitalist". Besides determining the level of contribution of x_0, the capitalist may have the additional role in certain enterprise design problems of choosing and implementing an incentive scheme. In other instances it will be the agents $i \in N$, nicknamed "workers", who will have the authority to institute an incentive scheme. The nature of the enterprise design problem will, of course, depend on where this authority is vested.

Given a pre-enterprise Ω, by an *incentive scheme* for Ω we mean any continuous function $r: \bar{X} \to \mathfrak{R}^n$. When r is an incentive scheme for Ω, the ith component function $r_i: \bar{X} \to \mathfrak{R}$ will be called the *incentive* determined by r for agent i; and, for any ordered pair $\delta = (x_0, r)$, the function $u[\delta]_i: \bar{X} \to \mathfrak{R}$ defined by $u[\delta]_i(x) = u_i(x_i, r_i(x_0, x))$ will be referred to as the *effective utility* determined by δ for agent $i (i \in N)$.

The incentive schemes analyzed in this chapter will all be *sharecropping* (i.e. *output-sharing*) *schemes*, i.e. incentive schemes r given by $r_i(\bar{x}) = \lambda_i f(\bar{x})$, where $\lambda_i \in \mathfrak{R}_+$ is the *share* of agent i in the output f and $\Sigma\lambda_i \leqslant 1$ ($\bar{x} \in \bar{X}$, $i \in N$). We denote $\Lambda = \{\lambda \in \mathfrak{R}^n_+ \mid \Sigma\lambda_i \leqslant 1\}$ for the set of "share systems". Notationally we will identify $\lambda = \{\lambda_i\}_N$ with the sharecropping scheme $\{\lambda_i f\}_N$ it iseomorphically determines in the fashion just indicated.

Our next task is to introduce the general notions of adjustment process, adjustment maps and of enterprises determined through sharecropping schemes. Our intent is to utilize various game-theoretic solution concepts in summarizing the (equilibrium) behavior of an enterprise once a sharing scheme is instituted. Several possibilities are of interest in this regard, but the most appropriate ones to begin with would seem to be the noncooperative or Nash solution and the cooperative (or Pareto) solution allowing lump-sum transfers of income among agents. Since results for this cooperative case turn out to be straightforward corollaries to the corresponding results for the noncooperative solution, we concentrate mostly on the noncooperative case, later deriving in a very simple fashion from this case corresponding results for the cooperative case.

Let Ω be the pre-enterprise of definition 1, and take any ordered pair $\delta = (x_0, \lambda)$, with $x_0 \in X_0$ and $\lambda \in \Lambda$. Given any $x = (x_1, \ldots, x_n) \in X$, consider, for each $i \in N$, the problem

$$\underset{X_i}{\text{maximize}}\, u[\delta]_i(x_i, x^i). \tag{1}$$

When, for each $i \in N$ and each $x \in X$, this maximization problem has a unique solution $\alpha_i[\delta](x^i) \in X_i$, a family of n reaction maps $\alpha_i[\delta]: X^i \to X_i$ is determined, from which we define the noncooperative *adjustment process* $\alpha[\delta]: X \to X$ through

$$\alpha[\delta](x) = \{\alpha_i[\delta](x^i)\}_N \qquad (x \in X). \tag{2}$$

The noncooperative nature of the adjustment process of $\alpha[\delta]$ stems from the specification of the optimization problem (1) defining the reactions $\alpha_i[\delta](x^i)$ of the members $i \in N$ to a given collective behavior $x \in X$. Namely, it stems from the fact that each i reacts by taking x^i (and, of course, x_0 and λ) as given.

Now, with Ω as above, let $\Delta(\Omega) \subset X_0 \times \Lambda$ be the largest set of points $\delta = (x_0, \lambda)$ such that $\alpha[\delta]$ is an adjustment process, i.e. for each $i \in N$ and each $x \in X$ the maximization problem (1) has a unique solution $\alpha_i[\delta](x^i) \in X_i$. An element $\delta \in \Delta(\Omega)$ will be called an *enterprise design* (w.r.t. Ω), and the ordered pair $\underline{\Omega}(\delta) = (\Omega, \delta)$ will be called the (*sharecropping*) *enterprise* determined by the design δ. (Whenever we speak of an enterprise $\Omega(\delta)$, it is to be understood that Ω is a pre-enterprise and $\delta \in \Delta(\Omega)$.)

By the *adjustment map* of the pre-enterprise Ω we will mean the map $\alpha : \Delta(\Omega) \times X \to X$ defined by

$$\alpha(\delta, x) = \alpha[\delta](x) \qquad (\delta \in \Delta(\Omega), x \in X). \tag{3}$$

When $\alpha[\delta]$ is an adjustment process, a fixed point $x = \alpha[\delta](x) \in X$ of $\alpha[\delta]$ will be called an *equilibrium* of the pre-enterprise Ω and the enterprise $\Omega(\delta)$. Of special interest is the case where enterprise equilibrium is unique, thus allowing enterprise designs to be evaluated unambiguously (in terms of output, profit or utility levels) at their respective enterprise equilibria. To focus on this case, we define $\underline{\Delta}(\Omega) \subset \underline{\Delta}(\Omega)$ to be the set of enterprise design δ for which the enterprise $\underline{\Omega}(\delta)$ has a *unique* equilibrium $\underline{x}(\delta)$. From this we define the *equilibrium map* $\underline{x} : \underline{\Delta}(\Omega) - X$ through

$$\underline{x}(\delta) = \alpha[\delta](x(\delta)) \qquad (\delta \in \underline{\Delta}(\Omega)), \tag{4}$$

and the *equilibrium product* $\underline{f}: \underline{\Delta}(\Omega) - \mathfrak{R}$ through

$$\underline{f}(\delta) = f(x_0, \underline{x}(\delta)) \qquad (\delta = (x_0, \lambda) \in \underline{\Delta}(\Omega)). \tag{5}$$

The remainder of the chapter begins by providing conditions (section 3) under which the adjustment map of a pre-enterprise is continuous.

The next section (section 4) identifies a class of pre-enterprises Ω for which each choice of a $\delta \in X_0 \times \Lambda$ determines an enterprise $\underline{\Omega}(\delta)$ possessing a unique equilibrium $\underline{x}(\delta) \in X$. From then on we work within this class of pre-enterprises, first studying the continuity (section 5), smoothness (section 6), and monotonicity (section 7) of $\underline{x}$ as a function of δ. In parallel, we study similar properties of the equilibrium value $f(\delta)$ of enterprise product as a function of δ. Finally, we study (section 8) the stability of enterprise (noncooperative) equilibrium. Corresponding results for the cooperative solution concept are obtained in section 9.

Since we will often require differentiability in the sequel, we need the following:

2. Definition. A pre-enterprise Ω will be said to be *smooth* at $x \in X$ if there exists an open (box) nbd $V = \prod V_i \subset X$ of x such that, for each $x_0 \in X_0$,

$f(x_0, \cdot)$ is twice continuously differentiable on V, and, for each $i \in N$, w_i is twice continuously differentiable on V_i with $w_i''(x_i) < 0$. A pre-enterprise Ω will be said to be *smooth* if it is smooth at every $x \in X$.

2. Continuity of adjustment

Let Ω be a pre-enterprise and consider the adjustment map $\alpha: X_0 \times \Lambda \times X \to X$ defined in (3). In this section we study the continuity of α, both as an interesting matter in its own right and as a necessary prelude to the analysis of continuity and stability of equilibrium to follow. The continuity of the adjustment map of a pre-enterprise is characterized by the following:

3. Theorem. Let Ω be a pre-enterprise and let $'\Delta \subset \Delta(\Omega)$ be closed in $X_0 \times \Lambda$. The restriction $'\alpha$ of the adjustment map $\alpha: \Delta(\Omega) \times X \to X$ to $'\Delta \times X$ is continuous iff $'\alpha(K) \subset \mathfrak{R}^n$ is bounded for every compact $K \subset {}'\Delta \times X$.

Proof. "Only if" is obvious. To see "if", first note that, as $'\Delta \times X$ is closed in the Hausdorff k-space $\mathfrak{R} \times \mathfrak{R}^n \times \mathfrak{R}^n$, $'\Delta \times X$ is also a Hausdorff k-space (see Nagata, 1968).

Hence, taking any compact $K \subset {}'\Delta \times X$, $'\alpha(K)$ bounded, it suffices (see Nagata, 1968, exercise 17, p. 148) to show that α is continuous on K. Now the closure H of K in $\mathfrak{R}^n$ is compact. Thus, by Fundamental Continuity Theorem II of Sertel (1975), each coordinate function $'\alpha_i (i \in N)$ of $'\alpha$ is upper-semicontinuous when considered as a mapping into the space of closed nonempty subsets of X_i. Since $\alpha: \Delta(\Omega) \times X \to X$ is a point-to-point mapping, this means that each coordinate function $'\alpha_i$, hence $'\alpha$ itself, is continuous on K. This completes the proof. □

The key to continuity of α is thus a certain type of boundedness. We pursue this further below. First note that, since f is concave, the one-sided derivatives of the restrictions $\lambda_i f(\cdot, \bar{x}^i)$: $X_i \to \mathfrak{R}$ of the incentive function $\lambda_i f$ exist for every $i \in N$ and $\bar{x}^i \in \bar{X}^i$; we denote the left-hand such derivative by $f_i'(\cdot, \bar{x}^i)$.

4. Definition. Let Ω be a pre-enterprise. For any $\Delta \subset X_0 \times \Lambda$ we define

$$\beta(\Delta) = \{B = B_\Delta \times B_X \mid \varnothing \neq B_\Delta \subset \Delta \text{ is compact}, \ \varnothing = B_X \subset X\} \tag{6}$$

and, for any $\beta \subset \beta(\Delta)$, we say that Ω is β-*bounded* (on Δ) iff, for each $i \in N$,

X_i has an infimal element and, unless X_i also has a supremal element, for every $B \in \beta$ it owns points $\hat{x}_i, \hat{y}_i \in X_i$ with $\hat{x}_i \geqslant \hat{y}_i$ such that

$$\sigma_i(B) = \sup\{\lambda_i f_i'(\bar{x}) \mid (x_0, \lambda) \in B_\Delta, \hat{y}_i \leqslant x_i \in X_i, x^i \in \pi_{X^i}(B_X)\} \tag{7}$$

exists and satisfies $\sigma_i(B) \leqslant -w_i'(x_i)$. Of particular interest are the families

$$\beta_1(\Delta) = \{B \in \beta(\Delta) \mid B_X \text{ is singleton}\} \tag{8}$$

and

$$\beta_2(\Delta) = \{B \in \beta(\Delta) \mid B_X \text{ is compact}\}, \tag{9}$$

and the notions of $\beta_1(\Delta)$- and $\beta_2(\Delta)$-boundedness (on subsets $\Delta \subset X_0 \times \Lambda$). Evidently, $\beta_2(\Delta)$-boundedness implies $\beta_1(\Delta)$-boundedness for any $\Delta \subset X_0 \times \Lambda$.

Note that, if X is compact, then Ω is B-bounded on every $\Delta \subset X_0 \times \Lambda$. The essential import of β-boundedness is embodied in the following two propositions.

5. Proposition. Let Ω be a pre-enterprise, and take any $\Delta \subset X_0 \times \Lambda$ and any $\beta \subset \beta(\Delta)$. If Ω is β-bounded on Δ, then every $B \in \beta$ is a subset of $\Delta(\Omega) \times X$ and $\alpha(B)$ is bounded in X.

Proof. Assume that Ω is β-bounded on Δ, and take any $B = B_\Delta \times B_X \in \beta$ and any $i \in N$. If X_i is not compact, then for any $\delta = (x_0, r) \in B_\Delta$ and any $x \in B_X$, as $u[\delta]_i(\cdot, x^i)$ is strictly concave and, consequently, left-differentiable, β-boundedness implies

$$w_i'(x_i) + r_i'(x_0, x_i, x^i) < w_i'(\hat{x}_i) + r_i'(x_0, \hat{x}_i, x^i) \leqslant 0 \tag{10}$$

whenever $x_i \in X_i$ exceeds $\hat{x}_i$ (as given for B in definition 4). Thus, (1) has no solution

$$\alpha_i[\delta](x^i) > \hat{x}_i, \quad \text{so } \alpha_i[\delta](x^i) \in [\inf X_i, \hat{x}_i],$$

on which compact nonvacuous set the continuous $u[\delta]_i(\cdot, x^i)$ in fact attains a maximum. The set $[\inf X_i, \hat{x}_i]$ being convex and the maximand $u[\delta]_i(\cdot, x^i)$ strictly concave, the maximum is attained at a unique point, which is evidently $\alpha_i[\delta](x^i)$. Similarly, if X_i is compact, (1) yields a unique solution $\alpha_i[\delta](x^i) \in X_i$. We conclude that α is well-defined on B, i.e. $B \subset \Delta(\Omega) \times X$, and that $\alpha(B)$ is bounded. □

In fact, continuing with the domain of definition of the adjustment map, and turning to its continuity, in the context of β_1- and β_2-boundedness, respectively, we have:

6. Proposition. Given a pre-enterprise Ω, let $\Delta \subset X_0 \times \Lambda$ be closed. (i) If Ω is $\beta_1(\Delta)$-bounded, then $\Delta \subset \Delta(\Omega)$. (ii) If Ω is $\beta_2(\Delta)$-bounded, then the adjustment map $\alpha: \Delta(\Omega)\times X \to X$ is continuous on $\Delta \times X$.

Proof. (i) Apply proposition 5. (ii) Assuming that Ω is $\beta_2(\Delta)$-bounded, hence $\beta_1(\Delta)$-bounded, (i) gives $\Delta \subset \Delta(\Omega)$. Using proposition 5, the restriction of the adjustment map α of Ω to any compact $K \subset \Delta \times X$ has $\alpha(K) \subset X$ bounded, so that theorem 3 applies to complete the proof. □

In particular, it is useful to note

7. Corollary. Given a pre-enterprise Ω, let $\delta \in X_0 \times \Lambda$. (i) If Ω is $\beta_1(\delta)$-bounded, then $\Omega(\delta)$ is an enterprise. (ii) If Ω is $\beta_2(\delta)$-bounded then the adjustment process $\alpha[\delta]: X \to X$ is continuous.

3. Existence and uniqueness of equilibrium

Let Ω be a pre-enterprise and take any $(x_0, \lambda) \in X_0 \times \Lambda$ such that $\underline{\Omega}(x_0, \lambda)$ is an enterprise. Let $P \subset N$ be the set of agents i for which $\lambda_i > 0$. From the definition of an enterprise it is clear that, for each $i \in N \setminus P$, there is a unique $\tilde{x}_i \in X_i$ such that

$$w_i(\tilde{x}_i) = \sup_{X_i} w_i, \tag{11}$$

i.e. $\tilde{x}_i = \alpha_i[\lambda_i, x_0](x^i)$ for every $x^i \in x^i$. Write $\tilde{x}^P = \{\tilde{x}_i\}_{N \setminus P}$ and consider the following problem:

$$\underset{x_P \in X_P}{\text{maximize}}\, f(x_P, \tilde{x}^P; x_0) + \sum_P \frac{w_i(x_i)}{\lambda_i}. \tag{12}$$

8. Proposition. Let Ω be a smooth pre-enterprise. The equilibria of $\underline{\Omega}(\lambda, x_0)$ are precisely the points $\tilde{x} = (\tilde{x}_P, \tilde{x}^P)$ solving (11) and (12) ($\tilde{x}^P$ solving (11) and $\tilde{x}_P$ solving (12)).

Proof. From the definition of an equilibrium, and referring to (1) and (2), we see that a point $\tilde{x}\in X$ is an equilibrium of $\underline{\Omega}(x_0,\lambda)$ iff

$$w_i(\tilde{x}_i)+\lambda_i f(x_0,\tilde{x})=\sup_{X_i}\left[w_i+\lambda_i f(x_0,\cdot,\tilde{x}^i)\right] \tag{13}$$

obtains for each $i\in N$. For $i\in N\setminus P$, eq. (13) is equivalent to (11). For $i\in P$ one obtains the same (necessary and sufficient) Kuhn–Tucker conditions from (13) as from (12). [For example, when $X_i=\mathfrak{R}$ for each $i\in N$, (2) and (3) yield $w_i'(\tilde{x}_i)+\lambda_i f_i(x_0,\tilde{x})=0$ for each $i\in N$ as a necessary and sufficient condition for $\tilde{x}$ to be an equilibrium of $\underline{\Omega}(x_0,\lambda)$.] □

In establishing a sufficient condition for the existence and boundedness of sharecropping equilibria, we make use of its *uniqueness*, and this is a straightforward fact which we settle right away. Given a pre-enterprise Ω and any $(x_0,\lambda)\in X_0\times\Lambda$, if $\underline{\Omega}(x_0,\lambda)$ is an enterprise, then its equilibria will, as we saw in proposition 8, be precisely the solutions to (11) and (12). Since X is convex and the maximands in (11) and (12) are strictly concave, (11) and (12) clearly have at most one solution, i.e. by proposition 8, $\underline{\Omega}(x_0,\lambda)$ has at most one equilibrium when $\underline{\Omega}(x_0,\lambda)$ is an enterprise. We now state the main result of this section.

9. Theorem. Let Ω be a smooth pre-enterprise and take any $\Delta\subset X_0\times\Lambda$. If Ω Is $\beta(\Delta)$-bounded (see definition 4), then $\Delta\subset\underline{\Delta}(\Omega)$, i.e. $\underline{\Omega}(\delta)$ has a unique equilibrium $x(\delta)$ for each $\delta\in\Delta$, and the set $\underline{x}(K)\subset X$ of equilibria is bounded for every compact $K\subset\Delta$.

Proof. Since $\beta(\Delta)$-boundedness implies both $\beta_1(\Delta)$- and $\beta_2(\Delta)$-boundedness, we see from propositions 5 and 6 that $\Delta\subset\Delta(\Omega)$ and that the adjustment map $\alpha:\Delta(\Omega)\times X\to X$ is continuous on $\Delta\times X$.

Now take any compact $K\subset\Delta$. By definition 4, $K\times X\in\beta(\Delta)$, so that, from proposition 5, $\alpha(K\times X)\subset X$ is bounded. Let H be the closed convex hull of $\alpha(K\times X)$. Then H is compact and, for each $\delta\in K$, $\alpha[\delta](H)\subset H$.Since $\alpha[\delta]$ is continuous on H, we see from this and Brouwer's Fixed Point Theorem that there is, for each $\delta\in K$, a fixed point $\tilde{x}=\alpha[\delta](\tilde{x})\in H$. Clearly, for each $\delta\in K$, such a fixed point is the unique equilibrium of $\underline{\Omega}(\delta)$. Since all such equilibria lie in the compact H, we also see that $\underline{x}(K)$ is bounded in X, completing the proof. □

The reader will note that smoothness of the pre-enterprise Ω in theorem 9 is only required to insure uniqueness of enterprise equilibria. The following example shows that, indeed, multiple equilibria may arise for nonsmooth pre-enterprises, raising several interesting issues concerning the evaluation of enterprise designs at equilibrium.

10. Example (log-linear pre-enterprises). A pre-enterprise Ω is called *log-linear* iff it has the form:

1. $X_i = \mathcal{R}_+ (i \in \bar{N})$;
2. $u_i(x_i, r_i) = -b_i x_i^{\beta_i} + r_i$, with $b_i > 0$ $(i \in \bar{N})$, $\beta_0 \geqslant 1$ and $\beta_i > 1$ $(i \in N)$;
3. $f(\bar{x}) = \prod x_i^{\eta_i}$ with $\eta_i > 0$ $(i \in \bar{N})$ and $\Sigma \eta_i \leqslant 1$.

If Ω is log-linear, then $\Delta(\Omega) = \Lambda \times X_0$. However, Ω is not smooth at the origin and for some $\delta \in X_0 \times \Lambda$, there are multiple enterprise equilibria. In fact, the equilibria of each enterprise $\Omega(\delta)$, $\delta \in X_0 \times \Lambda$ are given explicitly as $\underline{x}(\delta) = 0$ and $\underline{x}(\delta) = \tilde{\underline{x}}(\delta)$ where

$$\tilde{\underline{x}}_i(x_0, \lambda) = \left[(C_i \lambda_i)^{\gamma_0} x_0^{\eta_0} \prod (C_j \lambda_j)^{\eta_j / \beta_j} \right]^{1/\gamma_i} \tag{14}$$

for any $i \in N$, with

$$C_j = \frac{\eta_j}{b_j \beta_j}; \qquad \gamma_j = \beta_j \gamma_0 \qquad (j \in N) \tag{15}$$

and

$$\gamma_0 = 1 - \Sigma (\eta_j / \beta_j). \tag{16}$$

Thus, generally corresponding to a sharecropping design $\delta = (x_0, \lambda) > 0$, the enterprise $\underline{\Omega}(\delta)$ will have two equilibria, one being positive and the other being zero in each coordinate. Of these, it turns out that $\underline{x}(\delta) = 0$ is unanimously $(i \in \bar{N})$ inferior to $\underline{x}(\delta) = \tilde{\underline{x}}(\delta)$. Moreover, $\underline{x}(\delta) = 0$ is repellent whereas $\underline{x}(\delta) = \tilde{\underline{x}}(\delta)$ is a stable point whose domain of attraction is dense in X. Thus, it is without hazard in this case that we disregard $\underline{x}(\delta) = 0$ as "unrepresentative" of enterprise behavior and define the equilibrium map $\underline{x}$ through $\underline{x}(\delta) = \tilde{\underline{x}}(\delta)$. In general, of course, some caution must be exercised in selecting a "representative" equilibrium from among multiple enterprise equilibria. These matters are dealt with in depth in (Kleindorfer and Sertel, 1976).

11. Corollary. Let Ω be a smooth pre-enterprise such that, for each $i \in N$,

1. X_i is compact

or

2. X_i has an infimal element and, for each $x_0 \in X$, $\sigma = \sup\{ f_i'(x_0, x) \mid x \in X\}$ exists satisfying $\sigma \leqslant -w_i'(\hat{x}_i)$ for some $\hat{x}_i \in X_i$.

Then $\underline{\Delta}(\Omega) = X_0 \times \Lambda$.

Proof. The hypotheses in corollary 11 imply that Ω is $\beta(\{x_0\}\times\Lambda)$-bounded for every $x_0\in X_0$. Thus, theorem 9 implies $\{x_0\}\times\Lambda\subset\underline{\Delta}(\Omega)$ for every $x_0\in X_0$. Since $\underline{\Delta}(\Omega)\subset X_0\times\Lambda$, we see that $\underline{\Delta}(\Omega)=X_0\times\Lambda$. □

We will see additional classes of pre-enterprise below for which, as in corollary 11, the domain $\underline{\Delta}(\Omega)$ of the equilibrium map $\underline{x}$ is the entire design set $X_0\times\Lambda$. On the other hand, this is not always the case as the following example shows.

12. Example. Let the elements of a pre-enterprise $\Omega=\langle\bar{N},\bar{X},u,f\rangle$ satisfy:
1. $\bar{N}=\{0,1,2\}$;
2. $X_i=\mathcal{R}_+$, $i=0,1,2$;
3. w_i is defined by $w_i(x_i)=-x_i-0.01e^{-x_i}$, $x_i\in X_i$, $i=1,2$;
4. f is defined by $f(x)=x_0+5x_2-(x_1-x_2)^2$, $\bar{x}\in\bar{X}$.

Then Ω is a pre-enterprise. Moreover, for each $(x_0,\lambda)\in\Lambda\times X_0$, the adjustment process $\alpha[x_0,\lambda]$ is well defined $(i\in N)$ and is given to a close approximation by

$$\alpha_1[x_0,\lambda](x_2)\cong\max\left[0,x_2-\frac{1}{2\lambda_1}\right],\qquad x_2\in X_2;\tag{17}$$

$$\alpha_2[x_0,\lambda](x_1)\cong\max\left[0,x_1-\frac{1-5\lambda_2}{2\lambda_2}\right],\qquad x_1\in X_1.\tag{18}$$

However, for $\lambda=(0.5,0.5)$, no equilibrium exists, as may be verified directly or by noting that the solution to (12) does not exist for λ as given and $x_0>0$. Thus, $\underline{\Delta}(\Omega)\neq X_0\times\Lambda$, even though $\Delta(\Omega)=X_0\times\Lambda$.

4. Continuity of equilibrium: completely regular pre-enterprises

In this section we investigate the continuity of the equilibrium map $\underline{x}$ of a pre-enterprise Ω. For simplicity we restrict attention to the case (see, for example, corollary 11) where $\underline{\Delta}(\Omega)=X_0\times\Lambda$. First we characterize (theorem 13) the continuity of $\underline{x}$ in terms of its boundedness on certain compact sets. When $\underline{x}$ is continuous on $X_0\times\Lambda$ we call Ω (sharecropping) completely regular (definition 14). By demonstrating sufficient conditions for this continuity, in corollary 15, we indicate a broad class of completely regular pre-enterprises. Finally, we examine (example 16) quadratic pre-enterprises as an example of complete regularity.

13. Theorem. Let Ω be a smooth pre-enterprise with $\underline{\Delta}(\Omega)=X_0\times\Lambda$. The equilibrium map $\underline{x}$ of Ω is continuous if $\underline{x}\,(Y_0\times\Lambda)\subset X$ is bounded for each compact $Y_0\subset X_0$.

Proof. If $\underline{x}$ is continuous, then $\underline{x}(Y_0 \times \Lambda)$ is compact (hence, bounded) for each compact $Y_0 \subset X_0$, so that "only if" is clear. To see "if", assume that $\underline{x}(Y_0 \times \Lambda)$ is bounded for each compact $Y_0 \subset X_0$. Since $X_0 \times \Lambda \subset \mathfrak{R}^{n+2}$ is a k-space (see Nagata, 1968, exercise 17, p. 148), it suffices to show that $\underline{x}$ is continuous on $Y_0 \times \Lambda$ for each compact $Y_0 \subset X_0$. Take any compact $Y_0 \subset X_0$, and denote the (compact) closure of $\underline{x}(\Lambda \times Y_0)$ by K. Now, by definition 1, para. 2, for each $i \in N$, X_i is of one of the forms: (i) $[-\infty, b_1]$; (ii) $\mathfrak{R}$; (iii) $[a_i, +\infty]$; or (iv) $[a_i, b_i]$, where $a_i, b_i \in \mathfrak{R}$ with $a_i \leqslant b_i$. By proposition 8, a characterization of $y = \underline{x}(x_0, \lambda)$ for any $(x_0, \lambda) \in Y_0 \times \Lambda$ is a system of n Kuhn–Tucker conditions (similar to (19)–(21) below) involving the continuous functions w_i' and $f_i'(i \in N)$ and no strict inequalities. For example, if X_i is of the form (iv), then the Kuhn–Tucker conditions for i may be represented as

$$(y_i - a_i)(w_i'(y_i) + \lambda_i f_i'(x_0, y))(y_i - b_i) = 0; \tag{19}$$

$$(w_i'(y_i) + \lambda_i f_i'(x_0, y))(y_i - a_i) \geqslant 0; \tag{20}$$

$$(w_i'(y_i) + \lambda_i f_i'(x_0, y))(y_i - b_i) \geqslant 0. \tag{21}$$

From the above it is easily checked that the equilibrium map $\underline{x}$ has closed graph $\Gamma \subset X_0 \times \Lambda \times \underline{x}(X_0 \times \Lambda)$. Thus, $\Gamma \subset (Y_0 \times \Lambda \times K)$ is closed, and this implies that $\underline{x}$ is continuous on $Y_0 \times \Lambda$ (see Dugundji, 1966, XI.2.7, pp. 228).
□

14. Definition. A pre-enterprise Ω will be called (*sharecropping*) *completely regular* iff $\underline{\Delta}(\Omega) = X_0 \times \Delta$ and the equilibrium map $\underline{x}$: $X_0 \times \Lambda | X$ is continuous. (Thus, for a completely regular pre-enterprise, the equilibrium product map $\underline{f}$: $X_0 \times \Lambda \to \mathfrak{R}$ (see (5)) is also continuous.)

15. Corollary. Let Ω be a smooth pre-enterprise which is $\beta(X_0 \times \Lambda)$-bounded. For example, a pre-enterprise whose each $i \in N$ satisfies

1. X_i is compact,

or

2. X_i is bounded below and, for each compact $Y_0 \subset X_0$, $\sigma = \sup\{f_i'(\bar{x}) | \bar{x} \in Y_0 \times X\}$ exists, satisfying $\sigma \leqslant -w_i'(\hat{x}_i)$ for some $\hat{x}_i \in X_i$.

Then Ω is sharecropping completely regular and the equilibrium set $\underline{x}(X_0 \times \Lambda)$ is bounded for each compact $Y_0 \subset X_0$.

Proof. Since Λ is compact, theorem 9 (see also corollary 11) implies $\underline{\Delta}(\Omega) = X_0 \times \Lambda$ with the equilibrium set $\underline{x}(Y_0 \times \Lambda)$ bounded for each compact $Y_0 \subset X_0$. The proof is completed by applying theorem 13. □

Corollary 15 demonstrates only sufficient conditions for a pre-enterprise to be completely regular. The log-linear pre-enterprises introduced in example 10, although completely regular, do not fall in the class identified by corollary 15. This is true also of the quadratic pre-enterprises introduced immediately below.

16. Example. Consider a *quadratic pre-enterprise*, i.e. a pre-enterprise Ω such that, for each $i \in N$, $X_i = \mathfrak{R}$ with w_i quadratic of the form

$$w_i(x_i) = a_i(x_i)^2 + b_i x_i + c_i \qquad (a_i, b_i, c_i \in \mathfrak{R}) \tag{22}$$

and, for each $x_0 \in x_0$, $f(\cdot\,; x_0)$ quadratic of the form

$$f(\bar{x}) = x^t A(x_0)x + 2B(x_0)x + C(x_0), \tag{23}$$

where $A(x_0)$ and $B(x_0)$ are, respectively, $n \times n$ and $1 \times n$ real matrices and $C(x_0) \in \mathfrak{R}$, all three functions A, B and C being twice continuously differentiable. [Note that, by definition 1, para. 3, $a_i < 0$ for each $i \in N$, and that, by definition 1, para. 4, $A(x_0)$ is negative semi-definite for each $x_0 \in X_0$.]

Now, for each $i \in N$, $X_i = \mathfrak{R}$ and $u[(x_0, \lambda)]_i$ is strictly concave for each $(x_0, \lambda) \in X_0 \times \Lambda$, so the optimization problems (1) are solved by setting

$$\frac{\partial u[x_0, \lambda](\cdot, x^i)}{\partial x_i} = 2a_i x_i + 2b_i + 2\lambda_i\left(\sum_j A_{ij}(x_0)x_j + B_i(x_0)\right)$$

$$= 0 \qquad (i \in N), \tag{24}$$

where $A_{ij}(x_0)$ and $B_i(x_0)$ are the components of $A(x_0)$ and $B(x_0)$, respectively. Solving for x_i, we obtain, for each $(x_0, \lambda, x^i) \in X_0 \times \Lambda \times X^i$ and $i \in N$,

$$\alpha_i[x_0, \lambda](x^i) = -\frac{\lambda_i\left[\sum_j{}^i (A_{ij}(x_0)) + B_i(x_0)\right] + b_i}{a_i + \lambda_i A_{ii}(x_0)}. \tag{25}$$

In particular, as $a_i < 0$ and $A_{ii}(x_0) \leqslant 0$, the denominator in (25) is nonzero. Thus, the adjustment process is well defined and $\underline{\Omega}(x_0, \lambda)$ is an enterprise for each $(x_0, \lambda) \in (X_0 \times \Lambda)$.

Taking any $(x_0, \lambda) \in X_0 \times \Lambda$, according to (25), the equilibrium $\underline{x}(x_0, \lambda)$ (of $\underline{\Omega}(x_0, \lambda)$) must satisfy

$$\underline{x}(x_0, \lambda) = Q(x_0, \lambda)\underline{x}(x_0, \lambda) + q(x_0, \lambda), \tag{26}$$

where $Q(x_0, \lambda) = L(x_0, \lambda)(A(x_0) - D(x_0))$ with $L(x_0, \lambda)$ and $D(x_0)$ $n \times n$

diagonal matrices whose (i,i)th components are $-\lambda_i/(a_i+\lambda_i A_{ii}(x_0))$ and $A_{ii}(x_0)$, respectively, and where $q(x_0,\lambda)$ is an $n\times 1$ matrix with ith component $-(\lambda_i B_i(x_0)+b_i)/(a_i+\lambda_i A_{ii}(x_0))$. Now it can be shown (Kleindorfer and Sertel, 1976) that $Q(x_0,\lambda)$ has real eigenvalues, each of which is less than 1. In particular, $+1$ is not an eigenvalue of $Q(\lambda,x_0)$ so that $I-Q(\lambda,x_0)$ has an inverse. Thus, by (26),

$$\underline{x}(x_0,\lambda)=[I-Q(x_0,\lambda)]^{-1}q(x_0,\lambda). \tag{27}$$

This much says that $\underline{\Delta}(\Omega)=X_0\times\Lambda$. Actually Q and q are continuous functions of (x_0,λ) and, thus, so is $\underline{x}$. We conclude that Ω is sharecropping completely regular.

5. Smoothness of equilibrium and adjustment

In this section we investigate the smoothness, i.e. continuous differentiability, of the equilibrium map of a completely regular pre-enterprise and establish this smoothness on an open dense subset of the design set $\underline{\Delta}(\Omega)=X_0\times\Lambda$. Similarly, the smoothness of enterprise adjustment is established on an open dense set of X.

17. Theorem. Let Ω be a smooth pre-enterprise which is sharecropping completely regular. The equilibrium map $\underline{x}$ of Ω is then continuously differentiable (with Jacobian matrix given as in (30)) on a dense open set $\underline{\Delta}\subset\underline{\Delta}(\Omega)=X_0\times\Lambda$.

Proof. Define $\underline{\Delta}(\Omega)\setminus\underline{\Delta}^*$ as the set of points $\delta=(x_0,\lambda)\in\underline{\Delta}(\Omega)$ so that, for some $i\in N$, no matter which nbd U of δ one takes; $(*)$: the image $\underline{x}_i(U)$ intersects the interior int X_i of X_i and owns $\sup x_i$ or $\inf x_i$. (Thus, if $X=\mathcal{R}^n$, then $\inf X_i$ and $\sup X_i$ are nonexistent for each $i\in N$ and $\underline{\Delta}^*=\underline{\Delta}(\Omega)$.) Now $\underline{\Delta}(\Omega)\setminus\underline{\Delta}^*\subset\underline{\Delta}(\Omega)$ is closed. For suppose a sequence in $\underline{\Delta}(\Omega)\setminus\underline{\Delta}^*$ converges, say to a point δ (where, of course, $\delta\in\underline{\Delta}(\Omega)$), and suppose that δ has a nbd U such that (*) above fails for each $i\in N$, i.e. $\delta\in\underline{\Delta}^*$. Then all but a finite number of points in the sequence belong to $\underline{\Delta}^*$, a contradiction. Thus, $\underline{\Delta}^*$ is open in $\underline{\Delta}(\Omega)$. To see that it is dense in $\underline{\Delta}(\Omega)$ and that $\underline{\Delta}(\Omega)\setminus\underline{\Delta}^*$ has no interior, define $(\underline{\Delta}(\Omega)\setminus\underline{\Delta}^*)_i$ to be the set of points $\delta\in\underline{\Delta}(\Omega)$ such that (*) obtains for each nbd U of δ. Now $\underline{\Delta}(\Omega)\setminus\underline{\Delta}^*=\bigcup_N(\underline{\Delta}(\Omega)\setminus\underline{\Delta}^*)_i$, so all we need show is that, arbitrarily fixing $i\in N$, $(\underline{\Delta}(\Omega)\setminus\underline{\Delta}^*)_i$ has no interior in $\underline{\Delta}(\Omega)$. So, take any $\delta\in(\underline{\Delta}(\Omega)\setminus\underline{\Delta}^*)_i$, and let U be any nbd of δ. By definition of $(\underline{\Delta}(\Omega)\setminus\underline{\Delta}^*)_i$, U owns points δ such that $x_i(\delta)\in\operatorname{int}X_i$. But, by continuity of

$\underline{x}$, $(\underline{\Delta}(\Omega)\setminus\underline{\Delta}^*)_i \subset \underline{x}_i^{-1}(\{\inf X_i, \sup X_i\})$, so $U \subset (\underline{\Delta}(\Omega)\setminus\underline{\Delta}^*)_i$ cannot hold, i.e. $U \cap \underline{\Delta}^* \neq \varnothing$ and we see that $(\underline{\Delta}(\Omega)\setminus\underline{\Delta}^*)$ has no interior.

To see that $\underline{x}$ is continuously differentiable on $\underline{\Delta}^*$, take any $\delta' \in \underline{\Delta}^*$, let $U \subset \underline{\Delta}(\Omega)$ be a nbd of δ' with $\underline{x}_i(U)$ contained in int X_i, $\{\inf X_i\}$ or $\{\sup X_i\}$ for each $i \in N$, and define $G = \{i \in N \mid \underline{x}_i(U) \subset \text{int } X_i\}$, $H = \{i \in N \mid \underline{x}_i(U) = \inf X_i\}$ and $H' = \{i \in N \mid \underline{x}_i(U) = \sup X_i\}$. For each $\delta = (x_0, \lambda) \in U$, the conditions defining $\underline{x}(\delta)$ are then simply

$$w_i'(\underline{x}_i(\delta)) + \lambda_i f_i'(x_0, \underline{x}(\delta)) = 0 \qquad (i \in G), \tag{28G}$$

$$\underline{x}_i(\delta) = \inf X_i \qquad (i \in H), \tag{28H}$$

$$\underline{x}_i(\delta) = \sup X_i \qquad (i \in H'), \tag{28H'}$$

and these are satisfied, in particular, by $\delta = \delta'$. Now for each $i \in H \cup H'$, x_i is constant, hence certainly continuously differentiable on U. Also, given (28H) and (28H′), we may rewrite (28G) as

$$w_i'(\underline{x}_i(\delta)) + \lambda_i f_i'(x_0, \underline{x}_G(\delta), \tilde{x}^G(\delta)) = 0 \qquad (\delta \in U, i \in G), \tag{29}$$

where $\tilde{x}^G(\delta) = (\underline{x}_H(\delta), \underline{x}_{H'}(\delta))$, and by the Implicit Function Theorem, there exists a nbd $V \subset U$ of δ' and a continuously differentiable function $\xi: V \to X_G$ for which $\underline{x}_G(\delta) = \xi(\delta)$ satisfies (29). Clearly ξ is nothing but the restriction of $\underline{x}_G$ to V. So much shows that $\underline{x} = (\underline{x}_G, \underline{x}^G)$ is continuously differentiable on $\underline{\Delta}^*$. In fact, the Implicit Function Theorem gives the following explicit Jacobian matrix for $\underline{x} = \underline{x}(\delta)$ at $\delta = (x_0, \lambda)$:[9]

$$J_{\underline{x}}(\delta) = \begin{bmatrix} \dfrac{\partial \underline{x}_1}{\partial x_0} & \dfrac{\partial \underline{x}_1}{\partial \lambda_1} & \cdots & \dfrac{\partial \underline{x}_1}{\partial \lambda_n} \\ \vdots & \vdots & \vdots & \vdots \\ \dfrac{\partial \underline{x}_n}{\partial x_0} & \dfrac{\partial \underline{x}_n}{\partial \lambda_1} & \cdots & \dfrac{\partial \underline{x}_n}{\partial \lambda_n} \end{bmatrix}$$

$$= -I_G(\underline{H}_w + S_\lambda \underline{H}_f)^{-1}$$

$$\times \begin{bmatrix} \lambda_1 f_1'(x_0, x) & f_1'(x_0, x) & 0 & \cdots & 0 \\ \lambda_2 f_2'(x_0, \underline{x}) & 0 & f_2'(x_0, \underline{x}) & \cdots & 0 \\ \vdots & \vdots & \vdots & \ddots & \vdots \\ \lambda_n f_n'(x_0, \underline{x}) & 0 & 0 & \cdots & f_n'(x_0, \underline{x}) \end{bmatrix}, \tag{30}$$

[9]The reader will note from definition 2 that the Hessian $\underline{H}_w$ of Σw_i is negative definite. From this and the concavity of f, the matrix $\underline{H}_w + S_\lambda \underline{H}_f$ in (30) is negative definite, in particular, nonsingular.

where $\underline{x}=\underline{x}(\delta)$, I_G is the $n\times n$ diagonal matrix with (i,i)th element unity for $i\in G$ and all other elements zero, S_λ is the $n\times n$ diagonal matrix with (i,i)th element equal to λ_i, and where $\underline{H}_w$ and $\underline{H}_f$ are the Hessian matrices of Σw_i and f, respectively, both Hessians being evaluated at $\underline{x}(\delta)$. □

N.B. Since $\partial x_i/\partial\lambda_j=0$ for each $j\in H\cup H'$ and $i\in N$, we may actually write

$$J_{\underline{x}(x_0,\cdot)}(x_0,\lambda)=-I_G(\underline{H}_w+S_\lambda\underline{H}_f)^{-1}$$
$$\times\begin{bmatrix} f_1'(x_0,\underline{x}) & 0 & \cdots & 0 \\ 0 & f_2'(x_0,\underline{x}) & \cdots & 0 \\ \vdots & \vdots & \ddots & \vdots \\ 0 & 0 & & f_n'(x_0,\underline{x}) \end{bmatrix} I_G \quad (31)$$

whenever we fix the component x_0 of $\delta=(x_0,\lambda)$.

It follows from theorem 17, of course, that the equilibrium product map $\underline{f}$ of a completely regular smooth pre-enterprise is also continuously differentiable on $\underline{\Delta}^*$.

Our next proposition establishes conditions for enterprise adjustment to be smooth. These will be useful in our stability analysis below.

18. Proposition. Let Ω be a smooth pre-enterprise which is $\beta_2(X_0\times\Lambda)$-bounded. Then, for each $\delta\in\Delta(\Omega)$, the adjustment process $\alpha[\delta]$ (of the enterprise $\Omega(\delta)$) is continuously differentiable (with Jacobian matrix given as in (33)) on a dense set $X^*(\delta)\subset X$.

Proof. Take any $\delta\in\Delta(\Omega)$. By proposition 6, $\alpha[\delta]$ is continuous, and we can now imitate the proof of theorem 17. Define $X\setminus X^*(\delta)$ as the set of points $x\in X$ such that, for some $i\in N$, $(*)$: no matter which (box) nbd $U=\prod U_i$ of x one takes, the image $\alpha_i[\delta](U^i)$ intersects the interior int X_i of X_i and owns sup X_i or inf X_i. As in theorem 17, $X^*(\delta)$ is shown to be an open dense set on which $\alpha[\delta]$ is continuously differentiable. In this instance, however, the following conditions replace (28):

$$w_i'(\alpha_i[\delta](x^i))+\lambda_i f_i'(x_0,\alpha_i[\delta](x^i),x^i)=0 \qquad (i\in G), \qquad (32G)$$
$$\alpha_i[\delta](x^i)=\inf X_i \qquad (i\in H), \qquad (32H)$$
$$\alpha_i[\delta](x^i)=\sup X_i \qquad (i\in H'), \qquad (32H')$$

where $G=\{i\in N\mid\alpha_i[\delta](U^i)\subset\text{int } X_i\}H=\{i\in N\mid\alpha_i[\delta](U^i)=\inf X_i\}$ and $H'=\{i\in N\mid\alpha_i[\delta](U^i)=\sup X_i\}$.

From (32) the Implicit Function Theorem gives the following explicit Jacobian matrix for $\alpha[\delta], \delta=(x_0, \lambda), \in \Delta(\Omega)$, at $x \in X$:

$$J_{\alpha[\delta]}(x) = \begin{bmatrix} \frac{\partial \alpha_1[\delta]}{x_1} & \cdots & \frac{\partial \alpha_1[\delta]}{\partial x_n} \\ \vdots & \vdots & \vdots \\ \frac{\partial \alpha_n[\delta]}{\partial x_1} & & \frac{\partial \alpha_n[\delta]}{\partial x_n} \end{bmatrix}$$

$$= I_G F(\delta, x)\big(H_f(x_0, x) - D_f(x_0, x)\big), \tag{33}$$

where I_G is the $n \times n$ diagonal matrix with (i, i)th element unity for $i \in G$ and all other elements zero, $F(\delta, x)$ is the $n \times n$ diagonal matrix with (i, i)th element equal to[10] $-\lambda_i/(w_i''(x_i)+\lambda_i f_{ii}''(x_0, x))$, $H_f(x_0, x)$ is the Hessian of $f(x_0, x)$ w.r.t. x, and $D_f(x_0, x)$ is the $n \times n$ diagonal matrix with (i, i)th element equal to $f_{ii}''(x_0, x)(x \in X, \delta=(x_0, \lambda) \in \Delta(\Omega))$, so that $H_f - D_f$ is obtained from H_f by zeroing out its diagonal elements. □

N.B. Since $\partial \alpha_i[\delta]/\partial x_j = 0$ for each $j \in H \cup H'$ and $i \in N$, we may rewrite (33) as

$$J_{\alpha[\delta]}(x) = -I_G F(\delta, x)\big[H_f(x_0, x) - D_f(x_0, x)\big] I_G. \tag{34}$$

6. Monotonicity of equilibrium and equilibrium product

In this section we study the equilibrium map $\underline{x}$ and equilibrium product map f of a completely regular pre-enterprise from the viewpoint of when the equilibrium contributions $\underline{x}_i$ $(i \in N)$ and the equilibrium product f are nondecreasing for certain upward adjustments in the shares λ. In contrast with the previous sections, f has to be given special attention here, since its investigated properties do not follow from those of $\underline{x}$ as they have done up to here.

19. Theorem. Let Ω be a smooth pre-enterprise which is sharecropping completely regular and assume for some agent $i \in N$ that (the marginal product) $f_i' \geqslant 0$. Then, fixing $x_0 \in X_0$, for each fixed value $\hat{\lambda}^i$ of shares to other agents (in N^i), x_i is monotonically nondecreasing in λ_i (i.e. monotonically nonincreasing in $\lambda_0 = 1-(\lambda_i + \Sigma_{N^i}^i \hat{\lambda}_j)$), $\lambda \in \Lambda$.

[10] Note from definition 2 that $w_i'' + \lambda_i f_{ii}'' < 0$.

Proof. Since $\underline{x}_i$ is continuous, it suffices to show the desired monotonicity on a dense subset of $\underline{\Delta}(\Omega)$. By theorem 17, $\underline{\Delta}^* \subset \underline{\Delta}(\Omega)$ is dense. Thus, the set $(\underline{\Delta}^*)_+$ of points in $\underline{\Delta}^*$ with $\lambda_j > 0$ for each $j \in N$ is also dense in $\underline{\Delta}(\Omega)$. We now prove theorem 19 by showing that $\partial \underline{x}_i / \partial \lambda_i \geqslant 0$ on $(\underline{\Delta}^*)_+$. (By theorem 17, the partial derivative in question exists on $\underline{\Delta}^* \supset (\underline{\Delta}^*)_+$.)

Taking any $\delta \in (\underline{\Delta}^*)_+$ and denoting the characteristic function of G by $\chi_G (\chi_G(i) = 1$ if $i \in G$ and $\chi_G(i) = 0$ if $i \in N \setminus G)$, from (30) we may write

$$\frac{\partial \underline{x}(\delta)}{\partial \lambda_i} = -\chi_G(i)\left[\left(\underline{H}_w + S_\lambda \underline{H}_f\right)^{-1}\right]_{ii} f_i'(x_0, \underline{x}(\delta)), \tag{35}$$

where $[(\underline{H}_w + S_\lambda \underline{H}_f)^{-1}]_{ii}$ is the (i, i)th component of the bracketed matrix. Now the partial derivative in (35) is zero if $i \in N \setminus G$, so assume $i \in G$. Since λ is positive in each component, S_λ^{-1} exists and

$$\left(\underline{H}_w + S_\lambda \underline{H}_f\right)^{-1} = \left(S_\lambda^{-1} \underline{H}_w + \underline{H}_f\right)^{-1} S_\lambda^{-1}. \tag{36}$$

Thus,

$$\left[\left(\underline{H}_w + S_\lambda \underline{H}_f\right)^{-1}\right]_{ii} = \left[\left(S_\lambda^{-1} \underline{H}_w + \underline{H}_f\right)^{-1}\right]_{ii} \frac{1}{\lambda_i}. \tag{37}$$

Since $S_\lambda^{-1} \underline{H}_w$ is negative definite and $\underline{H}_f$ negative semi-definite, their sum is negative definite, so the diagonal term $[(S_\lambda^{-1} \underline{H}_w + \underline{H}_f)^{-1}]_{ii}$ is negative. Regarding (35) and recalling the hypothesis that $f_i' \geqslant 0$, (37) implies that the partial derivative in (35) is non-negative, and this completes the proof. □

20. Theorem. Let Ω be a smooth pre-enterprise which is sharecropping completely regular. Then the equilibrium product f of Ω is nondecreasing for proportional increases in workers' shares. [Formally, taking any $x_0 \in X_0$ and $\mu \in \Lambda$, and defining the function $Q_\mu : [0, 1] \to \mathfrak{R}$ through $Q_\mu(h) = \underline{f}(x_0, h\mu)$, Q_μ is nondecreasing.]

Proof. Given any $x_0 \in X_0$ and $\mu \in \Lambda$, take any $h \in [0, 1]$. Now f is continuously differentiable (c.d.) and, by theorem 17, $\underline{x}$ is c.d. on the open dense set $\underline{\Delta}^* \subset \underline{\Delta}(\Omega)$, so f is c.d. at points arbitrarily close to $(x_0, h\mu)$, say at $(y_0, s\nu) \in \underline{\Delta}^* (y_0 \in X_0, s \in [0, 1], \nu \in \Lambda)$, whence Q_ν is c.d. at s. By continuity of f and the fact that $\underline{\Delta}^*$ is dense in $\underline{\Delta}(\Omega)$, it therefore suffices to show that $\mathrm{d}Q_\nu / \mathrm{d}h \geqslant 0$ at $h = s$. Now, from the Chain Rule, we have

$$\frac{\mathrm{d}Q_\nu(s)}{\mathrm{d}h} = \sum_i \frac{\partial f}{\partial \underline{x}_i} \sum_j \frac{\partial \underline{x}_i}{\partial \lambda_j} \frac{\partial \lambda_j}{\partial h}$$

$$= \sum_i \frac{\partial f}{\partial \underline{x}_i} \sum_j \frac{\partial \underline{x}_i}{\partial \lambda_j} \nu_j \tag{38}$$

or, in matrix notation,

$$\frac{\mathrm{d}Q_\nu(s)}{\mathrm{d}h}=[\nabla f(y_0,s\nu)]^t \underline{J}_x(x_0,s\nu)S_\nu, \tag{39}$$

where $[\nabla f]^t=(f_1',\ldots,f_n')$, J_x (given by (31)) is the Jacobian of $\underline{x}$ w.r.t. λ, and S_ν is the $n\times n$ diagonal matrix with (i,i)th element ν_i. Substituting (31) for $\underline{J}_x$, we obtain:

$$\frac{\mathrm{d}Q_\nu(s)}{\mathrm{d}h}=[\nabla f]^t I_G(\underline{H}_w+S_{s\nu}\underline{H}_f)^{-1}S_\nu I_G\nabla f. \tag{40}$$

Now, in (40), $S_\nu^{-1}\underline{H}_w+s\underline{H}_f$ is negative definite, and therefore so is its inverse, $(\tilde{\underline{H}}_w+S_{s\nu}\tilde{\underline{H}}_f)^{-1}S_\nu$. Therefore, from (40), $\mathrm{d}Q_\nu(s)/\mathrm{d}h\geqslant 0$, as desired. □

21. Theorem. Let Ω be a completely regular smooth pre-enterprise such that, for some $M\subset N$, $\bar{f}_{ij}''=0$ unless i and j belong to the same "department" M or $M^c=N\setminus M$. Then the equilibrium product f of Ω is nondecreasing for proportional increases in the shares λ_M (resp. λ_{M^c}) of the workers in department M (resp. M^c), $\lambda\in\Lambda$.

Proof (sketch). Fix $x_0\in X_0$. The hypothesis says that the Hessian H_f of f is block-diagonal, of the form

$$H_f=\left[\begin{array}{c|c} H_{f,M^c} & 0 \\ \hline 0 & H_{f,M}\end{array}\right], \tag{41}$$

so $\underline{H}_w+S_\lambda\underline{H}_f$ in (31) is of similar block-diagonal form, and so is its inverse $(\underline{H}_w+S_\lambda\underline{H}_f)^{-1}$. Thus, (31) gives $\partial\underline{x}_i/\partial\lambda_j=0$ unless i and j belong to the same department, M or M^c. Thus, fixing the shares of workers in M^c, say at $\hat{\lambda}_{M^c}$, a unique equilibrium behavior $\underline{x}_{M^c}(\hat{\lambda}_{M^c})$ is determined for M^c – independent of the behavior x_M of M. Now, we may treat M as the personnel of a "subpre-enterprise" $\Omega_M(x_0,\hat{\lambda}_{M^c})$ of Ω (as parameterized by the fixed $\hat{\lambda}_{M^c}$ and x_0), and $\Omega_M(x_0,\hat{\lambda}_{M^c})$ will turn out to be completely regular, as Ω is so. What we wish to show is that $\bar{f}(x_0,\lambda_M;\hat{\lambda}_{M^c})=f(x_0,\underline{x}_M(\lambda_M);\underline{x}_{M^c}(\lambda_{M^c}))$ does not decrease when λ_M is increased proportionately. Now, treating this function as the "equilibrium product map" $f_M(\cdot;x_0)=\bar{f}(x_0,\cdot;\hat{\lambda}_{M^c})$ of $\Omega_M(x_0,\hat{\lambda}_{M^c})$, from theorem 20 one obtains the desired monotonicity for $f_M(x_0,\cdot)$ and, thus, for $\underline{f}$. □

The following example illustrates the above monotonicity results for the log-linear pre-enterprises introduced in example 10, this time allowing for aggregate factors.

22. Example. A pre-enterprise Ω will be called *log-linear with aggregate labor* iff it fits the form:

1. $X_i = \mathfrak{R}_+ \ (i \in \bar{N})$;
2. $u_i(x_i, r_i) = -b_i x_i^{\beta_i} + r_i$ with $b_i > 0 \ (i \in \bar{N})$, and $\beta_i > 1 \ (i \in N)$;
3. $f(\bar{x}) = x_0^{\eta_0}(\Sigma a_i x_i)^{\eta_1}$ with $a_i > 0 \ (i \in N)$, $\eta_0, \eta_1 > 0$ and $\eta_0 + \eta_1 \leqslant 1$.

Let Ω be a log-linear pre-enterprise with aggregate labor for which $\beta_i = \beta > 1$ for all $i \in N$. The sharecropping equilibrium map $\underline{x}$ and equilibrium product $\underline{f}$ are given by

$$\underline{x}_i(x_0, \lambda) = \frac{(\lambda_i a_i \eta_1 / \beta b_i)^{1/(\beta-1)} x_0^{\eta_0/(\beta-\eta_1)}}{\left[\Sigma a_j \left(\dfrac{\lambda_j a_j \eta_1}{\beta b_j}\right)^{1/(\beta-1)}\right]^{(1-\eta_1)/(\beta-\eta_1)}}$$

$$((x_0, \lambda) \in X_0 \times \Lambda, i \in N) \tag{42}$$

and

$$\underline{f}(x_0, \lambda) = x_0^{\eta_0 \beta/(\beta-\eta_1)} \left[\sum a_i \left(\frac{\lambda_i a_i \eta_1}{\beta b_i}\right)^{1/(\beta-1)}\right]^{\eta_1(\beta-1)/(\beta-\eta_1)}$$

$$(x_0, \lambda) \in X_0 \times \Lambda). \tag{43}$$

N.B. In this case $\underline{x}_i$ is nonincreasing in $\lambda_j \ (j \in N^i)$. Contrast this with (14) in example 10.

7. Stability of equilibrium

This section defines the notion of stability of enterprise equilibrium and provides sufficient conditions for global stability to obtain.[11] Following this, the quadratic pre-enterprise is used in providing an example of unstable equilibrium.

23. Remark–definition. We follow Bhatia and Szegö (1970) in our definition of terms related to stability. In particular, for a pre-enterprise Ω and

[11]Although for reasons of brevity we analyze only global stability here, much weaker sufficient conditions for local stability and attraction are obtained in Kleindorfer (1980). These are essentially those obtained in the original version of this paper, and require simply that the matrix $H_f(x_0, \tilde{x}) - 2D_f(x_0, \tilde{x})$ be positive semi-definite at the equilibrium $\tilde{x} = \underline{x}(\delta)$. ($H_f - 2D_f$ is simply the matrix H_f with the signs of the diagonal elements reversed.) This condition is always satisfied when $N = \{1, 2\}$ since for any 2×2 matrix H_f, $H_f \leqslant 0$ implies $H_f - 2D_f \geqslant 0$, as the reader may easily verify.

any $\delta \in \underline{\Delta}(\Omega)$, we say that the enterprise equilibrium $x(\delta)$ is *stable* iff, for every nbd $V \subset X$ of $\underline{x}(\delta)$, there exists a nbd $U \subset V$ of $\underline{x}(\delta)$ with $\alpha[\delta](U) \subset U$; and $\underline{x}(\delta)$ is said to be an *attractor* iff there exists a nbd $V \subset X$ of $\underline{x}(\delta)$ such that $\lim_{k \to \infty} \alpha[\delta]^k(x) = \underline{x}(\delta)$ whenever $x \in V$, where $\alpha[\delta]^k: X \to X$ is the k-fold composition of $\alpha[\delta]$ with itself. (The notions of *local* and *global attraction* are defined relative to the domain of attraction V.) Finally, $\underline{x}(\delta)$ is said to be (*globally*) *asymptotically stable* iff it is both stable and an attractor (a global attractor).

We start with a fundamental result of Gabay and Moulin (1980), adapted to our notation.

24. Theorem (Gabay and Moulin, 1980, theorem 4.7). Let Ω be a smooth pre-enterprise and take any $\delta = (x_0, \lambda) \in \underline{\Delta}(\Omega)$. Suppose that the Hessian matrix $\underline{H}_w + S_\lambda \underline{H}_f$ defined in (30) is strictly diagonally dominant for all $x \in X$, i.e.

$$|w_i''(x_i) + \lambda_i f_{ii}''(x_0, x)| > \sum_{j \neq i} |\lambda_i f_{ij}''(x_0, x)| \qquad (x \in X, i \in N). \tag{44}$$

Then the equilibrium $\tilde{x} = \underline{x}(\delta)$ of the enterprise $\underline{\Omega}(\delta)$ is globally asymptotically stable.

25. Remark. Gabay and Moulin prove their result for general games in extensive form. The underlying game here is specified by the (effective) utility functions $\{w_i(x_i) + \lambda_i f(x_0, x) \mid i \in N\}$ and the strategy spaces $\{X_i \mid i \in N\}$. Although Gabay and Moulin only treat explicitly the case where $X_i = [0, \infty)$ their result is easily generalized to the case where $X_i = \mathfrak{R}$ or X_i is a compact interval.

26. Example (unstable equilibrium). Let the elements of a quadratic pre-enterprise Ω (see example 16) satisfy the following:

1. $\bar{N} = \{0, 1, 2, 3\}$, $X_0 = \{\sqrt{2}\}$;
2.

i	1	2	3
a_i	$-1/3$	$-1/3$	$-1/3$
b_i	0	0	0
c_i	0	0	0

3. $a(x_0) = \begin{bmatrix} -2 & -4 & -2 \\ -4 & -10 & -4 \\ -2 & -4 & -5 \end{bmatrix}$; $\quad B(x_0) = [37 \quad 74 \quad 74]$; $\quad C(x_0) = 0$.

Then, fixing λ at $\lambda = (\frac{1}{3}, \frac{1}{4}, \frac{1}{4})$ it can be verified from (25) that

$$\alpha[x_0, \lambda](x) = Q(x_0, \lambda)x + q(x_0, \lambda) \qquad (x \in X), \tag{45}$$

where Q and q are defined following (26) and, in this case, given by

$$Q(x_0, \lambda) = \begin{bmatrix} 0 & -\frac{4}{3} & -\frac{2}{3} \\ -\frac{4}{11} & 0 & -\frac{4}{11} \\ -\frac{1}{3} & -\frac{2}{3} & 0 \end{bmatrix}; \qquad q(x_0 \lambda) = \begin{bmatrix} \frac{37}{3} \\ \frac{74}{11} \\ \frac{37}{3} \end{bmatrix}. \tag{46}$$

From (27) the unique equilibrium of $\Omega(\lambda, x_0)$ is

$$\underline{x}(x_0, \lambda) = [I - Q(x_0, \lambda)]^{-1} q(x_0, \lambda) = [3 \quad 4 \quad 10]'. \tag{47}$$

Since (45) is a linear system, the adjustment process $\alpha[\delta]$ is stable at equilibrium iff its spectral radius $\rho(Q(\delta)) < 1$. But, it can be verified that $\rho(Q(\delta)) \cong 1.11345$ in this case, so $\alpha[\delta]$ is unstable for $\lambda = (\frac{1}{3}, \frac{1}{4}, \frac{1}{4})$.

8. Cooperative behavior

We have until now dealt exclusively with adjustment processes characterized by noncooperative behavior. This section briefly sketches corresponding results for the case where enterprise adjustment is characterized by cooperative behavior amongst agents $i \in N$. Such results are of interest in comparing the consequences of cooperative and noncooperative behavior, especially in the context of a labor-managed firm where cooperative behavior amongst worker–partners could be a defensible assumption.

We first define cooperative behavior for agents $i \in N$ through a corresponding game-theoretic solution concept.

27. Definition. Let Ω be a pre-enterprise and let $\delta = (x_0, \lambda) \in X_0 \times \Lambda$ be any enterprise design. Then a *cooperative solution* at δ is any (Pareto-efficient) solution $(\hat{x}, \hat{t}) \in X \times T(x, \delta)$ to the following vector maximization problem with transferable utility:

$$\underset{\substack{x \in X \\ t \in T(x, \delta)}}{\text{maximize}} \{w_i(x_i) + \lambda_i f(x_0, x) + t_i\}_{i \in N}, \tag{48}$$

where, for $x \in X$,

$$T(x,\delta)=\{t\in \mathfrak{R}^n \mid \Sigma t_j=0, w_i(x_i)+\lambda_i f(x_0,x)+t_i \geqslant U_i \quad (i\in N)\},$$

where U_i represents the reservation utility level for agent $i \in N$.

Thus, if $t=(t_1,\ldots,t_n)\in T(x,\delta)$ is the vector of lump-sum transfers at (x,δ), then t_i represents the amount *paid to* agent i. These transfers must satisfy reservation utility level constraints $u_i(x_i, \lambda_i f(x_0,x)+t_i)\geqslant U_i$ (see definition 1, para. 2). It is natural to assume that $U_i \geqslant \sup_{X_i} w_i(x_i)$, which is the utility level which agent i could assure himself of by quitting the personnel N and maximizing w_i independently. If $U_i \geqslant \sup w_i$, then it also follows that if $t\in T(x,\delta)$, then $\lambda_i f(x_0,x)+t_i \geqslant 0$ for $i\in N$, a condition which disallows agent i from paying out (as a lump-sum transfer) more than he earns. [N.B. if $U_i \geqslant \sup w_i$, then $t\in T(x,\delta)$ implies $0 \leqslant w_i(x_i)+\lambda_i f(x_0 x) + t_i - U_i \leqslant w_i(x_i) - \sup w_i + \lambda_i f(x_0,x)+t_i \leqslant \lambda_i f(x_0,x)+t_i$.]

Now given the additively separable form of the utility functions $u_i = w_i + r_i$ (see definition 1), it is easily verified[12] that if $(\hat{x},\hat{t})$ solves (48), then $\hat{x}$ solves

$$\max_{x\in X} \Sigma \left[w_i(x_i)+\lambda_i f(x_0,x) = \max_{x\in X}(1-\lambda_0)f(x_0,x)+\Sigma w_i(x_i)\right], \quad (49)$$

where $\lambda_0 = 1-\Sigma\lambda_i$ is the capitalist's share of output. It follows from the strict concavity of the maximand in (49) that if a solution to (49) exists it is unique. Denote by $\underline{\hat{\Delta}}(\Omega)\subset X_0\times\Lambda$ the set of enterprise designs of a given pre-enterprise Ω for which the cooperative solution at δ exists. The following proposition parallels proposition 8 in providing a characterization of cooperative solutions.

28. Proposition. Let Ω be a pre-enterprise and take any $\delta\in\underline{\hat{\Delta}}(\Omega)$. The cooperative solution $\underline{\hat{x}}(\delta)\in X$ is determined by $w_i(\underline{\hat{x}}(\delta))=\sup_{X_i} w_i$ if $1-\lambda_0 = 0$ (i.e. if $\lambda_i=0$, $i\in N$) and, if $1-\lambda_0>0$, by the solution to

$$\max_{x\in X}\left[f(x_0,x)+\Sigma \frac{w_i(x_i)}{1-\lambda_0}\right]. \quad (50)$$

Proof. If $\lambda_i=0$, $i\in N$, then (49) implies that $\underline{\hat{x}}_i(\delta)$ must maximize w_i for each $i\in N$. If $1-\lambda_0>0$, we may divide through by $1-\lambda_0$ in (49) without affecting the solution $\underline{\hat{x}}_i(\delta)$ to (49). □

[12] See the Appendix of this book for additional discussion and proof of a similar proposition for cooperative choice of designs.

Comparing (11) and (12) with proposition 28 we see immediately that the cooperative solution $\hat{\underline{x}}(\delta)$ is obtained as a solution to the same formal problem as the noncooperative solution $\underline{x}(\delta)$. Indeed, extending the domain of definition of $\underline{x}(\delta)$, we may write formally from (50) and (12) that

$$\hat{\underline{x}}(x_0,\lambda_1,\ldots,\lambda_n)=\underline{x}(x_0,1-\lambda_0,1-\lambda_0,\ldots,1-\lambda_0). \tag{51}$$

Thus, the cooperative solution for $\delta=(x_0,\lambda)$ is the same as the same as the non-cooperative solution for $\bar{\delta}=(x_0,(1-\lambda_0)\underline{e})$, where $\underline{e}$ is an n-vector whose each component is unity. From this equivalence result, all of the preceding results for the noncooperative case carry over directly to the cooperative case. Moreover, since $1-\lambda_0=\Sigma\lambda_j\geqslant\lambda_i\ (i\in N)$, it can be shown as in theorem 20 that

$$f(x_0,\hat{\underline{x}}(\delta))\geqslant f(x_0,\underline{x}(\delta))\quad \text{for } \delta\in\hat{\underline{\Delta}}(\Omega)\cap(\Omega).$$

Also, by definition 27 of a cooperative solution, all agents $i\in N$ could be made better off (through appropriate lump-sum transfers) at $\hat{\underline{x}}(\delta)$ than they would be at $\underline{x}(\delta)$. Thus, *ceteris paribus*, both capitalist and workers alike are better off (at any design $\delta\in\hat{\underline{\Delta}}(\Omega)\cap\underline{\Delta}(\Omega)$) if the workers cooperate than if they do not; output is also higher.

9. Closing remarks

In our introductory remarks we indicated several areas of interest which could benefit from the equilibrium analysis presented here. It seems worthwhile to return briefly to this matter now in view of our results.

First let us see how these results apply in posing and solving enterprise design problems. If we take the (unique) equilibrium $\underline{x}(\delta)$ as being "representative" of the enterprise $\underline{\Omega}(\delta)$, as seems reasonable when $\underline{x}(\delta)$ is stable, then alternative enterprise designs $\delta\in\underline{\Delta}(\Omega)$ can be evaluated from one or another point of view in terms of $\underline{x}(\delta)$. Adopting this equilibrium approach, we may, for example, state the profit-maximizing (sharecropping) enterprise design problem (i.e. the design problem as seen from agent 0's point of view) as follows:

$$\underset{\delta\in\underline{\Delta}(\Omega)}{\text{maximize}}\left[w_0(x_0)+f(x_0,\underline{x}(\delta))\right]. \tag{52}$$

Similarly, if we adopted the viewpoint of agents $i\in N$, we would obtain the following vector maximization problem as the design problem of interest:

$$\underset{\delta\in\underline{\Delta}(\Omega)}{\text{maximize}}\,\{u[\delta]_i(\underline{x}(\delta))\}_{i\in N}. \tag{53}$$

Actually, not all designs $\delta \in \underline{\Delta}(\Omega)$ may be feasible in such problems, e.g. because the enterprise must attract its workers from a labor market. Nonetheless, (52) and (53) indicate the general nature of optimal enterprise design problems: a class of feasible designs is given, and some set of preferences regarding representative, i.e. equilibrium, outcomes of designs from the given class is then used to determine maximal or optimal designs. These matters are investigated in detail in Kleindorfer and Sertel (1979) for various classes of incentive schemes and from the point of view of various interest groups. It should be apparent, however, that the results of the present paper are crucial in even being able to state such problems, as well as in determining their solutions as a function of parameters of interest.[13] As a case in point, the existence of solutions to (52) and (53) is a simple matter of compactness of $\underline{\Delta}(\Omega)$ and continuity of $\underline{x}(\delta)$, conditions for which were established in corollary 15.

A second matter of interest is extending our analysis to incorporate risk.[14] This turns out to be straightforward, so we will outline the basic idea here. Suppose $\{(\theta_i, \xi_i) | i \in \bar{N}\}$ is a family of real-values random variables and let the utility function of definition 1, para. 2 $\{u_i | i \in \bar{N}\}$ be of the form

$$u_i(x_i, r_i) = \mathrm{E}[w_i(\theta_i, x_i) + r_i], \tag{54}$$

where E is the expectation operator. Assuming that each agent $i \in \bar{N}$ has *ex ante* impression $\xi_i f$ of enterprise production, we see that, for each agent $i \in \bar{N}$, the effective utility function under sharing is

$$u[\delta]_i(x) = \mathrm{E}[w_i(\theta_i, x_0) + \lambda_i \xi_i f(\bar{x})], \tag{55}$$

which, if $\mathrm{E}(\xi_i) > 0$, is clearly equivalent to the effective utility function

$$\bar{u}[\delta]_i(x) = \bar{w}_i(x_i) + \lambda_i f(\bar{x}), \tag{56}$$

with $\bar{w}_i(x_i) = \mathrm{E}w_i(\theta_i, x_i)/\mathrm{E}(\xi_i)$. From this we see that all the results of this chapter are applicable here by simply taking $w_i = \bar{w}_i$ in definition 1, para. 2. Also, when agents' impressions of production take the general form $f(\xi_i, \bar{x})$, then as long as $\mathrm{E}f(\xi_i, \bar{x}) = f(\bar{x})$ for every agent $i \in N$, so that expectations concerning technological uncertainty are unanimous, the effective utility functions of interest are all of the form

$$\bar{u}[\delta]_i(x) = \bar{w}_i(x_i) + \lambda_i \bar{f}(\bar{x}), \tag{57}$$

[13] The reader can verify that no problem arises with the above analysis if x_0 is understood to be a vector, e.g. of input factors purchased at price p. Then, if $w_0(x_0) = -px_0$, the parameters whose variations are of interest would include p.

[14] For the analysis of a related sharing problem under risk, see Wilson (1968).

with $\bar{w}_i(x_i) = Ew_i(\theta_i, x_i)$ and $\bar{f}(\bar{x})$ as above. Again (57) is clearly of suitable form for a direct application of the results of this study.

References

Arrow, K.J. (1975) "Vertical Integration and Communication", *Bell Journal of Economics*, 6, no. 1, 173–183.

Bardham, P.K. and T.N. Srinivasan (1971) "Crop Sharing Tenancy in Agrieulture: A Theoretical and Empirical Analysis", *American Economic Review*, 61, no. 1, 48–64.

Bell, C. and P. Zusman (1976) "Contracts for Sharing Output and Risks: A Bargaining Theoretic Approach", mimeo, I.B.R.D.

Bhatia, N.P. and G.P. Szegö (1970) *Stability Theory of Dynamical Systems* (Springer-Verlag, New York).

Canes, M.E. (1975) "The Simple Economics of Incentive Contracting: Note", *American Economic Review*, 65, no. 3, 478–483.

Cheung, S.N.S. (1969) *The Theory of Share Tenancy* (University of Chicago Press, Chicago).

Diamond, P. (1967) "The Role of a Stock Market in a General Equilibrium Model with Technological Uncertainty", *American Economic Review*, 57, 759–776.

Dugundji, J. (1966) *Topology* (Allyn and Bacon, Boston).

Gabay, D. and H. Moulin (1980), "On the Uniqueness and Stability of Nash Equilibria in Non-Cooperative Games", in A. Bensoussan, P.R. Kleindorfer and C.S. Tapiero, eds., *Applied Stochastic Control in Management Science and Econometrics* (North-Holland, Amsterdam).

Gately, D. (1974) "Sharing the Gains from Regional Cooperation", *International Economic Review*, 15, no. 1, 195–208.

Georgescu-Roegen, N. (1960) "Economic Theory and Agrarian Economics", *Oxford Economic Papers*, 12, 1–40.

Hsiao, J.C. (1975) "The Theory of Share Tenancy Revisited", *Journal of Political Economy*, 83, no. 5, 1023–1032.

Ichiishi, T. (1977) "Coalition Structure in a Labor-Managed Market Economy", *Econometrica*, 45, 341–360.

Kleindorfer, P.R. (1980) "Stability of Equilibrium for Sharecropping Enterprises", mimeo, University of Pennsylvania.

Kleindorfer, P.R. and M.R. Sertel (1976) "Equilibrium Analysis of Sharecropping", IIM Preprint Series 1/76/33, International Institute of Management, West Berlin. (See Chapter 6 of this book.)

Kleindorfer, P.R. and M.R. Sertel (1978) "Enterprises and Pre-enterprises", Preprint Series IIM/dp 78-38, International Institute of Management, West Berlin.

Kleindorfer, P.R. and M.R. Sertel (1979a) "Profit-Maximizing Design of Enterprises Through Incentives", *Journal of Economic Theory*, 20, 318–339. (See Chapter 4 of this book.)

Kleindorfer, P.R. and M.R. Sertel (1979b) "Value-added Sharing Enterprises", Preprint Series IIM/dp 79-81, International Institute of Management, West Berlin. (See Chapter 9 of this book.)

Mirrlees, J.A. (1974) "Notes on Welfare Economics, Information and Uncertainty", in: M. Balch, D. McFadden and S. Wu, eds., *Essay in the Economics of Uncertainty* (North-Holland, Amsterdam), ch. 9.

Mirrlees, J.A. (1976) "The Optimal Structure of Inventives and Authority Within an Organization", *Bell Journal of Economics*, 7, no. 1, 105–131.

Nagata, J. (1968) *Modern General Topology* (North-Holland, Amsterdam).

Newberry, D.M.G. (1976) "Risk Sharing, Sharecropping and Uncertain Markets", mimeo, Stanford.

Rao, C.H. (1971) "Uncertainty, Entrepreneurship and Sharecropping in India", *Journal of Political Economy*, 79, no. 3, 578–598.

Ross, S.A. (1973) "The Economic Theory of Agency: The Principal's Problem", *American Economic Review*, 63, no. 2, 134–139.

Sertel, M.R. (1975) "The Fundamental Continuity of Optimization on a Compact Space I", *Journal of Optimization Theory and Applications*, 16, no. 5–6 (*MR* 52, No. 9032).

Sondermann, D. (1974) "Economics of Scale and Equilibria in Coalition Production Economics", *Journal of Economic Theory*, 8, no. , 259–291.

Stiglitz, J.E. (1974) "Incentives and Risk Sharing in Sharecropping", *Review of Economic Studies*, 61, no. 2, 219–256.

Stiglitz, J.E. (1975) "Incentives, Risks, and Information: Notes Toward a Theory of Hierarchy", *Bell Journal of Economics*, 6, no. 2, 552–579.

Tulkens, H. (1979) "Information Exchanges in a Negotiation Model of Transfrontier Pollution", in: K. Krippendorff, ed., *Communication and Control in Social Processes* (Gordon and Breach Science Publishers, London).

Vanek, J. (1970) *The General Theory of Labor Managed Market Economies* (Cornell University Press, Ithaca).

Varga, R.S. (1962) *Matrix Iterative Analysis* (Prentice-Hall, Englewood Cliffs, N.J.).

Wilson, R. (1968) "The Theory of Syndicates", *Econometrica*, 36, no. 1, 119–132.

CHAPTER 7

Workers' enterprises facing competitive capitalism*

MURAT R. SERTEL,† TAMER BAŞAR and HASAN SELBUZ

1. Introduction

The economic institution of workers' management has received increasing attention, since it offers an alternative to capitalism and to the form of socialism depending on the centralized direction of economic activity. The general idea of workers' management has been applied with some amount of success, not only in Yugoslavia, where nationwide it has become a rule rather than an exception, but even in the US, e.g. in the plywood industry (Bernstein, 1976). While the trend in Western Europe has been inclined more in the direction of workers' participation in industrial decision-making than toward complete and direct workers' management, here again the widespread operation of producers' cooperatives would be difficult not to mention in any proper modern, or even current, historical account.[1] Certainly, the Mondragon experience of the Basques in Spain stands out as an

*This chapter is based on the authors' study (partially supported by the Ministry of Enterprises) with the same title, appearing as Technical Report No. 44 of the Applied Mathematics Division, Marmara Scientific and Technical Research Institute, Gebze-Kocaeli, Turkey, September 1978.

†The listing of authors is embarrassing to the first-listed, who otherwise sticks strictly to alphabetical orderings. The paper on which the chapter is based actually got printed during his absence, and his co-authors were as kind as ever, this time in their betalpha. The original paper has been referenced widely enough that a reordering of things now would be impractical, but at least subsequent works (e.g. Chapter 8) of the authors require no such notes.

[1]It is also of interest to note that Domar (1966) has analyzed "Soviet collectives" as producers' cooperatives.

unignorable success story of workers' enterprises flourishing in the midst of present-day capitalism.[2] Finally, regarding developing countries, one might recall that workers' management, although officially adopted as a target by the previous regimes in Peru and Chile, had to topple along with the regime in both cases. The present Turkish governmental objective of converting at least some state enterprises into workers' enterprises stands on stage against such a background. [*Post scriptum*: The above words were written in September 1978. Now see the Preface.]

Our concern in this study is simply the economic theory of workers' enterprises or of labor-managed firms. The accumulated theory in this area is still relatively scant and, if we leave aside a few works dealing mainly with the financial aspects of labor-managed firms (falling outside our present interests), is represented fairly for our present purposes by three main contributions: Ward (1958), Domar (1966) and Vanek (1970). This literature is internally consistent in a number of ways from which we will depart here. Considering a price-taking labor-managed firm whose output Y is taken as numéraire, these works recognize that the workers' income from such an enterprise will amount to the residual of output that remains after all factors other than labor have been paid for. Summarily regarding these other factors as capital goods, rented at an externally given rental $\rho>0$ in quantity K, the total income of the workers from the enterprise in question amounts to the value added by labor, expressed as

$$V=Y-\rho K.$$

The output term Y here is understood, in standard fashion, to depend through a production function F, not only on the input K, but also on the aggregate labor L expended in production by the workers of the enterprise:

$$Y=F(K,L).$$

So far we have no modeling disagreement with the received theory. We beg to disagree, however, with the jump that leads to the typical characterization of the labor-managed firm as a concern which maximizes V/L. This jump

[2] Taking the foundation of the first industrial Mondragon Cooperative as the starting point, "it is within a period of just over 20 years that the Mondragon Cooperatives have grown into a group which employs today roughly 16,000 people" (Oakeshott, 1978, p. 9). In the group there are agricultural and housing cooperatives, a chain of cooperative stores, and schools and educational institutions organized as cooperatives. They have become Spain's leading supplier of consumer durables and producers of machine tools, as well as manufacturers of many other types of equipment and components for sale either within the group or outside. Perhaps the most interesting aspect of the Mondragon Cooperatives is their most successful workers' bank – the Caja Laboral Popolar – which is the first of its kind (Oakeshott, 1978).

could be justified if workers had no utility for leisure, or suffered no disutility from work, whilst they enjoyed a utility from some positive share in V, received as individual income, and if the workers were all to contribute the same constant amount of labor, say a unit work-day of fixed duration, to the production process in the enterprise, regardless of the fashion in which they were remunerated for their efforts. For, in that case, L could be measured as $L = N \cdot 1 = N$, simply as the number N of workers, in which case $Y = F(K, N)$, and $V/L = V/N$ would truly represent, as a maximand, the interests of the purely income-seeking workers each of whom constitutes a homogeneous unit work-day of productive labor.

In the fashion of Kleindorfer and Sertel (1976) and Dirickx and Sertel (1977), however, our understanding of a worker here is an economic agent who values not only income but also leisure. Thus, just how much labor the workers of an enterprise may be expected to contribute will depend on the operating incentive scheme within the enterprise, since it is through the manner in which such an incentive scheme ties workers' incomes to their work that the workers will reckon in choosing their respective contributions of labor to the production process in the enterprise. Dealing with such workers, it is no longer possible, independently of the incentive scheme utilized, to figure just what labor input a worker will be contributing. Under these circumstances it is clear that we may no longer take L to be represented by the number N of workers, and certainly V/L will no longer measure the value added per worker generated by the enterprise. In fact, the quotient $[F(K, L) - \rho K]/N$, although correctly measuring the quantity in question, ceases to be justifiable as a valid objective function for a firm run by and for its workers. For, considering any such firm with a given number N of workers, the quotient indicated grows incessantly as a function of L/N, and any attempt to maximize this quotient is certain to overwork the workers, if not to work them to death, a consequence which could hardly serve as a goal for leisure-appreciating workers or any workers' council claiming to further their interests and accountable to their general assembly.

Being forced to abandon the characterization of a labor-managed firm as a concern maximizing value added per worker, we must agree on a sensible notion of such a firm. In fact, we focus attention on the notion of a *workers' enterprise* by which we mean *an enterprise whose workers and partners coincide*.

Now, workers' enterprises may institute various types of internal incentives. An extremely interesting class of internal incentive schemes is defined by assigning (*ex ante*) to each worker–partner some share in the value added (by labor) generated in the enterprise. Under such "sharing schemes" the relation of a typical worker–partner's income to his work contribution is generally dependent upon the work contributions of his fellow worker–partners, so that the equilibrium outcome (in terms of the behavior of all the participants, the consequent output, incomes, utilities, etc.) under such an incentive scheme may be analyzed and evaluated by employing one or another suitable game-theoretic solution concept, as in Kleindorfer and Sertel (1976) and Dirickx and Sertel (1977). We analyze workers' enterprises with value added sharing elsewhere (Kleindorfer and Sertel, 1978).

The workers' enterprises we study here utilize, in contrast, "individualistic" incentives, i.e. address each worker–partner with an incentive function stipulating the worker–partner's income as dependent on his own labor contribution only (independent of his fellow's behavior). In fact, we consider two types of individualistic internal incentive scheme which a workers' enterprise may adopt. In the case of a "workers' enterprise with internal wages", a worker–partner's income is determined pure and simple as the product of his labor contribution with a wage. The wage is stipulated by the general assembly of worker–partners, and may vary from one individual to another. In a "workers' enterprise with internal wages and quotas", on the other hand, the general assembly stipulates not only such internal wages, but also "quotas" of labor contributions up to which the wage is operative and beyond which there is no incentive to work.

As soon as we briefly specify the technological and preferential data with which we will be working, and assume price-taking behavior, all in section 2, we begin constructing table 7.1. Here, in three columns, we tabulate the fourteen-dimensional equilibrium outcome for three kinds of enterprise each utilizing n_i workers putting in labor of type $i \in M = \{1,\ldots,m\}$. In section 3 we compute column 1, pertaining to the competitive capitalistic enterprise; in section 4 we do the same for the workers' enterprise with internal wages; and in section 5 we make corresponding computations for the workers' enterprise with internal wages and quotas. The fourteen dimensions of outcome here, covering incomes and utilities of the agents as well as various input and output levels, are displayed in terms of their competitive capitalistic values, making most comparisons reasonably transparent. (The remaining comparisons are computed out in the text of sections 3–5.) So far, the results of Dirickx and Sertel (1977) are corroborated and extended to our present case with many types of labor.

At this point we introduce the question raised by Sertel (1978) regarding the relative size of the three kinds of enterprise, in terms of the number of workers or worker–partners, when these agents are allowed to move from one kind of enterprise to another, paying their colleagues in the enterprise of entry, if necessary, to enter. In the present study we extend the results of Sertel (1978) to the case with m types of labor, and find, once again, that it is difficult to sustain the hypothesis that the workers' enterprises will behave pathologically.

The "pathology" we refer to has to do with the behavior of "labor-managed firms" facing a complement of business in the form of an increased price of their output. The "folklore" of the topic seems to have it that the labor-managed firm will contract output under such circumstances, at least in the "short run". Such behavior might readily be classified as disturbing from the viewpoint of a Walrasian price equilibrium, at least as far as the stability of equilibrium prices is concerned. Leaving folklore aside, it is clear, as Ward (1958) has argued for the "Illyrian firm", that the number N of worker–partners will appear, if anything, excessive from the viewpoint of any current worker–partner, whenever the output price increases (the rental ρ decreases) in a firm maximizing $(F(K,N)-\rho K)/N$ in the short run where K is fixed.[3] While it is not clear that the fixity of K, rather than of N, most appropriately describes the short run for a labor-managed firm, a correct evaluation of the prospects for workers' enterprises certainly calls for a careful examination of the folkloric or the Wardian hypothesis claiming what might rightly be regarded as sickly behavior on the part of such enterprises in an economy.

Concentrating on the long run, here we deal with a large mixed economy to which ρ is a given, incorporating a competitive capitalistic sector alongside a bivariate workers' sector, and we investigate the general equilibrium outcomes for the various sectors (with the given ρ), again corroborating Sertel (1978). In particular, we find that, considering the sectors of workers' enterprises with internal wages and with or without quotas, they are constant-proportional in the number of worker(–partners) of a typical enterprise to the typical enterprise in the capitalistic sector, so that they increase or decrease their number of worker–partners, K and output in the same direction as their competitive capitalistic counterparts, which is hardly pathological. This occupies us through sections 6 and 7, in which we mix first a large sector of workers' enterprises with internal wages, then also one of workers' enterprises with internal wages and quotas, with a large competitive capitalistic economy, and we tabulate general equilibrium outcomes (with given ρ) in table 7.2, now listing the general equilibrium relative

[3]We refer back to the labor-managed firm maximizing value added per worker–partner in a world where every worker(–partner) carries with him the same given labor contribution, independent of incentives, and cares only for income, itself a fraction of the firm's residual output after capital goods have been paid for at given prices.

values of four more outcomes in addition to the fourteen outcomes of table 7.1. As a result, workers' enterprises of the types considered here come out with no communal disadvantages, and certainly with no handicaps from the workers' viewpoint, when compared with their competitive capitalistic counterparts. Imitating Sertel (1978), it should be easy for the reader to see that a perturbation of the given prices in the "short run", from a long-run equilibrium where all the firms have settled at their respective levels of employment of capital goods and of labor, will lead, *mutatis mutandis*, all the firms to adjust perfectly normally, so long as the share (or worker–partnership deed) market functions competitively. With the technical detail involved in the present chapter the task of establishing this for the "short run" amounts to more tedium and repetition than analysis, and so we spare the reader the details. (The reader will note that when K is fixed at its respective long-run equilibrium values for the various types of firm we study, one simply deals with F and V as evaluated at the proper K and reaches the same qualitative economic results as in the long run.) Again, of course, no Wardian (1958) pathology arises, since the workers' enterprises adjust their membership of various sorts of worker–partner in the same direction and by the same percentage as the typical capitalistic enterprise adjusts its corresponding work force, the supply of output, etc. responding with the according common sense.

Finally, section 8 records a summary and a few closing remarks, and the study ends with appendices A and B which provide proofs for the stability of the equilibrium relative sizes in the workers' enterprise with internal wages and the workers' enterprise with internal wages and quotas.

2. Basic data and framework

We consider an enterprise employing m types of productive labor with n_i workers of type $i \in M = \{1,\ldots,m\}$. The labor contribution of the jth worker of type i is denoted by x_{ij}, $j \in N_i = \{1,\ldots,n_i\}$, and the aggregate labor of workers of type i is denoted as L_i, i.e. $L_i = \sum_{N_i} x_{ij}$. The enterprise is equipped with a production function $Y = F(K, L_1,\ldots,L_m)$ of the log-linear form

$$Y = K^{\alpha} \prod_{M} L_i^{\beta_i} \qquad \left(0 < \alpha,\ \beta = \sum_{M} \beta_i,\ \alpha + \beta < 1\right), \tag{1}$$

where Y stands for the output of a single commodity and K for the quantity of capital goods employed. The workers all like income and dislike work, exhibiting preferences as represented by the utility function

$$u_{ij} = y_{ij} - x_{ij}^{\gamma} \qquad (1<\gamma) \tag{2}$$

for the jth worker of type i, whose income, measured in units of the output, is denoted by y_{ij}.

The enterprise is a price-taker both in selling its output and in renting capital goods. Taking the price of output as unity, we let ρ stand for the rental on capital goods. Thus, the value added generated by the enterprise is given as

$$V = Y - \rho K \qquad (\rho > 0). \tag{3}$$

3. The competitive capitalistic enterprise

In the enterprise we consider here, we envisage a profit-maximizing capitalist responsible for decisions regarding the employment of capital goods. Since profit is

$$\Pi = V - \sum_M w_i L_i, \tag{4}$$

where w_i denotes any given (positive) wage for labor of type $i \in M$, the profit-maximizing level of K is that which maximizes value added (V), a strictly concave function of K. Now, the first-order conditions of the maximization in question yield

$$\tilde{K} = \left(\frac{\alpha}{\rho} \prod_M L_i^{\beta_i}\right)^{1/(1-\alpha)} \tag{5}$$

as the profit-maximizing quantity of capital goods at the rental ρ. By substituting $\tilde{K}$ for K in Y, V and Π, we obtain, respectively,

$$\tilde{Y} = \left[\left(\frac{\alpha}{\rho}\right)^{\alpha} \prod_M L_i^{\beta_i}\right]^{1/(1-\alpha)}, \tag{6}$$

$$\tilde{V} = (1-\alpha)\tilde{Y}, \tag{7}$$

$$\tilde{\Pi} = \tilde{V} - \sum_M w_i L_i. \tag{8}$$

Facing any given wage vector $w = (w_1, \ldots, w_m)$, the profit-maximizing capitalist thus exhibits the following demand for labor of type i:

$$\bar{L}_i = \frac{\beta_i}{w_i} \bar{Y}, \tag{9}$$

where $\bar{Y}$ is the profit-maximizing output given by

$$\bar{Y} = \left[\left(\frac{\alpha}{\rho} \right)^{\alpha} \prod_{M} \left(\frac{\beta_k}{w_k} \right)^{\beta_k} \right]^{1/(1-\alpha-\beta)}. \tag{10}$$

As to the supply of labor by a typical, say jth, worker of type $i \in M$ facing a wage w_i, i.e. an income function $y_{ij} = w_i x_{ij}$, maximization of the worker's utility u_{ij} gives

$$\underline{x}_i = \left(\frac{w_i}{\gamma} \right)^{1/(\gamma-1)}. \tag{11}$$

Thus, the supply of labor by the n_i workers of type i adds up to

$$\underline{L}_i = n_i \left(\frac{w_i}{\gamma} \right)^{1/(\gamma-1)}. \tag{12}$$

Thinking in terms of a competitive capitalistic economy whose typical firms are copies of our present enterprise, the labor markets will be equilibrated by wages $w = (w_1, \ldots, w_m)$ solving the following m equations of supply and demand for our m types of labor:

$$\bar{L}_i = \underline{L}_i \qquad (i \in M). \tag{13}$$

We solve these equations in standard fashion, first obtaining

$$w_i = \left[\gamma \left(\frac{\beta_i}{n_i} \bar{Y} \right)^{\gamma-1} \right]^{1/\gamma}, \tag{14}$$

substituting this in (10) and solving now to get the competitive capitalistic equilibrium output

$$\underline{\bar{Y}} = \left[\left(\frac{\alpha}{\rho} \right)^{\alpha\gamma} \prod_{M} \left(\frac{\beta_k n_k^{\gamma-1}}{\gamma} \right)^{\beta_k} \right]^{1/\delta}, \tag{15}$$

as well as the competitive capitalistic equilibrium wages

$$\underline{\bar{w}}_i = \left[\gamma \left(\frac{\beta_i}{n_i} \underline{\bar{Y}} \right)^{\gamma-1} \right]^{1/\gamma} \qquad (i \in M), \tag{16}$$

where

$$\delta = \gamma(1-\alpha) - \beta. \tag{17}$$

Finally, for the competitive capitalistic equilibrium values $\underline{\bar{x}}_i$, $\underline{\bar{y}}_i$, $\underline{\bar{L}}_i$, $\underline{\bar{K}}$, $\underline{\bar{V}}$, $\underline{\bar{u}}_i$, $\underline{\bar{U}}_i$, $\underline{\bar{U}}$ and $\underline{\bar{\Pi}}$ of the typical ith type of workers' employment level, income, the aggregate input level of the ith type of labor, the quantity of capital goods rented, value-added, utility of a typical ith type of worker, aggregate utility of workers of type i, total utility of the workers' class and profit, respectively, we mechanically fill out the appropriate entries in the first column of table 7.1.

An important "efficiency" property of the competitive capitalistic enterprise, which should be noted at this point, is that its equilibrium behavior uniquely maximizes the quantity

$$\tilde{Z} = \tilde{V} - \sum_{M} \sum_{N_i} x_{ij}^{\gamma}, \tag{18}$$

which we call the *communal surplus*. (Regarding the appropriateness of communal surplus as a measure of efficiency, see the Appendix to this book.) This fact will later be utilized in section 5. The competitive capitalistic equilibrium value $\underline{\bar{Z}}$ of communal surplus is also listed in table 7.1 as the twelfth entry of column 1. The last two entries of column 1 list the competitive capitalistic equilibrium values of the productivity of the ith type of labor ($\underline{\bar{Y}}/\underline{\bar{L}}_i$) and the output capital ratio ($\underline{\bar{Y}}/\underline{\bar{K}}$).

4. The workers' enterprise with internal wages

The enterprise we consider in this section is a workers' enterprise, so that its workers coincide with its partners. We envisage a *workers' council* vested with the authority not only to decide about the utilization level K of capital goods, but also to set a wage system internal to the enterprise. Evidently, the communal income of the worker–partners is bounded above by value added, and any sensible workers' council will exhaust this quantity by distributing it among the worker–partners. As the internal incentive scheme of the enterprise, we fix attention to a wage system, i.e. we agree that the income of the jth worker of type i will be of the form

$$y_{ij} = w_i x_{ij} \qquad (j \in N_i, i \in M) \tag{19}$$

for some positive wage w_i. To clearly express the dictum that the workers' council will exhaust value added in payments to the worker–partners, let us not neglect to note that

$$\sum_{M} \sum_{N_i} y_{ij} = V. \tag{20}$$

According to just what criteria the workers' council chooses K and the internal wage system of the enterprise is a matter affording a genuine

Table 7.1
Equilibrium outcomes of three types of enterprise at common size n.

Equilibrium outcome \ Enterprise	Competitive capitalistic enterprise	Workers' enterprise with internal wages	Workers' enterprise with Internal wages and quotas
Wage (of a typical worker of type i) w_i	$\underline{\bar{w}}_i=\left[\gamma\left(\frac{\beta_i}{n_i}\underline{\bar{Y}}\right)^{\gamma-1}\right]^{1/\gamma}$	$\underline{\tilde{w}}_i^0=\left(\frac{1-\alpha}{\beta}\right)^{[(\gamma-1)(1-\alpha)]/\delta}\underline{\bar{w}}_i$	$\underline{\bar{\omega}}_i^0=\left(1+\frac{\lambda_i}{\beta_i}\varepsilon\right)\underline{\bar{w}}_i$
Labor (input of a typical worker of type i) x_i	$\underline{\bar{x}}_i=\left(\frac{\beta_i}{\gamma n_i}\underline{\bar{Y}}\right)^{1/\gamma}$	$\underline{\tilde{x}}_i^0=\left(\frac{1-\alpha}{\beta}\right)^{(1-\alpha)/\delta}\underline{\bar{x}}_i$	$\underline{\bar{x}}_i^0=\underline{\bar{x}}_i$
Income (of a typical worker of type i) y_i	$\underline{\bar{y}}_i=\frac{\beta_i}{n_i}\underline{\bar{Y}}$	$\underline{\tilde{y}}_i^0=\left(\frac{1-\alpha}{\beta}\right)^{\gamma(1-\alpha)/\delta}\underline{\bar{y}}_i$	$\underline{\bar{y}}_i^0=\left(1+\frac{\lambda_i}{\beta_i}\varepsilon\right)\underline{\bar{y}}_i$
Aggregate labor (input of workers of type i) L_i	$\underline{\bar{L}}_i=\left[\frac{\beta_i n_i^{\gamma-1}}{\gamma}\underline{\bar{Y}}\right]^{1/\gamma}$	$\underline{\tilde{L}}_i^0=\left(\frac{1-\alpha}{\beta}\right)^{(1-\alpha)/\delta}\underline{\bar{L}}_i$	$\underline{\bar{L}}_i^0=\underline{\bar{L}}_i$
Capital goods input K	$\underline{\bar{K}}=\left(\frac{\alpha}{\rho}\right)\underline{\bar{Y}}$	$\underline{\tilde{K}}^0=\left(\frac{1-\alpha}{\beta}\right)^{\beta/\delta}\underline{\bar{K}}$	$\underline{\bar{K}}^0=\underline{\bar{K}}$
Output Y	$\underline{\bar{Y}}=\left[\left(\frac{\alpha}{\rho}\right)^{\alpha\gamma}\prod_M\left(\frac{\beta_k n_k^{\gamma-1}}{\gamma}\right)^{\beta_k}\right]^{1/\delta}$	$\underline{\tilde{Y}}^0=\left(\frac{1-\alpha}{\beta}\right)^{\beta/\delta}\underline{\bar{Y}}$	$\underline{\bar{Y}}^0=\underline{\bar{Y}}$
Value added V	$\underline{\bar{V}}=(1-\alpha)\underline{\bar{Y}}$	$\underline{\tilde{V}}^0=\left(\frac{1-\alpha}{\beta}\right)^{\beta/\delta}\underline{\bar{V}}$	$\underline{\bar{V}}^0=\underline{\bar{V}}$

Utility (of a typical worker of type i) u_i	$\underline{\bar{u}}_i=\frac{(\gamma-1)\beta_i}{\gamma n_i}\underline{\bar{Y}}$	$\underline{\tilde{u}}_i^0=\left(\frac{1-\alpha}{\beta}\right)^{\gamma(1-\alpha)/\delta}\underline{\bar{u}}_i$	$\underline{\bar{u}}_i^0=\left(1+\frac{\lambda_i\gamma}{\beta_i(\gamma-1)}\varepsilon\right)\underline{\bar{u}}_i$
Aggregate utility (of group i) U_i	$\underline{\bar{U}}_i=\frac{(\gamma-1)\beta_i}{\gamma}\underline{\bar{Y}}$	$\underline{\tilde{U}}_i^0=\left(\frac{1-\alpha}{\beta}\right)^{\gamma(1-\alpha)/\delta}\underline{\bar{U}}_i$	$\underline{\bar{U}}_i^0=\left(1+\frac{\lambda_i\gamma}{\beta_i(\gamma-1)}\varepsilon\right)\underline{\bar{U}}_i$
Total utility (of workers) U	$\underline{\bar{U}}=\frac{(\gamma-1)\beta}{\gamma}\underline{\bar{Y}}$	$\underline{\tilde{U}}^0=\left(\frac{1-\alpha}{\beta}\right)^{\gamma(1-\alpha)/\delta}\underline{\bar{U}}$	$\underline{\bar{U}}^0=\frac{\delta}{\beta(\gamma-1)}\underline{\bar{U}}$
Profit Π	$\underline{\bar{\Pi}}=\varepsilon\underline{\bar{Y}}$	$\underline{\tilde{\Pi}}^0=0$	$\underline{\bar{\Pi}}^0=0$
Communal surplus Z	$\underline{\bar{Z}}=\frac{\delta}{\gamma}\underline{\bar{Y}}$	$\underline{\tilde{Z}}^0=\sigma^{\varepsilon\gamma/\delta}\underline{\bar{Z}}$	$\underline{\bar{Z}}^0=\underline{\bar{Z}}$
Y/L_i	$\left(\frac{\underline{\bar{Y}}}{\underline{\bar{L}}_i}\right)=\left[\frac{\gamma}{\beta_i n_i^{\gamma-1}}\underline{\bar{Y}}^{\gamma-1}\right]^{1/\gamma}$	$\left(\frac{\underline{\tilde{Y}}^0}{\underline{\tilde{L}}_i^0}\right)=\left(\frac{\beta}{1-\alpha}\right)^{\varepsilon/\delta}\left(\frac{\underline{\bar{Y}}}{\underline{\bar{L}}_i}\right)$	$(\underline{\bar{Y}}^0/\underline{\bar{L}}_i^0)=(\underline{\bar{Y}}/\underline{\bar{L}}_i)$
Y/K	ρ/α	ρ/α	ρ/α

$$\sigma\equiv\left[\left(\frac{1-\alpha}{\beta}\right)^{(1-\alpha)}\left(\frac{\beta(\gamma-1)}{\delta}\right)^{\delta/\gamma}\right]^{1/\varepsilon}.$$

variety of real characterizations associable with a multitude of internal political structures which might manifest themselves in this regard. Certainly, one of these criteria is the maximization of the communal utility

$$U=\sum_M \sum_{N_i} u_{ij} \tag{21}$$

of the enterprise participants. We regard this as a reasonable working assumption and adopt it for the present analysis.

Combining (2) and (20), the maximand of the workers' council may thus be expressed as

$$U=V-\sum_M \sum_{N_i} x_{ij}^{\gamma}. \tag{22}$$

Now, recalling (3) and (1), we see that (22) identifies a function strictly concave in K, whose maximization dictates the choice of K precisely in the same fashion as in the case of (5), so that the behavior of the present enterprise in the capital goods rental market coincides completely with that of the capitalistic enterprise examined in the previous section.

With K adjusted in this manner, output and value added are determined again as $\tilde{Y}$ and $\tilde{V}$, respectively (see (6) and (7), respectively). Thus, in selecting the wage system, the workers' council focuses attention on the maximization of

$$\tilde{U}=\tilde{V}-\sum_M \sum_{N_i} x_{ij}^{\gamma}. \tag{23}$$

Now, at any wage system $w=(w_1,\ldots,w_m)$, the supply of labor is again as expressed by (11) and (12), for the ith type of labor. Thus, x_{ij} in (23) reduces for each $j \in N_i$ to $\underline{x}_i$ $(i \in M)$, and, utilizing also (12), the maximand of the workers' council boils down to

$$\underline{\tilde{U}}=(1-\alpha)\left[\left(\frac{\alpha}{\rho}\right)^{\alpha} \prod_M \left(n_i\left(\frac{w_i}{\gamma}\right)^{1/(\gamma-1)}\right)^{\beta_i}\right]^{1/(1-\alpha)} - \sum_M n_i\left(\frac{w_i}{\gamma}\right)^{\gamma/(\gamma-1)}, \tag{24}$$

and of course this expression has to be maximized subject to the constraint that all value added will be distributed among the worker–partners as wages, that is

$$(1-\alpha)\left[\left(\frac{\alpha}{\rho}\right)^{\alpha}\prod_{M}\left(n_i\left(\frac{w_i}{\gamma}\right)^{1/(\gamma-1)}\right)^{\beta_i}\right]^{1/(1-\alpha)}$$

$$=\sum_{M} n_i\left(\frac{1}{\gamma}\right)^{1/(\gamma-1)} w_i^{\gamma/(\gamma-1)}. \qquad (25)$$

This constrained maximization problem is easily checked to admit the following unique solution as the internal wages to be instituted by the workers' council:

$$\underline{\tilde{w}}_i^0=\left(\frac{1-\alpha}{\beta}\right)^{[(\gamma-1)(1-\alpha)]/\delta}\underline{\bar{w}}_i \qquad (i\in M). \qquad (26)$$

(Recall that $\underline{\bar{w}}_i$ is the competitive capitalistic equilibrium wage for labor of type i, as recorded in (16)).

With this information in hand, again it is merely a mechanical task to reckon the outcomes $\underline{\tilde{x}}_i^0$, $\underline{\tilde{L}}_i^0$, $\underline{\tilde{V}}^0$, $\underline{\tilde{\Pi}}^0$, $\underline{\tilde{y}}_i^0$, $\underline{\tilde{u}}_i^0$, $\underline{\tilde{w}}_i^0$ corresponding to the workers' enterprise with internal wages as displayed in the appropriate row of table 7.1.

We see from table 7.1 that the present enterprise operates at uniformly higher wages than the enterprise of the last section, the workers all contribute more effort, the aggregate labor input of each type is now greater, and so the capital goods input and, thereby, the output are also greater. In fact, not only is a greater value added and a higher income for each worker produced by the present enterprise, but despite the higher level of individual workers' efforts that all this involves, the workers' enterprise with internal wages renders a greater utility for each worker than the competitive capitalistic enterprise. All this amounts to a clear improvement of the workers' lot as compared to their fortunes in the competitive capitalistic enterprise. In view of the fact that the present enterprise appropriates the whole of communal surplus to its workers, paying no profits to a capitalist, it is perhaps not a cause of astonishment that this enterprise is able to make its workers better off than the competitive capitalistic enterprise. As we had remarked at the end of section 3, however, the equilibrium behavior of the competitive capitalistic enterprise had *uniquely* maximized the communal surplus, as a consequence of which we already know that the present enterprise, inducing a different equilibrium behavior, must fail to maximize the quantity in question – which is confirmed by comparing the communal surplus entries of the two types of enterprise as displayed in table 7.1. Finally, the last two entries of the first two columns of table 7.1 indicate that the output/capital ratio in the workers' enterprise with internal wages coincides with the one in the competitive capitalistic enterprise of the same size, whereas the productivity of each type of labor in the workers' enterprise with internal wages is below its counterpart in the competitive capitalistic enterprise.

5. The workers' enterprise with internal wages and quotas

The design principles of the enterprise we wish to consider in this section have already been strongly suggested by the ultimate paragraphs of the last two sections. Since, in a workers' enterprise, the whole communal surplus is at the disposal of the workers, this quantity $\tilde{Z}$ is maximized uniquely at the competitive capitalistic employment $\underline{\bar{x}}$, and since $\underline{\tilde{x}}^0$ exceeds $\underline{\bar{x}}$ in every coordinate, it is quite transparent that the decentralized labor-contribution decisions of the worker–partners in the workers' enterprise with internal wages lead them all to overwork themselves. Surely there exists a mechanism inducing the work levels corresponding to $\underline{\bar{x}}$, while distributing enough income to the worker–partners so that they are uniformly better off than even in the workers' enterprise with internal prices. This can be seen by considering a *wage-quota* system (ω, x^*) with $\omega, x^* \in R^m$, by which we mean a system

$$y_{ij} = \begin{cases} \omega_i x_{ij}, & x_{ij} \leqslant x_i^* \\ \omega_i x_i^*, & x_{ij} \geqslant x_i^* \end{cases} \qquad (j \in N_i, i \in M) \tag{27}$$

of income functions for the worker–partners. Simply choosing the *quota* $x^* = \underline{\bar{x}}$ and setting ω_i equal to

$$\omega_i^0 = \left(\frac{(1-\alpha)\beta_i}{\beta n_i}\right)\frac{\underline{\bar{Y}}}{x_i^*}, \tag{28}$$

i.e. computing from table 7.1,

$$\omega_i^0 = \frac{(1-\alpha)}{\beta}(\gamma)^{1/\gamma}\left[\left(\frac{\beta_i}{n_i}\right)\left(\left(\frac{\alpha}{\rho}\right)^{\alpha\gamma}\prod_M\left(\frac{\beta_k n_k^{\gamma-1}}{\gamma}\right)^{\beta_k}\right)^{1/\delta}\right]^{(\gamma-1)/\gamma}, \tag{29}$$

it can be checked that the worker–partners facing such a wage-quota system settle precisely at the behavior $x^0 = \underline{\bar{x}}$ and are remunerated in proportion to the parameter β_i / n_i (associated with the type $i \in M$ of labor contributed) and so as to exhaust exactly the quantity $\underline{\bar{V}}$ – as a consequence of which the ith type of worker achieves the utility $u_i^0 > \underline{\tilde{u}}_i^0 > \underline{\bar{u}}_i$.

In fact, the wage-quota system (ω^0, x^0) is not unique – unless M is singleton – in steering the worker–partners to (the communal-surplus-maximizing behavior) $\underline{\bar{x}}$, and efficiently (exhaustively) paying out $\underline{\bar{V}}$ to the worker–partners so as to make them all better off than in the workers' enterprise with internal wages. For all these tasks are accomplished by any wage-quota system (ω, x^*) satisfying

$$\omega_i > \underline{\tilde{w}}_i^0 \qquad (i \in M), \tag{30}$$

$$\sum_M n_k \omega_k x_k^* = \underline{\bar{V}}, \tag{31}$$

$$x_i^* = \underline{\bar{x}}_i \qquad (i \in M). \tag{32}$$

Accordingly, we call any workers' enterprise employing a wage-quota system satisfying (30)–(32) a *workers' enterprise with internal wages and quotas*. Apparently, any such wage-quota system could be characterized uniquely by a distribution vector

$$\mu = \left\{ 0 \leqslant \mu_{ij} \leqslant 1, j \in N_i, i \in M, \sum_M \sum_{N_i} \mu_{ij} = 1 \right\},$$

where μ_{ij} stands for the relative portion of the capitalist's profit $\underline{\bar{\Pi}}$ to be appropriated, as a base-pay, for the jth worker of type i. Hence, such a distribution yields a total income of

$$\underline{\bar{y}}_{ij}^0 = \underline{\bar{y}}_i + \mu_{ij} \underline{\bar{\Pi}} \tag{33}$$

for the jth worker of type i, and using the values for $\underline{\bar{y}}_i$ and $\underline{\bar{\Pi}}$ from the appropriate entries of table 7.1, we compute the imputed wage $\underline{\bar{\omega}}_{ij}^0$ of the jth worker of type i, at the competitive capitalistic employment level $\underline{\bar{x}}_i$, to be

$$\underline{\bar{\omega}}_{ij}^0 = \frac{\underline{\bar{y}}_{ij}^0}{\underline{\bar{x}}_i} = \left(1 + \frac{n_i \mu_{ij}}{\beta_i} \varepsilon \right) \underline{\bar{w}}_i \qquad (i \in M). \tag{34}$$

Assuming that the portion of the capitalist's profit $\underline{\bar{\Pi}}$ to be appropriated for the n_i workers of type i $(i \in M)$ is distributed evenly among those workers, μ_{ij} becomes independent of $j \in N_i$ (i.e. $\mu_{ij} = \mu_i$), and then (34) takes the form

$$\underline{\overline{\omega}}_i{}^0 = \left(1 + \frac{\lambda_i}{\beta_i}\varepsilon\right)\underline{\overline{w}}_i \qquad (i \in M), \tag{35}$$

where

$$\lambda_i = n_i \mu_i \qquad (i \in M). \tag{36}$$

We display the (imputed) wage $\underline{\overline{\omega}}_i^0$, given by (35) in terms of the distribution vector $\lambda = \{\lambda_1, \ldots, \lambda_m\}$, in the appropriate entry of the third column of table 7.1. For this wage-quota system, which is characterized completely by the distribution vector λ, we mechanically fill out the remaining entries of the last column of table 7.1. It should be noted that a workers' enterprise with internal wages and quotas duplicates competitive capitalism in every aspect other than profit, the (imputed) wages and the incomes and utilities of the workers. Of course, the present type of enterprise leads to a zero profit and nonunique (imputed) wages, incomes and utilities for the workers, depending on what distribution, λ, it adopts as a policy of base payment.

6. General equilibrium: workers' enterprises with internal wages facing competitive capitalism

This section considers an economy consisting of many workers' enterprises with internal wages coexisting alongside many competitive capitalistic enterprises – a large mixed economy. The purpose is to study this economy at (general) competitive equilibrium. So, we assume there to be no collusion amongst agents or enterprises. There are $m+2$ commodities, namely a composite "output" with unit price, a capital good with an externally given price ρ, and m types of labor traded in the capitalistic sector at the "prices" $\underline{\overline{w}}_1, \ldots, \underline{\overline{w}}_m$. Thus, one thing we must do is to determine the general equilibrium values of $\underline{\overline{w}}_i$ $(i \in M)$.

The presence of a large sector of workers' enterprises, however, genuinely distinguishes our "mixed" economy from the usual capitalistic economy whose equilibrium analysis has so thoroughly been refined. For, apart from the usual labor markets in which various types of labor are traded at their respective competitive equilibrium prices $\underline{\overline{w}}_i$, a whole sector of workers in our economy enter contracts forming workers' enterprises in which they set internal wages $\underline{\tilde{w}}_i^0$ and find their livelihood by contributing their labor to production in their respective enterprises. Clearly, then, this process of the formation of firms must be at rest as a fundamental prerequisite for our economy to be at equilibrium. By a rest position of this process we mean a position in which no worker or worker–partner has an incentive to switch from one firm to another. It is to be understood, of course, that while entering into or exiting from a firm in the capitalistic sector is, by the nature of this sector, free for every worker, a workers' enterprise with internal wages may wish to exact an entrance fee from newly joining partners or be willing to be charged a severance compensation by worker–partners it wishes to buy out.

To analyze this matter somewhat more clearly, consider a workers' enterprise with internal wages consisting of $\Sigma_M b_i$ worker–partners altogether, b_i of which are of type i ($i \in M$). From table 7.1 we see (by writing b_i for n_i ($i \in M$)) that a typical worker–partner of type i in this enterprise enjoys a utility

$$\underline{\tilde{u}}_i^0(b) = \frac{\beta_i}{b_i} A g(b) \tag{37}$$

at the internal equilibrium of the enterprise, where

$$A = (\gamma - 1)\left[\left(\frac{\alpha}{\rho}\right)^{\gamma\alpha}\left(\frac{1-\alpha}{\gamma\beta}\right)^{\gamma(1-\alpha)} \prod_M \beta_k^{\beta_k}\right]^{1/\delta}, \tag{38}$$

$$g(b) = \left(\prod_M b_k^{\beta_k}\right)^{(\gamma-1)/\delta}. \tag{39}$$

To save both the reader and ourselves from a swamp of numerical analysis and the like, henceforth we ignore the fact that the numbers b_i are actually integral valued, and we pretend that they may lie anywhere along the non-negative real line. This allows us to think of the effect of a "marginal" worker–partner entering or exiting the enterprise in terms of derivatives.[4] In particular, in these terms the marginal entrant worker–partner of type $j \in M$ will cause a loss of equilibrium utility equal to

$$-\frac{\partial \underline{\tilde{u}}_i^0}{\partial b_j} = \begin{cases} \left(1 - \dfrac{(\gamma-1)\beta_i}{\delta}\right)\dfrac{\underline{\tilde{u}}_i^0}{b_i} & (i = j), \\ -\dfrac{(\gamma-1)\beta_j}{\delta b_j}\underline{\tilde{u}}_i^0 & (i \neq j), \end{cases} \tag{40}$$

[4]Rather than finite differences of nonintegral powers which would be correct but would unfortunately lead us to messy equations whose solutions are beyond our practical reach. Actually, in the examples that we have considered such an approximation turns out to be realistic even when the enterprise has few participants. The reader may confirm this for himself in the case where, for instance, there are two types of labor, $n_1 = n_2 = 25$, $\alpha = 1/3$, $\beta_1 = 1/4$, $\beta_2 = 1/5$ and $\gamma = 2$.

for the typical worker–partner of type $i \in M$. The net total loss of utility for the present worker–partners of the enterprise caused by the entry of a marginal worker–partner of type $j \in M$ is thus

$$\tilde{S}_j(b) = -\sum_M b_i \frac{\partial \underline{\tilde{u}}_i^0}{\partial b_j} = \frac{\gamma\varepsilon}{\delta} \underline{\tilde{u}}_j^0(b), \tag{41}$$

which is the minimal price at which the enterprise is willing to accept an extra worker–partner of type $j \in M$. Hence, we regard $\tilde{S}_j(b)$ as the *supply price* of a *share* of type j in a workers' enterprise of size $b = (b_1, \ldots, b_m)$ with internal wages. (This is also the maximal amount which the enterprise is willing to pay as severance compensation to buy out a marginal partner of type j.)

Perhaps the first thing to settle at this point is that the equilibrium sizes b and b' of any two workers' enterprises with internal wages will coincide. This is actually easy to see. For suppose that a marginal worker–partner of type j in a workers' enterprise of size $b = (b_1, \ldots, b_m)$ stands to gain $\underline{\tilde{u}}_j^0(b') - \underline{\tilde{u}}_j^0(b)$ from a potential movement from his enterprise to a similar enterprise of size $b' = (b'_1, \ldots, b'_m)$. The net cost of this move to the worker in question would be $\tilde{S}_j(b') - \tilde{S}_j(b)$, the supply price $\tilde{S}_j(b')$ of a share of type j in the workers' enterprise of size b' less the corresponding quantity $\tilde{S}_j(b)$ for the workers' present enterprise (of size b), the latter being received by the worker's sale of his present partnership share. Now, at equilibrium, the worker is to have no incentive to make the move in question, i.e. the net benefit $\underline{\tilde{u}}_j^0(b') - \underline{\tilde{u}}_j^0(b)$ is to just balance the cost $\tilde{S}_j(b') - \tilde{S}_j(b)$ of the move. But from (41) we have

$$\tilde{S}_j(b') - \tilde{S}_j(b) = \frac{\gamma\varepsilon}{\delta} \left[\underline{\tilde{u}}_j^0(b') - \underline{\tilde{u}}_j^0(b) \right], \tag{42}$$

where $(\gamma\varepsilon/\delta) < 1$. Thus, at equilibrium, both sides of (42) must vanish for each $j \in M$, and the reader may check that this obtains precisely when $b_j = b'_j$ for every $j \in M$.

Turning for a moment to the capitalistic sector, since the wage for any type of labor may not differ at equilibrium from one capitalistic enterprise to another, similar reasoning, in this case from (16), will show that the equilibrium sizes of the capitalistic enterprises will all be the same.

The key matter at hand is to equilibrate the size $a = (a_1, \ldots, a_m)$ of the capitalistic enterprises with $b = (b_1, \ldots, b_m)$ of the workers' enterprise with internal wages, and to determine the equilibrium share prices p_i of the latter enterprises for workers of type $i \in M$. To this end, we formulate the demand price

$$\tilde{D}_j(a,b)=\tilde{\underline{u}}_j^0(b)-\underline{u}_j(a) \tag{43}$$

for a share of type j of partnership in a workers' enterprise (of size b) with internal wages, as exhibited by a typical worker of type j in a capitalistic enterprise (of size a). This, of course, is the maximal amount which the worker in question is willing to pay for his promotion from a worker in the capitalistic sector to a worker–partner in a workers' enterprise with internal wages. Equilibrium requires, once again, an equation

$$\tilde{D}_j(a,b)=\tilde{S}_j(b) \qquad (j\in M) \tag{44}$$

of demand and supply for each type of partnership share in workers' enterprises with internal wages.[5] Spelling this out in terms of (38), (39), (41), (43) and table 7.1, we have

$$\beta_j A\left[\frac{g(b)}{b_j}-\frac{1}{a_j}\left(\frac{\beta}{1-\alpha}\right)^{\gamma(1-\alpha)/\delta}g(a)\right]=\left(\frac{\gamma\varepsilon}{\delta}\right)\left(\frac{\beta_j}{b_j}\right)Ag(b); \tag{45}$$

in other words,

$$\frac{b_j}{a_j}=B\frac{g(b)}{g(a)} \qquad (j\in M), \tag{46}$$

where

$$B=\frac{\beta(\gamma-1)}{\delta}\left(\frac{1-\alpha}{\beta}\right)^{\gamma(1-\alpha)/\delta}. \tag{47}$$

Thus, writing t_j for b_j/a_j and denoting $(t_1,\ldots,t_m)$ by t, (46) becomes

$$t_j=Bg(t) \qquad (j\in M). \tag{48}$$

So,

$$g(t)=\left(\prod_M t_j^{\beta_j}\right)^{(\gamma-1)/\delta}=(Bg(t))^{\beta(\gamma-1)/\delta}, \tag{49}$$

which solves uniquely for

$$g(t)=B^{\beta(\gamma-1)/\gamma\varepsilon}, \tag{50}$$

[5] Furthermore, this equilibrium will be stable, a result which is proven in appendix A of this chapter.

whose substitution into (48) determines, for every $j \in M$,

$$\frac{b_j}{a_j} = \left[\left(\frac{1-\alpha}{\beta}\right)^{(1-\alpha)}\left(\frac{\beta(\gamma-1)}{\delta}\right)^{\delta/\gamma}\right]^{1/\varepsilon}. \tag{51}$$

We have just determined the *equilibrium relative enterprise size* (b_j/a_j) in terms of the basic data α, β and γ given to us.[6] We assign the letter σ to denote this important (positive) constant of our system. It is difficult to overstate the significance of the existence of such a systemic constant – an invariant of the type of labor and a variant only of the technical parameters α and β and the preferential parameter γ of the system. For one thing, it is now clear that at equilibrium a workers' enterprise with internal wages cannot exhibit the "pathological behavior" ascribed to labor-managed firms in the literature and the folklore of this area of economics: at equilibrium, workers' enterprise with internal wages varies its size (in terms of worker–partners) precisely in the same fashion as does a capitalistic enterprise. In fact, (51) gives a unit equilibrium elasticity

$$\frac{\mathrm{d}b_j}{\mathrm{d}a_j}\cdot\frac{a_j}{b_j} = 1 \tag{52}$$

of b_j with respect to a_j $(j \in M)$.

We may ask, of course, whether at equilibrium the workers' enterprise with internal wages will be larger or smaller than the capitalistic enterprise. The complete answer to this question is furnished by the fact that

$$0 < \sigma < 1, \tag{53}$$

whereby the workers' enterprise with internal wages will be a proportionally shrunken model of the capitalistic enterprise, at equilibrium $(b_j = \sigma a_j < a_j,\ j \in M)$. For, since σ is obviously positive, verifying (53) amounts to showing $\sigma < 1$. To this end, since $1/\varepsilon > 0$, it suffices to show that

$$s = \left(\frac{1-\alpha}{\beta}\right)^{(1-\alpha)}\left(\frac{\beta(\gamma-1)}{\delta}\right)^{\delta/\gamma} < 1.$$

Considering s as a function of β, first note that $s = 1$ when $\beta = 1 - \alpha$, and now check that the slope

$$\frac{\mathrm{d}s}{\mathrm{d}\beta} = \frac{s}{\gamma}\ln\frac{\delta}{(\gamma-1)\beta}$$

[6] Check that, in terms of the example of footnote 4, if (b_1, b_2) is an equilibrium relative size for the workers' enterprise, then, in the world where the numbers of workers' are integer-valued, this is true of $(\text{int}\, b_1, \text{int}\, b_2)$, where "int" reads "the greatest integer less than or equal to".

is positive for $\beta \in (0, 1-\alpha)$, and vanishes at $\beta = 1-\alpha$; conclude that $s < 1$ for $\beta \in (0, 1-\alpha)$, as was to be shown.

Now that we have determined the equilibrium size of the workers' enterprises with internal wages relative to that of the capitalistic enterprises, it is possible to evaluate the first two columns of table 7.2 subject to the equilibrium relative size equation (51), as we do in the first fourteen entries of the first two columns of table 7.2. The last four entries in these columns do not appear in table 7.1. Before we examine these new entries, we turn to a comparison of the first fourteen entries of table 7.2, regarding their values in the two sectors.

The internal wages $\underline{\tilde{w}}_i^0$ in the workers' sector are clearly all proportionately higher than the competitive capitalistic wages $\underline{\overline{w}}_i$, since the ratio $\underline{\tilde{w}}_i^0/\underline{\overline{w}}_i = [\delta/\beta(\gamma-1)]^{(\gamma-1)/\delta}$ exceeds unity. By the same token, the employment levels $\underline{\tilde{x}}_i^0$ of each type $i \in M$ in the workers' sector with internal wages all proportionately exceed their counterparts in the competitive capitalistic sector. It follows, of course, that the workers' incomes $\underline{\tilde{y}}_i^0$ of each type $i \in M$ in the workers' sector with internal wages all exceed the incomes $\underline{\overline{y}}_i$ of the same type of workers in the competitive capitalistic sector. Again, the utilities $\underline{\tilde{u}}_i^0$ of the worker–partners in the workers' sector with internal wages are all proportionately higher than the utilities $\underline{\overline{u}}_i$ of their colleagues of the same type in the competitive capitalistic sector. Since profits are nil in any workers' sector, there is little more to say on this score other than to recognize that the profits in any capitalistic sector will exceed this quantity.

Now the ratio $\underline{\tilde{L}}_i^0/\underline{\overline{L}}_i$ of the aggregate labor input of type i in the workers' sector with internal wages to that in the competitive capitalistic sector is a positive power, at equilibrium, of the quantity

$$Q = \left(\frac{1-\alpha}{\beta}\right)^{\gamma}\left(\frac{\beta(\gamma-1)}{\delta}\right)^{\gamma-1}.$$

This quantity is unity at $\beta = 1-\alpha$, and a decreasing function of β in the interval $(0, 1-\alpha]$, so we see that $\underline{\tilde{L}}_i^0/\underline{\overline{L}}_i > 1$ for our basic data. By the same token, the equilibrium ratios $\underline{\tilde{K}}^0/\underline{\overline{K}}$, $\underline{\tilde{Y}}^0/\underline{\overline{Y}}$ and $\underline{\tilde{V}}^0/\underline{\overline{V}}$ all exceed unity. The ratios $\underline{\tilde{U}}_i^0/\underline{\overline{U}}_i$ and $\underline{\tilde{U}}^0/\underline{\overline{U}}$ are both positive powers of the quantity

$$Q' = Q\left(\frac{\delta}{\beta(\gamma-1)}\right)^{\varepsilon(\gamma-1)/(1-\alpha)}.$$

Since we already know that $Q > 1$, and since $\delta > \beta(\gamma-1)$ and $\varepsilon(\gamma-1)/(1-\alpha) > 0$, it is clear that $Q' > 1$, so $\underline{\tilde{U}}_i^0 > \underline{\overline{U}}_i$ and $\underline{\tilde{U}}^0 > \underline{\overline{U}}$.

Table 7.2
Equilibrium outcomes of three types of enterprise at their respective equilibrium sizes.

Equilibrium outcome \ Enterprise	Competitive capitalistic enterprise	Workers' enterprise with internal wages	Workers' enterprise with internal wages and quotas
Wage (of a typical worker of type i) w_i	$\underline{\bar{w}}_i=\left[\gamma\left(\frac{\beta_i}{a_i}\underline{\bar{Y}}\right)^{\gamma-1}\right]^{1/\gamma}$	$\underline{\tilde{w}}_i^0=\left(\frac{\delta}{\beta(\gamma-1)}\right)^{(\gamma-1)/\gamma}\underline{\bar{w}}_i$	$\underline{\bar{\omega}}_i^0=\left(1+\frac{\lambda_i}{\beta_i}\varepsilon\right)\underline{\bar{w}}_i$
Labor (input of a typical worker of type i) x_i	$\underline{\bar{x}}_i=\left(\frac{\beta_i}{\gamma a_i}\underline{\bar{Y}}\right)^{1/\gamma}$	$\underline{\tilde{x}}_i^0=\left(\frac{\delta}{\beta(\gamma-1)}\right)^{1/\gamma}\underline{\bar{x}}_i$	$\underline{\bar{x}}_i^0=\underline{\bar{x}}_i$
Income (of a typical work of type i) y_i	$\underline{\bar{y}}_i=\frac{\beta_i}{a_i}\underline{\bar{Y}}$	$\underline{\tilde{y}}_i^0=\frac{\delta}{\beta(\gamma-1)}\underline{\bar{y}}_i$	$\underline{\bar{y}}_i^0=\left(1+\frac{\lambda_i}{\beta_i}\varepsilon\right)\underline{\bar{y}}_i$
Aggregate labor (input of workers of type i) L_i	$\underline{\bar{L}}_i=\left(\frac{\beta_i a_i^{\gamma-1}}{\gamma}\underline{\bar{Y}}\right)^{1/\gamma}$	$\underline{\tilde{L}}_i^0=\left[\left(\frac{\beta(\gamma-1)}{\delta}\right)^{\gamma-1}\left(\frac{1-\alpha}{\beta}\right)^{\gamma}\right]^{(1-\alpha)/\gamma\varepsilon}\underline{\bar{L}}_i$	$\underline{\bar{L}}_i^0=\underline{\bar{L}}_i$
Capital goods input K	$\underline{\bar{K}}=\left(\frac{\alpha}{\rho}\right)\underline{\bar{Y}}$	$\underline{\tilde{K}}^0=\left(\frac{\beta(\gamma-1)}{\delta}\right)^{\gamma-1}\left(\frac{1-\alpha}{\beta}\right)^{\gamma}]^{\beta/\gamma\varepsilon}\underline{\bar{K}}$	$\underline{\bar{K}}^0=\underline{\bar{K}}$
Output Y	$\underline{\bar{Y}}=\left[\left(\frac{\alpha}{\rho}\right)^{\alpha\gamma}\prod_M\left(\frac{\beta_k a_k^{\gamma-1}}{\gamma}\right)^{\beta_k}\right]^{1/\delta}$	$\underline{\tilde{Y}}^0=\left[\left(\frac{\beta(\gamma-1)}{\delta}\right)^{\gamma-1}\left(\frac{1-\alpha}{\beta}\right)^{\gamma}\right]^{\beta/\gamma\varepsilon}\underline{\bar{Y}}$	$\underline{\bar{Y}}^0=\underline{\bar{Y}}$
Value added V	$\underline{\bar{V}}=(1-\alpha)\underline{\bar{Y}}$	$\underline{\tilde{V}}^0=\left[\left(\frac{\beta(\gamma-1)}{\delta}\right)^{\gamma-1}\left(\frac{1-\alpha}{\beta}\right)^{\gamma}\right]^{\beta/\gamma\varepsilon}\underline{\bar{V}}$	$\underline{\bar{V}}^0=\underline{\bar{V}}$

Utility (of a typical worker of type i) u_i	$\underline{\bar{u}}_i = \dfrac{(\gamma-1)\beta_i}{\gamma a_i}\underline{\bar{Y}}$	$\underline{\tilde{u}}_i^0 = \dfrac{\delta}{\beta(\gamma-1)}\underline{\bar{u}}_i$	$\underline{\bar{u}}_i^0 = \left(1+\dfrac{\lambda_i\gamma}{\beta_i(\gamma-1)}\varepsilon\right)\underline{\bar{u}}_i$
Aggregate utility (of group i) U_i	$\underline{\bar{U}}_i = \dfrac{(\gamma-1)\beta_i}{\gamma}\underline{\bar{Y}}$	$\underline{\tilde{U}}_i^0 = \dfrac{\delta\sigma}{\beta(\gamma-1)}\underline{\bar{U}}_i$	$\underline{\bar{U}}_i^0 = \left(1+\dfrac{\lambda_i\gamma}{\beta_i(\gamma-1)}\varepsilon\right)\underline{\bar{U}}_i$
Total utility (of workers) U	$\underline{\bar{U}} = \dfrac{(\gamma-1)\beta}{\gamma}\underline{\bar{Y}}$	$\underline{\tilde{U}}^0 = \dfrac{\delta\sigma}{\beta(\gamma-1)}\underline{\bar{U}}$	$\underline{\bar{U}}^0 = \dfrac{\delta}{\beta(\gamma-1)}\underline{\bar{U}}$
Profit Π	$\underline{\bar{\Pi}} = \varepsilon\underline{\bar{Y}}$	$\Pi^0 = 0$	$\underline{\bar{\Pi}}^0 = 0$
Communal surplus Z	$\underline{\bar{Z}} = \dfrac{\delta}{\gamma}\underline{\bar{Y}}$	$\underline{\tilde{Z}}^0 = \sigma\underline{\bar{Z}}$	$\underline{\bar{Z}}^0 = \underline{\bar{Z}}$
$Y(n)/L_i(n)$	$\left(\dfrac{\underline{\bar{Y}}}{\underline{\bar{L}}_i}\right) = \left[\dfrac{\gamma}{\beta_i a_i^{\gamma-1}}\underline{\bar{Y}}^{\gamma-1}\right]^{1/\gamma}$	$\dfrac{\underline{\tilde{Y}}^0}{\underline{\tilde{L}}_i^0} = \left[\left(\dfrac{\delta}{\gamma-1}\right)^{\gamma-1}\left(\dfrac{\beta}{1-\alpha}\right)^{\gamma}\right]^{1/\gamma}\dfrac{\underline{\bar{Y}}}{\underline{\bar{L}}_i}$	$(\underline{\bar{Y}}^0/\underline{\bar{L}}_i^0) = \underline{\bar{Y}}/\underline{\bar{L}}_i$
$Y(n)/K(n)$	ρ/α	ρ/α	ρ/α
$K(n)/N$	$\dfrac{\underline{\bar{K}}(a)}{A} = \left(\dfrac{\alpha}{\rho}\right)\underline{\bar{Y}}(a)/A$	$\dfrac{\underline{\tilde{K}}^0(b)}{B} = \dfrac{\delta}{(\gamma-1)(1-\alpha)}\dfrac{\underline{\bar{K}}(a)}{A}$	$(\underline{\bar{K}}^0(c)/C) = \underline{\bar{K}}(a)/A$
$Y(n)/N$	$\underline{\bar{Y}}(a)/A$	$\left(\dfrac{\underline{\tilde{Y}}^0(b)}{B}\right) = \dfrac{\delta}{(\gamma-1)(1-\alpha)}\left(\dfrac{\underline{\bar{Y}}(a)}{A}\right)$	$(\underline{\bar{Y}}^0(c)/C) = \underline{\bar{Y}}(a)/A$
$Z(n)/N$	$\left(\dfrac{\underline{\bar{Z}}(a)}{A}\right) = \dfrac{\delta}{\gamma}\underline{\bar{Y}}/A$	$(\underline{\tilde{Z}}^0(b)/B) = \underline{\bar{Z}}(a)/A$	$(\underline{\bar{Z}}^0(c)/C) = \underline{\bar{Z}}(a)/A$
Share price p_i	–	$\underline{\tilde{p}}_i^0 = \dfrac{\beta_i\sigma}{\beta b_i}\varepsilon\underline{\bar{Y}}\left(\dfrac{b}{\sigma}\right)$	$\underline{\bar{p}}_i^0 = \dfrac{\lambda_i}{c_i}\varepsilon\underline{\bar{Y}}(c)$

$N = \sum_M n_i; \quad A = \sum_M a_i; \quad B = \sum_M b_i; \quad C = \sum_M c_i.$

The equilibrium ratio $\tilde{\underline{Z}}^0/\underline{\bar{Z}}$ of the communal surplus in the workers' sector with internal wages to that in the competitive capitalistic sector is precisely the equilibrium relative enterprise size which we already saw to be less than one. Hence, the communal surplus $\tilde{\underline{Z}}^0$ of the (smaller) workers' enterprise with internal wages falls below the communal surplus $\underline{\bar{Z}}$ of the (larger) competitive capitalistic enterprise. Now, turning to the thirteenth entry in the first two columns of table 7.2, we observe that although the equilibrium output $\tilde{\underline{Y}}^0(b)$ of the workers' enterprise with internal wages exceeds $\underline{\bar{Y}}(a)$ of the competitive capitalistic enterprise, its equilibrium aggregate labor input $\tilde{\underline{L}}_i^0(b)$ of each type exceeds its competitive capitalistic level $\underline{\bar{L}}_i(a)$ by a greater proportion so that the equilibrium average product $\tilde{\underline{Y}}^0(b)/\tilde{\underline{L}}_i^0$ of each type of labor in a workers' enterprise with internal wages is below its competitive capitalistic counterpart $\underline{\bar{Y}}(a)/\underline{\bar{L}}_i(a)$.

Turning to the last four entries in the first two columns of table 7.2, it is most interesting just now to regard the seventeenth entries recording the communal surplus per worker generated by the two types of enterprise. We see that the equilibrium communal surplus per worker, $\tilde{\underline{Z}}^0(b)/B$, generated in a workers' enterprise with internal wages just equals $\underline{\bar{Z}}(a)/A$ generated in a competitive capitalistic enterprise. In fact, the workers' enterprise, having settled at an equilibrium relative size below that of the competitive capitalistic enterprise, sets higher wages, at which the workers all work more and hire more capital goods, producing a larger output and value added, but the increase in the typical workers' labor contribution is pushed to just that point at which the workers' enterprise with internal wages duplicates the communal surplus per worker in the competitive capitalistic enterprise. It follows that the output per worker (sixteenth entries) and the capital goods utilized per worker (fifteenth entries) are higher in the workers' enterprise with internal wages than in the competitive capitalistic enterprise. While the workers' enterprise with internal wages utilizes more capital goods per worker at equilibrium than does the competitive capitalistic enterprise, it is important to note (fourteenth entries) that the equilibrium average product of capital is the same, $\tilde{\underline{Y}}^0(b)/\tilde{\underline{K}}^0(b)=\underline{\bar{Y}}(a)/\underline{\bar{K}}(a)$, in the two types of enterprise. Thus, the capital/output ratios in the two sectors – the competitive capitalistic sector and the sector consisting of workers' enterprises with internal wages – will coincide at equilibrium. Finally, the last entries of the first two columns of table 7.2 restate that it is free for a worker to join a competitive capitalistic enterprise as a worker, and record the equilibrium share price of worker–partnership of type i in a workers' enterprise with internal wages.

7. General equilibrium: workers' enterprises with internal wages and quotas facing competitive capitalism

Our task in this section is, roughly, to do for a workers' enterprise with internal wages and quotas what we did in the previous section for a workers' enterprise with internal wages. Thus, we extend the economy considered in the previous section by attaching to it a large sector of workers' enterprises with internal wages and quotas, and again assume no collusion between agents and enterprises. Since now also workers' enterprises with internal wages and quotas may be formed, our notion of a rest point for the process of formation of firms has to be sharpened so as to further require that no worker has an incentive to switch to and from a workers' enterprise with internal wages and quotas. This means that the share market for worker–partnership in the newly attached sector must also be at equilibrium. So, first we determine the equilibrium relative size of the workers' enterprises with internal wages and quotas. Equipped with this information, we will then be able to fill out the final column of table 7.2.

The main fact we establish is that, for each $j \in M$, the equilibrium size $\bar{\underline{c}}_j^0$ of the jth group of worker–partners in a workers' enterprise with internal wages and quotas will coincide with the equilibrium size $\bar{\underline{a}}_j$ of the jth group of workers in a competitive capitalistic enterprise, and this independently of the distribution $\lambda = (\lambda_1, \ldots, \lambda_m)$ of base pay to the worker–partners in the workers' enterprises with internal wages and quotas.

To see this, in similar fashion to (41) and using table 7.1, we first form the supply price $\underline{\bar{S}}_j^0(c)$ for a share of the jth type of worker–partnership in a workers' enterprise with internal wages and quotas and of size $c = (c_1, \ldots, c_m)$:

$$\underline{\bar{S}}_j^0(c) = -\sum_M c_i \frac{\partial \bar{\underline{u}}_i^0}{\partial c_j} = \frac{\lambda_j}{c_j} \varepsilon \underline{\bar{Y}}(c). \tag{54}$$

Then we form the demand price $\underline{\bar{D}}_j^0(a, c)$ of a jth type of worker in a competitive capitalistic enterprise (of size a) for such a share

$$\begin{aligned}\underline{\bar{D}}_j^0(a,c) &= \bar{\underline{u}}_j^0(c) - \bar{\underline{u}}_j(a) \\ &= \left(\frac{\lambda_j \varepsilon}{c_j} + \frac{(\gamma-1)\beta_j}{\gamma c_j}\right)\underline{\bar{Y}}(c) - \frac{(\gamma-1)\beta_j}{\gamma a_j}\underline{\bar{Y}}(a).\end{aligned} \tag{55}$$

Now, equating the supply price $\underline{\bar{S}}_j^0(c)$ to the demand price $\underline{\bar{D}}_j^0(a, c)$ for each

$j \in M$ gives

$$\frac{c_j}{a_j} = \frac{\overline{Y}(c)}{\underline{Y}(a)} = \prod_M \left(\frac{c_k}{a_k}\right)^{\beta_k(\gamma-1)/\delta} \tag{56}$$

for each $j \in M$, which clearly determines

$$c = a, \tag{57}$$

i.e. the workers' enterprises with internal wages and quotas copy, at equilibrium, the size of the competitive capitalistic enterprise.[7]

It is no surprise, therefore, that the first fourteen entries of the third column of table 7.2 copy exactly the third column of table 7.1, and that the next three entries in the third column of table 7.2 copy exactly the corresponding entries in the first column of table 7.1. As for the very last entry of the third column of table 7.2, the equilibrium share price of worker–partnership of type j in a workers' enterprise with internal wages and quotas, it is obtained by evaluating (54) subject to (57).

This share price exceeds (resp. equals, falls below) the corresponding share price for a worker–partnership in a workers' enterprise with internal wages accordingly as λ_j exceeds (resp. equals, falls below) β_j/β. It may be checked that this price differential precisely measures the utility differential of a jth type of worker–partner between the two types of workers' enterprises at equilibrium, washing out any incentive for worker–partners to switch from one type of workers' enterprise to another.

Since the workers' enterprise with internal wages and quotas replicates all physical aspects (excluding distributional and welfare aspects, i.e. incomes and utilities of participants) of the competitive capitalistic enterprise at equilibrium, we see again that there can be nothing "pathological" about the behavior of such a workers' enterprise at equilibrium.

A very interesting aspect of workers' enterprises with internal wages and quotas is that, as a form of economic institution, they afford a great degree of flexibility in matters of distribution and welfare in a manner completely independent of the "physical" running of economic affairs: the choice of λ is an entirely internal issue for such enterprises, and one such enterprise may pursue, say, in egalitarian welfare policy (by setting λ so as to minimize an indicator of welfare differentials between worker–partners), while another might settle at a different λ.

[7] This equilibrium size can also be shown to be stable (see appendix B of this chapter).

8. Summary and closing remarks

This study aimed to present a complete economic comparison between two types of workers' enterprise and a capitalistic enterprise equipped with the same technology and embedded in the same competitive mixed economy. Comparisons have proceeded in two steps: first producing table 7.1, and then table 7.2. Table 7.1 displays the partial equilibrium outcome for three kinds of enterprise as a function of the enterprise size expressed in terms of the number of workers of various types employed. The first column of the table presents the values taken by fourteen economic variables in the case of a competitive capitalistic enterprise at equilibrium. The second column, pertaining to a workers' enterprise with internal wages, presents equilibrium values of the same variables in terms of their respective sizes for the competitive capitalistic enterprise. Column 3 does likewise for a workers' enterprise with internal wages and quotas. In this analysis the workers' enterprise with internal wages and quotas replicates the competitive capitalistic enterprise in all physical aspects of its outcome. The part of output accruing as profits in the competitive capitalistic enterprise, however, is now distributed in lump-sum payments to the worker–partners, and the entries of column 3 are expressed in terms of the shares λ_i according to which this sum is distributed to groups of workers of type i which internally share equally. The workers all come out better off than workers in the competitive capitalistic enterprise, so long as the shares λ_i are all positive.

It is noteworthy that the workers' enterprise with internal wages and quotas replicates the efficiency property of the competitive capitalistic enterprise in that it too maximizes communal surplus. In contrast, the workers' enterprise with internal wages, of column 2, fails to maximize communal surplus. In particular, its adopted incentive scheme leads its worker–partners to overwork themselves, employing more capital goods and generating a greater physical output and value added, gaining a greater material affluence than in the competitive capitalistic enterprise, but at the loss of so much of the pleasures of leisure that, although they are better off than they would be in the competitive capitalistic enterprise, they could all be made better off by reorganizing themselves as a workers' enterprise with internal wages and quotas and setting $(\lambda_1,\ldots,\lambda_m)$ so that, for instance, $\lambda_i=\beta_i/\beta$. Such a distribution of workers' income amongst the various types of labor would duplicate that in a competitive capitalistic enterprise and a workers' enterprise with internal wages, in both of which the share of output (or of that of value added) received by a type of aggregate labor input (L_i), is proportional to the marginal product (or marginal value added) of that type of labor input.

A comparison of labor productivities (Y/L_i) between the competitive capitalistic enterprise and the workers' enterprise with internal wages and quotas finds that they coincide type for type – an unsurprising result since Y and L_i coincide in the two kinds of enterprise. The productivities Y/L_i in the workers' enterprise with internal wages, however, all fall below their respective competitive capitalistic levels. Finally, it is of interest that the output/capital ratio Y/K resulting from the choice of output and capital input levels by the three kinds of enterprise are all the same.

Our interenterprise comparisons at the second stage, using table 7.2, first pass through an equilibration of relative enterprise size and a share price of worker–partnership in the two kinds of workers' enterprise, when workers are allowed to move from one enterprise to another, even if at the cost of a compensation to the present worker–partners exacted by a workers' enterprise through the sale of a worker–partnership share. Construed as a perfect market, the market for shares in workers' enterprises equilibrates the relative sizes of the three kinds of enterprise, so as to yield an exact match between the number of workers of any given type in a competitive capitalistic enterprise and the number of worker–partners of the same type in a workers' enterprise with internal wages and quotas; but this number is uniformly – in fact proportionately – smaller in a workers' enterprise with internal wages. The equilibrium share price for any type of worker–partnership coincides for the two kinds of workers' enterprise when we set $\lambda_i = \beta_i/\beta$ in the workers' enterprise with internal wages and quotas. Since the workers' enterprise with internal wages and quotas copies even the size of the competitive capitalistic enterprise at equilibrium, the first fourteen economic variables of table 7.2, evaluated at the mentioned equilibrium, just copy table 7.1 for the columns corresponding to the two kinds of enterprise. Since there is no worker–partnership, and hence no price for a share thereof, in a capitalistic enterprise, of the four new variables tabulated in table 7.2, there remain only the *per capita* quantities of capital goods employed, output and communal surplus to be compared between the capitalistic and the workers' enterprises. Of course, having already seen how the workers' enterprise with internal wages and quotas has copied the competitive capitalistic enterprise in the economic magnitudes considered so far, we already know that the last mentioned three equilibrium *per capita* quantities show no differences between these two kinds of enterprise. So much completes the comparison of the first and last columns of table 7.2.

Turning to the middle column which pertains to the workers' enterprise with internal wages at equilibrium, the first fourteen economic variables tabulated preserve their relative magnitudes *vis-à-vis* their corresponding values in the neighboring columns, as we had seen with regard to table 7.1. In the *per capita* utilization of capital goods, the workers' enterprise with internal wages surpasses the other two kinds of enterprise, as it does in the output *per capita* it generates. Interestingly enough, the three kinds of enterprise generate precisely the same communal surplus *per capita* when they settle at their respective equilibrium sizes, so that none suffers from any relative inefficiency in this regard.

Placing ourselves in the position of a society contemplating which, if any, kind of workers' enterprise to permit or foster, in conclusion, allowing relative enterprise sizes to equilibrate, some matters are clear and some will invoke further criteria for a sensible choice. First of all, both kinds of workers' enterprise considered here make their workers happier than they would be in a capitalistic enterprise (provided that every λ_i is positive). In fact, setting $\lambda_i = \beta_i/\beta$ for each i, the two kinds of workers' enterprise considered promise an equal improvement in the well-being of a worker–partner offering labor of the same type. Furthermore, this happens at no loss in the communal surplus generated per worker. So far workers' enterprises offer a clear superiority over capitalistic enterprises from the viewpoint of workers, and they offer no inferiority even after expropriated profit-earners are all exactly compensated for a switch from capitalism to any of the two kinds of workers' enterprises considered. To apply one of the typical – though often irrelevant – tests of an economist, now compare labor productivities across our three types of enterprise. For any given type i of labor, Y/L_i in the capitalistic enterprise coincides with that in the workers' enterprise with internal wages and quotas, but the corresponding productivity in a workers' enterprise with internal wages is inferior. We have already gone through the utility comparisons in the three types of enterprise, and from the viewpoint of nonparticipants in any enterprise we see that a workers' enterprise with internal wages offers a superiority over its two rivals in the output it supplies to the rest of society per participant it incorporates. And its providing a greater output per capita dampens, for the workers' enterprise with internal wages, its societal loss in economic growth potential by settling at a higher capital/output ratio.

What may look so far to be in favor of the workers' enterprises with internal wages is a balance which may be contested on account of a sufficiently intensive social preference to create jobs subject to a binding constraint on capital goods at the disposal of the society. For a workers' enterprise with internal wages uses more capital goods per job-partnership than its two rivals here. If the social preference to create jobs is strong enough, one of the rival types of economic organization will be a sensible social choice. The question of *which* will depend on whose utilities count more, the profit earners' or the workers'. So long as expropriated profit-earners are exactly compensated for a switch from capitalistic enterprises to workers' enterprises with internal wages and quotas, in fact there will be a social indifference regarding the transition, independent of the relative importance of workers' and profit-earners' utilities. If the profit-earners are to be undercompensated (resp. overcompensated), however, then workers' enterprises with internal wages and quotas will be favored (resp. disfavored) by any society where the happiness of workers outweighs that of profit-earners. Similarly, a society in which the utilities of profit-earners outweigh those of workers will stick to competitive capitalism (resp. switch to workers' enterprises with internal wages and quotas) so long as the compensation in question falls below (resp. above) the exact compensation.

These comparisons are extended elsewhere to further types of workers' enterprises obtained by instituting systems of value-added sharing (Başar, Selbuz and Sertel, 1978, and Sertel, 1978). The former of these also reconfirms that there is no pathology (of the sort which earlier sections have described) in the behavior of workers' enterprises *vis-à-vis* price fluctuations in a mixed economy incorporating a competitive capitalistic sector coexisting with a sector of workers' enterprises – a pathology clearly discarded in Sertel (1978) whose results have been extended here.

Appendix A

In this appendix we provide a proof for stability of the equilibrium relative enterprise size $(b_j/a_j)=\sigma$ $(j\in M)$ for the workers' enterprise with internal wages. In particular, we establish the validity of a natural algorithm which takes a workers' enterprise with internal wages, originally at disequilibrium group sizes, asymptotically to the stable equilibrium size $(b_j^*=\sigma a_j,\ j\in M)$. To this end, suppose that, in the mixed economy, there exists a workers' enterprise with internal wages of size $b\neq b^*=\sigma a$, where $a=(a_1,\dots,a_m)$ denotes the size of a competitive capitalistic enterprise taken as reference. Now, at disequilibrium, the supply price of at least one type of partnership (say the jth) in the workers' enterprise with internal wages will exceed or fall below the demand price for a similar share. In the case where it exceeds, the natural reaction of the workers' enterprise in question would be to buy out some of its worker–partners of type j. In the case where the supply price falls below the demand price for any type of partnership, however, the dynamics of the market forces the workers' enterprise to admit new worker–partners of that type.

Thus, we observe from the preceding discussion that the direction of change in the number of worker–partners of each type is strictly governed by the sign of the difference between the supply and demand prices for that type of worker–partnership. To be more precise, the relation

$$\operatorname{sgn}\left[\dot{b}_j\right] = -\operatorname{sgn}\left[\tilde{S}_j(b) - \tilde{D}_j(a,b)\right] \qquad (j \in M) \tag{A1}$$

holds, where $\dot{b}_j$ denotes the (continuous) rate of change in the number of worker–partners of type j, and sgn denotes the sign function. Since (from (41) and (43)) the difference between supply and demand prices is

$$\tilde{S}_j(b) - \tilde{D}_j(a,b) = \underline{u}_j(a) - \frac{(\gamma-1)\beta}{\delta}\underline{\tilde{u}}_j^0(b) \qquad (j \in M), \tag{A2}$$

it follows that the sign of $\dot{b}_j$ is determined by whether the quantity

$$\tilde{\chi}_j(b) = \underline{u}_j(a) \Big/ \frac{(\gamma-1)\beta}{\delta}\underline{\tilde{u}}_j^0(b) \tag{A3}$$

exceeds or falls below unity. When this ratio is identically one, then $\dot{b}_j$ should of course be zero. Now, introducing the notation

$$b^* = (b_1^*, \ldots, b_m^*) = \sigma a \tag{A4}$$

for the equilibrium size of the enterprise, we obtain from appropriate entries of table 7.1 the following expression for $\tilde{\chi}_j(b)$:

$$\tilde{\chi}_j(b) = \frac{b_j}{b_j^*}\sigma^{(\gamma-1)\beta/\delta}\underline{Y}\left(\frac{b^*}{\sigma}\right) \Big/ \underline{Y}(b) = \frac{b_j}{b_j^*}\left[\prod_M\left(\frac{b_k^*}{b_k}\right)^{\beta_k}\right]^{(\gamma-1)/\delta}$$
$$(j \in M). \tag{A5}$$

Since one would also expect the magnitude of $\dot{b}_j$ to be proportional to the magnitude of $\tilde{\chi}_j$, a natural path that the workers' enterprise with internal wages should follow in arriving at the equilibrium sizes (if stable at all) is dictated by the algorithm

$$\dot{b}_j = -\log\tilde{\chi}_j(b) \qquad (j \in M). \tag{A6}$$

We now show that, for this set of intercoupled differential equations, the unique equilibrium solution $b_j = b_j^*$ $(j \in M)$ is asymptotically stable.

This would have been an easy result to prove if we had

$$\tilde{\chi}_j(b)\begin{cases} >1, & \text{whenever } b_j > b_j^*, \\ <1, & \text{whenever } b_j < b_j^*, \end{cases}$$

independent of all the other b_i, $i \in M$, $i \neq j$. Unfortunately, however, this turns out not to be the case. In fact, it so happens that the supply price for a type of partnership (say the jth) might be below the demand price $\tilde{D}_j(a, b)$ at disequilibrium, thus dictating the enterprise to admit more worker–partners of type j, even though $b_j > b_j^*$. But, in the long run, such abnormalities die out and the equilibrium solution is asymptotically stable, as is shown below.

To this end we introduce the function

$$V = \tfrac{1}{2} \sum_M \beta_i b_i^* \left(\log \frac{b_i}{b_i^*} \right)^2 \tag{A7}$$

which is clearly positive definite, since $V \geqslant 0$ and $V = 0$ if and only if $b = b^*$. Attempting to obtain an expression for the rate of change of V on the path (A6) we first have

$$\dot{V} = \sum_M \beta_i \dot{b}_i \frac{b_i^*}{b_i} \log \frac{b_i}{b_i^*}$$

and, using (A6) and (A7), we arrive at the expression

$$\dot{V} = -\sum_M \beta_i \frac{b_i^*}{b_i} \left(\log \frac{b_i}{b_i^*} \right)^2 + \left(\sum_M \beta_i \frac{b_i^*}{b_i} \log \frac{b_i}{b_i^*} \right) \left(\frac{\gamma - 1}{\delta} \sum_M \beta_k \log \frac{b_k}{b_k^*} \right),$$

which can also be written as

$$\dot{V} = -\sum_M \beta_i \sigma_i (\log \sigma_i)^2 + \frac{(\gamma - 1)\beta}{\delta} \left(\sum_M \beta_i \sigma_i \log \sigma_i \right) \left(\sum_M \frac{\beta_k}{\beta} \log \sigma_k \right), \tag{A8}$$

where σ_i $(i \in M)$ is defined as

$$\sigma_i = b_i^* / b_i \qquad (i \in M). \tag{A9}$$

We now show that $\dot{V}$ is negative, unless $\sigma_i = 1$ for all $i \in M$, in which case it is clearly zero. If the second additive term in (A8) is nonpositive, then the negative definiteness of $\dot{V}$ is apparent. If the said term is positive, however, since $(\gamma-1)\beta<\delta$ we obtain the bound

$$\dot{V}<-\sum_{M}\beta_i\sigma_i(\log\sigma_i)^2+\left(\sum_{M}\beta_i\sigma_i\log\sigma_i\right)\left(\sum_{M}\frac{\beta_k}{\beta}\log\sigma_k\right)$$

$$=-\sum_{i\neq k}\frac{\beta_i\beta_k}{\beta}\sigma_i(\log\sigma_i)\left(\log\frac{\sigma_i}{\sigma_k}\right)$$

$$=-\sum_{i>k}\frac{\beta_i\beta_k}{\beta}[\sigma_i\log\sigma_i-\sigma_k\log\sigma_k]\log\frac{\sigma_i}{\sigma_k}, \qquad \text{(A10)}$$

the maximum value of which is zero and is attained for $\sigma_i=\sigma_k$ $(i, k\in M)$. Since it also follows from the first term of (A8) that $\dot{V}$ cannot vanish at points other than the equilibrium point $\sigma_i=1$ $(i\in M)$, $\dot{V}$ is negative definite on the solution path of (A6), and hence V is a Liapunov function. Then, asymptotic stability of the equilibrium solution $b_j=b_j^*$ $(j\in M)$ follows from standard results on Liapunov theory (La Salle and Lefschetz, 1961).

Appendix B

In this appendix we provide a proof for the stability of the equilibrium enterprise size $c_j=c_j^*=a_j$ $(j\in M)$ for the workers' enterprise with internal wages and quotas. The proof actually parallels the one given in appendix A, since what replaces (A5) is the same with only b_i's replaced by c_i's and b_i^*'s by c_i^*'s. To see this, we first construct the counterpart of (A2) using (54) and (55):

$$\underline{\bar{S}}_j^0(c)-\underline{\bar{D}}_j^0(a,c)=\frac{(\gamma-1)\beta_j}{\gamma}\left(\frac{\bar{Y}(c^*)}{c_j^*}-\frac{\bar{Y}(c)}{c_j}\right) \qquad (j\in M). \qquad \text{(B1)}$$

Then, the counterpart of (A3) is

$$\underline{\bar{x}}_j^0(c)=\frac{c_j}{c_j^*}\frac{\bar{Y}(c^*)}{\bar{Y}(c)}=\frac{c_j}{c_j^*}\left[\prod_{M}\left(\frac{c_k^*}{c_k}\right)^{\beta_k}\right]^{(\gamma-1)/\delta} \qquad (j\in M), \qquad \text{(B2)}$$

which verifies our claim. Hence, it follows from appendix A that the equilibrium solution $c_j=c_j^*$ $(j\in M)$ of the algorithm

$$\dot{c}_j=-\log\underline{\bar{x}}_j^0(c) \qquad (j\in M)$$

is asymptotically stable, thereby proving stability of the equilibrium enterprise size $c=a$.

References

Başar, T., H. Selbuz and M.R. Sertel (1978) "Workers' Cooperatives and Semi-Cooperatives Facing Competitive Capitalism", Technical Report No. 45, Applied Mathematics Division, Marmara Scientific and Industrial Research Institute, Gebze-Kocaeli, Turkey. (See Chapter 8 of this book.)

Bernstein, P. (1976) *Workplace Democratization: Its Internal Dynamics* (School of Social Sciences, University of California, Irvine).

Dirickx, Y.M.I. and M.R. Sertel (1978) "Comparative Political Economy of Capitalism, Communism, Slavery, and Colonialism in a Nutshell", *Recherches Economiques de Louvain*, 44, no. 3.

Domar, E. (1966) "The Soviet Collective Farm", *American Economic Review*, 56, 734–754.

Kleindorfer, P.R. and M.R. Sertel (1976) "Equilibrium Analysis of Sharecropping", IIM Preprint Series I/76/33, International Institute of Management, West Berlin. (See Chapter 6 of this book.)

Kleindorfer, P.R. and M.R. Sertel (1978) "Value-added Sharing Enterprises", Preprint Series No. DP 78-38, International Institute of Management, West Berlin. (See Chapter 9 of this book.)

Kleindorfer, P.R. and M.R. Sertel (1979) "Profit-maximizing Design of Enterprises through Incentives", *Journal of Economic Theory*, 20, 318–339. (See Chapter 4 of this book.)

La Salle, J. and S. Lefschetz (1961) *Stability by Liapunov's Direct Method* (Academic Press, New York).

Oakeshott, R. (1978) *The Prospect and the Conditions for Successful Co-operative Production* (Co-operative Union Ltd. Publishers, Congress 78, Great Britain).

Sertel, M.R. (1978) "The Relative Size and Share Price of a Workers' Enterprise Facing Competitive Capitalism", paper presented at the Second Bosphorus Workshop on Industrial Democracy, Istanbul. (See Chapter 2 of this book.)

Vanek, J. (1970) *The General Theory of Labor Managed Market Economies* (Cornell University Press).

Ward, B. (1958) "The Firm in Illyria: Market Syndicalism", *American Economic Review*, 48, 566–589.

CHAPTER 8

Workers' cooperatives and semi-cooperatives facing competitive capitalism*

TAMER BAŞAR, HASAN SELBUZ and MURAT R. SERTEL

1. Introduction

An earlier paper by Sertel, Başar and Selbuz (1978) has developed an economic theory of workers' enterprises utilizing "individualistic" incentive schemes of two types: internal wages, and internal wages and quotas. It analyzed their equilibrium behavior when they coexist, in the same competitive mixed economy, with capitalistic enterprises equipped with the same technology. One of the important conclusions to be drawn from that paper is that workers' enterprises of both types behave normally in face of price fluctuations, in contrast to the "pathological behavior" ascribed to such firms in face of increased prices of their outputs in the "short-run" (see Ward, 1958).

The present chapter works with the general model of Sertel, Başar and Selbuz (1978), but this time under a "nonindividualistic" incentive scheme. In particular, we investigate the internal equilibrium behavior of workers' cooperatives and semi-cooperatives that adopt "value-added sharing"[1] as the internal incentive scheme. Such an incentive scheme assigns (*ex ante*) to

*This chapter is based on the authors' study (partially supported by the Ministry of Enterprises) with the same title, appearing as Technical Report No. 45 of the Applied Mathematics Division, Marmara Scientific and Technical Research Institute, Gebze-Kocaeli, Turkey, November 1978.

[1] Kleindorfer and Sertel (1978) develop this type of sharing for nine types of enterprises but these do not include workers' semi-cooperatives.

each worker–partner some share in the value added generated in the enterprise. Consequently, a worker–partner's income depends not only on his individual labor contribution, but also on the work contributions of his fellow worker–partners. The equilibrium outcome under such an incentive scheme is analyzed and evaluated using game-theoretic solution concepts.

In a workers' cooperative, worker–partners show cooperative behavior both individually within each labor group and between labor groups, thus resulting in a total utility-maximizing level of labor inputs. In a workers' semi-cooperative, however, decisions concerning the employment level of individual worker–partners are made noncooperatively among different types of labor groups, while cooperation is retained within each group. Hence, in this case, the noncooperative (Nash) solution concept is adopted between groups, and the cooperative solution concept is used within each labor group.

Paralleling the analysis of Sertel, Başar and Selbuz (1978), we first introduce the technological and preferential data in section 2, and outline in section 3 the derivation of the equilibrium outcomes of the economic quantities for the competitive capitalistic enterprise employing m types of labor, and n_i workers of type i. After listing these values in the first column of table 8.1, we turn to determine the equilibrium behavior of a workers' cooperative equipped with the same technology and employing the same number of worker–partners of each type as in the capitalistic enterprise. In this context, we observe that, as far as the equilibrium outcomes are concerned, workers' cooperatives are copies of workers' enterprises with internal wages and quotas which are extensively analyzed in Sertel, Başar and Selbuz (1978). The equilibrium values of fourteen economic magnitudes are displayed in columns 2 and 3 of table 8.1, first in terms of a general group-share vector λ (column 2) and then, for shares that are proportional for each labor group i, to the elasticity β_i of output with respect to that group's labor (column 3).

The internal equilibrium behavior of workers' semi-cooperatives is analyzed in section 4, and the equilibrium values of the economic magnitudes of interest are displayed in the last column of table 8.1, again in terms of a general group-share vector λ. A discussion is included as to the comparison of these values with the corresponding ones obtained for the other two types of enterprise.

Section 5 is devoted to determining the relative size of the three kinds of enterprise, in terms of the number of workers or worker–partners, when these agents are allowed to move from one kind of enterprise to another, paying their colleagues in the enterprise of entry, if necessary, to enter. One result in this context is that the equilibrium group sizes of a workers' cooperative and a competitive capitalistic enterprise are the same, thus echoing the result of Sertel, Başar and Selbuz (1978), since the workers' cooperative is no different than a workers' enterprise with internal wages and quotas, in terms of the equilibrium values of economic magnitudes, even though the internal incentive schemes are different in the two types of enterprise.

For workers' semi-cooperatives, it is shown that the relative equilibrium size is such that the semi-cooperative is a proportionately shrunken model of the competitive capitalistic enterprise, once again dispelling the pathology ascribed to the behavior of such enterprises in face of price fluctuations (see Ward, 1958; Vanek, 1970). The equilibrium values of our eighteen economic magnitudes at the relative equilibrium sizes of the three types of enterprise are displayed in appropriate columns and entries in table 8.2, and certain comparisons are included in section 6. Finally, section 7 is devoted to a few closing remarks on some aspects of the results obtained in this chapter.

2. Basic data and framework

The typical enterprise under consideration in this chapter employs m types of productive labor with n_i workers of type $i \in M = \{1, \ldots, m\}$. The labor contribution of the jth worker of type i is denoted by $x_{ij}, j \in N_i = \{1, \ldots, n_i\}$, and the aggregate labor of workers of type i is denoted as $L_i = \sum_{N_i} x_{ij}$. The enterprise is equipped with a production function

$$Y = K^{\alpha} \prod_M L_i^{\beta_i} \qquad \left(0 < \alpha, \beta_i, \beta = \sum_M \beta_i, \alpha + \beta < 1\right), \tag{1}$$

where Y and K denote, respectively, the output (of a single commodity) and the quantity of capital goods employed. The workers all like income and dislike work, exhibiting preferences as represented by the utility function

$$u_{ij} = y_{ij} - x_{ij}^{\gamma} \qquad (1 < \gamma) \tag{2}$$

for the jth worker of type i, whose income, measured in units of the output, is denoted by y_{ij}.

The enterprise is assumed to be a price-taker, both in selling its output and in renting capital goods. Taking the price of output as unity, we let the positive quantity ρ stand for the rental on capital goods. Thus, the value added by labor in the enterprise is given by

$$V = Y - \rho K. \tag{3}$$

Then, in terms of the value added (by labor), we define the communal surplus as

$$Z = V - \sum_M \sum_{N_i} x_{ij}^{\gamma}. \tag{4}$$

3. Internal equilibrium behavior of the workers' cooperative

In this section we first briefly outline, from Sertel, Başar and Selbuz (1978), the derivation of equilibrium outcomes for the economic magnitudes of the competitive capitalistic enterprise, listed in the first column of table 8.1, and then we investigate the equilibrium behavior of a typical workers' cooperative in a mixed economy.

In the competitive capitalistic enterprise, we have a profit-maximizing capitalist responsible for decisions regarding the employment of capital goods. Since profit is

$$\Pi = V - \sum_M w_i L_i, \tag{5}$$

where w_i denotes any given (positive) wage for labor of type $i \in M$, we determine the profit-maximizing level of K by maximizing the value added V, finding the unique solution

$$\tilde{K} = \left(\frac{\alpha}{\rho} \prod_M L_i^{\beta_i} \right)^{1/(1-\alpha)}. \tag{6}$$

At this level of employment of capital goods, the output, value added and profit are, respectively, given by

$$\tilde{Y} = \left[\left(\frac{\alpha}{\rho} \right)^{\alpha} \prod_M L_i^{\beta_i} \right]^{1/(1-\alpha)}, \tag{7}$$

$$\tilde{V} = (1-\alpha)\tilde{Y}, \tag{8}$$

$$\tilde{\Pi} = \tilde{V} - \sum_M w_i L_i. \tag{9}$$

Now, at a given wage vector $w = (w_1, \ldots, w_m)$, the demand for labor of type $i \in M$ is

$$\bar{L}_i = \frac{\beta_i}{w_i} \bar{Y}, \tag{10}$$

where $\overline{Y}$ is the profit-maximizing output given by

$$\overline{Y} = \left[\left(\frac{\alpha}{\rho} \right)^{\alpha} \prod_{M} \left(\frac{\beta_k}{w_k} \right)^{\beta_k} \right]^{1/\varepsilon} \tag{11}$$

and

$$\varepsilon = 1 - \alpha - \beta, \tag{12}$$

while the supply of labor of type $i \in M$ is given by

$$\underline{L}_i = n_i \left(\frac{w_i}{\gamma} \right)^{1/(\gamma - 1)}. \tag{13}$$

Thinking in terms of a competitive capitalistic economy whose typical firms are copies of our present enterprise, the labor markets will thus be equilibrated by wages $w = (w_1, \ldots, w_m)$ solving the m equations

$$\overline{L}_i = \underline{L}_i \qquad (i \in M), \tag{14}$$

which then yield the competitive capitalistic equilibrium output

$$\underline{\overline{Y}} = \left[\left(\frac{\alpha}{\rho} \right)^{\alpha\gamma} \prod_{M} \left(\frac{\beta_k n_k^{\gamma-1}}{\gamma} \right)^{\beta_k} \right]^{1/\delta}, \tag{15}$$

where

$$\delta = \gamma(1 - \alpha) - \beta. \tag{16}$$

The competitive capitalistic equilibrium values of all the other economic magnitudes can now be determined, mechanically, in terms of $\underline{\overline{Y}}$, and are listed in the first column of table 8.1. We should note at this point that the equilibrium employment levels,

$$x_{ij} = \bar{x}_i = \left(\frac{\beta_i}{\gamma n_i} \, \underline{\overline{Y}} \right)^{1/\gamma} \qquad (j \in N_i, i \in M), \tag{17}$$

in the competitive capitalistic enterprise uniquely maximize the communal surplus $\tilde{Z}$ evaluated at the profit-maximizing capital goods level $\tilde{K}$.

We now investigate the internal equilibrium behavior of a workers' cooperative equipped with the same technology and having again n_i workers (now worker–partners) of each type i, as in the preceding competitive capitalistic enterprise. In the workers' cooperative we envisage a *workers' council* responsible for decisions concerning both the utilization level K of capital goods and the distribution of value added V among the worker-partners so as to exhaust this quantity (V) totally. We assume that the

Table 8.1
Equilibrium outcomes of the three types of enterprise at common size n.

Enterprise / Equilibrium outcome	Competitive Capitalistic Enterprise	Workers' cooperative: General λ	Workers' cooperative: $\lambda_i = \beta_i/\beta\ (i \in M)$	Workers' semi-cooperative (general λ)
Wage (of a typical worker of type i) w_i	$\underline{\overline{w}}_i = \left[\gamma\left(\frac{\beta_i}{n_i}\underline{\overline{Y}}\right)^{\gamma-1}\right]^{1/\gamma}$	$\underline{\overline{\omega}}_i^0 = \frac{(1-\alpha)\lambda_i}{\beta_i}\underline{\overline{w}}_i$	$\underline{\overline{\omega}}_i^0 = \left(\frac{1-\alpha}{\beta}\right)\underline{\overline{w}}_i$	$\underline{\tilde{\omega}}_i^* = \left(\frac{1-\alpha}{\beta}\right)\left[\lambda_i\prod_M \lambda_k^{\beta_k/\delta}\right]^{(\gamma-1)/\gamma}\underline{\overline{w}}_i$
Labor (input of a typical worker of type i) x_i	$\underline{\overline{x}}_i = \left(\frac{\beta_i}{\gamma n_i}\underline{\overline{Y}}\right)^{1/\gamma}$	$\underline{\overline{x}}_i^0 = \underline{\overline{x}}_i$	$\underline{\overline{x}}_i^0 = \underline{\overline{x}}_i$	$\underline{\tilde{x}}_i^* = \left[\lambda_i\prod_M \lambda_k^{\beta_k/\delta}\right]^{1/\gamma}\underline{\overline{x}}_i$
Income (of a typical worker of type i) y_i	$\underline{\overline{y}}_i = \frac{\beta_i}{n_i}\underline{\overline{Y}}$	$\underline{\overline{y}}_i^0 = \frac{(1-\alpha)\lambda_i}{\beta_i}\underline{\overline{y}}_i$	$\underline{\overline{y}}_i^0 = \left(\frac{1-\alpha}{\beta}\right)\underline{\overline{y}}_i$	$\underline{\tilde{y}}_i^* = \frac{(1-\alpha)\lambda_i}{\beta_i}\left[\prod_M \lambda_k^{\beta_k/\delta}\right]\underline{\overline{y}}_i$
Aggregate labor (input of workers of type i) L_i	$\underline{\overline{L}}_i = \left[\frac{\beta_i n_i^{\gamma-1}}{\gamma}\underline{\overline{Y}}\right]^{1/\gamma}$	$\underline{\overline{L}}_i^0 = \underline{\overline{L}}_i$	$\underline{\overline{L}}_i^0 = \underline{\overline{L}}_i$	$\underline{\tilde{L}}_i^* = \left[\lambda_i\prod_M \lambda_k^{\beta_k/\delta}\right]^{1/\gamma}\underline{\overline{L}}_i$
Capital goods input K	$\underline{\overline{K}} = \left(\frac{\alpha}{\rho}\right)\underline{\overline{Y}}$	$\underline{\overline{K}}^0 = \underline{\overline{K}}$	$\underline{\overline{K}}^0 = \underline{\overline{K}}$	$\underline{\tilde{K}}^* = \left[\prod_M \lambda_k^{\beta_k/\delta}\right]\underline{\overline{K}}$
Output Y	$\underline{\overline{Y}} = \left[\left(\frac{\alpha}{\rho}\right)^{\alpha\gamma}\prod_M\left(\frac{\beta_k n_k^{\gamma-1}}{\gamma}\right)^{\beta_k}\right]^{1/\delta}$	$\underline{\overline{Y}}^0 = \underline{\overline{Y}}$	$\underline{\overline{Y}}^0 = \underline{\overline{Y}}$	$\underline{\tilde{Y}}^* = \left[\prod_M \lambda_k^{\beta_k/\delta}\right]\underline{\overline{Y}}$
Value added V	$\underline{\overline{V}} = (1-\alpha)\underline{\overline{Y}}$	$\underline{\overline{V}}^0 = \underline{\overline{V}}$	$\underline{\overline{V}}^0 = \underline{\overline{V}}$	$\underline{\tilde{V}}^* = \left[\prod_M \lambda_k^{\beta_k/\delta}\right]\underline{\overline{V}}$

Utility (of a worker of type i) u_i	$\underline{\bar{u}}_i = \frac{(\gamma-1)\beta_i}{\gamma n_i}\underline{\bar{Y}}$	$\underline{\bar{u}}_i^0 = \left[\frac{\gamma(1-\alpha)\lambda_i}{\beta_i} - 1\right] \times \frac{\underline{\bar{u}}_i}{(\gamma-1)}$	$\underline{\bar{u}}_i^0 = \frac{\delta}{\beta(\gamma-1)}\underline{\bar{u}}_i$	$\underline{\tilde{u}}_i^* = \frac{\lambda_i\delta_i}{\beta_i(\gamma-1)}\left[\prod_M \lambda_k^{\beta_k/\delta}\right]\underline{\bar{u}}_i$
Aggregate utility (group i) U_i	$\underline{\bar{U}}_i = \frac{(\gamma-1)\beta_i}{\gamma}\underline{\bar{Y}}$	$\underline{\bar{U}}_i^0 = \left[\frac{\gamma(1-\alpha)\lambda_i}{\beta_i} - 1\right] \times \frac{\underline{\bar{U}}_i}{(\gamma-1)}$	$\underline{\bar{U}}_i^0 = \frac{\delta}{\beta(\gamma-1)}\underline{\bar{U}}_i$	$\underline{\tilde{U}}_i^* = \frac{\lambda_i\delta_i}{\beta_i(\gamma-1)}\left[\prod_M \lambda_k^{\beta_k/\delta}\right]\underline{\bar{U}}_i$
Total utility (of workers) U	$\underline{\bar{U}} = \frac{(\gamma-1)\beta}{\gamma}\underline{\bar{Y}}$	$\underline{\bar{U}}^0 = \frac{\delta}{\beta(\gamma-1)}\underline{\bar{U}}$	$\underline{\bar{U}}^0 = \frac{\delta}{\beta(\gamma-1)}\underline{\bar{U}}$	$\underline{\tilde{U}}^* = \frac{\delta t^{\epsilon\gamma/\delta}}{\beta(\gamma-1)}\underline{\bar{U}}$
Profit Π	$\underline{\bar{\Pi}} = \epsilon\underline{\bar{Y}}$	$\underline{\bar{\Pi}}^0 = 0$	$\underline{\bar{\Pi}}^0 = 0$	$\underline{\tilde{\Pi}}^* = 0$
Communal surplus Z	$\underline{\bar{Z}} = \frac{\delta}{\gamma}\underline{\bar{Y}}$	$\underline{\bar{Z}}^0 = \underline{\bar{Z}}$	$\underline{\bar{Z}}^0 = \underline{\bar{Z}}$	$\underline{\tilde{Z}}^* = t^{\epsilon\gamma/\delta}\underline{\bar{Z}}$
Y/L_i	$\left(\frac{\underline{\bar{Y}}}{\underline{\bar{L}}_i}\right) = \left[\frac{\gamma}{\beta_i n_i^{\gamma-1}}\underline{\bar{Y}}^{\gamma-1}\right]^{1/\gamma}$	$(\underline{\bar{Y}}^0/\underline{\bar{L}}_i^0) = (\underline{\bar{Y}}/\underline{\bar{L}}_i)$	$(\underline{\bar{Y}}^0/\underline{\bar{L}}_i^0) = (\underline{\bar{Y}}/\underline{\bar{L}}_i)$	$\left(\frac{\underline{\tilde{Y}}^*}{\underline{\tilde{L}}_i^*}\right) = \left(\frac{1}{\lambda_i}\right)^{1/\gamma} \times \left[\prod_M \lambda_k^{\beta_k/\delta}\right]^{(\gamma-1)/\gamma}\left(\frac{\underline{\bar{Y}}}{\underline{\bar{L}}_i}\right)$
Y/K	ρ/α	ρ/α	ρ/α	ρ/α

$$t \equiv \left[\left(\prod_M \lambda_k^{\beta_k/\delta}\right)\sum_M \lambda_k\delta_k/\delta\right]^{\delta/\gamma\epsilon}$$

workers' council adopts "value-added sharing" as the internal incentive scheme of the enterprise, in which case the income of the jth worker of type i will be determined from

$$y_{ij}=\mu_{ij}V \qquad (j\in N_i, i\in M) \tag{18}$$

for some positive share μ_{ij}. Here we should also note the constraint

$$\sum_M \sum_{N_i} \mu_{ij}=1, \tag{19}$$

which says that the value added will be exhausted in payments to the worker–partners.

Even though there exist several different criteria according to which the workers' council can determine the utilization level K of capital goods, the most reasonable one, in the present context, seems to be the maximization of the communal utility

$$U=\sum_M \sum_{N_i} u_{ij} \tag{20}$$

of the enterprise participants. This will be our working assumption, not only for the workers' cooperative, but also for the workers' semi-cooperative to be analyzed in section 4.

Using (18) in (2) and noting the constraint (19), we observe that the maximand of the workers' council may be expressed as

$$U=V-\sum_M \sum_{N_i} x_{ij}^{\gamma}. \tag{21}$$

Here $\partial U/\partial K$ vanishes exactly when $\partial V/\partial K$ does. Thus, the maximization of (21) gives again (6), so that the behavior of the present enterprise in the capital goods rental market coincides completely with that of the capitalistic enterprise, regardless of how the shares μ_{ij} $(j\in N_i, i\in M)$ are chosen.

With K adjusted in this manner, output and value added are determined again as $\tilde{Y}$ and $\tilde{V}$, respectively (see (7) and (8), respectively). Now, by the very nature of a workers' cooperative, the worker–partners will act cooperatively in choosing their labor inputs. This means choosing the levels of individual labor contributions so as to maximize the communal surplus $\tilde{U}$ given by

$$\tilde{U}=\tilde{V}-\sum_M \sum_{N_i} x_{ij}^{\gamma}=(1-\alpha)\tilde{Y}-\sum_M \sum_{N_i} x_{ij}^{\gamma}, \tag{22}$$

independent of the way in which $\tilde{V}$ is shared, i.e. independent of the shares

μ_{ij} $(j \in N_i, i \in M)$. Differentiating $\tilde{U}$ with respect to x_{ij} $(j \in N_i, i \in M)$ and setting the resulting expression equal to zero, we obtain the cooperative solution of labor inputs

$$x_{ij} = \tilde{x}_i = \left(\frac{\beta}{\gamma n_i} \tilde{Y} \right)^{1/\gamma} \qquad (j \in N_i, i \in M). \tag{23}$$

Solving (23) and (7) for $\tilde{Y}$, the resulting equilibrium output $\underline{\overline{Y}}^0$ of the workers' cooperative yields the relation

$$\underline{\overline{Y}}^0 = \underline{\overline{Y}}. \tag{24}$$

That is to say, the equilibrium output level of a workers' cooperative coincides with the equilibrium output level of a competitive capitalistic enterprise of the same size. To determine the equilibrium level of labor input of each type, we merely use (24) in (23), obtaining

$$\underline{\overline{x}}_{ij}^0 = \underline{\overline{x}}_i^0 = \underline{\overline{x}}_i = \left(\frac{\beta_i}{\gamma n_i} \underline{\overline{Y}} \right)^{1/\gamma} \qquad (j \in N_i, i \in M). \tag{25}$$

It can easily be checked that (25) actually gives the unique solution to maximizing (22), since it is the unique solution of the first-order conditions, while the Hessian matrix is negative definite at the solution point.

We have just seen that employment levels (25) maximizing communal surplus are attained in the workers' cooperative regardless of what share each worker–partner receives from the value added. For an incentive scheme to be implementable, however, it has to provide a typical worker–partner of type i $(i \in M)$ a utility no lower than what he would attain in the capitalistic enterprise. Hence, if we let λ_i $(i \in M, \Sigma_M \lambda_i = 1)$ denote the share of the ith labor group and assume that income allocated for a labor group is evenly divided among the worker–partners of that type, for the group share vector $\lambda = (\lambda_1, \ldots, \lambda_m)$ this requires the inequalities

$$\underline{\overline{u}}_i^0 = \frac{\lambda_i}{n_i} \underline{\overline{V}}^0 - \underline{\overline{x}}_i^{0\gamma} \geqslant \underline{\overline{u}}_i \qquad (i \in M), \tag{26}$$

where $\underline{\overline{V}}^0$ is defined by (8) and (24). A more direct restriction on λ can easily be obtained from (26) as

$$\lambda_i \geqslant \frac{\beta_i}{1 - \alpha} \qquad (i \in M). \tag{27}$$

There are in general many group share vectors that satisfy this natural restriction. One such choice would be to let each group share λ_i be proportional to β_i, i.e.

$$\lambda_i^0 = \frac{\beta_i}{\beta} \qquad (i \in M). \tag{28}$$

With $\underline{\bar{x}}_i^0$ and $\underline{\bar{Y}}^0$ as given by (25) and (24), respectively, it is then a mechanical task to determine, for the workers' cooperative, the equilibrium outcomes of all the remaining economic magnitudes listed in table 8.1, under the assumption that worker–partners of the same type of labor receive equal shares from value added. These equilibrium values are displayed in the second column of table 8.1, in terms of their counterparts in the capitalistic enterprise. The third column of table 8.1 displays the same quantities, evaluated for the specific group share vector (28). It should be noted that the first entries in both of these columns designate not the real wage, but the "imputed" wage determined by dividing $\underline{\bar{Y}}_i^0$ into $\underline{\bar{x}}_i^0$. It is for this reason that a different symbol ($\underline{\bar{\omega}}_i^0$) is used in these entries as compared to the first entry of column 1.

We observe from both the second and third columns of table 8.1 that a workers' cooperative duplicates competitive capitalism in every aspect other than profit, the (imputed) wages and the incomes and the utilities of the workers. Of course, the present type of enterprise leads to a zero profit, and the incomes, (imputed) wages and utilities of worker–partners could all be higher than their counterparts in the capitalistic enterprise by appropriate choice of the group share vector λ. The choice λ^0, given by (28), stands out as one such policy that results in uniformly higher income, wages and utilities for all the worker–partners of the workers' cooperative as compared with the capitalistic enterprise.

4. Internal equilibrium behavior of a workers' semi-cooperative

Roughly speaking, a workers' semi-cooperative is a workers' enterprise whose members of a common type cooperate within their respective groups but behave noncooperatively as such groups. That is to say, in a workers' semi-cooperative, decisions concerning the employment levels of individual worker–partners are made noncooperatively among different types of labor groups, while cooperation is retained within each group. In this section we analyze the internal behavior of this type of workers' enterprise accommodating again n_i worker–partners of labor type i $(i \in M)$ and adopting "value-added sharing" as the internal incentive scheme.

The workers' council still determines the utilization level of capital goods by maximizing the total utility of the worker–partners (or of any given group receiving a certain share of V), and hence the functional form (6) will provide the optimal level of capital goods employed in the workers' semi-cooperative too. Using this in (2) together with (18) and (8) now yields the utility of a typical jth worker–partner of type i to be

$$\tilde{u}_{ij} = \mu_{ij}\tilde{V} - x_{ij}^{\gamma} \qquad (j \in N_i, i \in M), \tag{29}$$

where μ_{ij} denotes the share of that worker–partner, as introduced above in section 3. Since there is cooperation among worker–partners of a particular labor type, the quantity that is of greatest interest for the present analysis is the total utility of worker–partners of type i ($i \in M$), given by

$$\tilde{U}_i = \lambda_i \tilde{V} - \sum_{N_i} x_{ij}^{\gamma} \qquad (i \in M), \tag{30}$$

where the group-share vector $\lambda = (\lambda_1, \ldots, \lambda_m)$ obeys

$$\lambda_i = \sum_{N_i} \mu_{ij} \qquad (i \in M). \tag{31}$$

Since we adopt the cooperative solution concept within each group and the noncooperative (Nash) solution concept between groups, the first-order conditions that the desired solution should satisfy are

$$\frac{\partial \tilde{U}_i}{\partial x_{ij}} = \frac{\lambda_i \beta_i}{L_i} \tilde{Y} - \gamma x_{ij}^{\gamma-1} = 0 \qquad (j \in N_i, i \in M), \tag{32}$$

which can also be written as

$$x_{ij} = \left(\frac{\lambda_i \beta_i}{\gamma L_i} \tilde{Y} \right)^{1/(\gamma-1)} \qquad (j \in N_i, i \in M). \tag{33}$$

This indicates that the optimal labor input levels do not depend on the index j. With this property in hand we can write L_i as

$$L_i = \sum_{N_i} x_{ij} = n_i x_i \qquad (i \in M) \tag{34}$$

which, when used in (33), yields the labor input level of a typical worker–partner of type i as a function of $\tilde{Y}$:

$$\tilde{x}_i = \left(\frac{\lambda_i \beta_i}{\gamma \eta_i} \tilde{Y} \right)^{1/\gamma} \qquad (i \in M). \tag{35}$$

If (34) and (35) are used in (7), the resulting equation in terms of $\tilde{Y}$ admits the unique solution

$$\underline{\tilde{Y}}^* = \left[\left(\frac{\alpha}{\rho} \right)^{\alpha\gamma} \prod_M \left(\frac{\lambda_i \beta_i \eta_i^{\gamma-1}}{\gamma} \right)^{\beta_i} \right]^{1/\delta} \tag{36}$$

as the equilibrium output of the enterprise and as a function of the group-share vector λ. A more illuminating version of (36), in terms of the equilibrium output of the capitalistic enterprise of same size $\{n_i\}_{i=1}^m$, gives

$$\underline{\tilde{Y}}^* = \left(\prod_M \lambda_i^{\beta_i/\delta} \right) \underline{\bar{Y}}. \tag{37}$$

If this expression is used in (35), we obtain, in view of (17), the equilibrium employment level of a typical worker–partner of type i to be

$$\underline{\tilde{x}}_i^* = \left(\frac{\lambda_i \beta_i}{\gamma n_i} \underline{\tilde{Y}}^* \right)^{1/\gamma} = \left(\lambda_i \prod_M \lambda_k^{\beta_k/\delta} \right)^{1/\gamma} \underline{\bar{x}}_i \qquad (i \in M), \tag{38}$$

and finally the equilibrium level of value added by the enterprise can be expressed in terms of the value added, $\underline{\bar{V}}$, of the competitive capitalistic enterprise:

$$\underline{\tilde{V}}^* = (1-\alpha)\underline{\tilde{Y}}^* = \left(\prod_M \lambda_i^{\beta_i/\delta} \right) \underline{\bar{V}} \qquad (i \in M). \tag{39}$$

We have so far shown that the employment levels $\underline{\tilde{x}}_i^*$ $(i \in M)$ uniquely satisfy the first-order conditions associated with the "cooperative-Nash" optimization problem that the worker–partners of the enterprise solve. It can, moreover, be shown that the solutions described by (38) also satisfy the second-order (sufficiency) conditions that involve negative definiteness of the $(n_i \times n_i)$-Hessian matrix of $\tilde{U}_i$ for each $i \in M$.

The three economic values ($\underline{\tilde{x}}_i^*$, $\underline{\tilde{Y}}^*$ and $\underline{\tilde{V}}^*$), determined at the internal equilibrium of the worker's semi-cooperative, as well as the seven magnitudes, $\underline{\tilde{L}}_i^*$, $\underline{\tilde{K}}^*$, $\underline{\tilde{U}}_i^*$, $\underline{\tilde{U}}^*$, $\underline{\tilde{Z}}^*$, $\underline{\tilde{Y}}^*/\underline{\tilde{L}}_i^*$ and $\underline{\tilde{Y}}^*/\underline{\tilde{K}}^*$, directly obtainable from those three, are tabulated in the appropriate entries of the fourth column of table 8.1. We readily observe that all these equilibrium values are dependent only on the group-share vector λ, but not on how each group share is split among worker–partners of a particular group; that is to say, they depend on the μ_{ij}'s only through the relation $\Sigma_{N_i} \mu_{ij} = \lambda_i$ $(i \in M)$.

On the other hand, the equilibrium values of individual income and utility levels do in fact depend on the distribution of value added among different worker–partners contributing the same type of labor. The equilibrium income level of a jth worker–partner of type i will be given by

$$\underline{\tilde{y}}_{ij}^{*}=\mu_{ij}\underline{\tilde{V}}^{*}=\frac{(1-\alpha)\mu_{ij}n_i}{\beta_i}\left(\prod_{M}\beta_k^{\beta_k/\delta}\right)\underline{\bar{y}}_i \qquad (j\in N_i, i\in M), \tag{40}$$

and the same worker–partner's utility level will be

$$\begin{aligned}\underline{\tilde{u}}_{ij}^{*}&=\underline{\tilde{y}}_{ij}^{*}-(\underline{\tilde{x}}_{ij}^{*})^{\gamma}\\&=\left[\frac{\mu_{ij}n_i}{\beta_i}\gamma(1-\alpha)-\lambda_i\right]\frac{1}{(\gamma-1)}\left(\prod_{M}\lambda_k^{\beta_k/\delta}\right)\underline{\bar{u}}_i \qquad (j\in N_i, i\in M),\end{aligned} \tag{41}$$

where $\underline{\bar{y}}_i$ and $\underline{\bar{u}}_i$ denote, respectively, the equilibrium income and utility levels of a typical worker of type i in the capitalistic enterprise.

Since worker–partners belonging to the same labor class act cooperatively in a workers' semi-cooperative, a most reasonable assumption to be made at this stage is

$$\mu_{ij}=\mu_i=\frac{\lambda_i}{n_i} \qquad (j\in N_i, i\in M). \tag{42}$$

So, from now on, we only consider the value-added sharing incentive schemes that distribute equal shares to worker–partners contributing the same type of labor. In this case, expressions (40) and (41) take the forms, respectively,

$$\underline{\tilde{y}}_{ij}^{*}=\underline{\tilde{y}}_{i}^{*}=\frac{(1-\alpha)\lambda_i}{\beta_i}\left(\prod_{M}\lambda_k^{\beta_k/\delta}\right)\underline{\bar{y}}_i \qquad (i\in M) \tag{43}$$

and

$$\underline{\tilde{u}}_{ij}^{*}=\underline{\tilde{u}}_{i}^{*}=\frac{\lambda_i\delta_i}{(\gamma-1)\beta_i}\left(\prod_{M}\lambda_k^{\beta_k/\delta}\right)\underline{\bar{u}}_i \qquad (i\in M), \tag{44}$$

which depend only on the group-share vector λ. The new term, δ_i, used in (44) is defined by

$$\delta_i=\gamma(1-\alpha)-\beta_i \qquad (i\in M). \tag{45}$$

These expressions (the equilibrium income level $\underline{\tilde{y}}_i^{*}$ and utility $\underline{\tilde{u}}_i^{*}$ of a typical worker–partner of type i) are displayed in the appropriate entries of column 4 of table 8.1. The remaining two entries of this column, which we have so far not yet seen, are the profits, which are clearly zero in this case, and the (imputed) wages. As already mentioned in section 3, the (imputed) wage of a typical worker of type i is determined by dividing his equilibrium income into his equilibrium labor input. In the present case this gives the (imputed) wage level

$$\underline{\tilde{\omega}}_i^* = \frac{\tilde{y}_i^*}{\underline{\tilde{x}}_i^*} = \left(\frac{1-\alpha}{\beta}\right)\left(\lambda_i \prod_M \lambda_k^{\beta_k/\delta}\right)^{(\gamma-1)/\gamma} \underline{\overline{w}}_i \qquad (i \in M), \tag{46}$$

for a typical worker–partner of type i, in terms of the wage of a similar worker in the corresponding capitalistic enterprise.

We are now in a position to compare the fourth column of table 8.1 with its first column, i.e. the equilibrium outcomes of the economic quantities in a workers' semi-cooperative with their corresponding values in the competitive capitalistic enterprise employing the same number of workers of each type. First of all, in both enterprises the output/capital ratio is the same. Furthermore, since the quantity $\prod_M \lambda_k^{\beta_k/\delta}$ is strictly less than unity, the equilibrium levels of output and value added, and the utilization level of capital goods, are lower in the workers' semi-cooperative than their corresponding values in the capitalistic enterprise. By the same token, the equilibrium labor input of each type of worker–partner is lower in the workers' semi-cooperative, as a result of which we arrive at the important conclusion that the communal surplus is smaller in the workers' enterprise, since it was uniquely maximized at the capitalistic labor input levels. This then implies that the coefficient of $\underline{\overline{Z}}$ in the twelfth entry of the fourth column of table 8.1 is strictly less than unity for any possible group-share vector λ, i.e.

$$\frac{1}{\delta}\left(\sum_M \lambda_i \delta_i\right)\left(\prod_M \lambda_i^{\beta_i/\delta}\right) < 1 \qquad \left(\lambda_i > 0, \sum_M \lambda_i = 1\right). \tag{47}$$

We will have occasion to make use of this inequality in the next section.

The comparisons that we have made so far, and the conclusions drawn from them, are valid for all positive group-share vectors λ summing to unity. For the remaining economic values (such as (imputed) wages, individual income and utility levels, productivity of each type of labor), however, no unambiguous conclusions can be drawn for all such λ. In particular, whether the worker–partners would all enjoy at least the income and utility level of their colleagues in the capitalistic sector is very much dependent on the choice of λ. Of course, the choice of λ is at the discretion of the workers' council. How, then, should the council choose it to make "everybody happy"? Is there, in fact, such a choice? More will be said on this in the next section where we study general equilibrium with the worker–partnership share market of Sertel (1978) operative.

5. General equilibrium: workers' cooperatives and semi-cooperatives facing competitive capitalism

In this section we determine the general equilibrium sizes of workers' cooperatives and semi-cooperatives relative to that of analogous capitalistic enterprises, thereby determining the general equilibrium values of the economic magnitudes of interest, paralleling an analysis employed in section 6 of Sertel, Başar and Selbuz (1978). That is to say, we consider a large mixed economy comprising many workers' cooperatives and semi-cooperatives alongside many competitive capitalistic enterprises, and by a general equilibrium position of such an economy we mean a position in which no worker or worker–partner has any incentive to switch from one firm to another. In the formation of this general equilibrium, it is of course assumed that a worker is always free to enter a capitalistic enterprise or leave it, while such might not be the case for workers' cooperatives and semi-cooperatives, with the decisions regarding the levels of entrance fees for different types of incoming worker–partners and severance compensations for outgoing worker–partners being determined in a market of worker–partnership deeds (see Sertel, 1978).

Let us first develop our general equilibrium analysis regarding a workers' semi-cooperative consisting of a total of $\Sigma_M d_i$ worker–partners, d_i of which are of type i, under the natural assumption that the share allocated from value added to each labor group is divided equally among the worker–partners belonging to that group. Then, if the workers' semi-cooperative is in general equilibrium with a typical competitive capitalistic enterprise of size $\Sigma_M a_i$, the following demand and supply equation for a worker–partnership share should hold for each type of labor:

$$\tilde{D}_i^*(a,d)=\tilde{S}_i^*(d) \qquad (i\in M). \tag{48}$$

Here $\tilde{D}_i^*$ and $\tilde{S}_i^*$ stand, respectively, for the demand price and supply price for the ith type of partnership share in the workers' semi-cooperative, and $a=(a_1,\dots,a_m)$ and $d=(d_1,\dots,d_m)$ denote, respectively, the vectors of group sizes in a typical competitive capitalistic enterprise and workers' semi-cooperative. Specifically,

$$\tilde{D}_i^*(a,d)=\underline{\tilde{u}}_i^*(d)-\underline{\bar{u}}_i(a) \qquad (i\in M) \tag{49}$$

and

$$\tilde{S}_i^*(d)=-\sum_{j=1}^{m} d_j\frac{\partial \underline{\tilde{u}}_j^*(d)}{\partial d_i} \qquad (i\in M), \tag{50}$$

where $\bar{u}_i(a)$ and $\underline{\tilde{u}}_i^*(d)$ are the utility levels of a typical worker of type i, respectively, in a capitalistic enterprise of size a and a workers' semi-cooperative of size d, as displayed, respectively, in the eighth entry of the first column of table 8.1, with n_j replaced by a_j $(j \in M)$, and the eighth entry of the fourth column of table 8.1 (or equivalently, by (44)), with n_j replaced by d_j $(j \in M)$. Now, if expression (44) for $\underline{\tilde{u}}_i^*(d)$ is used in (49) and (50), we obtain, respectively,

$$\tilde{D}_i^*(a,d) = \underline{\tilde{u}}_i^*(d) - \frac{\beta_i(\gamma-1)}{\gamma_i\delta_i}\left[\prod_M \left(\frac{1}{\lambda_k}\right)^{\beta_k/\delta}\right]\underline{\tilde{u}}_i^*(d) \tag{51}$$

and

$$\tilde{S}_i^*(d) = \left[1 - \frac{\beta_i(\gamma-1)}{\delta\delta_i\lambda_i}\sum_M \lambda_k\delta_k\right]\underline{\tilde{u}}_i^*(d). \tag{52}$$

In view of these expressions, the equilibrium relation (48) becomes

$$\frac{1}{\delta}\left(\sum_M \lambda_k\delta_k\right)\underline{\tilde{u}}_i^*(d) = \left[\prod_M \left(\frac{1}{\lambda_k}\right)^{\beta_k/\delta}\right]\underline{\tilde{u}}_i^*(a) \qquad (i \in M), \tag{53}$$

and by further use of (44), and invoking the sixth and eighth entries of the first column of table 8.1 in (53), we obtain the set of equations

$$\begin{aligned}\frac{d_i}{a_i} &= \left(\frac{1}{\delta}\right)\left(\prod_M \lambda_k^{\beta_k/\delta}\right)\left(\sum_M \lambda_k\delta_k\right)\left[\frac{\underline{Y}(d)}{\underline{Y}(a)}\right]\\ &= \left(\frac{1}{\delta}\right)\left(\prod_M \lambda_k^{\beta_k/\delta}\right)\left(\sum_M \lambda_k\delta_k\right)\left[\prod_M \left(\frac{d_k}{a_k}\right)^{\beta_k(\gamma-1)/\delta}\right] \qquad (i \in M),\end{aligned} \tag{54}$$

the solution of which yields the equilibrium size ratios d_i/a_i $(i \in M)$, which are clearly seen to be dependent on the group-share vector λ, but independent of the subindex i. Hence, denoting this common ratio for all types of labor by t (i.e. $t = d_i/a_i$ $(i \in M)$), we have the equation

$$\delta t = \left[\left(\prod_M \lambda_k^{\beta_k/\delta}\right)\left(\sum_M \lambda_k\delta_k\right)\right] t^{\beta(\gamma-1)/\delta}, \tag{55}$$

the unique solution of which is

$$\frac{d_i}{a_i} = t = \left[\left(\frac{1}{\delta}\right)\left(\prod_M \lambda_k^{\beta_k/\delta}\right)\left(\sum_M \lambda_k\delta_k\right)\right]^{\delta/\gamma\varepsilon} \qquad (i \in M). \tag{56}$$

We thus obtain the result that the equilibrium relative enterprise size ($d_i/a_i = t$) is an invariant of the type of labor, and of the group sizes of the capitalistic enterprise, depending only on the system parameters α, β_i and γ, and on the group-share vector λ. This implies that, at equilibrium, the workers' semi-cooperative varies its size (in terms of worker–partners) precisely in the same fashion as does a capitalistic enterprise.[2]

With regard to the magnitude of t, we readily have the result

$$0<t<1, \tag{57}$$

for all group size vectors λ, a fact which follows directly from (47) since t is its positive power. Thus, we have the conclusion that, regardless of what group-share vector λ the workers' semi-cooperative adopts as an internal policy, it will always be a shrunken model of a competitive capitalistic enterprise operating in the same mixed economy. Furthermore, since each semi-cooperative obeying the ratio (56) will be in equilibrium with the capitalistic enterprise, it now easily follows that such semi-cooperatives will also be in general equilibrium among themselves, the relative group sizes, of course, depending on what group-share vector λ each adopts as an internal policy.

The equilibrium values of the economic magnitudes of a workers' semi-cooperative in general equilibrium with a competitive capitalistic enterprise of size $a=(a_1,\ldots,a_m)$ can now be determined by re-evaluating the fourth column of table 8.1 at the relative size ratio (56) and with n_i replaced by d_i. The corresponding results are displayed in the first fourteen entries of the fourth column of table 8.2, which just replicate those of the first column of table 8.1 with n_i replaced by a_i ($i \in M$). The last four rows of table 8.2 display, in sequence, the capital goods utilized per worker, output per worker, communal surplus per worker and the equilibrium share price of a worker–partnership of type i in the corresponding enterprise at general equilibrium. The worker–partnership share price is clearly zero in a capitalistic enterprise, and is determined according to the relation

$$\tilde{P}_i^* = \underline{\tilde{u}}_i^*(ta) - \underline{\bar{u}}_i(a) \tag{58}$$

in the workers' semi-cooperative.

Comparing the corresponding entries of the first and fourth columns of table 8.2, we first observe that, regardless of the value of the group-share vector λ, communal surplus per worker is the same in both enterprises. A similar equality also holds for the equilibrium average product of capital.

[2]It can also be shown exactly as in appendix A of Sertel, Başar and Selbuz (1978) that the equilibrium relative enterprise size t is stable for all admissible λ.

Table 8.2
Equilibrium outcomes of three types of enterprise at their respective equilibrium sizes.

Equilibrium outcome \ Enterprise	Competitive capitalistic enterprise of size a	Workers' cooperative of size $c = a$		Workers' semi-cooperative of size $d = ta$	
		General λ	$\lambda_i = \beta_i/\beta \ (i \in M)$	General λ	$\lambda_i = \left(\frac{\beta_i}{\delta_i}\right)\left[\sum_M \left(\frac{\beta_k}{\delta_k}\right)\right] \quad (i \in M)$
Wage (of a typical worker of type i) w_i	$\underline{\bar{w}}_i = \left[\gamma\left(\frac{\beta_i}{a_i}\underline{\bar{Y}}\right)^{\gamma-1}\right]^{1/\gamma}$	$\underline{\bar{\omega}}_i^0 = \frac{(1-\alpha)\lambda_i}{\beta_i}\underline{\bar{w}}_i$	$\underline{\bar{\omega}}_i^0 = \left(\frac{1-\alpha}{\beta}\right)\underline{\bar{w}}_i$	$\underline{\tilde{\omega}}^*_i = \left(\frac{1-\alpha}{\beta_i}\right) \times \left[\frac{\lambda_i\delta}{\sum_M \lambda_k\delta_k}\right]^{(\gamma-1)/\gamma} \underline{\bar{w}}_i$	$\underline{\tilde{\omega}}_i^* = \left(\frac{1-\alpha}{\beta}\right) \times \left[\frac{\delta}{\delta_i}\right]^{(\gamma-1)/\gamma}\left[\frac{\beta}{\beta_i}\right]^{1/\gamma} \underline{\bar{w}}_i$
Labor (input of a typical worker of type i) x_i	$\underline{\bar{x}}_i = \left[\frac{\beta_i}{\gamma a_i}\underline{\bar{Y}}\right]^{1/\gamma}$	$\underline{\bar{x}}_i^0 = \underline{\bar{x}}_i$	$\underline{\bar{x}}_i^0 = \underline{\bar{x}}_i$	$\underline{\tilde{x}}_i^* = \left[\frac{\lambda_i\delta}{\sum_M \lambda_k\delta_k}\right]^{1/\gamma} \underline{\bar{x}}_i$	$\underline{\tilde{x}}_i^* = \left[\frac{\beta_i\delta}{\beta\delta_i}\right]^{1/\gamma} \underline{\bar{x}}_i$
Income (of a worker of type i) y_i	$\underline{\bar{y}}_i = \frac{\beta_i}{a_i}\underline{\bar{Y}}$	$\underline{\bar{y}}_i^0 = \frac{(1-\alpha)\lambda_i}{\beta_i}\underline{\bar{y}}_i$	$\underline{\bar{y}}_i^0 = \left(\frac{1-\alpha}{\beta}\right)\underline{\bar{y}}_i$	$\underline{\tilde{y}}_i^* = \left(\frac{\lambda_i}{\beta_i}\right)\left[\frac{(1-\alpha)\delta}{\sum_M \lambda_k\beta_k}\right]\underline{\bar{y}}_i$	$\underline{\tilde{y}}_i^* = \left[\frac{(1-\alpha)\delta}{\beta\delta_i}\right]\underline{\bar{y}}_i$
Aggregate labor (input of workers of type i) L_i	$\underline{\bar{L}}_i = \left[\frac{\beta_i a_i^{\gamma-1}}{\gamma}\underline{\bar{Y}}\right]^{1/\gamma}$	$\underline{\bar{L}}_i^0 = \underline{\bar{L}}_i$	$\underline{\bar{L}}_i^0 = \underline{\bar{L}}_i$	$\underline{\tilde{L}}_i^* = t\left[\frac{\lambda_i\delta}{\sum_M \lambda_k\delta_k}\right]^{1/\gamma} \underline{\bar{L}}_i$	$\underline{\tilde{L}}_i^* = t^*\left[\frac{\beta_i\delta}{\beta\delta_i}\right]^{1/\gamma} \underline{\bar{L}}_i$
Capital goods input K	$\underline{\bar{K}} = \left(\frac{\alpha}{\rho}\right)\underline{\bar{Y}}$	$\underline{\bar{K}}^0 = \underline{\bar{K}}$	$\underline{\bar{K}}^0 = \underline{\bar{K}}$	$\underline{\tilde{K}}^* = \frac{t\delta}{\sum_M \lambda_k\delta_k}\underline{\bar{K}}$	$\underline{\tilde{K}}^* = \frac{\delta t^*}{\beta}\left[\sum_M \frac{\beta_k}{\delta_k}\right]\underline{\bar{K}}$

Output Y	$\underline{\bar{Y}}=\left[\left(\frac{\alpha}{\rho}\right)^{\alpha\gamma}\prod_{M}\left(\frac{\beta_k a_k}{\gamma}\right)^{\beta_k}\right]^{1/\delta}$	$\underline{\bar{Y}}^0=\underline{\bar{Y}}$	$\underline{\bar{Y}}^0=\underline{\bar{Y}}$	$\underline{\tilde{Y}}^*=\frac{t\delta}{\sum_M \lambda_k\delta_k}\underline{\bar{Y}}$	$\underline{\tilde{Y}}^*=\frac{\delta t^*}{\beta}\left[\sum_M \frac{\beta_k}{\delta_k}\right]\underline{\bar{Y}}$
Value added V	$\underline{\bar{V}}=(1-\alpha)\underline{\bar{Y}}$	$\underline{\bar{V}}^0=\underline{\bar{V}}$	$\underline{\bar{V}}^0=\underline{\bar{V}}$	$\underline{\tilde{V}}^*=\frac{t\delta}{\sum_M \lambda_k\delta_k}\underline{\bar{V}}$	$\underline{\tilde{V}}^*=\frac{\delta t^*}{\beta}\left[\sum_M \frac{\beta_k}{\delta_k}\right]\underline{\bar{V}}$
Utility (of a worker of type i) u_i	$\underline{\bar{u}}_i=\frac{(\gamma-1)\beta_i}{\gamma a_i}\underline{\bar{Y}}$	$\underline{\bar{u}}_i^0=\left[\frac{\gamma(1-\alpha)\lambda_i}{\beta_i}-1\right]\times\frac{\underline{\bar{u}}_i}{(\gamma-1)}$	$\underline{\bar{u}}_i^0=\left[\frac{\delta}{\beta(\gamma-1)}\right]\underline{\bar{u}}_i$	$\underline{\tilde{u}}_i^*=\left[\frac{\delta}{\sum_M \lambda_k\delta_k}\right]\times\left[\frac{\lambda_i\delta_i}{\beta_i(\gamma-1)}\right]\underline{\bar{u}}_i$	$\underline{\tilde{u}}_i^*=\frac{\delta}{\beta(\gamma-1)}\underline{\bar{u}}_i$
Aggregate utility (of group i) U_i	$\underline{\bar{U}}_i=\frac{(\gamma-1)\beta_i}{\gamma}\underline{\bar{Y}}$	$\underline{\bar{U}}_i^0=\left[\frac{\gamma(1-\alpha)\lambda_i}{\beta_i}-1\right]\times\frac{\underline{\bar{U}}_i}{(\gamma-1)}$	$\underline{\bar{U}}_i^0=\left[\frac{\delta}{\beta(\gamma-1)}\right]\underline{\bar{U}}_i$	$\underline{\tilde{U}}_i^*=\left[\frac{t\delta}{\Sigma\lambda_k\delta_k}\right]\times\left[\frac{\lambda_i\delta_i}{\beta_i(\gamma-1)}\right]\underline{\bar{U}}_i$	$\underline{\tilde{U}}_i^*=\frac{\delta}{\beta(\gamma-1)}\underline{\bar{U}}_i$
Total utility (of workers) U	$\underline{\bar{U}}=\frac{(\gamma-1)\beta}{\gamma}\underline{\bar{Y}}$	$\underline{\bar{U}}^0=\frac{\delta}{\beta(\gamma-1)}\underline{\bar{U}}$	$\underline{\bar{U}}^0=\left[\frac{\delta}{\beta(\gamma-1)}\right]\underline{\bar{U}}$	$\underline{\tilde{U}}^*=\frac{t\delta}{\beta(\gamma-1)}\underline{\bar{U}}$	$\underline{\tilde{U}}^*=\frac{\delta}{\beta(\gamma-1)}\underline{\bar{U}}$
Profit Π	$\underline{\bar{\Pi}}=\varepsilon\underline{\bar{Y}}$	$\underline{\bar{\Pi}}^0=0$	$\underline{\bar{\Pi}}^0=0$	$\underline{\tilde{\Pi}}^*=0$	$\underline{\tilde{\Pi}}^*=0$
Communal surplus Z	$\underline{\bar{Z}}=\frac{\delta}{\gamma}\underline{\bar{Y}}$	$\underline{\bar{Z}}^0=\underline{\bar{Z}}$	$\underline{\bar{Z}}^0=\underline{\bar{Z}}$	$\underline{\tilde{Z}}^*=t\underline{\bar{Z}}$	$\underline{\tilde{Z}}^*=t^*\underline{\bar{Z}}$
Y/L_i	$\left(\frac{\underline{\bar{Y}}}{\underline{\bar{L}}_i}\right)=\left[\frac{\gamma}{\beta_i a_i^{\gamma-1}}\underline{\bar{Y}}^{\gamma-1}\right]^{1/\gamma}$	$\left(\frac{\underline{\bar{Y}}^0}{\underline{\bar{L}}_i^0}\right)=\left(\frac{\underline{\bar{Y}}}{\underline{\bar{L}}_i}\right)$	$\left(\frac{\underline{\bar{Y}}^0}{\underline{\bar{L}}_i^0}\right)=\left(\frac{\underline{\bar{Y}}}{\underline{\bar{L}}_i}\right)$	$\left(\frac{\underline{\tilde{Y}}^*}{\underline{\tilde{L}}_i^*}\right)=\left(\frac{1}{\lambda_i}\right)^{1/\gamma}\times\left(\frac{\delta}{\sum_M \lambda_k\delta_k}\right)^{(\gamma-1)/\gamma}\left(\frac{\underline{\bar{Y}}}{\underline{\bar{L}}_i}\right)$	$\left(\frac{\underline{\tilde{Y}}^*}{\underline{\tilde{L}}_i^*}\right)=\frac{\delta}{\beta}\left(\frac{\delta_i\beta}{\delta\beta_i}\right)^{1/\gamma}\times\left[\sum_M \frac{\beta_k}{\delta_k}\right]\left(\frac{\underline{\bar{Y}}}{\underline{\bar{L}}_i}\right)$

Table 8.2 (*continued*)

Enterprise / Equilibrium outcome	Competitive capitalistic enterprise of size a	Workers' cooperative of size $c=a$		Workers' semi-cooperative of size $d=ta$	
		General λ	$\lambda_i=\beta_i/\beta\ (i\in M)$	General λ	$\lambda_i=\left(\frac{\beta_i}{\delta_i}\right)\left[\sum_M\left(\frac{\beta_k}{\delta_k}\right)\right]\ (i\in M)$
Y/K	ρ/α	ρ/α	ρ/α	ρ/α	ρ/α
K/N	$\left(\frac{\underline{\bar{K}}}{A}\right)=\left(\frac{\alpha}{\rho}\right)\left(\frac{\underline{\bar{Y}}}{A}\right)$	$\left(\frac{\underline{\bar{K}}^0}{C}\right)=\left(\frac{\underline{\bar{K}}}{A}\right)$	$\left(\frac{\underline{\bar{K}}^0}{C}\right)=\left(\frac{\underline{\bar{K}}}{A}\right)$	$\left(\frac{\underline{\tilde{K}}^*}{D}\right)=\left(\frac{\delta}{\sum_M\lambda_k\delta_k}\right)\left(\frac{\underline{\bar{K}}}{A}\right)$	$\left(\frac{\underline{\tilde{K}}^*}{D}\right)=\frac{\delta}{\beta}\times\left[\sum_M\frac{\beta_k}{\delta_k}\right]\left(\frac{\underline{\bar{K}}}{A}\right)$
Y/N	$\underline{\bar{Y}}/A$	$\left(\frac{\underline{\bar{Y}}^0}{C}\right)=\left(\frac{\underline{\bar{Y}}}{A}\right)$	$\left(\frac{\underline{\bar{Y}}^0}{C}\right)=\left(\frac{\underline{\bar{Y}}}{A}\right)$	$\left(\frac{\underline{\tilde{Y}}^*}{D}\right)=\left(\frac{\delta}{\sum_M\lambda_k\delta_k}\right)\left(\frac{\underline{\bar{Y}}}{A}\right)$	$\left(\frac{\underline{\tilde{Y}}^*}{D}\right)=\frac{\delta}{\beta}\times\left[\sum_M\frac{\beta_k}{\delta_k}\right]\left(\frac{\underline{\bar{Y}}}{A}\right)$
Z/N	$\left(\frac{\underline{\bar{Z}}}{A}\right)=\frac{\delta}{\gamma}\left(\frac{\underline{\bar{Y}}}{A}\right)$	$(\underline{\bar{Z}}^0/C)=(\underline{\bar{Z}}/A)$	$(\underline{\bar{Z}}^0/C)=(\underline{\bar{Z}}/A)$	$(\underline{\tilde{Z}}^*/D)=(\underline{\bar{Z}}/A)$	$(\underline{\tilde{Z}}^*/D)=(\underline{\bar{Z}}/A)$
Share price p_i	—	$\underline{\bar{P}}_i^0=[(1-\alpha)\lambda_i-\beta_i]\frac{\underline{\bar{Y}}}{c_i}$	$\underline{\bar{P}}_i^0=\left(\frac{\beta_i\varepsilon}{\beta}\right)\frac{\underline{\bar{Y}}}{c_i}$	$\underline{\tilde{P}}_i^*=\left[\frac{\lambda_i\delta_i\delta}{\sum_M\lambda_k\delta_k}-\beta_i(\gamma-1)\right]\frac{t\underline{\bar{Y}}}{\gamma d_i}$	$\underline{\tilde{P}}_i^*=\left[\frac{\beta_i t^*}{\beta d_i}\right]\varepsilon\underline{\bar{Y}}$

$$N=\sum_M n_i;\ A=\sum_M a_i;\ C=\sum_M c_i;\ D=\sum_M d_i;\ t=\left[\left(\prod_M\lambda_k^{\beta_k/\delta}\right)\sum_M\frac{\gamma_k\delta_k}{\delta}\right]^{\delta/\gamma\varepsilon};\qquad t^*=\left[\left(\frac{\beta}{\delta}\right)^{\delta}\prod_M\left(\frac{\beta_k}{\delta_k}\right)^{\beta_k}\Big/\left[\sum_M\left(\frac{\beta_k}{\delta_k}\right)\right]^{\gamma(1-\alpha)}\right]^{1/\gamma\varepsilon}$$

The equilibrium labor input level for a worker–partner of type i $(i \in M)$ is lower in the workers' semi-cooperative as compared with that of a similar worker in a capitalistic enterprise, since

$$\lambda_i \delta \Big/ \Big(\sum_M \lambda_k \delta_k \Big) = [\lambda_i \delta_i - \lambda_i(\beta - \beta_i)] \Big/ \Big(\sum_M \lambda_k \delta_k \Big)$$

$$< \lambda_i \delta_i \Big/ \Big(\sum_M \lambda_k \delta_k \Big) < 1, \tag{59}$$

and this result holds, regardless of how value added is shared among different types of labor. By the same inequality, and since $t < 1$, the aggregate equilibrium labor input of each group, total capital goods used in production, the equilibrium level of production, the equilibrium level of value added, equilibrium output per worker–partner and capital goods used per worker–partner are all smaller in the workers' semi-cooperative. It should be noted that these conclusions are also valid for all possible values of λ. (Total utility of the worker–partners is also lower in the semi-cooperative but mainly because it accommodates less worker–partners than a capitalistic enterprise.)

No definite conclusions can be drawn from a comparison of the remaining entries of the two columns, unless specific values are assigned to the group-share vector λ. Specifically, if λ_i is chosen sufficiently small for a particular labor type i, the individual income and utility levels and imputed wages of a typical worker–partner of that labor type become lower in the workers' semi-cooperative than the corresponding levels in the capitalistic enterprise. A sufficiently large value of λ_i, on the other hand, will yield the reverse conclusion. But since a large share for one particular labor group will imply a low share for the remaining groups, the question of existence of a group-share vector λ that will make all worker–partners in the semi-cooperative better off in terms of their utilities becomes important. One such possible choice is

$$\lambda_i = \left(\frac{\beta_i}{\delta_i} \right) \Big/ \left(\sum_M \frac{\beta_k}{\delta_k} \right) \qquad (i \in M), \tag{60}$$

under which the utility level of a typical worker–partner of type i becomes

$$\underline{\tilde{u}}_i^*(ta) = \frac{\delta}{\beta(\gamma - 1)} \underline{\bar{u}}_i(a) \qquad (i \in M), \tag{61}$$

indicating that all worker–partners are better off in this semi-cooperative, since the quantity $\delta / [\beta(\gamma - 1)]$ is larger than unity. We now re-evaluate the entries of column 4 of table 8.2 at the specific group-share values (60) and list them in the corresponding entries of the fifth column. It should be observed that, in addition to the individual utility levels, the imputed wage for each labor type is also higher in the present semi-cooperative as compared with the corresponding value in the capitalistic enterprise. Finally, we note that the equilibrium share price of a worker–partnership of type i in the present enterprise is given by

$$\underline{\tilde{P}}_i^* = \frac{\beta_i t^*}{\beta d_i} \varepsilon \underline{Y}\left(\frac{d}{t^*}\right) \qquad (i \in M), \tag{62}$$

where t^* denotes the value of (56) evaluated at the share distribution (60).

Coming to a workers' cooperative of size $c=(c_1,\ldots,c_m)$ at general equilibrium in our mixed economy, we follow the same procedure and equate demand price $\bar{D}_i$ and supply price $\bar{S}_i$ of a worker–partnership share. Now

$$\begin{aligned}\bar{D}_i(a,c) &= \underline{\bar{u}}_i^0(c) - \underline{\bar{u}}_i(a)\\ &= \left[\left(\frac{\gamma}{\gamma-1}\right)\left(\frac{1-\alpha}{\beta_i}\right)\lambda_i - \frac{1}{\gamma-1}\right]\underline{\bar{u}}_i(c) - \underline{\bar{u}}_i(a) \qquad (i \in M)\end{aligned} \tag{63}$$

and

$$\bar{S}_i(c) = -\sum_{i=1}^{m} c_i \frac{\partial \underline{\bar{u}}_j^0}{\partial c_i} = \frac{(1-\alpha)\lambda_i - \beta_i}{c_i} \underline{\bar{Y}}(c) \qquad (i \in M). \tag{64}$$

The equalities

$$\bar{D}_i(a,c) = \bar{S}_i(c) \qquad (i \in M) \tag{65}$$

yield the set of equations

$$\frac{c_i}{a_i} = \frac{\underline{\bar{Y}}(c)}{\underline{\bar{Y}}(a)} = \prod_M \left(\frac{c_k}{a_k}\right)^{\beta_k(\gamma-1)/\delta} \qquad (i \in M) \tag{66}$$

from which the unique solution

$$c_i = a_i \qquad (i \in M) \tag{67}$$

follows. Hence, a workers' cooperative keeps, at equilibrium, the same group sizes as the capitalistic enterprise, and all the comparisons that we performed in section 3 are valid at general equilibrium also. The first fourteen entries of columns 2 and 3 of table 8.2 are now identical with the corresponding entries of table 8.1, only with n_i replaced by c_i. The last four entries can also be filled out mechanically by use of the first fourteen entries of each column. It is interesting just to note that the eighth entries of columns 3 and 5 are equal. That is to say, at general equilibrium the individual utility level of a typical worker–partner of type i in the cooperative that adopts $\lambda_i = \beta_i / \beta$ $(i \in M)$ as the internal value-added sharing scheme is equal to that in the semi-cooperative that adopts (60) instead. The equilibrium share prices of a worker–partnership of type i in the two types of enterprise are also equal, as can easily be detected from the last entries of columns 3 and 5.

It is rather tedious but straightforward to compute the "short-run" behavior of the three types of firms we have studied when their general equilibrium is perturbed by a change in relative prices and they have to stick to their respective general equilibrium levels of capital goods utilization. As in Sertel (1978) and Sertel, Başar and Selbuz (1978), the workers' firms behave qualitatively just like their capitalistic counterpart, dispelling once again with the Wardian (1958) pathology of perverse short-run behavior (in the form of a "backward-bending supply curve", etc.) for workers' enterprises – all of this, of course, with the worker–partnership deed market of Sertel (1978) operating competitively.

6. Closing remarks

This chapter has presented a complete economic comparison between workers' cooperatives and semi-cooperatives and capitalistic enterprises, all equipped with the same technology and embedded in the same competitive mixed economy. The results are displayed in tables 8.1 and 8.2, with the former devoted to the three types of enterprise of the same group sizes, and the latter to the case when the group sizes are in general equilibrium. At general equilibrium, the workers' cooperative adopts the same group sizes as the capitalistic enterprise, while the workers' semi-cooperative becomes its proportionately shrunken model, with communal surplus per worker identical in all three types of enterprise.

It is noteworthy that, by choosing the group-share vector λ so as to satisfy the ratios $\lambda_i / \lambda_j = \beta_i / \beta_j$ in the workers' cooperative and $\lambda_i / \lambda_j = (\beta_i / \beta_j)(\delta_j / \delta_i)$ in the workers' semi-cooperative, the equilibrium share price for every type of worker–partnership can be made to coincide for the two kinds of workers' enterprise. This implies that the utility levels of different types of worker–partners can be made equal in the two types of enterprise, all being relatively higher than the corresponding levels in the competitive capitalistic enterprise. Moreover, by a comparison of the appropriate entries of table II of Sertel, Başar and Selbuz (1978), it can easily be seen that these levels also coincide with the utility levels of worker–partners in a workers' enterprise with internal wages, and in a workers' enterprise with internal wages and quotas this distributes the capitalist's profit among its worker–partners in proportion to the β_i's (in lump-sum fashion). Hence, we can have a mixed competitive economy with four types of workers' enterprises, all in general equilibrium with the capitalistic enterprises, and with a single share price for each type of worker–partnership.

We finally note that, since the level of capital goods used in production is smaller in the workers' semi-cooperative as compared with the cooperative or the capitalistic enterprise (and even more so when compared with the workers' enterprise with internal wages), while the equilibrium level of average product of capital is the same in all these types of enterprise, a workers' semi-cooperative stands out as a sensible economic institution when the social preference stresses the creation of more jobs.

References

Kleindorfer, P.R. and M.R. Sertel (1978) "Value-Added Sharing Enterprises", Preprint Series No. DP 78-38, International Institute of Management, West Berlin. (See Chapter 9 of this book.)

Sertel, M.R. (1978) "Relative Size and Share Price of a Workers' Enterprise Facing Competitive Capitalism", paper presented at the Second Bosphorus Workshop in Industrial Democracy, Istanbul. (See Chapter 2 of this book.)

Sertel, M.R., T. Başar and H. Selbuz (1978) "Workers' Enterprises Facing Competitive Capitalism", Technical Report, No. 44, Marmara Scientific and Industrial Research Institute, Gebze-Kocaeli, Turkey. (See Chapter 7 of this book.)

Vanek, J. (1970) *The General Theory of Labor Managed Market Economies* (Cornell University Press).

Ward, B. (1958) "The Firm in Illyria: Market Syndicalism", *American Economic Review*, 48, 566–589.

CHAPTER 9

Value-added sharing enterprises*

PAUL R. KLEINDORFER and MURAT R. SERTEL

1. Introduction

This chapter examines the design of enterprises under alternative conditions governing their internal organization, but linked by the common assumptions that the incentive system through which enterprise participants are remunerated is based on sharing the value added by labor[1] and that workers in these enterprises determine their inputs to the production process cooperatively. These assumptions are motivated by the theory of the labor-managed firm as developed by Ward (1958), Domar (1966) and Vanek (1970). In this traditional theory,[2] each worker–partner of the firm is assumed to contribute a fixed amount of labor and, thus, all that need be decided relative to labor input is the size of the labor force. This, and other factor inputs, are assumed chosen by the labor-managed firm so as to maximize value added per worker, which is also the income each worker receives.

While continuing to assume value-added sharing as the incentive scheme linking enterprise participants, we depart from the traditional theory of the

*Paper prepared for the First International Conference on Economics of Workers' Management, Inter-University Centre, Dubrovnik, October 1978. A preliminary version of this paper was presented at the Second Bosphorus Workshop on Industrial Democracy (BWID-II), Bosphorus University, Istanbul, July 1978. Comments of BWID-II participants are gratefully acknowledged. Special thanks are due Felix FitzRoy for several helpful discussions.

[1]From here on we will abbreviate "value added by labor" to simply "value added".

[2]In both Domar (1966) and Vanek (1970, ch. 12) there are very healthy seeds sown for an analysis where labor contributions depend on incentives.

labor-managed firm on several other counts. Our first point of departure is that the inputs of participants in the enterprises studied here are not assumed fixed. Instead, the level of each participant's input (of, for example, labor, effort, or some other privately owned factor) is assumed to be chosen so as to balance income earned against the opportunities foregone (e.g. leisure) through participation in the enterprise. Thus, we assume here that workers attempt to maximize utility, a function of both their income and their input contribution, rather than just maximizing their income. In addition, we depart from the traditional literature in assuming that the inputs of different enterprise participants may enter enterprise production asymmetrically. Finally, we want to study and compare labor-designed enterprises with those designed to represent other interests, e.g. those of a central planning authority. As a result, we will need to consider a richer set of design possibilities than has been customary in the theory of the labor-managed firm.

As a starting point it is useful to relate our problem to the general problem of organizational design. This latter may be viewed as the problem of choosing and setting a number of design variables including authority structures, incentive schemes, information and monitoring systems, production technology, and personnel. Incorporating all of these design instruments in a single framework has proven to be difficult and studies of organizational design to date have typically considered only a very restricted class of design possibilities. The present chapter is no exception in this regard.

Our approach here will consider enterprises with technology and information systems fixed and where incentives are restricted to shares in value added.[3] The main issue we address is how such shares would or should be set as between workers and a financier (or central planning authority) who allocates or rents capital to the enterprise. We study this question by variously fixing the personnel and authority structure of the enterprise and then determining optimal share distributions from the viewpoint of various groups of enterprise participants (e.g. the workers or the financier). We then compare such enterprises at their corresponding optimal sharing schemes as to enterprise output and value added as well as participants' inputs, incomes and utilities. Finally, we examine which of the various enterprises so designed could coexist with a competitive capitalist sector, paying special attention to personnel movements between this sector and the enterprises in question. Our purpose in doing this is to compare the viability and

[3]A parallel analysis using internal wages as the enterprise incentive scheme (instead of value-added sharing) is contained in Sertel, Başar and Selbuz (1978). A comparison of (output-) sharing and internal wages is presented in Kleindorfer and Sertel (1979).

equilibrium size of various forms of labor-managed firm, as determined by their respective internal organizational design processes, in relation to competitive capitalism. Our main findings are summarized in section 6.

2. Basic data and framework

In this section we first specify basic data concerning the production technology and the agents' preferences, all of which amount to specifying the economic presystem which we will later equip with one or another of nine institutional set-ups whose consequences we will evaluate and compare.

To start with the agents of our presystem, we consider a number $n = n_1 + n_2 + \cdots + n_m$ of *workers*, where $N_i = \{1,\dots,n_i\}$ stands for the workers of group $i \in M = \{1,\dots,m\}$, the jth member of the ith group exhibiting a preference between income, y_{ij}, and work, $x_{ij} \geqslant 0$, as represented by the utility function

$$u_{ij} = y_{ij} - c_i x_{ij}^{\gamma_i} \qquad (i \in M,\ j \in N_i), \tag{1}$$

with $c_i > 0$ and $\gamma_i > 1$. As to the production technology of our presystem, it specifies output as

$$Y = K^{\alpha} \prod_{i \in M} L_i^{\beta_i} \qquad \left(0 < \alpha, \beta_i, \alpha + \sum_M \beta_i \leqslant 1\right), \tag{2}$$

where K stands for capital goods input and $L_i = \Sigma_{j \in N_i} x_{ij}$ stands for the aggregate input of the ith type of labor. The output Y is taken as numeraire, i.e. with unit price.

We assume that capital goods are rented from a price-dictating market at a rental $\rho > 0$, so *value added* (by labor) in units of Y is given by

$$V = Y - \rho K. \tag{3}$$

It is the sharing of V that provides the incentive schemes with which the above economic presystem will be equipped. In particular, the income, y_{ij}, of the jth member of the ith group of workers will consist of

$$y_{ij} = \mu_i V \qquad (i \in M,\ j \in N_i), \tag{4}$$

identical for all members of the same group, where the shares μ_i $(i = 1,\dots,m)$ as well as $\mu_0 = 1 - \Sigma_{i=1}^{m} n_i \mu_i$ are all non-negative, leaving

$$\pi = \mu_0 V \tag{5}$$

as the profit after all the factors (capital goods and labor) have been paid. We assume that there is an agent who decides on the magnitude of K and who attempts to maximize π in the process. Whether this is an entrepreneur in the usual sense or a bureaucrat hired to manage enterprise capital, we will nickname this agent "financier".

Once a sharing scheme $\mu=(\mu_0,\ldots,\mu_m)$ is fixed, we imagine that workers and financier adjust their behavior until an equilibrium is reached. It is at such enterprise equilibria, as defined through various game-theoretic solution concepts, that we then evaluate the consequences of instituting μ. Which game-theoretic solution concept best approximates the behavior of agents in value-added sharing enterprises is partly an empirical question, of course, and we will return to this issue after our more formal analysis has shown the implications of differing assumptions in this regard.

Now, from (1)–(3), workers' effective utility functions are given by

$$u_{ij}(x,K;\mu)=\mu_i(Y-\rho K)-c_i x_{ij}^{\gamma_i} \qquad (i\in M,\ j\in N_i), \tag{6}$$

where $x=(x_{11},\ldots,x_{1n_1},\ldots,x_{m1},\ldots,x_{mn_m})$ is the workers' joint behavior. We assume that workers choose their joint behavior x *cooperatively*, i.e. so as to maximize[4]

$$U=\sum_M\sum_{N_i}u_{ij}(x,K,\mu). \tag{7}$$

The financier is supposed to choose K so as to maximize profit π. At any given sharing scheme μ, workers' joint behavior x will depend on the decision K of the financier, as will K depend on x. Regarding the adjustment of workers' and the financier's behaviors to one another at any given μ, we consider three modes, corresponding to the workers being von Stackelberg leader, the financier being von Stackelberg leader, and the Nash solution (with neither as a leader). We also study the case where workers and financier cooperate in the choice of x and K and show this to be a special case of the von Stackelberg solution with labor leading. Which ever of these solution concepts we use, we will refer to the resulting collective behavior (x,K) as an *enterprise equilibrium*.

The next section presents and compares the equilibrium outcomes corresponding, at any given μ, to each of the solution concepts of interest. It is on the basis of this information that, in the section thereafter, we will be able to determine the sharing system that would be chosen, should the authority to design μ be given to either the financier, the workers, or to an agency representing their communal interests, and to evaluate and compare

[4]The fact that workers' utility is separable in income and leisure, with constant marginal utility of income, implies that maximizing (7) will yield a collective behavior x which, together with *ex post* lump-sum transfers of income, can Pareto dominate any other behavior and set of lump-sum transfers. See Kleindorfer and Sertel (1976) and Groves (1978) for discussions.

the equilibrium outcomes under the various institutional set-ups that arise from the three alternative modes of adjustment between K and x and the three possible ways of designing μ in each case.

3. Comparisons at any common sharing system

In this section we work with a given sharing system μ with $0 \leqslant \mu_0 \leqslant 1$, and compare the outcomes of value-added sharing according to μ under the types of solution, mentioned above, to the ensuing game between the financier and the workers, the workers cooperating among themselves. Toward all this, first we compute the reaction $\overline{K}(L)$ of the financier to the aggregate labor input $L = \prod_M L_i^{\beta_i}$ of the workers. The first-order condition for maximizing profit, $\pi = \mu_0 V$, gives

$$\overline{K}(\ell) = \left(\frac{\alpha}{\rho}\right)^{1/(1-\alpha)} \ell, \tag{8}$$

a linear function of the aggregate

$$\ell = L^{1/(1-\alpha)} = \left(\prod_M L_i^{\beta_i}\right)^{1/(1-\alpha)}. \tag{9}$$

Substituting $\overline{K}(\ell)$ for K in Y and V gives, respectively,

$$\overline{Y}(\ell) = \left(\frac{\alpha}{\rho}\right)^{1/(1-\alpha)} \ell \tag{10}$$

and

$$\overline{V}(\ell) = (1-\alpha)\overline{Y}(\ell) = \left[(1-\alpha)\left(\frac{\alpha}{\rho}\right)^{\alpha/(1-\alpha)}\right]\ell. \tag{11}$$

Turning now to the workers, at any given level of K and at any positive $\mu^0 = 1 - \mu_0$, their cooperative behavior $\underline{x}$ is found by maximizing

$$U = \sum_M \sum_{N_i} u_{ij} = \mu^0 V - \sum_M c_i \sum_{N_i} x_{ij}^{\gamma_i}, \tag{12}$$

which is easily computed to be the behavior $\underline{x}$ with $\underline{x}_{ij} = \underline{x}_i$, $j \in N_i$, and

$$\underline{x}_i = \left[\frac{\mu^0 \beta_i K^\alpha \underline{L}(K;\mu^0)}{n_i c_i \gamma_i}\right]^{1/\gamma_i} \qquad (i \in M), \tag{13}$$

where

$$\underline{L}(K;\mu^0) = (D\mu^0 K^\alpha)^{\theta/(1-\theta)} \tag{14}$$

with

$$D=\left(\prod_M n_i^{\beta_i}\left(\frac{\theta_i}{n_i c_i}\right)^{\theta_i}\right)^{1/\theta}; \tag{15}$$

$$\theta=\sum_M \theta_i; \qquad \theta_i=\frac{\beta_i}{\gamma_i} \qquad (i\in M); \tag{16}$$

and from which we define the parameter

$$\zeta=1-\alpha-\theta>0, \tag{17}$$

where $\zeta>0$ follows from (2) and (16).

From $\underline{L}(K;\mu^0)$ we also obtain $\underline{\ell}(K;\mu^0)=(\underline{L}(K;\mu^0))^{1/(1-\alpha)}$ as the reaction of the aggregate ℓ chosen cooperatively by the workers facing a capital goods input level K. Inverting $\underline{\ell}(K;\mu^0)$ to obtain K as a function of ℓ gives, equivalently,

$$\underline{K}(\ell;\mu^0)=\left[\frac{\ell^{(\zeta+\alpha\theta)/\theta}}{(\mu^0 D)}\right]^{1/\alpha}, \tag{18}$$

and, by substituting $\underline{K}(\ell;\mu^0)$ for K in Y and V, we get, respectively,

$$\underline{Y}(\ell;\mu^0)=\frac{\ell^{(1-\alpha)/\theta}}{(\mu^0 D)} \tag{19}$$

and

$$\underline{V}(\ell;\mu^0)=\underline{Y}(\ell;\mu^0)-\rho\underline{K}(\ell;\mu^0). \tag{20}$$

Now when the workers each provide a zero labor input, they all achieve zero utility and $U=0$. It will be useful to know the minimal total income that they, as a group, must receive in order to provide, at minimal total disutility $\Sigma_M c_i \Sigma_{n_i} x_{ij}^{\gamma_i}$ of work, any given level L of aggregate labor input without achieving less utility U than when none of them participates positively in production. This quantity we refer to, in the fashion of Dirickx and Sertel (1978), as the *subsistence income*, denoting it by S.

As a function of L, we find $S(L)$ by minimizing $\Sigma_M n_i c_i x_i^{\gamma_i}$, where $x_i=x_{ij}$ of the typical (jth) member of the ith group of workers, subject to $\Pi_M(n_i x_i)^{\beta_i}=L$. The solution to this simple minimization problem, expressed as a function of ℓ, is

$$S(\ell)=(\theta/D)\ell^{(1-\alpha)/\theta}. \tag{21}$$

With $\bar{V}(\ell)$, $\underline{V}(\ell)$ and $S(\ell)$ in hand, we can now identify the three solutions of interest. We start with the *Nash solution*

$$\bar{\underline{\ell}}(\mu^0)=\left[\left(\frac{\alpha}{\rho}\right)^{\alpha/(1-\alpha)}(\mu^0 D)\right]^{\theta/\zeta}, \tag{22}$$

which is obtained for any fixed $\mu^0 \in [0,1]$ as the (unique) solution to the equation

$$\bar{K}(\ell)=\underline{K}(\ell;\mu^0). \tag{23}$$

From (21) and (22) we compute value added at the Nash solution to be

$$\bar{V}(\bar{\underline{\ell}}(\mu^0))=\underline{V}(\bar{\underline{\ell}}(\mu^0);\mu^0)=(1-\alpha)\left[\left(\frac{\alpha}{\rho}\right)^{\alpha}(\mu^0 D)^{\theta}\right]^{1/\zeta}. \tag{24}$$

Similarly, other quantities of interest (output, utility, etc.) can be obtained from (21), and these are all tabulated in table 9.1.

Turning to the von Stackelberg solutions, when the workers lead, their total income is $\mu^0\bar{V}(\ell)$ and, since they determine their labor inputs cooperatively, their class utility becomes

$$\bar{U}(\ell;\mu^0)=\mu^0\bar{V}(\ell)-S(\ell). \tag{25}$$

Thus, when the workers lead, they choose ℓ so as to maximize $\bar{U}(\ell;\mu^0)$. For any positive μ^0 the solution $\bar{\ell}(\mu^0)$ to this maximization problem is again unique and, in fact,

$$\bar{\ell}(\mu^0)=\bar{\underline{\ell}}(\mu^0), \tag{26}$$

so that the *von Stackelberg solution with workers leading* coincides with the Nash solution (22). Moreover, when capital and labor cooperate, jointly maximizing *communal surplus* (see Dirickx and Sertel, 1978)

$$Z=\Pi+U=\mu_0 V+\mu^0 V-S=V-S, \tag{27}$$

it is easy to see that the resulting *cooperative solution* will be the labor-leading solution with $\mu^0=1$ (and $K=\bar{K}(\bar{\ell}(1))$).

When the financier leads, his utility, i.e. the profit, is $\mu_0\underline{V}(\ell;\mu^0)$, the maximization of which, subject to the constraint that workers' incomes exceed the subsistence level $S(\ell)$, gives

$$\underline{\ell}(\mu^0)=\begin{cases}\left[\left(\dfrac{\alpha}{\rho(1-\theta)}\right)^{\alpha/(1-\alpha)}(\mu^0 D)\right]^{\theta/\zeta}, & \text{if } \alpha\leqslant(1-\theta)^2,\\[2ex] \left[\left(\dfrac{1-\theta}{\rho}\right)^{\alpha/(1-\alpha)}(\mu^0 D)\right]^{\theta/\zeta}, & \text{if } \alpha\geqslant(1-\theta)^2,\end{cases} \tag{28}$$

Table 9.1

Comparing the outcomes of solution concepts at a common $\mu^0 \in [0, 1]$.

	Labor leading or Nash[a] cooperative (at $\mu^0 = 1$)	Capital leading[b] $[\alpha \leqslant (1-\theta)^2]$	Capital leading[b] $[\alpha \geqslant (1-\theta)^2]$
1. Output	$\bar{Y}[\mu^0] = \left[\left(\frac{\alpha}{\rho}\right)^{\alpha} (\mu^0 D)^{\theta}\right]^{1/\zeta}$	$\underline{Y}[\mu^0] = \left(\frac{1}{1-\theta}\right)^{\alpha/\zeta} \bar{Y}[\mu^0]$	$\underline{Y}[\mu^0] = \left(\frac{1-\theta}{\alpha}\right)^{\alpha/\zeta} \bar{Y}[\mu^0]$
2. Value added	$\bar{V}[\mu^0] = (1-\alpha)\bar{Y}[\mu^0]$	$\underline{V}[\mu^0] = \frac{\zeta}{1-\theta}\underline{Y}[\mu^0]$	$\underline{V}[\mu^0] = \theta \underline{Y}[\mu^0]$
3. Capital	$\bar{K}[\mu^0] = \frac{\alpha}{\rho}\bar{Y}[\mu^0]$	$\underline{K}[\mu^0] = \frac{\alpha}{\rho(1-\theta)}\underline{Y}[\mu^0]$	$\underline{K}[\mu^0] = \left(\frac{1-\theta}{\rho}\right)\underline{Y}[\mu^0]$
4. Labor input (of a typical worker of type i)	$\bar{x}_i[\mu^0] = \left[\frac{\theta_i}{n_i c_i}\mu^0 \bar{Y}[\mu^0]\right]^{1/\gamma_i}$	$\underline{x}_i[\mu^0] = \left[\frac{\theta_i}{n_i c_i}\mu^0 \underline{Y}[\mu^0]\right]^{1/\gamma_i}$	$\underline{x}_i[\mu^0] = \left[\frac{\theta_i}{n_i c_i}\mu^0 \underline{Y}[\mu^0]\right]^{1/\gamma_i}$
5. Aggregate labor (of workers of type i)	$\bar{L}_i[\mu^0] = n_i \bar{x}_i[\mu^0]$	$\underline{L}_i[\mu^0] = n_i \underline{x}_i[\mu^0]$	$\underline{L}_i[\mu^0] = n_i \underline{x}_i[\mu^0]$
6. Output–capital ratio	$\bar{Y}[\mu^0]/\bar{K}[\mu^0] = \rho/\alpha$	$\underline{Y}[\mu^0]/\underline{K}[\mu^0] = \rho(1-\theta)/\alpha$	$\underline{Y}[\mu^0]/\underline{K}[\mu^0] = \rho/(1-\theta)$
7. Output–labor ratio (for type i labor)	$\bar{Y}[\mu^0]/\bar{L}_i[\mu^0] = \left[\frac{c_i}{\theta_i \mu^0}\left(\frac{\bar{Y}[\mu^0]}{n_i}\right)^{\gamma_i - 1}\right]^{1/\gamma_i}$	$\underline{Y}[\mu^0]/\underline{L}_i[\mu^0] = \left[\frac{c_i}{\theta_i \mu^0}\left(\frac{\underline{Y}[\mu^0]}{n_i}\right)^{\gamma_i - 1}\right]^{1/\gamma_i}$	$\underline{Y}[\mu^0]/\underline{L}_i[\mu^0] = \left[\frac{c_i}{\theta_i \mu^0}\left(\frac{\underline{Y}[\mu^0]}{n_i}\right)^{\gamma_i - 1}\right]^{1/\gamma_i}$
8. Income (of a typical worker of type i)	$\bar{y}_i[\mu^0] = \mu_i \bar{V}[\mu^0]$	$\underline{y}_i[\mu^0] = \mu_i \underline{V}[\mu^0]$	$\underline{y}_i[\mu^0] = \mu_i \underline{V}[\mu^0]$
9. Utility (of a typical worker of type i)	$\bar{u}_i[\mu] = \left(\mu_i(1-\alpha) - \frac{\mu^0\theta_i}{n_i}\right)\bar{Y}[\mu^0]$	$\underline{u}_i[\mu] = \left(\mu_i \frac{\zeta}{1-\theta} - \frac{\mu^0\theta_i}{n_i}\right)\underline{Y}[\mu^0]$	$\underline{u}_i[\mu] = 0$
10. Workers' aggregate utility	$\bar{U}[\mu^0] = \zeta\mu^0\bar{Y}[\mu^0]$	$\underline{U}[\mu^0] = \frac{(1-\theta)^2 - \alpha}{1-\theta}\mu^0\underline{Y}[\mu^0]$	$\underline{U}[\mu^0] = 0$
11. Profit	$\bar{\Pi}[\mu^0] = (1-\mu^0)\bar{V}[\mu^0]$	$\underline{\Pi}[\mu^0] = (1-\mu^0)\underline{V}[\mu^0]$	$\underline{\Pi}[\mu^0] = (1-\mu^0)\underline{V}[\mu^0]$
12. Communal surplus	$\bar{Z}[\mu^0] = (1-\alpha-\theta\mu^0)\bar{Y}[\mu^0]$	$\underline{Z}[\mu^0] = \left(\frac{\zeta}{1-\theta} - \theta\mu^0\right)\underline{Y}[\mu^0]$	$\underline{Z}[\mu^0] = (1-\mu^0)\theta\underline{Y}[\mu^0]$

[a]All quantities are evaluated at $\bar{\ell}(\mu^0)$, e.g. $\bar{Y}[\mu^0] = \bar{Y}(\bar{\ell}(\mu^0))$.

[b]All quantities are evaluated at $\underline{\ell}(\mu^0)$, e.g. $\underline{Y}[\mu^0] = \underline{Y}(\underline{\ell}(\mu^0); \mu^0)$.

[c]$\mu = (\mu_0, \mu_1, \ldots, \mu_n)$ such that $\Sigma n_i \mu_i = \mu^0$.

as the *von Stackelberg solution with capital leading.* When $\alpha \geqslant (1-\theta)^2$ workers earn only subsistence income and $U=0$. Otherwise their income exceeds the subsistence level and $U>0$. Again the results of substituting (28) into various quantities of interest are tabulated in table 9.1.

Our next task will be to compare the magnitudes of the quantities listed in table 9.1. For this a geometric analysis is useful. In fig. 9.1 below we show the general relationship between the functions $\bar{V}$, $\underline{V}(\cdot\,;\mu^0)$, and S and the solutions $\bar{\ell}(\mu^0)$, $\underline{\ell}(\mu^0)$, and $\bar{\underline{\ell}}(\mu^0)$. Fig. 9.1(a) illustrates the case $\alpha \leqslant (1-\theta)^2$.

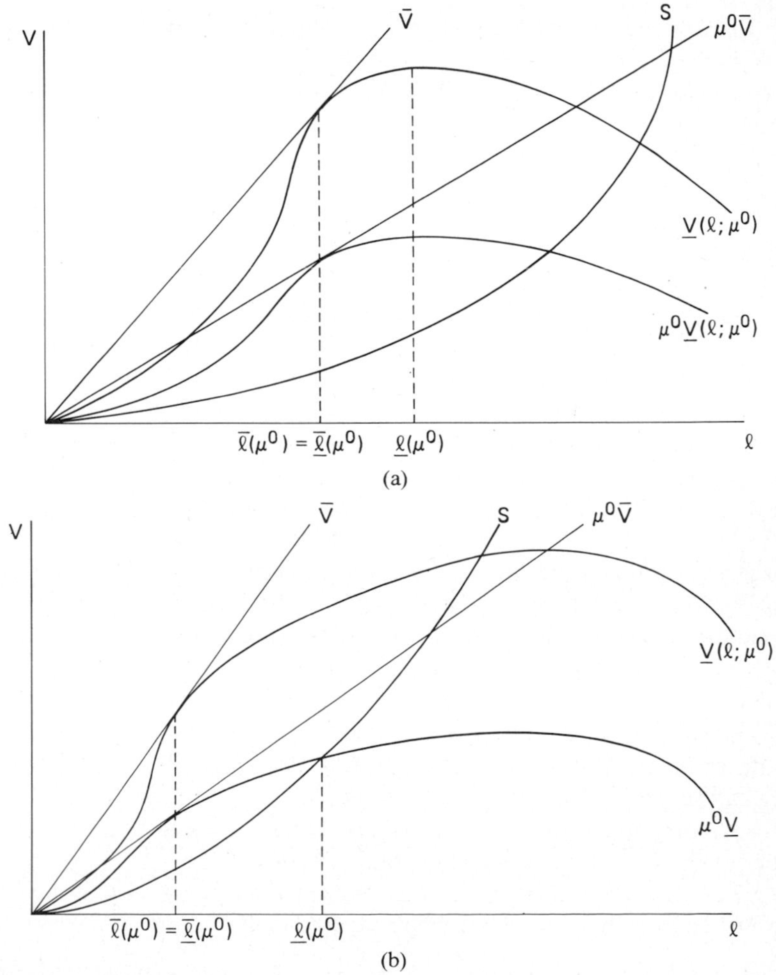

Figure 9.1. Comparing solution concepts at a common $\mu^0 \in (0,1)$. (a) The case $[\alpha \leqslant (1-\theta)^2]$. (b) The case $[\alpha > (1-\theta)^2]$.

In this case the profit-maximizing labor input $\underline{\ell}(\mu^0)$ (which is also the labor input at which $\underline{V}(\cdot;\mu^0)$ and $\mu^0\underline{V}(\cdot;\mu^0)$ are maximized, since these are proportional to profit) occurs at a point where workers' income $\mu^0\underline{V}(\underline{\ell}(\mu^0);\mu^0)$ is above subsistence. Fig. 9.1(b) illustrates the case $\alpha>(1-\theta)^2$, where the unconstrained profit-maximizing solution fails to provide subsistence requirements for the workers.

The geometry of fig. 9.1 is characterized through the following results, which are verified in appendix A.

P1. Fix $\mu^0\in[0,1]$. Then $\bar{V}(\ell)\geqslant\underline{V}(\ell;\mu^0)$ for all $\ell\geqslant 0$, with $\bar{V}(\ell)=\underline{V}(\ell;\mu^0)$ if and only if $\ell=0$ or $\ell=\bar{\underline{\ell}}(\mu^0)$. Moreover, if $\mu^0>0$, then $\bar{V}$ and $\underline{V}(\cdot;\mu^0)$ (and therefore also $\mu^0\bar{V}$ and $\mu^0\underline{V}(\cdot;\mu^0)$) have the same positive slope at $\ell=\underline{\ell}(\mu^0)$ $=\underline{\ell}(\mu^0)$.

P2. $\bar{V}$ and S are monotonically increasing, with $\bar{V}$ linear and S strictly convex; for any $\mu^0\in(0,1]$, $\mu^0\bar{V}(\ell)=S(\ell)$ at precisely two points: $\ell=0$ and a unique positive ℓ depending on μ^0.

P3. Fix $\mu^0\in(0,1]$. Then $\underline{V}(\cdot;\mu^0)$ is first convex and thereafter concave. Furthermore, $\mu^0\underline{V}(\ell;\mu^0)=S(\ell)$ at precisely two points: $\ell=0$ and a unique positive ℓ. Between these two points of intersection $\mu^0\underline{V}(\ell;\mu^0)$ exceeds $S(\ell)$.

We can now compare the results of labor leading (or the Nash solution) with capital leading at any common workers' share $\mu^0\in(0,1]$. (We delay our comparisons of these with the cooperative solution until later.)

Theorem 1. Comparing the results corresponding to the solution concepts, labor leading, capital leading, and Nash, we find for the preferences and production technology in (1) and (2) that, when evaluated at any common $\mu^0\in(0,1]$, the Nash solution is identical with the labor-leading solution, and that:

(i) Output (Y), value added (V), capital (K), workers' inputs (x_i and L_i) and incomes (y_i), profits (Π), and output–labor ratios (Y/L_i) are all higher when capital leads than when labor leads.

(ii) Labor's total utility (U) and the output–capital ratio (Y/K) are higher when labor leads than when capital leads.

(iii) Participants' utilities (u_i) and communal surplus (Z) may be higher or lower when labor leads than when capital leads.

Proof. Fixing any $\mu^0\in(0,1]$, we will proceed by comparing the corresponding entries in table 9.1.

(*ad* i): First recall from (17) that $\zeta = 1 - \alpha - \theta > 0$. From table 9.1, therefore, $\bar{Y}[\mu^0] < \underline{Y}[\mu^0]$, and this implies that capital, workers' inputs, incomes, and output–labor ratios are also higher when capital leads than when labor leads. Finally, $\bar{V}[\mu^0] < \underline{V}[\mu^0]$ from the geometry of fig. 9.1, since (by P2) $\bar{V}(\bar{\ell}(\mu^0)) = \underline{V}(\bar{\ell}(\mu^0); \mu^0)$ and therefore the positive slope of $\underline{V}(\cdot; \mu^0)$ at $\bar{\ell}(\mu^0)$ implies

$$\bar{V}[\mu^0] \equiv \bar{V}(\bar{\ell}(\mu^0)) = \underline{V}(\bar{\ell}(\mu^0)) < \max\{\underline{V}(\ell; \mu^0) \mid \ell \geqslant 0\} \equiv \underline{V}[\mu^0]. \quad (29)$$

(*ad* ii): Since $\bar{Y}[\mu^0]/\bar{K}[\mu^0]$ is clearly greater than $\underline{Y}[\mu^0]/\underline{K}[\mu^0]$, we need only verify $\bar{U}[\mu^0] > \underline{U}[\mu^0]$. This follows since the von Stackelberg solution with workers leading $(\bar{\ell}(\mu^0))$ uniquely maximizes $\bar{U}(\ell)$. Moreover, workers' utility ($\bar{U}$ or $\underline{U}$) in fig. 9.1 is represented by the distance between $\mu^0 V$ and S, so that, from fig. 9.1, $\bar{U}(\ell)$ exceeds $\underline{U}(\ell)$ everywhere except at $\ell = 0$ and $\ell = \bar{\ell}(\mu^0)$. In particular,

$$\bar{U}[\mu^0] \equiv \bar{U}(\bar{\ell}(\mu^0)) > \bar{U}(\underline{\ell}(\mu^0)) > \underline{U}(\underline{\ell}(\mu^0)) \equiv \underline{U}[\mu^0]. \quad (30)$$

(*ad* iii): Our proof here, given in appendix B, consists of giving examples showing that utilities and communal surplus may be higher or lower when capital leads than when labor leads, depending on the particular preferences, technology and sharing system in question.

Remark 1. From the above we see that, for any fixed sharing scheme, some workers may prefer that capital leads if their total remuneration is just their share $\mu_i V$ of value added. In fact, however, the philosophy underlying the cooperative objective function (6) allows that *ex post* lump-sum transfers of income also take place among workers. In particular, since $\bar{U}[\mu^0] > \underline{U}[\mu^0]$ and, because of the form of the utility function (1), it is straightforward to show (as done, for example, in Kleindorfer and Sertel, 1978) that, for any fixed sharing scheme $(\mu_0, \ldots, \mu_m)$, there always exists a set of lump-sum income transfers with which each worker is better off when labor leads than when capital leads. In a similar vein, the cooperative solution entails communal surplus $Z = \bar{Z}[1]$ and, as we show below, this exceeds $\underline{Z}[\mu^0]$ for any $\mu^0 \in (0, 1]$. Thus, a lump-sum income transfer scheme can be designed so that everyone, workers and financier alike, prefers the cooperative solution to either capital-leading or labor-leading.

Remark 2. Since the Nash solution here coincides with the von Stackelberg solution with labor leading, we shall henceforth restrict attention to the two von Stackelberg solutions, with capital or labor leading, only occasionally referring to the Nash solution. (Generally, of course, the Nash solution need coincide with neither von Stackelberg solution.)

4. Comparisons at respective optimal sharing schemes

In this section we first determine, for the solution concepts of interest, optimal sharing schemes from the viewpoint of labor, of capital (i.e. of the financier), and of labor and capital in cooperation. Thereafter we compare the outcomes of these solution concepts at their respective optimal sharing schemes. The respective objectives of labor, capital, and the labor–capital "community" are taken to be workers' aggregate utility (U), profit (Π), and communal surplus (Z).

Theorem 2. Let preferences and production technology be given by (1) and (2). Then, evaluating workers' aggregate utility (U), profit (Π), and communal surplus (Z) at the respective enterprise equilibria corresponding to the von Stackelberg solution concept with labor leading (which coincides with the Nash solution) and that with capital leading, we find that:

(i) Both $\overline{U}[\mu^0]$ and $\underline{U}[\mu^0]$ achieve their maximum over $\mu^0 \in [0,1]$ at $\mu^0 = 1$. Thus, the optimal workers' share when labor chooses is $\mu^0 = 1$, irrespective of whether the solution concept representing enterprise equilibrium is labor leading or capital leading.

(ii) Both $\overline{\Pi}[\mu^0]$ and $\underline{\Pi}[\mu^0]$ achieve their maximum over $\mu^0 \in [0,1]$ at $\mu^0 = \theta/(1-\alpha)$. Thus, the optimal workers' share when the financier chooses is $\mu^0 = \theta/(1-\alpha) < 1$, irrespective of whether the solution concept representing enterprise equilibrium is labor leading or capital leading.

(iii) $\overline{Z}[\mu^0]$ achieves its maximum over $\mu^0 \in [0,1]$ at $\mu^0 = 1$. $\underline{Z}[\mu^0]$ achieves its maximum over $\mu^0 \in [0,1]$ at

$$\mu^0 = \begin{cases} \dfrac{1-\alpha-\theta}{(1-\alpha)(1-\theta)}, & \text{if } \alpha \leqslant (1-\theta)^2, \\[2ex] \dfrac{\theta}{(1-\alpha)}, & \text{if } \alpha \geqslant (1-\theta)^2. \end{cases} \tag{31}$$

(Thus, when labor leads communal surplus is maximized at the workers' share $\mu^0 = 1$, and when capital leads at the workers' share μ^0 in (31).)

Proof. Straightforward application of first-order conditions to the respective maximands, given in table 9.1, establishes the assertions. □

Remark 3. From theorem 2 and the definition of the cooperative solution (see (27)), we see that the cooperative solution coincides with the labor-leading solution when labor chooses the design ($\mu^0 = 1$). (The only difference between outcomes here would be in the distribution of V between π

and $\{y_i \mid i \in M\}$, with consequences also for $\{U_i \mid i \in M\}$. Apart from distributional matters, however, the two solutions are identical.) We therefore suppress special reference to the cooperative solution until section 5.

Notation. Henceforth we denote quantities evaluated at labor's optimal design, $\mu^0 = 1$, by a superscript asterisk (*) (e.g. $\underline{Y}^* = \underline{Y}[1]$); quantities evaluated at the capitalist's optimal design, $\mu^0 = \theta/(1-\alpha)$, by a subscript asterisk (e.g. $\underline{Y}_* = \underline{Y}[\theta/(1-\alpha)]$); and quantities evaluated at the communally optimal design by a superscript *and* a subscript asterisk (e.g. $\overline{Y}^*_* = \overline{Y}[1]$ and $\underline{Y}^*_*[\zeta/(\zeta+\alpha\theta)]$ or $\underline{Y}[\theta/(1-\alpha)]$ as α is $<$ or $\geqslant (1-\theta)^2$). From the starred quantities just defined, we also define the vectors Y^*, Y_*, Y^*_*, V^*, V_*, V^*_*, etc. as follows:

$$Y^* = (\overline{Y}^*, \underline{Y}^*); \qquad Y_* = (\overline{Y}_*, \underline{Y}_*); \qquad Y^*_* = (\overline{Y}^*_*, \underline{Y}^*_*);$$

$$V^* = (\overline{V}^*, \underline{V}^*); \qquad V_* = (\overline{V}_*, \underline{V}_*); \qquad V^*_* = (\overline{V}^*_*, \underline{V}^*_*); \quad \text{etc.}$$

Finally, for any vectors $x, y \in R^n$, $x \leqslant y$ means "$\leqslant$" applies componentwise to x and y.

Tables 9.2(a)–(c) provide a comparison of quantities of interest at the optimal sharing designs. These results are obtained simply from table 9.1 by substituting for μ^0 the optimal workers' share as given by theorem 2. In analogy with theorem 1, we now summarize comparisons of interest in the following theorem for the various optimal sharing schemes.

Theorem 3. Let all be as in theorem 2. Comparing labor-optimal, profit-maximizing, and communally optimal designs, we find that:

(i) Output (Y), value added (V), capital (K), workers' inputs (x_i and L_i, $i \in M$), and workers' aggregate utility (U) are highest at the labor-optimal design ($\mu^0 = 1$) and lowest at the profit-maximizing design ($\mu^0 = \theta/(1-\alpha)$), irrespective of whether capital leads or labor leads. That is,

$$x_{i*} \leqslant x^*_{i*} \leqslant x^*_i; \qquad L_{i*} \leqslant L^*_{i*} \leqslant L^*_i \qquad (i \in M);$$

$$Y_* \leqslant Y^*_* \leqslant Y^*; \qquad V_* \leqslant V^*_* \leqslant V^*; \qquad K_* \leqslant K^*_* \leqslant K^*; \qquad U_* \leqslant U^*_* \leqslant U^*.$$

(ii) When labor leads, the output–capital ratio (Y/K) is ζ/α; and when capital leads the output–capital ratio is $\max[\zeta(1-\theta)/\alpha, \zeta/(1-\theta)]$. In particular, the output–capital ratio is unaffected by the particular sharing scheme instituted.

(iii) The output–labor ratio for the ith group of workers (Y/L_i) is highest at the labor-optimal design (resp. at the profit-maximizing design) whenever $\gamma_i\theta$ is greater than (resp. is no greater than) $(1-\alpha)$, and this is so

Table 9.2(a)
Comparisons at respective optimal sharing schemes: labor leading or Nash.

	Labor-optimal design[a] $\mu^0=1$	Profit-maximizing design $\mu^0=\theta/(1-\alpha)$	Communally-optimal design $\mu^0=1$
1. Output	$\bar{Y}^*=\left[\left(\frac{\alpha}{\rho}\right)^{\alpha}D^{\theta}\right]^{1/\zeta}$	$\bar{Y}_*=\left(\frac{\theta}{1-\alpha}\right)^{\theta/\zeta}\bar{Y}^*$	$\bar{Y}^*_*=\bar{Y}^*$
2. Value added	$\bar{V}^*=(1-\alpha)\bar{Y}^*$	$\bar{V}_*=\left(\frac{\theta}{1-\alpha}\right)^{\theta/\zeta}\bar{V}^*$	$\bar{V}^*_*=\bar{V}^*$
3. Capital	$\bar{K}^*=\frac{\alpha}{\rho}\bar{Y}^*$	$\bar{K}_*=\left(\frac{\theta}{1-\alpha}\right)^{\theta/\zeta}\bar{K}^*$	$\bar{K}^*_*=\bar{K}^*$
4. Labor input (of a typical worker of type i)	$\bar{x}_i^*=\left[\frac{\theta_i}{n_ic_i}\bar{Y}^*\right]^{1/\gamma_i}$	$\bar{x}_{i*}=\left(\frac{\theta}{1-\alpha}\right)^{(1-\alpha)/\gamma_i\zeta}\bar{x}_i^*$	$\bar{x}^*_{i*}=\bar{x}_i^*$
5. Aggregate labor (of workers of type i)	$\bar{L}_i^*=n_i\bar{x}_i^*$	$\bar{L}_{i*}=\left(\frac{\theta}{1-\alpha}\right)^{(1-\alpha)/\gamma_i\zeta}\bar{L}_i^*$	$\bar{L}^*_{i*}=\bar{L}_i^*$
6. Output–capital ratio	$\bar{Y}^*/\bar{K}^*=\rho/\alpha$	$\bar{Y}_*/\bar{K}_*=\bar{Y}^*/\bar{K}^*$	$\bar{Y}^*_*/\bar{K}^*_*=\bar{Y}^*/\bar{K}^*$
7. Output–labor ratio (for type i labor)	$\frac{\bar{Y}^*}{\bar{L}_i^*}=\left[\frac{c_i}{\theta_i}\left(\frac{\bar{Y}^*}{n_i}\right)^{\gamma_i-1}\right]^{1/\gamma_i}$	$\frac{\bar{Y}_*}{\bar{L}_{i*}}=\left(\frac{\theta}{1-\alpha}\right)^{[\gamma_i\theta-(1-\alpha)]/\gamma_i\zeta}\frac{\bar{Y}^*}{\bar{L}_i^*}$	$\bar{Y}^*_*/L^*_{i*}=\bar{Y}^*/L_i^*$
8. Income (of a typical worker of type i)	$\bar{y}_i^*=\bar{\mu}_i^*\bar{V}^*$	$\bar{y}_{i*}=\left(\frac{\bar{\mu}_{i*}}{\bar{\mu}_i^*}\right)\left(\frac{\theta}{1-\alpha}\right)^{\theta/\zeta}\bar{y}_i^*$	$\bar{y}^*_{i*}=\bar{y}_i^*$
9. Utility (of a typical worker of type i)[b]	$\bar{u}_i^*=\left(\bar{\mu}_i^*(1-\alpha)-\frac{\theta_i}{n_i}\right)\bar{Y}^*$	$\bar{u}_{i*}=\frac{n_i\bar{\mu}_{i*}(1-\alpha)^2-\theta_i\theta}{n_i\bar{\mu}_i^*(1-\alpha)^2-\theta_i(1-\alpha)}\left(\frac{\theta}{1-\alpha}\right)^{\theta/\zeta}\bar{u}_i^*$	$\bar{u}^*_{i*}=\bar{u}_i^*$
10. Workers' aggregate utility	$\bar{U}^*=\zeta\bar{Y}^*$	$\bar{U}_*=\left(\frac{\theta}{1-\alpha}\right)^{(1-\alpha)/\zeta}\bar{U}^*$	$\bar{U}^*_*=\bar{U}^*$
11. Profit	$\bar{\Pi}^*=0$	$\bar{\Pi}_*=\left(\frac{\zeta}{1-\alpha}\right)\bar{V}_*$	$\bar{\Pi}^*_*=\bar{\Pi}^*$
12. Communal surplus	$\bar{Z}^*=\bar{U}^*$	$\bar{Z}_*=\left(1+\frac{\theta}{1-\alpha}\right)\left(\frac{\theta}{1-\alpha}\right)^{\theta/\zeta}\bar{Z}^*$	$\bar{Z}^*_*=\bar{Z}^*$

[a] This column also represents the cooperative solution as per remark 3.

[b] Evaluated at any fixed $\bar{\mu}_i^*$ and $\bar{\mu}_{i*}$ for which $\sum n_i\bar{\mu}_i^*=1$ and $\sum n_i\bar{\mu}_{i*}=\theta/(1-\alpha)$.

Table 9.2(b)

Comparisons at respective optimal sharing schemes: capital leading, $\alpha<(1-\theta)^2$.

	Labor-optimal design $\mu^0=1$	Profit-maximizing design $\mu^0=\theta/(1-\alpha)$	Communally-optimal design $\mu^0=(1-\alpha-\theta)/(1-\alpha)(1-\theta)=\zeta/(\zeta+\alpha\theta)$
1. Output	$\underline{Y}^*=\left[\left(\frac{\alpha}{\rho(1-\theta)}\right)^{\alpha} D^{\theta}\right]^{1/\zeta}$	$\underline{Y}_*=\left(\frac{\theta}{1-\alpha}\right)^{\theta/\zeta}\underline{Y}^*$	$\underline{Y}^*_*=\left(\frac{\zeta}{\zeta+\alpha\theta}\right)^{\theta/\zeta}\underline{Y}^*$
2. Value added	$\underline{V}^*=\left(\frac{\zeta}{1-\theta}\right)\underline{Y}^*$	$\underline{V}_*=\left(\frac{\theta}{1-\alpha}\right)^{\theta/\zeta}\underline{V}^*$	$\underline{V}^*_*=\left(\frac{\zeta}{\zeta+\alpha\theta}\right)^{\theta/\zeta}\underline{V}^*$
3. Capital	$\underline{K}^*=\frac{\alpha}{\rho(1-\theta)}\underline{Y}^*$	$\underline{K}_*=\left(\frac{\theta}{1-\alpha}\right)^{\theta/\zeta}\underline{K}^*$	$\underline{K}^*_*=\left(\frac{\zeta}{\zeta+\alpha\theta}\right)^{\theta/\zeta}\underline{K}^*$
4. Labor input (of a typical worker of type i)	$\underline{x}_i^*=\left[\frac{\theta_i}{n_i c_i}\underline{Y}^*\right]^{1/\gamma_i}$	$\underline{x}_{i*}=\left(\frac{\theta}{1-\alpha}\right)^{(1-\alpha)/\gamma_i\zeta}\underline{x}_i^*$	$\underline{x}^*_{i*}=\left(\frac{\zeta}{\zeta+\alpha\theta}\right)^{(1-\alpha)/\zeta}\underline{x}_i^*$
5. Aggregate labor (of workers of type i)	$\underline{L}_i^*=n_i\underline{x}_i^*$	$\underline{L}_i^*=\left(\frac{\theta}{1-\alpha}\right)^{(1-\alpha)/\gamma_i\zeta}\underline{L}_i^*$	$\underline{L}^*_{i*}=\left(\frac{\zeta}{\zeta+\alpha\theta}\right)^{(1-\alpha)/\zeta}\underline{L}_i^*$
6. Output–capital ratio	$\underline{Y}^*/\underline{K}^*=\rho(1-\theta)/\alpha$	$\underline{Y}_*/\underline{K}_*=\underline{Y}^*/\underline{K}^*$	$\underline{Y}^*_*/\underline{K}^*_*=\underline{Y}^*/\underline{K}^*$
7. Output–labor ratio (for type i labor)	$\frac{\underline{Y}^*}{\underline{L}_i^*}=\left[\frac{c_i}{\theta_i}\left(\frac{\underline{Y}^*}{n_i}\right)^{\gamma_i-1}\right]^{1/\gamma_i}$	$\frac{\underline{Y}_*}{\underline{L}_{i*}}=\left(\frac{\theta}{1-\alpha}\right)^{[\gamma_i\theta-(1-\alpha)]/\gamma_i\zeta}\frac{\underline{Y}^*}{\underline{L}_i^*}$	$\frac{\underline{Y}^*_*}{\underline{L}^*_{i*}}=\left(\frac{\zeta}{\zeta+\alpha\theta}\right)^{[\gamma_i\theta-(1-\alpha)]/\gamma_i\zeta}\frac{\underline{Y}^*}{\underline{L}_i^*}$
8. Income (of a typical worker of type i)[a]	$\underline{y}_i^*=\underline{\mu}_i^*\underline{V}^*$	$\underline{y}_{i*}=\frac{\underline{\mu}_{i*}}{\underline{\mu}_i^*}\left(\frac{\theta}{1-\alpha}\right)^{\theta/\zeta}\underline{y}_i^*$	$\underline{y}^*_{i*}=\frac{\underline{\mu}^*_{i*}}{\underline{\mu}_i^*}\left(\frac{\zeta}{\zeta+\alpha\theta}\right)^{\theta/\zeta}\underline{y}_i^*$
9. Utility (of a typical worker of type i)[a]	$\underline{u}_i^*=\left(\underline{\mu}_i^*\frac{\zeta}{1-\theta}-\frac{\theta_i}{n_i}\right)\underline{Y}^*$	$\underline{u}_{i*}=\frac{n_i\underline{\mu}_{i*}(1-\alpha)\zeta-\theta_i\theta(1-\theta)}{n_i\underline{\mu}_i^*(1-\alpha)\zeta-\theta_i(\zeta+\alpha\theta)}\left(\frac{\theta}{1-\alpha}\right)^{\theta/\zeta}\underline{u}_i^*$	$\underline{u}^*_{i*}=\frac{n_i\underline{\mu}^*_{i*}(\zeta+\alpha\theta)-\theta_i(1-\theta)}{n_i\underline{\mu}_i^*\zeta-\theta_i(1-\theta)}\left(\frac{\zeta}{\zeta+\alpha\theta}\right)^{(1-\alpha)/\zeta}\underline{u}_i^*$
10. Workers' aggregate utility	$\underline{U}^*=\left(\frac{(1-\theta)^2-\alpha}{1-\theta}\right)\underline{Y}^*$	$\underline{U}_*=\left(\frac{\theta}{1-\alpha}\right)^{(1-\alpha)/\zeta}\underline{U}^*$	$\underline{U}^*_*=\left(\frac{\zeta}{\zeta+\alpha\theta}\right)^{(1-\alpha)/\zeta}\underline{U}^*$
11. Profit	$\underline{\Pi}^*=0$	$\underline{\Pi}_*=\left(\frac{\zeta}{1-\alpha}\right)\underline{V}_*$	$\underline{\Pi}^*_*=\left(\frac{\alpha\theta}{(1-\alpha)\zeta}\right)\left(\frac{\zeta}{\theta(1-\theta)}\right)^{\theta/\zeta}\underline{\Pi}_*$
12. Communal surplus	$\underline{Z}^*=\underline{U}^*$	$\underline{Z}_*=\frac{(1-\alpha)\zeta-\theta^2(1-\theta)}{\theta[(1-\theta)^2-\alpha]}\left(\frac{\theta}{1-\alpha}\right)^{(1-\alpha)/\zeta}\underline{Z}^*$	$\underline{Z}^*_*=\left(\frac{(1-\theta)\zeta}{[(1-\theta)^2-\alpha]}\right)\left(\frac{\zeta}{\zeta+\alpha\theta}\right)^{(1-\alpha)/\zeta}\underline{Z}^*$

[a] Evaluated at any fixed $\bar{\mu}^*$, $\bar{\mu}^*_*$ and $\bar{\mu}_*$ for which $\Sigma n_i\bar{\mu}_i^*=1$, $\Sigma n_i\bar{\mu}_{i*}=\theta/(1-\alpha)$, and $\Sigma n_i\mu^*_{i*}=\zeta/(\zeta+\alpha\theta)$.

Table 9.2(c)
Comparisons at respective optimal sharing schemes: capital leading, $\alpha > (1-\theta)^2$.

	Labor-optimal design $\mu^0 = 1$	Profit-maximizing design $\mu^0 = \theta/(1-\alpha)$	Communally-optimal design $\mu^0 = \theta/(1-\alpha)$
1. Output	$\underline{Y}^* = \left[\left(\frac{1-\theta}{\rho}\right)^{\alpha} D^{\theta}\right]^{1/\zeta}$	$\underline{Y}_* = \left(\frac{\theta}{1-\alpha}\right)^{\theta/\zeta} \underline{Y}^*$	$\underline{Y}^*_* = \underline{Y}_*$
2. Value added	$\underline{V}^* = \theta \underline{Y}^*$	$\underline{V}_* = \left(\frac{\theta}{1-\alpha}\right)^{\theta/\zeta} \underline{V}^*$	$\underline{V}^*_* = \underline{V}_*$
3. Capital	$\underline{K}^* = \left(\frac{1-\theta}{\rho}\right)\underline{Y}^*$	$\underline{K}_* = \left(\frac{\theta}{1-\alpha}\right)^{\theta/\zeta} \underline{K}^*$	$\underline{K}^*_* = \underline{K}_*$
4. Labor input (of a typical worker of type i)	$\underline{x}_i^* = \left[\frac{\theta_i}{n_i c_i}\underline{Y}^*\right]^{1/\gamma_i}$	$\underline{x}_{i*} = \left(\frac{\theta}{1-\alpha}\right)^{(1-\alpha)/\gamma_i\zeta} \underline{x}_i^*$	$\underline{x}^*_{i*} = \underline{x}_{i*}$
5. Aggregate labor (of workers of type i)	$\underline{L}_i^* = n_i \underline{x}_i^*$	$\underline{L}_{i*} = \left(\frac{\theta}{1-\alpha}\right)^{(1-\alpha)/\gamma_i\zeta} \underline{L}_i^*$	$\underline{L}^*_{i*} = \underline{L}_{i*}$
6. Output–capital ratio	$\underline{Y}^*/\underline{K}^* = \rho/(1-\theta)$	$\underline{Y}_*/\underline{K}_* = \underline{Y}^*/\underline{K}^*$	$\underline{Y}^*_*/\underline{K}^*_* = \underline{Y}_*/\underline{K}_*$
7. Output–labor ratio (for type i labor)	$\frac{\underline{Y}^*}{\underline{L}_i^*} = \left[\frac{c_i}{\theta_i}\left(\frac{\underline{Y}^*}{n_i}\right)^{\gamma_i - 1}\right]^{1/\gamma_i}$	$\frac{\underline{Y}_*}{\underline{L}_{i*}} = \left(\frac{\theta}{1-\alpha}\right)^{[\gamma_i\theta-(1-\alpha)]/\gamma_i\zeta} \frac{\underline{Y}^*}{\underline{L}_i^*}$	$\underline{Y}^*_*/\underline{L}^*_{i*} = \underline{Y}_*/\underline{L}_{i*}$
8. Income (of a typical worker of type i)[a]	$\underline{y}_i^* = \underline{\mu}_i^* \underline{V}^*$	$\underline{y}_{i*} = \frac{\underline{\mu}_{i*}}{\underline{\mu}_i^*}\left(\frac{\theta}{1-\alpha}\right)^{\theta/\zeta} \underline{y}_i^*$	$\underline{y}^*_{i*} = \underline{y}_{i*}$
9. Utility (of a typical worker of type i)[a]	$\underline{u}_i^* = 0$	$\underline{u}_{i*} = 0$	$\underline{u}^*_{i*} = \underline{u}_{i*}$
10. Workers' aggregate utility	$\underline{U}^* = 0$	$\underline{U}_* = 0$	$\underline{U}^*_* = 0$
11. Profit	$\underline{\Pi}_* = 0$	$\underline{\Pi}_* = \left(\frac{\zeta}{1-\alpha}\right)\underline{V}_*$	$\underline{\Pi}^*_* = \underline{\Pi}_*$
12. Communal surplus	$\underline{Z}^* = 0$	$\underline{Z}_* = \underline{\Pi}_*$	$\underline{Z}^*_* = \underline{Z}_*$

[a]Evaluated at any fixed $\bar{\mu}^*$ and $\bar{\mu}_* = \bar{\mu}^*_*$ for which $\Sigma n_i \bar{\mu}_i^* = 1$ and $\Sigma n_i \bar{\mu}_{i*} = \theta/(1-\alpha)$.

irrespective of whether capital leads or labor leads. That is,

$$Y_*/L_{i*} \leqslant Y^*_*/L^*_{i*} \leqslant Y^*/L^*_i, \quad \text{if } \gamma_i\theta > (1-\alpha);$$

and

$$Y^*/L^*_i \leqslant Y^*_*/L^*_{i*} \leqslant Y_*/L_{i*}, \quad \text{if } \gamma_i\theta \leqslant (1-\alpha).$$

(iv) The incomes (y_i) and utilities (u_i) of workers of any fixed group $i \in M$ may be highest at either the labor-optimal, the profit-maximizing, or the communally-optimal design, depending on the particular preferences and production technology obtaining. However, total workers' income ($\mu^0 V$) is always highest at the labor-optimal design ($\mu^0 = 1$) and lowest at the capitalist-optimal design ($\mu^0 = \theta/(1-\alpha)$).

(v) Profit (Π) is highest at the profit-maximizing design ($\mu^0 = \theta/(1-\alpha)$) and lowest at the labor-optimal design ($\mu^0 = 1$), irrespective of whether capital leads or labor leads. That is,

$$\Pi^* \leqslant \Pi^*_* \leqslant \Pi_*.$$

(vi) Communal surplus is highest at the communally-optimal design. That is,

$$Z^*_* \geqslant \max\left[Z_*, Z^*\right].$$

Moreover, when labor leads, communal surplus is higher at the labor-optimal design than at the profit-maximizing design (i.e. $\bar{Z}^* > \bar{Z}_*$); and when capital leads, communal surplus may be higher or lower at the labor-optimal design ($\mu^0 = 1$) than at the capitalist-optimal design ($\mu^0 = \theta/(1-\alpha)$).

Proof. Most of the above assertions follow directly from table 9.2 or from the definition of the labor-optimal, profit-maximizing, or communally-optimal designs as maximizing, respectively, U, Π, and Z. The only nonobvious assertions are (iv) and, from (i) and (vi), the assertions that $\underline{U}^*_* > \underline{U}_*$ when $\alpha < (1-\theta)^2$ and that $\underline{Z}^*$ may exceed or be less than $\underline{Z}_*$. These we now verify.

Assertion (iv) simply records the fact that the relative orderings of y_i and u_i are not determined alone by the total workers' share μ^0, but also by the distribution of shares to each worker class, with the consequence that one or another group of workers may be made better off under some profit-maximizing or communally-optimal sharing schemes than under some labor-optimal sharing schemes, even though the latter always provides the highest aggregate welfare (U) and income ($\mu^0 V$) to the workers.[5] The

[5] See also remark 1 in this regard.

details of the proof here are analogous to those of theorem 1 (iii) and are hence omitted.

When $\alpha<(1-\theta)^2, \zeta=(1-\alpha-\theta)>(1-\theta)-(1-\theta)^2=\theta(1-\theta)$. Now, from table 9.2(b),

$$\frac{\underline{U}_*}{\underline{U}_*^*}=\left(\frac{\theta(1-\theta)}{1-\alpha-\theta}\right)^{(1-\alpha)/(1-\alpha-\theta)}, \tag{31}$$

so that $\underline{U}_*/\underline{U}_*^*<1$ whenever $\alpha<(1-\theta)^2$.

Concerning $\underline{Z}^*$ and $\underline{Z}_*$, we note from table 9.2(c) that $\underline{Z}^*<\underline{Z}_*$ whenever $\alpha\geqslant(1-\theta)^2$. So now assume $\alpha<(1-\theta)^2$. Then, from table 9.2(b), $\underline{Z}^*/\underline{Z}_*$ exceeds unity as α approaches $(1-\theta)^2$. To see that $\underline{Z}^*<\underline{Z}_*$ can also obtain, fix $\alpha\in(0,1)$ and let θ approach zero (so that $\alpha<(1-\theta)^2$ will certainly hold). Then, from table 9.2(b), $\underline{Z}^*/\underline{Z}_*$ approaches zero, and thus $\underline{Z}^*<\underline{Z}_*$ whenever θ is sufficiently small.

A further matter of interest is the comparison, at the optimal designs, of the equilibrium consequences resulting when labor leads with those resulting when capital leads. These are comparisons between corresponding entries in tables 9.2(a) and 9.2(b) (if $\alpha<(1-\theta)^2$) or table 9.2(c) (if $\alpha\geqslant(1-\theta)^2$). Happily, very little additional work is required to obtain these comparisons, since the profit-maximizing and labor-optimal designs are independent of whether capital or labor leads. Thus, theorem 1 provides complete informa-

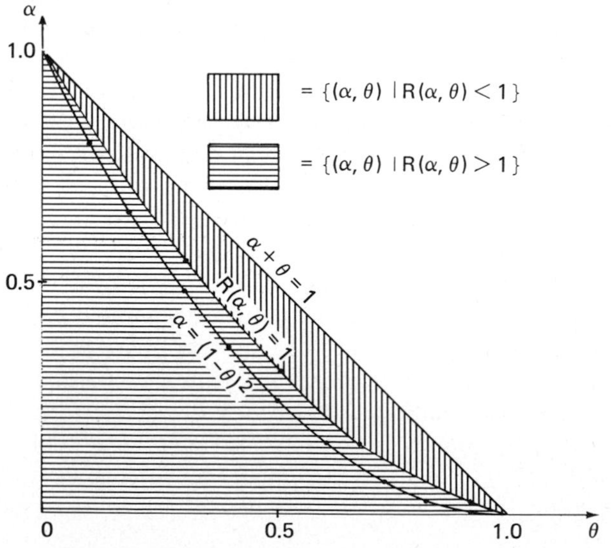

Figure 9.2. Comparing labor leading with capital leading.

tion in comparing the equilibrium consequences of either labor leading and profit-maximizing leading when considered at either the labor- or profit-maximizing design. For example, from theorem 1(i) output and value added are higher when capital leads than when labor leads, regardless of whether capital or labor chooses the design.

What theorem 1 does not answer are comparisons between profit-maximizing and labor leading at the communally optimal design, since here the optimal design is not the same when labor leads as when capital leads. As it turns out, however, no general dominance results are possible in this case. To illustrate, we consider the most important comparisons here, namely those involving value added (V) and communal surplus (Z). From tables 9.2(a)–(c) we obtain the following ratio $R(\alpha,\theta)$

$$R(\alpha,\theta)=\frac{\bar{V}^*_*}{\underline{V}^*_*}=\frac{\bar{Z}^*_*}{\underline{Z}^*_*}=\begin{cases}\left[\left(\dfrac{1-\alpha}{\zeta}\right)^{1-\alpha}(1-\theta)\right]^{1/\zeta}, & \text{if } \alpha<(1-\theta)^2,\\[2ex] \left[\left(\dfrac{1-\alpha}{\theta}\right)^{1-\alpha}(1-\theta)^{\alpha}\right]^{1/\zeta}, & \text{if } \alpha\geqslant(1-\theta)^2.\end{cases} \tag{32}$$

In fig. 9.2 we show the general shape of the regions where $R(\alpha,\theta)$ exceeds and is less than unity. The parameters α and θ are, of course, restricted by $\alpha>0$, $\theta>0$, and $\alpha+\theta<1$. When $R>1$ (resp. $R<1$) value added and communal surplus at the communally-optimal design are higher (resp. lower) when labor leads than when capital leads. Note, in particular, that $R>1$ whenever $\alpha<(1-\theta)^2$. More generally, we see from fig. 9.2 that R exceeds unity whenever $\alpha+\theta$ is sufficiently small (e.g. whenever $\alpha+\theta\leqslant 0.8$). Since from (16) $\alpha+\theta<\alpha+\Sigma\beta_i$, strongly decreasing returns to scale or high elasticities γ_i or workers' disutility with respect to effort, imply that, at the communally optimal design, both V and Z will be higher when labor leads than when profit-maximizing leads.

As a final matter of interest, we record here some general dominance results showing which internal adjustment process and which designer groups maximize various quantities.

Theorem 4. Let all be as in theorems 2 and 3. Then,

$$\underline{Y}^*\geqslant\max\left\{\bar{Y}^*,\bar{Y}_*,\bar{Y}^*_*,\underline{Y}_*,\underline{Y}^*_*\right\},$$

$$\underline{V}^*\geqslant\max\left\{\bar{V}^*,\bar{V}_*,\bar{V}^*_*,\underline{V}_*,\underline{V}^*_*\right\},$$

$$\underline{L}^*_i\geqslant\max\left\{\bar{L}^*_i,\bar{L}_{i*},\bar{L}^*_{i*},\underline{L}_{i*},\underline{L}^*_{i*}\right\}\qquad(i\in M),$$

$$\underline{x}_i^* \geqslant \max\{\bar{x}_i^*, \bar{x}_{i*}, \bar{x}_{i*}^*, \underline{x}_{i*}, \underline{x}_{i*}^*\} \qquad (i \in M),$$

$$\bar{U}^* = \bar{U}_*^* \geqslant \max\{\bar{U}_*, \underline{U}^*, \underline{U}_*, \underline{U}_*^*\},$$

$$\bar{Y}^*/\bar{K}^* = \bar{Y}_*^*/\bar{K}_*^* \geqslant \max\{\bar{Y}_*/\bar{K}_*, \underline{Y}^*/\underline{K}^*, \underline{Y}_*/\underline{K}_*, \underline{Y}_*^*/\underline{K}_*^*\},$$

$$\Pi_* \geqslant \max\{\bar{\Pi}^*, \bar{\Pi}_*, \bar{\Pi}_*^*, \underline{\Pi}^*, \underline{\Pi}_*^*\},$$

$$\bar{Z}^* = \bar{Z}_*^* \geqslant \max\{\bar{Z}_*, \underline{Z}^*, \underline{Z}_*, \underline{Z}_*^*\}.$$

Proof. Clear from the above discussion, theorem 1, and tables 9.2(a)–(c).

Remark 4. Note, as announced in remark 1, that the cooperative solution (which coincides with the labor-leading solution with labor-designed shares) maximizes communal surplus over all adjustment processes and designs. It also maximizes the output–capital ratio.

In concluding our discussion of the optimal designs it is important to note that the labor-optimal and the communally-optimal designs exhibit an ambiguity when capital leads, since $\mu^0 = 1$ implies that profit is zero irrespective of capital input. To continue to assume that a profit-maximizing financier would choose his capital input so as to maximize value added is therefore problematical. Rather, one might expect a minimum profit rate for his services to be determined in the market place. Alternatively, one might assume a bureaucrat, employed by the state, who was charged with maximizing enterprise profits. Note that, in any case, the providers of capital receive the rental ρK even when μ_0 and Π vanish. The issue discussed above is what additional remuneration is required for the financier in order that he take an active role in the capital-planning decision of the enterprise in question. This issue is obviated, of course, when the enterprise is labor-managed, and it is to such enterprises we now turn out attention.

5. Value-added sharing, labor management, and competitive capitalism

To this point we have studied various types of value-added sharing enterprises, differentiated by their internal adjustment processes and by the group of participants whose interests determine the choice of sharing scheme implemented. We now imagine, in turn, each of these various types of value-added sharing enterprises as forming a labor-managed sector of an economy coinhabited by a competitive capitalist sector. What we wish to determine is the equilibrium solution for these two sectors, assuming perfect mobility of labor between them.

The description of a labor-managed enterprise for us amounts to the workers' council becoming employer. Thus, hiring and firing is up to this council, in free negotiation, of course, with those to be hired or fired. Furthermore, the employment of the services of capital goods is again up to the workers' council or an appointed agent acting in its behalf, subject in this case to negotiation with parties offering the services of capital goods. Naturally, such a firm utilizes K so as to maximize V, which is equivalent, so long as $\mu^0 \in (0,1)$, to maximizing Π, as if an effective profit-maximizing agent were present. Our basic aim here is to see whether and how the various forms of value-added sharing enterprise studied above could coexist as labor-managed firms with competitive capital.

We proceed as follows.[6] We first fix the number of workers of each type in the two sectors and compute workers' utilities (and other quantities of interest) at the resulting competitive wage rates and internal sharing systems. We then allow labor to move between the two sectors until the utility of each worker of each skill type is equalized in all sectors. Workers are assumed to enter and exit the capitalistic sector freely, i.e. costlessly, while we allow enterprises in the value-added sharing sector to exact competitive entrance fees and to pay competitive severance compensations to workers in the equilibrating process just indicated.

Starting with the capitalist sector, we assume that in this sector the employment contract takes the form of wage incentives of the form $y_{ij} = w_i x_{ij}$, so that, using (1), labor supply is determined by maximizing

$$u_{ij} = w_i x_{ij} - c_i x_{ij}^{\gamma_i}, \tag{33}$$

which, through first-order conditions, yields

$$w_i x_i = \gamma_i c_i x_i^{\gamma_i} \tag{34}$$

as the income ("supply price" in the terminology of Dirickx and Sertel, 1978) that has to be given to a worker of type i for him to supply x_i.

The demand for labor is found by maximizing

$$\Pi = Y - \rho K - \sum_{i=1}^{m} a_i w_i x_i, \tag{35}$$

where a_i is the number of workers of type i employed by the capitalist firm. By maximizing Π over K and x_i, for the given w_i, the capitalist's demand for

[6] We follow here the development in Sertel, Başar and Selbuz (1978) to which the reader is referred for a more detailed discussion.

labor is determined. Equating this to the supply function (34) yields the competitive wage and corresponding inputs, outputs, utilities and profit. Details of this process for a similar model specification can be found in Sertel, Başar and Selbuz (1978) and they will not be repeated here. The competitive wage for type i workers, denoting $\underline{a}=(a_1,\ldots,a_m)$,

$$\hat{w}_i(\underline{a})=\frac{\beta_i\hat{Y}(\underline{a})}{x_i(\underline{a})} \qquad (i\in M), \tag{36}$$

where competitive output ($\hat{Y}$), labor input of type i ($\hat{L}_i$), and capital input ($\hat{K}$) all turn out to equal the respective values in table 9.2(a) for the labor-leading, labor-designed enterprise, evaluated at $n_i=a_i$ ($i\in M$). Thus, we have

$$\hat{Y}=\hat{Y}(\underline{a})=\bar{Y}^*=\left[\left(\frac{\alpha}{\rho}\right)^{\alpha}\left(\prod_M a_i^{\beta_i}\left(\frac{\theta_i}{a_i c_i}\right)^{\theta_i}\right)\right]^{1/\zeta}; \tag{37}$$

$$\hat{L}_i=a_i\hat{x}_i(\underline{a})=a_i\left(\frac{\theta_i}{a_i c_i}\hat{Y}\right)^{1/\gamma_i}; \qquad \hat{K}=\frac{\alpha}{\rho}\hat{Y}. \tag{38}$$

From these, all other quantities of interest are easily computed and are displayed in table 9.3. In particular, the utility of the typical worker i in the competitive capitalist sector is

$$\begin{aligned}\hat{u}_{ij}(\underline{a})&=\hat{w}_i\hat{x}_i(\underline{a})-c_i\hat{x}_i(\underline{a})^{\gamma_i}\\&=\hat{w}_i\left(\frac{\hat{L}_i(\underline{a})}{a_i}\right)-c_i\left(\frac{\hat{L}_i(\underline{a})}{a_i}\right)^{\gamma_i}\\&=\frac{\beta_i-\theta_i}{a_i}\hat{Y}(\underline{a}).\end{aligned} \tag{39}$$

Now we consider the value-added sharing sector, taking each of the types of enterprise of the previous sections in turn. We will actually work out only one case in detail, leaving to the reader the imitation of this for the other cases. The case we consider is where the value-added sharing sector consists entirely of enterprises which are labor-designed and in which the solution concept describing enterprise equilibrium is von Stackelberg with labor leading. As noted in remark 3, this is equivalent to the case of the cooperative solution. In fact, this seems to be the most interesting case from the viewpoint of labor management, since the cooperative solution assumes that communal surplus (which is shared entirely by the worker–partners of the labor-managed firm) is maximized with respect to both capital and labor inputs (see (27) in this regard).

Table 9.3
Competitive capitalist solution.

Output	$\hat{Y}=\left[\left(\frac{\alpha}{\zeta}\right)^{\alpha}\prod_{M} a_i^{\beta_i}\left(\frac{\theta_i}{a_i c_i}\right)^{\theta_i}\right]^{1/\zeta}$	Output–labor ratio (for type i labor)	$\frac{\hat{Y}}{\hat{L}_i}=\left[\frac{c_i}{\theta_i}\left(\frac{\hat{Y}}{a_i}\right)^{\gamma_i-1}\right]^{1/\gamma_i}$
Value added	$\hat{V}=(1-\alpha)\hat{Y}$	Income (of a typical worker of type i)	$\hat{y}_i=\frac{\beta_i}{a_i}\hat{Y}$
Capital	$\hat{K}=\frac{\alpha}{\rho}\hat{Y}$		
Labor input (of a typical worker of type i)	$\hat{x}_i=\left(\frac{\theta_i}{a_i c_i}\hat{Y}\right)^{1/\gamma_i}$	Utility (of a typical worker of type i)	$\hat{u}_i=\frac{\beta_i-\theta_i}{a_i}\hat{Y}$
Aggregate labor (of workers of type i)	$\hat{L}_i=a_i\hat{x}_i$	Workers' aggregate utility	$\hat{U}=(\beta-\theta)\hat{Y}$
		Profit	$\hat{\Pi}=(1-\alpha-\beta)\hat{Y}$
Output–capital ratio	$\hat{Y}/\hat{K}=\rho/\alpha$	Communal surplus	$\hat{Z}=\zeta\hat{Y}$

We denote the number of workers of type i employed by the typical enterprise in the labor-designed, value-added sharing sector as b_i, and we denote $\underline{b}=(b_1,\ldots,b_m)$. Then from table 9.2(a) the utility of workers of type i in this sector is

$$\begin{aligned}\bar{u}_{ij}(\underline{b})&=\mu_i\bar{V}^*(\underline{b})-c_i\bar{x}_i^*(\underline{b})^{\gamma_i}\\&=\left(\mu_i(1-\alpha)-\frac{\theta_i}{b_i}\right)\bar{Y}^*(\underline{b})\\&=\left(\mu_i(1-\alpha)-\frac{\theta_i}{b_i}\right)\left[\left(\frac{\alpha}{\rho}\right)^{\alpha}\left(\prod_{M} b_i^{\beta_i}\left(\frac{\theta_i}{b_i c_i}\right)^{\theta_i}\right)\right]^{1/\zeta}.\end{aligned}\tag{40}$$

Now we consider adjustment between the two sectors, treating both $\underline{a}$ and $\underline{b}$ as continuous variables in the process. First, we give a few definitions. The *demand price* for a worker–partnership of type i in the value-added sharing sector is defined as

$$D_i(\underline{a},\underline{b})=\bar{u}_{ij}(\underline{b})-\hat{u}_{ij}(\underline{a}),\tag{41}$$

and the *supply price* of a position in the same sector is defined as

$$S_i(\underline{b})=-\sum_{k\in M} b_k\frac{\partial\bar{u}_{kj}(\underline{b})}{\partial b_i}.\tag{42}$$

$D_i(\underline{a}, \underline{b})$ is the price a worker of type i would be willing to pay to move from the capitalist sector to the labor-managed value-added sharing sector. Since $\partial \bar{u}_{kj}(\underline{b})/\partial b_i$ is the change in utility for any worker of type k (of which there are b_k) when another type i worker joins the enterprise, the supply price (42) represents the least compensation which a labor-managed value-added sharing enterprise would require to accept another worker–partner of type i without causing any loss of welfare for any current worker–partner. At equilibrium[7] we must have

$$S_i(\underline{b}) = D_i(\underline{a}, \underline{b}) \qquad (i \in M). \tag{43}$$

From (40) we have

$$\frac{\partial \bar{u}_{kj}(\underline{b})}{\partial b_i} = \left[\left((1-\alpha)\frac{\partial \mu_k}{\partial b_i} + \frac{\theta_i}{b_i^2}\delta(i,k)\right) + \left(\frac{\beta_i - \theta_i}{b_i \zeta}\right)\left((1-\alpha)\mu_k - \frac{\theta_k}{b_k}\right)\right]\bar{Y}^*, \tag{44}$$

where $\delta(i,k)=0$ if $i \neq k$ and 1 if $i=k$. From (42), (44) and the fact that $\Sigma_M b_k \mu_k = \mu^0 = 1$ for the labor-designed enterprise, we have

$$S_i(\underline{b}) = -\left[(1-\alpha)\sum_{k \in M} b_k \frac{\partial \mu_k}{\partial b_i} + \frac{\beta_i}{b_i}\right]\bar{Y}^*. \tag{45}$$

On the other hand, from (39)–(41), $D_i(\underline{a}, \underline{b})$ is

$$D_i(\underline{a}, \underline{b}) = \left((1-\alpha)\mu_i - \frac{\theta_i}{b_i}\right)\bar{Y}^* - \left(\frac{\beta_i - \theta_i}{a_i}\right)\hat{Y}. \tag{46}$$

Equating (45) and (46) then yields the following characterization of equilibrium:

$$(1-\alpha)\left[\mu_i + \sum_{k \in M} b_k \frac{\partial \mu_k}{\partial b_i}\right] + \frac{\beta_i - \theta_i}{b_i} = \frac{\beta_i - \theta_i}{a_i}\frac{\hat{Y}}{\bar{Y}^*} \qquad (i \in M). \tag{47}$$

But for any labor-designed value-added sharing enterprise $\Sigma_M b_k \mu_k = \mu^0 = 1$ identically so that, no matter how shares are adjusted as new entrants join the enterprise,

$$\frac{\partial}{\partial b_i}\left(\sum_M b_k \mu_k(\underline{b})\right) = \mu_i + \sum_{k \in M} b_k \frac{\partial \mu_k}{\partial b_i} = 0, \tag{48}$$

and (47) reduces to

$$\frac{a_i}{b_i} = \frac{\hat{Y}}{\bar{Y}^*} = \prod_M \left(\frac{a_j}{b_j}\right)^{(\beta_j - \theta_j)/\zeta} \qquad (i \in M). \tag{49}$$

[7]See also Sertel, Başar and Selbuz (1978) for a discussion of adjustment towards and stability of equilibrium in a related context.

From this we also see that in equilibrium total employment in the two sectors satisfies

$$\frac{A}{B}=\frac{\sum_M a_i}{\sum_M b_i}=\frac{\hat{Y}}{\overline{Y}^*}, \tag{50}$$

where $A=\Sigma_M a_i$ and $B=\Sigma_M b_i$. From (49) and the fact that $\beta_j-\theta_j=\theta_j(\gamma_j-1)>0$ one easily deduces that $a_i=b_i$, $i\in M$, must hold at equilibrium, so that also $A=B$. From these results and (37)–(39) we obtain column 1 of table 9.4, which tabulates the ratios of quantities of interest for the labor-managed value-added sharing sector (at market equilibrium) to the corresponding quantities for the competitive capitalism sector.

The constant β in table 9.4 is defined by

$$\beta=\sum_M \beta_i, \tag{51}$$

so that, from (2), $1-\alpha\geqslant\beta$, with equality under constant returns to scale. Note also from (16), (51) and $\gamma_i>1$ that $\beta-\theta>0$. When $\alpha+\beta=1$, we have $\zeta=1-\alpha-\theta=\beta-\theta$ and $1-\alpha=\beta$. Thus, noting from table 9.3 that $\hat{\Pi}=0$ when $\alpha+\beta=1$, we see from table 9.4 that the cooperative solution is identical to the competitive capitalist solution. More generally, when $\alpha+\beta\leqslant 1$, we see that the cooperative labor-managed solution yields identical results to the competitive capitalist solution in all respects except distribution, where profits are lower and worker incomes and utilities higher for the labor-managed solution than for the competitive capitalist solution. Total communal surplus is always the same, however.

Similar computations to those above lead to the other four columns of table 9.4, where the constants E_i, $i=1,\ldots,4$, are given as follows, assuming $\alpha+\beta<1$:

$$E_1=\left(\frac{\theta}{1-\alpha}\right)^{\beta/(1-\alpha-\beta)}, \tag{52}$$

$$E_2=\left(\frac{(1-\theta)^2-\alpha}{\zeta}\left(\frac{1}{1-\theta}\right)^{(1-\theta)/\zeta}\right)^{\zeta/(1-\alpha-\beta)}, \tag{53}$$

$$E_3=\left(\frac{(1-\theta)^2-\alpha}{\zeta}\left(\frac{1}{1-\theta}\right)^{(1-\theta)/\zeta}\left(\frac{\theta}{1-\alpha}\right)^{(1-\alpha)/\zeta}\right)^{\zeta/(1-\alpha-\beta)}, \tag{54}$$

$$E_4=\left(\frac{(1-\theta)^2-\alpha}{\zeta}\left(\frac{1}{1-\theta}\right)^{(1-\theta)/\zeta}\left(\frac{\zeta}{\zeta+\alpha\theta}\right)^{(1-\alpha)/\zeta}\right)^{\zeta/(1-\alpha-\beta)}. \tag{55}$$

We show below that under constant returns to scale ($\alpha+\beta=1$) the labor-

Table 9.4
Comparing labor-management value-added sharing and competitive capitalism at equilibrium.

	Cooperative Labor leads Labor designs	Labor leads[a] Capital designs	Capital leads[b] Labor designs	Capital leads Capital designs	Capital leads[b] Community designs
$Y/\hat{Y}$	1	E_1	$\frac{\zeta(\zeta+\alpha\theta)}{\theta((1-\theta)^2-\alpha)}E_2$	$\frac{\zeta(\zeta+\alpha\theta)}{\theta((1-\theta)^2-\alpha)}E_3$	$\frac{\zeta(\zeta+\alpha\theta)}{\theta((1-\theta)^2-\alpha)}E_4$
$V/\hat{V}$	1	E_1	$\frac{\zeta^2}{\theta((1-\theta)^2-\alpha)}E_2$	$\frac{\zeta^2}{\theta((1-\theta)^2-\alpha)}E_3$	$\frac{\zeta^2}{\theta((1-\theta)^2-\alpha)}E_4$
$K/\hat{K}$	1	E_1	$\frac{\zeta(1-\alpha)}{\theta((1-\theta)^2-\alpha)}E_2$	$\frac{\zeta(1-\alpha)}{\theta((1-\theta)^2-\alpha)}E_3$	$\frac{\zeta(1-\alpha)}{\theta((1-\theta)^2-\alpha)}E_4$
$x_i/\hat{x}_i$	1	1	$\left(\frac{\zeta(1-\theta)}{(1-\theta)^2-\alpha}\right)^{1/\gamma_i}$	$\left(\frac{\zeta(1-\theta)}{(1-\theta)^2-\alpha}\right)^{1/\gamma_i}$	$\left(\frac{\zeta(1-\theta)}{(1-\theta)^2-\alpha}\right)^{1/\gamma_i}$
$L_i/\hat{L}_i$	1	$\frac{\theta}{1-\alpha}E_1$	$\left(\frac{\zeta(1-\theta)}{(1-\theta)^2-\alpha}\right)^{1/\gamma_i}E_2$	$\left(\frac{\zeta(1-\theta)}{(1-\theta)^2-\alpha}\right)^{1/\gamma_i}E_3$	$\left(\frac{\zeta(1-\theta)}{(1-\theta)^2-\alpha}\right)^{1/\gamma_i}E_4$
$\underline{Y}/\hat{\underline{Y}}$	1	1	$1-\theta$	$1-\theta$	$1-\theta$
$\frac{Y}{L_i}\Big/\frac{\hat{Y}}{\hat{L}_i}$	1	$\frac{1-\alpha}{\theta}$	$\left(\frac{\zeta(1-\theta)}{(1-\theta)^2-\alpha}\right)^{(\gamma_i-1)/\gamma_i}$	$\left(\frac{1-\alpha}{\theta}\right)\left(\frac{\zeta(1-\theta)}{(1-\theta)^2-\alpha}\right)^{(\gamma_i-1)/\gamma_i}$	$\left(\frac{\zeta+\alpha\theta}{\zeta}\right)\left(\frac{\zeta(1-\theta)}{(1-\theta)^2-\alpha}\right)^{(\gamma_i-1)/\gamma_i}$

$\Pi/\hat{\Pi}$	0	$\frac{\zeta}{1-\alpha-\beta}E_1$	0	$\frac{\zeta^3}{\theta(1-\alpha-\beta)\left((1-\theta)^2-\alpha\right)}E_3$	$\frac{\alpha\zeta^2}{(1-\theta)(1-\alpha-\beta)\left((1-\theta)^2-\alpha\right)}E_4$
$Z/\hat{Z}$	1	$\frac{(1-\alpha)^2-\theta^2}{\zeta(1-\alpha)}E_1$	$\frac{1-\alpha}{\theta}E_2$	$\frac{\zeta(1-\alpha)-\theta^2(1-\theta)}{\theta\left((1-\theta)^2-\alpha\right)}E_3$	$\frac{\zeta^2}{\theta\left((1-\theta)^2-\alpha\right)}E_4$
$\frac{Y}{A}\Big/\frac{\hat{Y}}{B}$	1	$\frac{1-\alpha}{\theta}$	$\frac{\zeta(1-\theta)}{(1-\theta)^2-\alpha}$	$\frac{\zeta(\zeta+\alpha\theta)}{\theta(1-\theta)^2-\alpha)}$	$\frac{(1-\theta)(\zeta+\alpha\theta)}{\left((1-\theta)^2-\alpha\right)}$
$\frac{V}{A}\Big/\frac{\hat{V}}{B}$	1	$\frac{1-\alpha}{\theta}$	$\frac{\zeta^2}{(1-\alpha)\left((1-\theta)^2-\alpha\right)}$	$\frac{\zeta^2}{\theta\left((1-\theta)^2-\alpha\right)}$	$\frac{(1-\theta)\zeta}{\left((1-\theta)^2-\alpha\right)}$
$\frac{K}{A}\Big/\frac{\hat{K}}{B}$	1	$\frac{1-\alpha}{\theta}$	$\frac{\zeta}{\left((1-\theta)^2-\alpha\right)}$	$\frac{\zeta(1-\alpha)}{\theta\left((1-\theta)^2-\alpha\right)}$	$\frac{\zeta+\alpha\theta}{\left((1-\theta)^2-\alpha\right)}$
$\frac{\Sigma b_i y_i}{A}\Big/\frac{\Sigma a_i \hat{y}_i}{B}$	$\frac{1-\alpha}{\beta}$	$\frac{1-\alpha}{\beta}$	$\frac{\zeta^2}{\beta\left((1-\theta)^2-\alpha\right)}$	$\frac{\zeta^2}{\beta\left((1-\theta)^2-\alpha\right)}$	$\frac{\zeta^2}{\beta\left((1-\theta)^2-\alpha\right)}$
$\frac{U}{A}\Big/\frac{\hat{U}}{B}$	$\frac{\zeta}{\beta-\theta}$	$\frac{\zeta}{\beta-\theta}$	ζ	ζ	ζ
$\frac{Z}{A}\Big/\frac{\hat{Z}}{B}$	1	$\frac{(1-\alpha)^2-\theta^2}{\theta\zeta}$	1	$\frac{\zeta(1-\alpha)-\theta^2(1-\theta)}{\theta\left((1-\theta)^2-\alpha\right)}$	$\frac{(1-\theta)\zeta}{\left((1-\theta)^2-\alpha\right)}$
A/B	1	$E_1^{(1-\alpha)/\beta}$	$\frac{1-\alpha}{\theta}E_2$	E_3	$\frac{\zeta}{\theta(1-\theta)}E_4$

[a] This column assumes $\alpha+\beta<1$.
[b] This column assumes $\alpha+\beta<1$ and $\alpha<(1-\theta)^2$.

managed, value-added sharing sector shrinks to extinction except for the cooperative case, i.e. the case natural to a labor-managed enterprise, labor leading and designing incentives so as to share value added among worker–partners.

We note that only the case where $\alpha<(1-\theta)^2$ is tabulated when capital leads (columns 3–5 of table 9.4). This is because when $\alpha\geqslant(1-\theta)^2$ workers receive only subsistence pay and $u_{ij}=0$ for every worker in the labor-managed sector (see table 9.1). Clearly, in equilibrium these workers would have no reason to stay and the capital-leading labor-managed sector would cease to exist.

The following lemma is of interest in interpreting the results in table 9.4.

Lemma 1. Assuming $\alpha+\beta<1$ and $\alpha<(1-\theta)^2$, the constants E_i, $i\in\{1,\ldots,4\}$, in (52)–(55) are all less than unity. Moreover, $\lim_{\alpha+\beta\to 1}E_i=0$, for each $i\in\{1,\ldots,4\}$.

Proof. See appendix C. □

From the above lemma and the final entry in table 9.4 (for A/B), we see that under constant returns to scale the only labor-managed, value-added sharing firm which remains viable is the cooperative firm. For the other four enterprise types in table 9.4, A/B goes to zero as $\alpha+\beta$ approaches unity.

As our final result we present comparisons of other key quantities of interest at equilibrium.

Theorem 5. Assume $\alpha+\beta<1$. Then, comparing competitive capitalism with labor-managed, value-added sharing enterprises, at equilibrium, we find that *per capita* values of output (Y/N), value added (V/N), and capital input (K/N), the capital–output ratio (K/Y), individual labor inputs (x_i), and the *per capital* values of worker incomes ($(\Sigma n_i y_i)/N$), workers' utility (U/N) and communal surplus (Z/N) are all at least as high in the labor-managed sector as they are in the capitalistic sector. Moreover, these results hold whether capital leads or labor leads and whether labor, capital or the labor–capital community chooses the enterprise design in the labor-managed sector.

Proof. All the assertions are straightforward consequences of table 9.4. For example, considering *per capita* output, we have

$$1-\alpha>\theta, \quad \text{so} \quad \frac{1-\alpha}{\theta}>1, \tag{56}$$

$$\zeta(1-\theta)-\big((1-\theta)^2-\alpha\big)=\alpha\theta>0, \quad \text{so} \quad \frac{\zeta(1-\theta)}{(1-\theta)^2-\alpha}>1, \tag{57}$$

$$(1-\theta)(\zeta+\alpha\theta)-\big((1-\theta)^2-\alpha\big)=\alpha\theta(2-\theta)>0, \quad \text{so} \quad \frac{(1-\theta)(\zeta+\alpha\theta)}{\big((1-\theta)^2-\alpha\big)}>1. \tag{58}$$

From this, table 9.4 shows that $Y/N \geqslant \hat{Y}/\hat{N}$ in all five columns, as asserted. □

6. Concluding remarks

Since much of our development has been quite technical, it may be useful to summarize our results in more qualitative, intuitive terms. After doing so, we will reflect on some open research issues raised by these results.

Our aim in this chapter has been to investigate the consequences for economic performance of various organizational design and adjustment processes. Keeping always to the assumption that remuneration for workers was through shares in value added and that workers cooperated in choosing their joint behavior, we studied the impact of various internal adjustment processes (between capital and labor) and of various authority structures governing the choice of incentive (or enterprise) design.

With respect to authority structures we studied the consequences of having incentive design chosen by labor, by a profit-maximizing financier or by a (cooperating) labor–capital coalition. The essential consequences of these three authority structures are fairly easily understood by recalling that labor chooses the enterprise design so that, evaluated at equilibrium, workers' aggregate utility is maximized. Similarly, the financier attempts to maximize profits, and the cooperative design is a compromise directed at maximizing the sum of profits and workers' aggregate utilities, i.e. communal surplus. Now when labor designs the enterprise, they appropriate all value added to themselves. The incentives for labor productivity are thus highest at the labor-optimal design. Given this, it is not surprising that we found (theorem 3) that the labor-optimal design maximized not only workers' aggregate utility, but also most physical quantities of interest, including output and value added. The profit-maximizing design maximized profits, of course, but was otherwise dominated fairly clearly by the labor-optimal design. When labor and capital cooperate in the design process, the labor-optimal design is chosen, though the distribution of value added between labor and capital may be different (through lump-sum transfers) than when labor rules the roost alone.

Turning now to the matter of alternative adjustment processes, we assume always that workers acted cooperatively among themselves, using side-payments as necessary to still the woes of any who were dissatisfied with the cooperative solution. Concerning the adjustment of labor and capital to one another, we considered four possibilities: the noncooperative or Nash solution, the cooperative solution, and the two von Stackelberg solutions with labor leading and with capital leading. Of these, the Nash and the cooperative solutions turned out to be special cases of the labor-leading solution. Comparing labor-leading and capital-leading solutions at a common sharing scheme, we found (see theorem 1) that if labor was able to choose its input first, with capital then being adjusted to this, then labor's interests (i.e. workers' aggregate utility) were served. On the other hand, allowing capital to have the dominant, first choice led to the maximization of most physical quantities of interest (excluding the output–capital ratio). The cooperative solution led to results intermediate between those of labor leading and capital leading.

Comparing across both adjustment processes and authority structures we found (in theorem 4) that most physical quantities of interest were maximized when labor designed the enterprise and capital led. Profits were maximized when the financier chose the enterprise design and when capital led. Aggregate utility measures, including communal surplus, were maximized at the cooperative design and adjustment process. We noted a certain conflict in these results as relates to maximizing physical quantities like output and value added, since the appropriate recipe for this would be labor-designed and capital-led. However, the labor-optimal design calls for zero profits, thus taking away the incentive from the financier to properly "lead" with capital. We noted that a market for entrepreneurs would have to impose constraints on minimal payments (e.g. in terms of residual shares in value added) to the financier in order for this set-up to work. Alternatively, a state-appointed capital-manager would have to be assumed, with sufficient bureaucratic incentives to motivate him to set capital properly.

In addition to the above comparative static comparisons (which assumed that a change in authority structure or adjustment process could be evaluated *ceteris paribus*), we also considered how enterprises with each of the various authority structures and adjustment processes would fare if they were labor-managed and had to compete in a labor market with a competitive capitalist sector for workers. The comparisons described above for the case of isolated value-added sharing enterprises were confirmed as well at market equilibrium. Two additional points also emerged. First, labor-managed, value-added sharing enterprises were not only viable relative to competitive capitalism, but also provided the same or higher *per capita* values for most quantities of interest, for output and value added in particular. The second point of interest is that if constant returns to scale obtain, then only the cooperative solution (both in adjustment and design) remains viable in competition with competitive capitalism. All other forms of labor-managed firm are unviable. Thus, to the extent that scale economies are exhausted in general equilibrium, any lack of cooperation internal to the labor-managed firm could be fatal. (All of this assumes that capitalist firms function without a hitch as well, of course.) Finally, none of these results has considered differences in monitoring and administrative costs between capitalist and labor-managed firms, or among the various forms of labor-managed enterprise considered. Consideration of these issues, as in Kleindorfer and Sertel (1979), is likely to change the tenor of the above results somewhat, but not in a completely predictable fashion. Monitoring costs (e.g. of workers' inputs) may be quite high for wage contracts in the capitalistic sector, but the costs of cooperation amongst workers can also be high. There would appear to be considerable returns here to empirical and experimental research.[8]

Some information on related results from the literature may shed some further light on our results. First, Sertel, Başar and Selbuz (1978) study exactly the same problem as here, but for internal prices (or wages) as the work incentive, and only for the case where labor leads and labor designs. This gives rise to effective utility functions of the form (32). When they allow a cooperative determination of labor inputs (the case they refer to as internal wages with quotas) they duplicate the cooperative solution studied here. This is simply because in both cases the maximand of interest is communal surplus (see (27)), and the individual effects of incentives (whether in the form of shares in value added, wages with quotas, or something else) are washed out by the assumption that labor inputs are determined cooperatively.

In a companion paper, Başar, Selbuz and Sertel (1979) have also studied the case of value-added sharing enterprises where workers adjust their inputs to one another internally in a noncooperative fashion. They show for the case when labor leads (so that capital is set after labor in such a way as to maximize value added), that such noncooperative behavior leads to a shrinking of all physical quantities (e.g. output and value added) in relation to the corresponding enterprise under cooperative behavior.[9] Thus,

[8]See Cable and FitzRoy (1978) for some preliminary empirical findings on this point.
[9]Kleindorfer and Sertel (1976) obtain similar results for output-sharing incentives.

cooperation is a good not only from the point of view of aggregate utility, but also from the viewpoint of output and value added.

In terms of general results, what seems to emerge from these papers taken together is the intuitive result that he who designs the enterprise will see his interests reflected in the product. If the interests of profitability or value-added maximization are foremost, then a profit-maximizing enterprise or a labor-managed enterprise with capital leading would be the designer's choice. Similarly, if workers' well-being is of prime interest, then a more labor-oriented design process is called for. None of this is at all surprising, which is reassuring from the point of view of the model formulation.

What we have not dealt with here are monitoring and information processing costs of alternative incentive systems, adjustment processes, and authority structures. Nor have we dealt with the very important issues of uncertainty and risk-aversion differences among workers and between workers and the financier or central planners. These are important areas for future research.

Appendix A

Here we prove the properties listed in the text concerning the geometry of fig. 9.1.

(*ad* P1). For $\mu^0=0$, P1 is obvious, so take any $\mu^0\in(0,1]$. Define the function $\Delta(\cdot;\mu^0): R_+ \to R$ through

$$\Delta(\ell;\mu^0)=\bar{V}(\ell)-\underline{V}(\ell;\mu^0)$$

$$=(1-\alpha)\left(\frac{\alpha}{\rho}\right)^{\alpha/(1-\alpha)}\ell-\frac{\ell^{(1-\alpha)/\theta}}{\mu^0 A}+\frac{\rho\ell^{[(1-\alpha)(1-\theta)]/\alpha\theta}}{(\mu^0 A)^{1/\alpha}}. \tag{A1}$$

From this we obtain

$$\frac{\partial\Delta(\ell;\mu^0)}{\partial\ell}=(1-\alpha)\left(\frac{\alpha}{\rho}\right)^{\alpha/(1-\alpha)}-\left(\frac{1-\alpha}{\theta(\mu^0 A)}\right)\ell^{\xi/\theta}$$

$$+\left(\frac{(1-\alpha)(1-\theta)}{\ell\theta}\right)\left(\frac{\rho}{(\mu^0 A)^{1/\alpha}}\right)\ell^{\xi/\alpha\theta}. \tag{A2}$$

Property (P1) is proven by showing (i) $\partial\Delta(\ell;\mu^0)/\partial\ell=0$ at $\ell=\bar{\underline{\ell}}(\mu^0)$, and (ii) that $\Delta(\ell;\mu^0)\geqslant 0$, for all $\ell\geqslant 0$, with $\Delta(\ell;\mu^0)=0$ only when $\ell=0$ or $\ell=\bar{\underline{\ell}}(\mu^0)$. Now one computes easily from (A2) that (i) holds. Moreover, $\partial\Delta(\ell;\mu^0)/\partial\ell$

>0 at $\ell=0^+$ and $\Delta(0;\mu^0)=\Delta(\underline{\ell}(\mu^0);\mu^0)=0$. Therefore, by Rolle's Theorem, there is an $\hat{\ell}\in(0,\underline{\ell}(\mu^0))$ at which $\partial\Delta(\hat{\ell};\mu^0)/\partial\ell=0$. Thus, $\partial\Delta(\ell;\mu^0)/\partial\ell$ has at least two zeros, $\underline{\ell}(\mu^0)$ and $\hat{\ell}$. Note also that if $\Delta(\ell;\mu^0)$ has any other zeros than $\ell=0$ and $\ell=\underline{\ell}(\mu^0)$, then $\partial\Delta/\partial\ell$ would, again by Rolle's Theorem, have to have at least three zeros. We show below, however, that $\partial\Delta/\partial\ell$ has at most two zeros, so also $\Delta(\cdot;\mu^0)$ can only have two zeros. Assuming this to be so, all that remains to see is that $\Delta(\ell;\mu^0)\geqslant 0$ for all $\ell\geqslant 0$. This is so for $\ell\in(0,\underline{\ell}(\mu^0))$ since the only zeros of $\Delta(\ell;\mu^0)$ are at 0 and $\underline{\ell}(\mu^0)$ and, from (A2), $\partial\Delta/\partial\ell>0$ for $\ell=0^+$. Similarly, one verifies easily that $\partial^2\Delta/\partial\ell^2>0$ at $\ell=\underline{\ell}(\mu^0)$ so that, together with $\partial\Delta/\partial\ell=0$ at $\underline{\ell}(\mu^0)$, we see that $\underline{\ell}(\mu^0)$ is a strict local minimum of Δ. In particular, $\Delta(\ell;\mu^0)>\Delta(\underline{\ell}(\mu^0);\mu^0)=0$ for some ℓ slightly larger than $\underline{\ell}(\mu^0)$. But then $\Delta(\ell;\mu^0)>0$ for all $\ell>\underline{\ell}(\mu^0)$ since the continuous $\Delta(\cdot;\mu^0)$ has no zeros beyond $\underline{\ell}(\mu^0)$. Thus, the proof of P1 is complete except for showing that $\partial\Delta(\ell;\mu^0)/\partial\ell$ has at most two zeros on R_+. Towards this, we note that $\partial\Delta/\partial\ell$ in (A2) is of the form

$$\delta(x)=a_0-a_1x+a_2x^{1/\alpha}, \tag{A3}$$

where $a_0, a_1, a_2>0$ and $x=\ell^{\zeta/\theta}$ is a monotonic transformation of ℓ. Since $\alpha<1$, $a_1x-a_2x^{1/\alpha}$ is strictly concave for $x>0$ and, therefore, $a_0=a_1x-a_2x^{1/\alpha}$ for at most two values of x. Thus, δ, and therefore also $\Delta(\cdot,\mu^0)$, has at most two zeros on R_+.

(*ad* P2). From (10) and (21) all that need be verified is that the exponent $(1-\alpha)/\theta$ in (21) exceeds unity. This follows since $1-\alpha\geqslant\Sigma\beta_i>\theta$ from (2) and (16).

(*ad* P3). Fixing $\mu^0\in(0,1]$, we compute

$$\frac{\mu^0\partial\underline{V}(\ell;\mu^0)}{\partial\ell}-\frac{\partial S(\ell)}{\partial\ell}$$
$$=\left(\frac{1-\alpha}{\theta}\right)\left(\frac{1-\theta}{A}\right)\ell^{\zeta/\theta}-\left(\frac{\mu^0\rho}{(\mu^0A)^{1/\alpha}}\right)\left(\frac{(1-\alpha)(1-\theta)}{\alpha\theta}\right)\ell^{\zeta/\alpha\theta}, \tag{A4}$$

so that, since $\zeta/\theta<\zeta/\alpha\theta$, $\mu^0\partial\underline{V}/\partial\ell-\partial S/\partial\ell$ is positive for $\ell>0$ sufficiently small. Also, from (20) and (21) one computes directly that $\mu^0\underline{V}(\ell;\mu^0)=S(\ell)$ occurs at precisely $\ell=0$ and

$$\dot{\ell}(\mu^0)=\left[\left(\frac{1-\theta}{\rho}\right)^{\alpha/(1-\alpha)}(\mu^0A)\right]^{\theta/(1-\alpha-\theta)}>0. \tag{A5}$$

Thus, between 0 and $\dot{\ell}(\mu^0)$, $\mu^0\underline{V}(\ell;\mu^0)$ exceeds $S(\ell)$. Continuing,

$$\frac{\mu^0\partial^2\underline{V}(\ell;\mu^0)}{\partial\ell^2}=\left(\frac{1-\alpha}{\theta}\right)\left(\frac{1-\alpha-\theta}{\theta A}\right)\frac{\ell^{\zeta/\theta}}{\ell}$$
$$-\left(\frac{\mu^0\rho}{(\mu^0 A)^{1/\alpha}}\right)\left(\frac{(1-\alpha)(1-\theta)}{\alpha\theta}\right)\left(\frac{1-\alpha-\theta}{\alpha\theta}\right)\frac{\ell^{\zeta/\alpha\theta}}{\ell},\tag{A6}$$

which is of the form

$$v(x)=\frac{b_1x-b_2x^{1/\alpha}}{x^{\theta/\zeta}},\tag{A7}$$

where $b_1, b_2>0$ and $x=\ell^{\zeta/\theta}$. Since $\alpha<1$, (A7) implies that $v(x)$ is positive for x small, and then becomes and stays negative. The same properties clearly carry over to $\mu^0\partial^2\underline{V}/\partial\ell^2$ in terms of ℓ. Thus, $\mu^0\underline{V}$ is first convex and then concave, and the proof of P3 is complete.

Appendix B

This appendix proves part (iii) of theorem 1 in section 3.

(*ad* iii). We present cases where $\bar{u}_i[\mu]/\underline{u}_i[\mu]$ and $\bar{Z}[\mu^0]/\underline{Z}[\mu^0]$ exceed unity and where they are less than unity.

Concerning $\bar{u}_i[\mu]/\underline{u}_i[\mu]$, we may first note that since $U[\mu^0]=\Sigma_{i=1}^m n_i u_i[\mu]$ and, from table 9.1, $\bar{U}[\mu^0]>\underline{U}[\mu^0]$, we must always have $\bar{u}_i[\mu]>\underline{u}_i[\mu]$ for some $i\in\{1,\ldots,m\}$. In fact, the reader may easily verify that if $\mu=(\mu_0,\mu_1,\ldots,\mu_m)$ is such that

$$\frac{n_i\mu_i}{\theta_i}=\frac{n_j\mu_j}{\theta_j},\qquad i,j\in\{1,\ldots,m\}\tag{B1}$$

then, from table 9.1,

$$\frac{\bar{u}_i[\mu]/\underline{u}_i[\mu]}{\bar{u}_j[\mu]/\underline{u}_j[\mu]}=1,\qquad i,j\in\{1,\ldots,m\},\tag{B2}$$

so that $U=\Sigma n_i u_i[\mu]$ and $\bar{U}[\mu]>\underline{U}[\mu]$ imply $\bar{u}_i[\mu]>\underline{u}_i[\mu]$ for all $i\in\{1,\ldots,m\}$. Thus, (B1) characterizes a case where *every* worker prefers the results of labor leading to those of capital leading.

To determine a case where $\bar{u}_i[\mu]/\underline{u}_i[\mu]$ is less than unity for some i, we define $\hat{\mu} = (\hat{\mu}_0, \dots, \hat{\mu}_m)$ through

$$\hat{\mu}_1 = \frac{\mu^0}{n_1}\left[\frac{(1-\alpha-\theta)-(\theta-\theta_i)(1-\theta)}{1-\alpha-\theta}\right] \tag{B3}$$

and

$$\hat{\mu}_j = \frac{\mu^0\theta_j}{n_j}\frac{1-\theta}{1-\alpha-\theta}, \qquad j \in \{2,\dots,m\}. \tag{B4}$$

Then it is easily verified that $\hat{\mu}_i \geqslant 0$ for all $i, \sum_{i=1}^m n_i\hat{\mu}_i = \mu^0$, and that $\bar{u}_j[\hat{\mu}] > \underline{u}_j[\hat{\mu}] = 0$ for $j \in \{2,\dots,m\}$. Thus, when capital leads $\hat{\mu}$ is just sufficient for subsistence requirements for $j \in \{2,\dots,m\}$ and $\hat{\mu}_1$ is therefore the maximum feasible share which agent 1 can receive for the given μ^0. We now verify that $\bar{u}_1[\hat{\mu}] < \underline{u}_1[\hat{\mu}]$ when θ_1 is sufficiently small and $(1-\theta)^2 < \alpha$.

We now compute from table 9.1

$$\frac{\bar{u}_1[\hat{\mu}]}{\underline{u}_1[\hat{\mu}]} = \frac{\hat{\mu}_1(1-\alpha) - \dfrac{\mu^0\theta_1}{a_1}}{\hat{\mu}_1\left(\dfrac{1-\alpha-\theta}{1-\theta}\right) - \dfrac{\mu^0\theta_1}{a_1}}\frac{\bar{Y}[\mu^0]}{\underline{Y}[\mu^0]} \tag{B5}$$

or, substituting from (B3) for $\hat{\mu}_1$,

$$\frac{\bar{u}_1[\hat{\mu}]}{\underline{u}_1[\hat{\mu}]} = \frac{(1-\alpha-\theta)^2 - \alpha\theta(\theta-\theta_1)}{(1-\alpha-\theta)\left[(1-\theta)^2-\alpha\right]}(1-\theta)\frac{\bar{Y}[\mu^0]}{\underline{Y}[\mu^0]}. \tag{B6}$$

Now when $\theta_1 = 0$, (B6) reduces to

$$\frac{\bar{u}_1[\hat{\mu}]}{\underline{u}_1[\hat{\mu}]} = \frac{\zeta+\alpha\theta}{\zeta}\frac{\bar{Y}[\mu^0]}{\underline{Y}[\mu^0]} = \frac{\bar{V}[\mu^0]}{\underline{V}[\mu^0]}, \tag{B7}$$

where the last equality follows from table 9.1 (for the case $(1-\theta)^2 > \alpha$). Since $\bar{V}[\mu^0] < \underline{V}[\mu^0]$, we see from (B6) and (B7) that $\bar{u}_1[\hat{\mu}] < \underline{u}_1[\hat{\mu}]$ whenever θ is sufficiently small. Thus, we have found a case where $\bar{u}_i[\mu] < \underline{u}_i[\mu]$ for some worker i.

Turning now to communal surplus, Z, we first note that when $\mu^0 = 1$, we have $Z = U$. Since $\bar{U}[\mu^0] > \underline{U}[\mu^0]$, for $\mu^0 \in (0,1]$ we therefore see that $\bar{Z}[\mu^0] > \underline{Z}[\mu]$ whenever μ^0 is sufficiently close to unity. To see that it is possible that $\bar{Z}[\mu^0] < \underline{Z}[\mu^0]$, consider the case where $\alpha = (1-\theta)^2$. Substituting $\alpha = (1$

$-\theta)^2$ and simplifying, yields from table 9.1

$$\frac{\bar{Z}[\mu^0]}{\underline{Z}[\mu^0]}=\frac{(2-\theta-\mu^0)}{(1-\theta)(1-\mu^0)}(1-\theta)^{(1-\theta)/[(1-\theta)-(1-\theta)^2]}$$
$$=\frac{(2-\theta-\mu^0)}{(1-\theta)(1-\mu^0)}(1-\theta)^{1/\theta}. \tag{B8}$$

Moreover, since $\lim_{\theta\to 0}(1-\theta)^{1/\theta}=1/e$, (B8) implies that

$$\lim_{\theta\to 0}\frac{\bar{Z}[\mu^0]}{\underline{Z}[\mu^0]}=\frac{(2-\mu^0)}{e(1-\mu^0)}, \tag{B9}$$

which is less than unity when μ^0 is close to zero. Thus, sufficiently small θ and μ^0 would ensure that communal surplus is higher when capital leads than when labor leads.

Appendix C

Proof of lemma 1. Take any parameters α, β and γ_i satisfying (1) and (2) and $(1-\theta)^2-\alpha>0$, so that $\alpha>0$, $\beta>0$, $\alpha+\beta\leqslant 1$, and $\zeta=1-\alpha-\theta>0$. Then we first verify that the quantity

$$Q=\left(\frac{(1-\theta)^2-\alpha}{\zeta}\right)^{\zeta}\left(\frac{1}{1-\theta}\right)^{1-\theta} \tag{C1}$$

is less than unity. To this end take logarithms to obtain

$$\ln Q=\zeta\ln\left(\frac{(1-\theta)^2-\alpha}{\zeta}\right)+(1-\theta)\ln\left(\frac{1}{1-\theta}\right). \tag{C2}$$

But

$$\frac{\partial\ln Q}{\partial\alpha}=1-\frac{\zeta}{(1-\theta)^2-\alpha}-\ln\left(\frac{(1-\theta)^2-\alpha}{\zeta}\right), \tag{C3}$$

which is strictly negative since

$$\ln x>1-\frac{1}{x},\qquad 0<x<1, \tag{C4}$$

and

$$\zeta-((1-\theta)^2-\alpha)=(1-\theta)-(1-\theta)^2>0. \tag{C5}$$

Moreover, when $\alpha=0$, (C2) implies

$$\ln Q|_{\alpha=0}=(1-\theta)\ln(1-\theta)+(1-\theta)\ln\left(\frac{1}{1-\theta}\right)=0. \tag{C6}$$

Since $\partial \ln Q/\partial\alpha<0, \ln Q<0$ whenever $\alpha>0$, as desired. We now proceed to the main assertions of lemma 1.

$E_1<1$ and $\lim_{\alpha+\beta\to 1}E_1=0$ are immediate since $1-\alpha>\theta$.

To see that $E_i<1$ and $\lim_{\alpha+\beta\to 1}E_i=0$, $i=2,3,4$, note that

$$E_i=Q^{1/(1-\alpha-\beta)}P_i, \qquad i=2,3,4, \tag{C7}$$

where

$$P_2=1; \qquad P_3=\left(\frac{\theta}{1-\alpha}\right)^{(1-\alpha)/(1-\alpha-\beta)};$$
$$P_4=\left(\frac{\zeta}{\zeta+\alpha\theta}\right)^{(1-\alpha)/(1-\alpha-\beta)}, \tag{C8}$$

so that $P_i\leqslant 1$, for all i. Since $Q<1$ for all α and β for which $\alpha+\beta\leqslant 1$, the assertion follows from (C7).

References

Başar, T., H. Selbuz and M. Sertel (1978) "Workers' Cooperatives Facing Competitive Capitalism", Technical Report, Marmara Scientific and Industrial Research Institute, Gebze, Turkey. (See Chapter 8 of this book.)

Cable, J.R. and F.R. FitzRoy (1978) "Productive Efficiency, Incentives and Employee Participation: A Study of West German Firms", dp-series no. dp/78-63, International Institute of Management, West Berlin.

Dirickx, Y.M.I. and M.R. Sertel (1978) "Comparative Political Economy of Capitalism, Communism, Slavery and Colonialism in a Nutshell", *Recherches Economiques de Louvain*, 44, no. 3.

Domar, E.D. (1966) "The Soviet Collective Farm as a Producer Cooperative", *The American Economic Review*, 56, 734–757.

Groves, T. (1978) "Efficient Collective Choice with Compensation", The Economic Series, Technical Report No. 258, Institute for Mathematical Studies in the Social Sciences, Stanford University.

Kleindorfer, P.R. and M.R. Sertel (1976) "Equilibrium Analysis of Sharecropping", preprint Series No. 1/76-63, International Institute of Management, West Berlin. (See Chapter 6 of this book.)

Kleindorfer, P.R. and M.R. Sertel (1978) "Pre-enterprises and Enterprises", dp-series no. dp/78-38, International Institute of Management, West Berlin.

Kleindorfer, P.R. and M.R. Sertel (1979) "Profit-Maximizing Design of Enterprises through Incentives", *The Journal of Economic Theory*, 20, 318–339. (See Chapter 4 of this book.)

Sertel, M., T. Başar and H. Selbuz (1978) "Workers' Enterprises Facing Competitive Capitalism", Technical Report No. 44, Marmara Scientific and Industrial Research Institute, Applied Mathematics Division, Gebze, Turkey. (See Chapter 8 of this book.)

Vanek, J. (1970) *The General Theory of Labor Managed Market Economics* (Cornell University Press, Ithaca).

Ward, B.N. (1958) "The Firm in Illyria: Market Syndicalism", *The American Economic Review*, 48, 566–589.

CHAPTER 10

Capitalism, communism and labor management in a dynamic nutshell under constant returns to scale

CARL CHIARELLA and MURAT R. SERTEL

1. Introduction

Our aim is to analyze some of the different political economies considered by Dirickx and Sertel (1978) (henceforth DS) in an intertemporal framework. We pose the various political economies as differential games between the agents of the particular economy, e.g. between workers and capitalists under the different forms of capitalism, between workers and workers' council under the different forms of labor management. Each agent (or group of agents) maximizes a discounted utility integral over an infinite horizon subject to his economic constraints. We analyze the equilibrium towards which certain solutions of various differential games tend as well as the stability properties of the equilibrium (solution). Where possible we draw phase diagrams which enable us to characterize the manner in which the main economic quantities behave through time. For those political economies whose dynamic behavior is governed by more than two differential equations (so that a phase diagram analysis is no longer possible) we have to be content with the knowledge that the equilibrium is locally asymptotically stable.

Our economic framework is that of the neoclassical one-sector growth model, one good only is produced and it may be either consumed or combined with labor in the productive process to produce further output. Thus, output Y is given by

$$Y = K^{\alpha} L^{\beta}, \quad \text{with } 0 < \alpha = 1 - \beta < 1, \tag{1}$$

Workers and Incentives, by M.R. Sertel

where K is the stock of productive capital and L is the amount of labor input. As in DS we assume constant returns to scale. If we assume that there are a workers each offering a fraction x of his total available labor $(0 \leqslant x \leqslant 1)$ then (1) can be written

$$Y = ak^{\alpha}x^{\beta}, \tag{2}$$

where we put $k = K/a$, the amount of capital per worker. Unlike the standard neoclassical world, our workers do not unstintingly offer all their available labor to the productive process, so we pose them as deriving disutility from work. It will therefore be instructive for comparison purposes to begin our analysis with a discussion of the neoclassical optimal growth model with leisure-liking workers.

2. Neoclassical optimal growth with a leisure dependent utility function

We consider the neoclassical economy equipped with a workers. A benevolent social planner will seek the labor participation ratio, x, and *per capita* consumption c so as to

$$\max_{c,x} \int_0^{\infty} e^{-\rho t} \log(c - x^{\gamma})\, dt \tag{3}$$

subject to the capital accumulation equation

$$\dot{k} = k^{\alpha}x^{\beta} - c \qquad (k(0) = k_0 \text{ given}) \tag{4}$$

showing output/capita $(k^{\alpha}x^{\beta})$ being divided between consumption *per capita* (c) and investment *per capita* $(\dot{k})$. The integrand of (3) is the typical worker's utility, time-discounted at a rate $\rho > 0$, the x^{γ} term representing disutility of work (reflecting utility of leisure). Throughout we assume $\gamma > 1$.

Defining the Hamiltonian

$$H = e^{-\rho t}\left[\log(c - x^{\gamma}) + \lambda(k^{\alpha}x^{\beta} - c)\right], \tag{5}$$

where $e^{-\rho t}\lambda(t)$ is the shadow price of k, the capital stock for worker, we readily obtain the necessary conditions for the maximum of (3) subject to (4), namely

$$\frac{1}{c - x^{\gamma}} = \lambda, \tag{6}$$

$$\frac{\gamma x^{\gamma - 1}}{c - x^{\gamma}} = \lambda\beta\left(\frac{k}{x}\right)^{\alpha}, \tag{7}$$

and

$$\dot{\lambda}=\lambda\left[\rho-\alpha\left(\frac{x}{k}\right)^{\beta}\right]. \tag{8}$$

Now (6) and (7) combine to give us the x, k mix along the optimal path, in fact,

$$x=\left(\frac{\beta}{\alpha}\right)^{e}k^{\alpha e}, \tag{9}$$

where $e=1/(\gamma-\beta)$.

Equation (9) shows us a concave relationship between x and k along the optimal path. Observing from (6) that

$$c=x^{\gamma}+1/\lambda, \tag{10}$$

we can use (9) and (10) to express the differential equations for k and λ as

$$\dot{k}=\left(1-\frac{\beta}{\gamma}\right)\left(\frac{\beta}{\gamma}\right)^{\beta e}k^{\alpha\gamma e}-\frac{1}{\lambda}, \tag{11}$$

$$\dot{\lambda}=\lambda\left(\rho-\alpha\left(\frac{\beta}{\gamma}\right)^{\beta e}k^{-\delta e}\right), \tag{12}$$

where $\delta=-(1-\gamma)\beta$.

The differential equations (11) and (12) together with the transversality condition

$$\lim_{t\to\infty} \mathrm{e}^{-\rho t}\lambda(t)k(t)=0$$

define the optimal path. Standard analysis reveals that the optimal path has the stable arms of the saddle point in the (k, λ) phase plane, illustrated in figure 10.1.

The optimal path tends to the equilibrium described by

$$\bar{k}_n=\left(\frac{\beta}{\gamma}\right)^{1/(\gamma-1)}\left(\frac{\alpha}{\rho}\right)^{1/e\delta}, \tag{13}$$

$$\bar{\lambda}_n=\left(1-\frac{\beta}{\gamma}\right)^{-1}\left(\frac{\beta}{\gamma}\right)^{-1/(\gamma-1)}\left(\frac{\alpha}{\rho}\right)^{-\alpha\gamma/\delta}, \tag{14}$$

with the equilibrium value of x being given by

$$\bar{x}_n=\left(\frac{\beta}{\gamma}\right)^{1/(\gamma-1)}\left(\frac{\alpha}{\rho}\right)^{\alpha/\delta}. \tag{15}$$

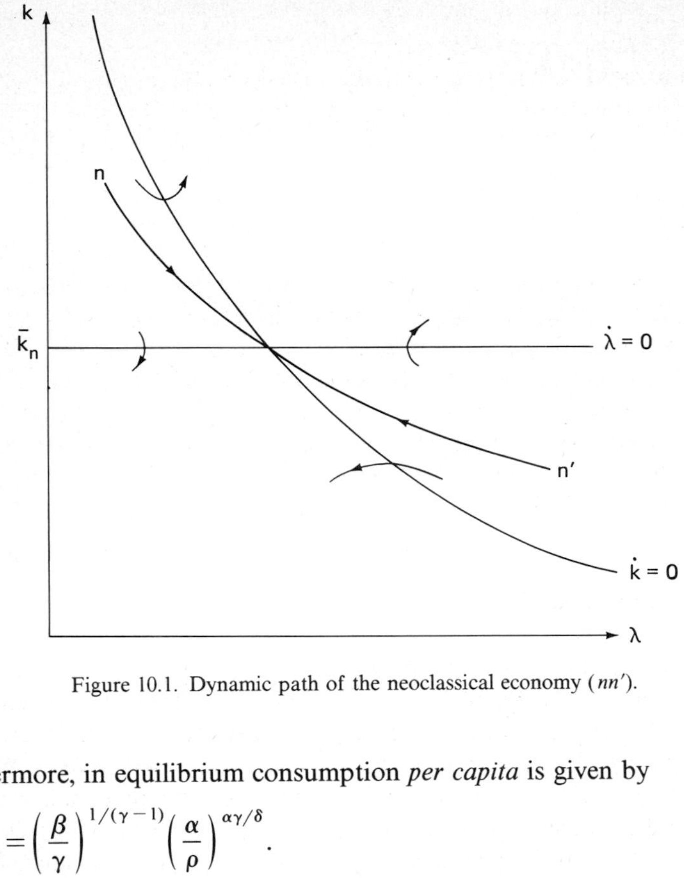

Figure 10.1. Dynamic path of the neoclassical economy (*nn*′).

Furthermore, in equilibrium consumption *per capita* is given by

$$\bar{c}_n = \left(\frac{\beta}{\gamma}\right)^{1/(\gamma-1)} \left(\frac{\alpha}{\rho}\right)^{\alpha\gamma/\delta}. \tag{16}$$

The broad features of the optimal path are the same as those of the standard neoclassical optimal growth model, k, x and c all declining or rising to their equilibrium values depending on whether k_0, the initial capital stock *per capita*, is greater or less than the equilibrium value $\bar{k}_n$. Finally, note that in the limit as $\gamma \to \infty$ the differential system (11) and (12) reduces to

$$\dot{k} = k^{\alpha} - 1/\lambda \tag{17}$$

and

$$\dot{\lambda} = \lambda(\rho - \alpha k^{-\beta}), \tag{18}$$

which is the differential system governing the optimal path of the standard neoclassical optimal growth model. This is expected, of course, since, bearing in mind that $0 \leqslant x \leqslant 1$, the utility function in (3) becomes the standard neoclassical one as $\gamma \to \infty$.

We should point out that an analysis of this problem using a far more general utility function than ours has been carried out by Chase (1967).

3. Capitalism

We model capitalism as a differential game in which the workers each decide on their respective labor inputs and capitalists take the investment decision, each group seeking to maximize a discounted utility integral over an infinite horizon. As in DS the different types of capitalism are distinguished from one another by the institutions which determine the wage, w. The different institutions correspond to different solution concepts for the differential game, e.g. Nash, capitalists as von Stackelberg leaders or workers as von Stackelberg leaders.

3.1. Competitive capitalism

In this version of capitalism the time path for the wage, $w(t)$, is determined by a Walrasion auctioneer. In the auction hall the auctioneer announces a $w(t)$. Given this $w(t)$ each worker chooses $x(t)$ so as to maximize his utility, thus coming up with a labor supply function at every point in time. Whilst given the same $w(t)$, the capitalists determine the amount of labor to be employed and the investment pattern so as to maximize their utility, coming up with a labor demand function at every point in time. The auctioneer ends up announcing $w(t)$ so as to equate labor demand and supply at each point in time.

Thus, given a wage time path $w(t)$, a typical worker seeks $x(t)$ so as to

$$\max_{x} \int_{0}^{\infty} e^{-\rho_1 t}(wx - x^{\gamma})\,dt, \tag{19}$$

where ρ_1 is the discount factor of a typical worker and we take workers' utility to be simply $wx - x^{\gamma}$. (All of our analysis in this and subsequent sections carries in its basic conclusions, only at the expense of computational complication, if we make workers' utility a concave function of $wx - x^{\gamma}$, such as $\log(wx - x^{\gamma})$ or $(wx - x^{\gamma})^{v}$, with $0 < v < 1$.) Now the typical worker under competitive capitalism, being subject to no differential equation constraint, maximizes the integral in (19) by choosing

$$x=\left(\frac{w}{\gamma}\right)^{1/(\gamma-1)}, \tag{20}$$

which displays for us the labor supply function.

The typical capitalist seeks labor input x, and his own consumption c so as to

$$\max_{x,c}\int_0^\infty e^{-\rho_2 t}\log c\,dt, \tag{21}$$

subject to the capital accumulation equation

$$\dot{K}=Y-wax-c, \tag{22}$$

where ρ_2 is the capitalists discount factor. For analytical convenience we have assumed a logarithmic utility function for the capitalists. The differential equation (22) shows output Y being split up between the total wage bill, wax, capitalists consumption, c, and investment, $\dot{K}$. In the scenario we envisage there are b (>1), say, capitalists and to be strictly correct we should write (22) as

$$\dot{K}=Y-wax-bc. \tag{23}$$

However, if in (22) we interpret a as the ratio of the number of workers to the number of capitalists, and K as the amount of capital owned by a typical capitalist then there will be no logical inconsistency. Alternatively, we may simply assume that there is just one capitalist competing against the a workers, and this is the viewpoint we shall henceforth adopt. As in section 2 we will find it more convenient to work in terms of k, the amount of capital per worker, in terms of which (22) becomes

$$\dot{k}=k^\alpha x^\beta-wx-c/a. \tag{24}$$

The capitalist must determine c and x so as to maximize his discounted Hamiltonian

$$H_2=e^{-\rho_2 t}\left[\log c+\lambda\left(k^\alpha x^\beta-wx-c/a\right)\right] \tag{25}$$

with respect to c and x, where $e^{-\rho_2 t}\lambda(t)$ is the capitalist's shadow price on k. Thus, maximization of H_2 with respect to c yields

$$\lambda c=a, \tag{26}$$

and maximization with respect to x gives

$$x=\left(\frac{w}{\beta}\right)^{-1/\alpha}k. \tag{27}$$

The differential equation for λ turns out to be

$$\dot{\lambda}=\lambda\left(\rho_2-\alpha\left(\frac{x}{k}\right)^{\beta}\right). \tag{28}$$

Given a wage time path $w(t)$, (26), (27) and the differential equations (24), (28) together with the transversality condition

$$\lim_{t\to\infty} e^{-\rho_2 t}\lambda(t)k(t)=0 \tag{29}$$

enable the capitalist to determine $k(t)$ and hence, via (27), his labor demand function $x(t)$.

The wage time path which equates labor supply and demand at every point in time will be such as to equate x in (20) to x in (27). Thus, eliminating w between these latter two equations we find that along the labor market clearing time path

$$x=\left(\frac{\beta}{\gamma}\right)^{e}k^{\alpha e}. \tag{30}$$

Referring back to (9) we observe that the relation between x and k is the same under competitive capitalism as in the neoclassical model of section 2. Of course, this does not mean that the time paths for x and k are the same under the two different economic systems; indeed, as we shall see shortly, they are different. All that we have shown is that the neoclassical and competitive capitalist economies mix labor and capital in the same proportions, but the actual amounts that are mixed in the two economic systems can and do differ.

Substituting (26), (27) and (30) into (24) and (28) we find that the differential equations for k and λ reduce to

$$\dot{k}=\alpha\left(\frac{\beta}{\gamma}\right)^{\beta e}k^{\alpha\gamma e}-1/\lambda \tag{31}$$

and

$$\dot{\lambda}=\lambda\left(\rho_2-\alpha\left(\frac{\beta}{\gamma}\right)^{\beta e}k^{-\delta e}\right), \tag{32}$$

which together with the transversality condition (29) completely determine the time paths for k and λ and thereby those for x, w and c. Comparing the differential system of competitive capitalism (31)–(32) with the corresponding differential system for the neoclassical economy (11)–(12), we see that the two systems are somewhat different in the differential equation for k

and hence will generate different time paths starting from the same initial value of k.

The equilibrium of the differential system (31)–(32) is given by

$$\bar{k}_A = \left(\frac{\beta}{\gamma}\right)^{1/(\gamma-1)} \left(\frac{\alpha}{\rho_2}\right)^{1/\delta e}, \tag{33}$$

$$\bar{\lambda}_A = \frac{1}{\alpha}\left(\frac{\beta}{\gamma}\right)^{-1/(\gamma-1)} \left(\frac{\rho_2}{\alpha}\right)^{\alpha\gamma/\delta}, \tag{34}$$

so that equilibrium values of x, w and c are

$$\bar{x}_A = \left(\frac{\beta}{\gamma}\right)^{1/(\gamma-1)} \left(\frac{\alpha}{\rho_2}\right)^{\alpha/\delta}, \tag{35}$$

$$\bar{w}_A = \beta\left(\frac{\alpha}{\rho_2}\right)^{\alpha/\beta}, \tag{36}$$

$$\bar{c}_A = a/\bar{\lambda}. \tag{37}$$

If we equate the discount factor ρ_2 of the capitalist to the rental on capital in the static framework of DS then we observe that the equilibrium values of k, x and w that we have obtained correspond precisely to those obtained by DS in their static version of competitive capitalism.

It is a straightforward matter to draw the phase diagram for the differential system (31)–(32) and show that the equilibrium $(\bar{k}_A, \bar{\lambda}_A)$ is a saddle point. Indeed the phase diagram will have the same general features as fig. 10.1. In fig. 10.2 we show just the stable arms of the saddle (AA') which constitute the dynamic path of competitive capitalism. We show, on the same diagram, the dynamic path of the neoclassical economy, (nn'), using the fact that

$$\bar{\lambda}_A = \frac{(1-\beta/\gamma)}{\alpha}\bar{\lambda}_n > \bar{\lambda}_n. \tag{38}$$

Note: Using arguments on the relative values of $\mathrm{d}k/\mathrm{d}\lambda$ in each economy we show in the appendix that the dynamic paths AA' and nn' never cross.

We see from fig. 10.2 that the qualitative features of the dynamic path are the same under competitive capitalism as under the neoclassical regime of optimal growth. Thus, given the same initial capital stock per worker, k_0, both economies have k declining (rising) to its equilibrium value $\bar{k}_A$ if k_0 is greater (less) than $\bar{k}_A$. The competitive capitalist economy, however, will start and finish with a higher value for the shadow price of capital.

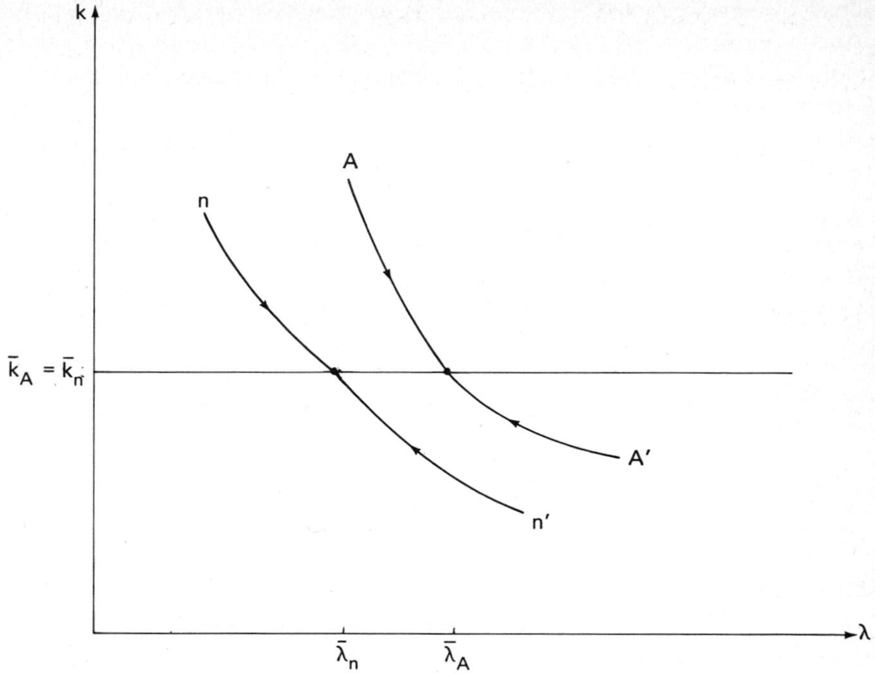

Figure 10.2. Dynamic paths of competitive capitalism (AA') and the neoclassical economy (nn').

3.2. Capitalism with monopsony capital

DS model this form of capitalism as one in which the workers are still price (i.e. wage) takers but the capitalists collude in the labor market and dictate the wage. We model this version of capitalism as the differential game of the previous section but with the capitalists as von Stackelberg leaders. Thus, the optimal reaction of a typical worker to a given wage time path is still given by (20). The typical capitalist, however, takes the wage time path not as given, but rather chooses it optimally subject to the workers' optimal reaction (20). Hence, the typical capitalist seeks c and x so as to

$$\max_{x,c} \int_0^\infty e^{-\rho_2 t} \log c \, dt$$

subject to

$$\dot{k} = k^\alpha x^\beta - \gamma x^\gamma - c/a, \tag{39}$$

where we have obtained the differential equation (39) by substituting (20) into the capitalists' accumulation equation (24) under competitive capitalism to eliminate w. (Alternatively we could have eliminated x and made w a control variable.)

Choosing c and x so as to maximize the discounted Hamiltonian

$$H_2 = \mathrm{e}^{-\rho_2 t}\left[\log c + \lambda\left(k^{\alpha}x^{\beta} - \gamma x^{\gamma} - c/a\right)\right], \tag{40}$$

the necessary conditions for the capitalist become, (26) as under competitive capitalism, together with

$$x = \left(\frac{1}{\gamma}\right)^{e}\left(\frac{\beta}{\gamma}\right)^{e} k^{\alpha e} \tag{41}$$

and, for λ, the differential equation

$$\dot{\lambda} = \lambda\left(\rho_2 - \left(\frac{1}{\gamma}\right)^{\beta e}\cdot\alpha\left(\frac{\beta}{\gamma}\right)^{\beta e} k^{-\delta e}\right). \tag{42}$$

Comparing (41) with (30) we see that, considered as a function of k,

$$x(k)_{\text{monopsony capitalism}} < x(k)_{\text{competitive capitalism}}, \tag{43}$$

i.e. at a given level of capital stock less labor is employed under monopsony capitalism than under competitive capitalism. It then follows from (20) that at a given level of capital stock a lower wage is realized under monopsony capitalism than under competitive capitalism. These facts are summarized in the schedules shown in fig. 10.3.

Substituting (26) and (41) into (40) the differential equation for k becomes

$$\dot{k} = \left(\frac{1}{\gamma}\right)^{\beta e}\left(1 - \frac{\beta}{\gamma}\right)\left(\frac{\beta}{\gamma}\right)^{\beta e} k^{\alpha\gamma e} - 1/\lambda. \tag{44}$$

It is interesting to observe that in the limit as $\gamma \to \infty$, the differential system (42)–(43) and the differential system (11)–(12) for the neoclassical economy tend to the same limit (17)–(18). Thus, in the limit as $\gamma \to \infty$, with a leisure *independent* utility function for workers, the dynamic path under monopsony capitalism will be the same as that under the neoclassical system.

The differential system (42)–(43) tends to the equilibrium

$$\bar{k}_{\mathrm{B}} = \gamma^{-1/(\gamma-1)}\bar{k}_{\mathrm{A}}, \tag{45}$$

$$\bar{\lambda}_{\mathrm{B}} = \gamma^{1/(\gamma-1)}\left(\frac{1-\beta}{1-\beta/\gamma}\right)\bar{\lambda}_{\mathrm{A}}. \tag{46}$$

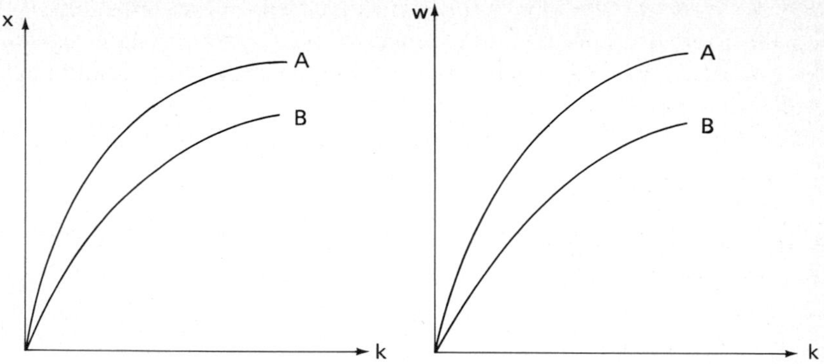

Figure 10.3. Competitive capitalism (A) and monopsony capitalism (B).

It follows immediately that the equilibrium values of x, w and c are

$$\bar{x}_{\mathrm{B}} = \gamma^{-1/(\gamma-1)} \bar{x}_{\mathrm{A}}, \tag{47}$$

$$\bar{w}_{\mathrm{B}} = \gamma^{-1} \bar{w}_{\mathrm{A}}, \tag{48}$$

$$\bar{c}_{\mathrm{B}} = \gamma^{-1/(\gamma-1)} \left(\frac{1-\beta/\gamma}{1-\beta} \right) \bar{c}_{\mathrm{A}}. \tag{49}$$

Clearly,

$$\bar{k}_{\mathrm{B}} < \bar{k}_{\mathrm{A}}; \qquad \bar{x}_{\mathrm{B}} < \bar{x}_{\mathrm{A}}; \qquad \bar{w}_{\mathrm{B}} < \bar{w}_{\mathrm{A}}, \tag{50}$$

but independent of parameter values there is no unambiguous relationship between $\bar{\lambda}_{\mathrm{B}}$ and $\bar{\lambda}_{\mathrm{A}}$ nor between $\bar{c}_{\mathrm{B}}$ and $\bar{c}_{\mathrm{A}}$. The function

$$f(\gamma) = \gamma^{1/(\gamma-1)}(1-\beta)/(1-\beta/\gamma),$$

which occurs in (46) declines monotonically from e (the exponential number) to $(1-\beta)$ as γ increases from 1 to ∞. Denoting by γ^* the value of γ such that $f(\gamma^*)=1$, we can assert that

$$\bar{\lambda}_{\mathrm{B}} \gtreqless \bar{\lambda}_{\mathrm{A}}, \quad \text{iff } \gamma \lesseqgtr \gamma^*, \tag{51a}$$

$$\bar{c}_{\mathrm{B}} \lesseqgtr c_{\mathrm{A}}, \quad \text{iff } \gamma \lesseqgtr \gamma^*. \tag{51b}$$

These equilibrium values for k, x and w correspond with those obtained by DS in their static version of monopsony capital.

The construction of the phase diagram for the differential system (42)–(43) is straightforward and we will obtain the familiar saddle point with the same features as shown in fig. 10.1. In fig. 10.4 we show the dynamic path of monopoly capitalism (BB') together with that of competitive capitalism

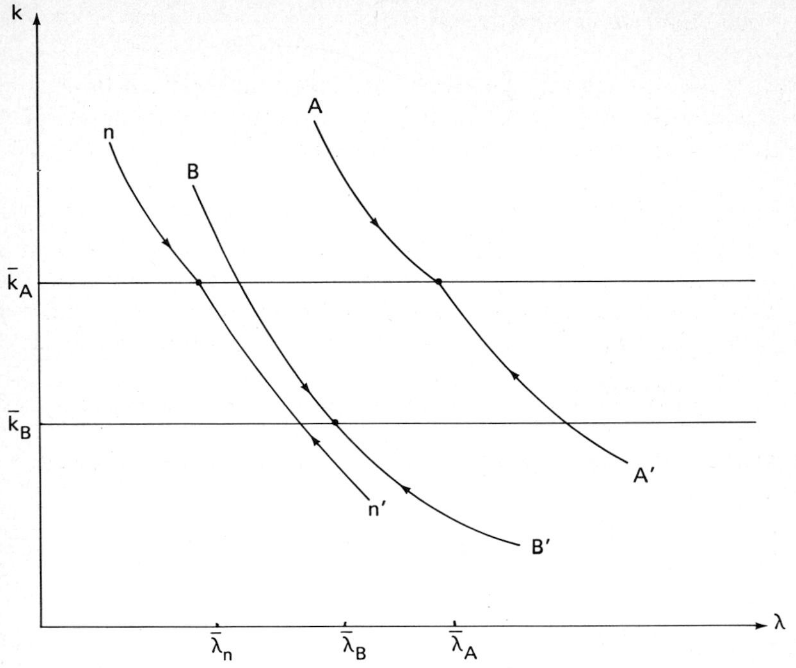

Figure 10.4. Dynamic paths of competitive capitalism (*AA′*), monopsony capitalism (*BB′*) and the neoclassical system (*nn′*).

(*AA′*), illustrating the case $\gamma > \gamma^*$. We show in the appendix that these two curves do not cross.

We see from fig. 10.4 that the dynamic paths under monopsony capitalism have the same qualitative features as under competitive capitalism except when the initial capital stock is such that $\bar{k}_B < \bar{k}_0 < \bar{k}_A$. In this case the quantities k, x and w *decline* towards their equilibrium values under monopsony capitalism whilst they *rise* towards equilibrium under competitive capitalism.

We also show in fig. 10.4 the dynamic path (*nn′*) of the neoclassical system. We have used the fact that

$$\bar{\lambda}_B = \gamma^{1/(\gamma-1)}\bar{\lambda}_n > \bar{\lambda}_n, \tag{52}$$

and information on the relative slopes of *nn′* and *BB′* which is given in the appendix.

3.3. Capitalism with monopoly labor

Now it is the workers who collude by forming a monopolistic labor union and dictating the wage to the capitalists. In other words, in terms of the differential game framework which we have developed, the workers become von Stackelberg leaders.

Thus, the capitalists, taking the wage w as given and seeking x and c so as to maximize the utility integral (21), will react as under competitive capitalism, i.e. according to equations (26), (27), (24) and (28). The workers then seek to maximize the utility of a typical worker subject to these conditions. Now taking account of (27) a typical worker's utility integral becomes

$$\int_0^{\infty} e^{-\rho_1 t}(\beta k^{\alpha} x^{\beta} - x^{\gamma})\,dt. \tag{53}$$

The workers seek x so as to maximize (53) subject to the differential equation constraints

$$\dot{k} = \alpha k^{\alpha} x^{\beta} - 1/\lambda \tag{54}$$

and

$$\dot{\lambda} = \lambda\left(\rho_2 - \alpha\left(\frac{x}{k}\right)^{\beta}\right). \tag{55}$$

The differential equation (54) is obtained by substituting (26) and (27) into the differential equation (24).

The workers solve their optimization problem by forming the Hamiltonian

$$H = e^{-\rho_2 t}\left[\beta k^{\alpha} x^{\beta} - x^{\gamma} + \eta_1(\alpha k^{\alpha} x^{\beta} - 1/\lambda) + \eta_2 \lambda\left(\rho_2 - \alpha\left(\frac{x}{k}\right)^{\beta}\right)\right], \tag{56}$$

where $\eta_1 e^{-\rho_1 t}$ and $\eta_2 e^{-\rho_2 t}$ are Lagrange multipliers. The interpretation of $\eta_1 e^{-\rho_1 t}$ as the workers' shadow price on k is clear, but the interpretation of $\eta_2 e^{-\rho_1 t}$ as a shadow price on λ is not so apparent since λ is itself a shadow price. Maximizing H with respect to x we obtain

$$x = \left(\frac{\beta}{\gamma}\right)^{e} k^{\alpha e}\left[\beta + \alpha\eta_1 - \frac{\alpha\lambda\eta_2}{k}\right]^{e}. \tag{57}$$

On comparing with (30) we see that the relation between x and k differs from the corresponding one under competitive capitalism by the appearance of the last factor on the right-hand side of (57). The differential equations for η_1 and η_2 turn out to be

$$\dot{\eta}_1 - \rho_1\eta_1 = -\alpha\left(\frac{x}{k}\right)^{\beta}\left[\beta + \alpha\eta_1 + \frac{\beta\lambda\eta_2}{k}\right] \tag{58}$$

and

$$\dot{\eta}_2 - \rho_1\eta_2 = -\frac{\eta_1}{\lambda^2} - \eta_2\left(\rho_2 - \alpha\left(\frac{x}{k}\right)^{\beta}\right). \tag{59}$$

The dynamic motion of capitalism under monopoly labor is governed by the differential equations (54), (55), (58) and (59) for k, λ, η_1 and η_2, respectively, with x given in terms of these by (57). Since we are now dealing with a differential system in four-dimensional space it is impossible to draw a phase diagram as we have done for all the other systems considered up to this point. We shall determine the equilibrium point of the differential system for k, λ, η_1 and η_2 and then analyze its local stability properties.

After some lengthy calculations we find that the differential system (54)–(55), (58)–(59), has the equilibrium point given by

$$\bar{k}_c = \theta^{1/(\gamma-1)}\bar{k}_A, \tag{60a}$$

$$\bar{\lambda}_c = \theta^{-1/(\gamma-1)}\bar{\lambda}_A, \tag{60b}$$

$$\bar{\eta}_1 = \left(\frac{\rho_1}{\rho_2} - \beta\right)\Big/\left(\alpha + \beta\frac{\rho_2}{\rho_1}\right), \tag{60c}$$

$$\bar{\eta}_2 = \bar{\eta}_1/\rho_1\lambda^2, \tag{60d}$$

where we define

$$\theta = \frac{\alpha(\rho_1/\rho_2 - 1) + \beta\rho_2/\rho_1}{\alpha + \beta\rho_2/\rho_1}. \tag{61}$$

From (57) we have the equilibrium level of x:

$$\bar{x}_c = \theta^{1/(\gamma-1)}\bar{x}_A. \tag{62}$$

In the special case of equal discount factors $\rho_1 = \rho_2 = \rho$ we find that $\theta = \beta$ and hence

$$\bar{x}_c = \beta^{1/(\gamma-1)}\bar{x}_A < \bar{x}_A, \tag{63a}$$

$$\bar{k}_c = \beta^{1/(\gamma-1)}\bar{k}_A < \bar{k}_A. \tag{63b}$$

Now this result does *not* agree with the corresponding static result of DS who found that $\bar{x}_c = \bar{x}_A$ and $\bar{k}_c = \bar{k}_A$, so that in their static version capitalism with monopoly labor reproduces the outcome of competitive capitalism.

Since there are four differential equations governing the dynamic motion of capitalism under monopoly labor it is impossible to carry out a stability analysis of the equilibrium using phase plane analysis. The most we can do is a local stability analysis by linearizing the differential system (54)–(55), (58)–(59) about the equilibrium (60a–d). Examination of the eigenvalues of the resulting linear system indicate that the equilibrium is a saddle point in four-dimensional $(k, \lambda, \eta_1, \eta_2)$ space. Hence, invoking a theorem due to Rockafellor (1976) we can assert that the stable arm of the saddle point is the dynamic path of capitalism under monopoly labor. The details of the calculations involved are set out in Chiarella (1980). We stress that all of this stability analysis is local and we have only shown that the solution of the workers' optimization problem exists locally around the equilibrium (60a–d). The question of the global existence of such a solution remains open.

4. Communism and labor management

Now we pose communism and cooperative labor management as differential games. Both have the common difference from capitalism that capitalists no longer decide on how much capital or labor to hire, these decisions are now taken by bodies either imposed upon the workers or elected to represent the workers' collective interests. The systems considered here differ among themselves in that communism pays workers wages, while in the labor-managed political economy workers are remunerated by communal value added per worker minus investment per worker.

4.1. Communism

In communism the "dictatorship of the proletariat" expropriates the capitalists and through its central committee seeks the optimal investment and wage paths. In all of this it acts in the name and interests of the workers. The typical individual worker still reacts as under competitive capitalism and, given a wage time path w, will determine his labor contribution x so as to maximize the utility integral (19). Thus, the worker's optimal reaction to a given wage time path is still summarized by eq. (20).

The central committee acting as a von Stackelberg leader takes into account the workers' reaction to each w time path when seeking the w which will maximize a typical worker's utility integral. Thus, the central committee seeks $w(t)$ so as to

$$\max_{w} \int_0^{\infty} \mathrm{e}^{-\rho t}(wx - x^{\gamma})\,\mathrm{d}t, \tag{64}$$

subject to the accumulation equation

$$\dot{k} = k^{\alpha}x^{\beta} - wx, \tag{65}$$

and the typical worker's reaction

$$x = \left(\frac{w}{\gamma}\right)^{1/(\gamma-1)} \tag{66}$$

to w. We allow the central committee to adopt a discount factor ρ which may be different from that of a typical worker. However, since we do not allow the workers to save, this difference turns out not to make a difference in the final analysis.

Using (66) to eliminate x from (64) and (65), the central committee's optimal control problem becomes

$$\max_{\omega} \int_0^{\infty} \mathrm{e}^{-\rho t}(\gamma - 1)\omega\,\mathrm{d}t, \tag{67}$$

subject to

$$\dot{k} = k^{\alpha}\omega^{\beta/\gamma} - \gamma\omega, \tag{68}$$

where we set

$$\omega = \left(\frac{w}{\gamma}\right)^{\gamma/(\gamma-1)}. \tag{69}$$

Maximizing the Hamiltonian

$$H = \mathrm{e}^{-\rho t}\left[(\gamma-1)\omega + \lambda\left(k^{\alpha}\omega^{\beta/\gamma} - \gamma\omega\right)\right] \tag{70}$$

with respect to ω, where $\mathrm{e}^{-\rho t}\lambda(t)$ is the central committee's shadow price on capital per worker, yields

$$\frac{\beta}{\gamma}k^{\alpha}\omega^{(\beta-\gamma)/\gamma} = \frac{\gamma\lambda + 1 - \gamma}{\lambda}. \tag{71}$$

Substituting (66) and (69) into (71) we find that the optimal capital–labor mix in the communist economy is given by

$$x = \left(\frac{\beta}{\gamma}\right)^{e} k^{\alpha e}\left(\frac{\lambda}{\gamma\lambda + 1 - \gamma}\right)^{e}, \tag{72}$$

which differs from (30), the corresponding relation under competitive capitalism, by the last factor on the right-hand side.

The differential equation for λ turns out to be

$$\dot{\lambda}=\lambda\left(\rho-\alpha\frac{\omega^{\beta/\gamma}}{k^{\beta}}\right). \tag{73}$$

Using (71) to eliminate ω from the differential equations (68) and (73) we obtain that k and λ satisfy the differential equations

$$\dot{k}=\left(\frac{\beta}{\gamma}\right)^{\beta e}k^{\alpha\gamma e}\left(\frac{\gamma\lambda+1-\gamma}{\lambda}\right)^{-\gamma e}\left(\frac{(\gamma-\beta)\lambda+1-\gamma}{\lambda}\right) \tag{74}$$

and

$$\dot{\lambda}=\lambda\left[\rho-\alpha\left(\frac{\gamma}{\beta}\right)^{-\beta e}\left(\frac{\lambda\gamma+1-\gamma}{\lambda}\right)^{-\beta e}k^{-\delta e}\right]. \tag{75}$$

The equilibrium of the differential system (74)–(75) is described by

$$\bar{k}_{\mathrm{D}}=\beta^{1/(1-\gamma)}\bar{k}_{\mathrm{A}}>\bar{k}_{\mathrm{A}}, \tag{76}$$

$$\bar{\lambda}_{\mathrm{D}}=(\gamma-1)/(\gamma-\beta), \tag{77}$$

so that

$$\bar{x}_{\mathrm{D}}=\beta^{1/(1-\gamma)}\bar{x}_{\mathrm{A}}>\bar{x}_{\mathrm{A}}, \tag{78}$$

$$\bar{w}_{\mathrm{D}}=\beta^{-1}\bar{w}_{\mathrm{A}}>\bar{w}_{\mathrm{A}}. \tag{79}$$

We observe that the equilibrium values of k, x and w differ from the corresponding ones under competitive capitalism. This result contrasts with that obtained by DS for their static nutshell; there the outcomes of communism and competitive capitalism coincided.

It is not possible to make any definitive assertion about the relation between $\bar{\lambda}_{\mathrm{D}}$ and $\bar{\lambda}_{\mathrm{A}}$, since $\bar{\lambda}_{\mathrm{A}}$, eq. (34) involves an extra parameter, ρ_2. In fact, of all the political economies we consider, communism is the only one in which the equilibrium value of λ does *not* depend on the discount factor.

The phase diagram of the differential system (74)–(75) is shown in fig. 10.5, where we see the familiar saddle point. The stable arms of the saddle, DD', constitute the dynamic path of the communist economy, this being the unique path satisfying the transversability condition

$$\lim_{t\to\infty}\mathrm{e}^{-\rho t}\lambda(t)k(t)=0. \tag{80}$$

The only point in the construction of the phase diagram requiring some comment is that the asymptote $\tilde{k}$ satisfies

$$\tilde{k}=\left(\frac{\beta}{\gamma}\right)^{1/(\gamma-1)}\bar{k}_{\mathrm{D}}<\bar{k}_{\mathrm{D}}. \tag{81}$$

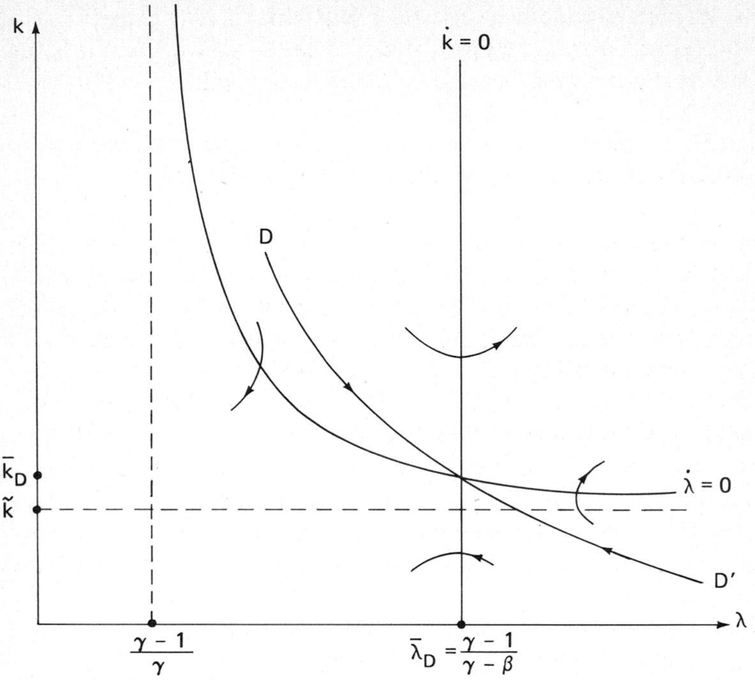

Figure 10.5. Dynamic path of the communist economy (*DD′*).

Since there is no definite relation between $\bar{\lambda}_D$ and $\bar{\lambda}_A$ it is not possible to make any comparison of *AA′* and *DD′* on the same diagram. However, some comparisons with the competitive capitalist economy are possible. If the initial capital stock is such that $\bar{k}_A < \bar{k}_0 < \bar{k}_D$, then the two economies move in opposite directions, k, x and w *rising* in the communist economy whilst declining in the competitive capitalist economy to their equilibrium values. For k_0 in any other interval the two economies move in the same direction. Considering eq. (72), which gives the optimal capital–labor mix in the communist economy, the factor $\lambda/(\gamma\lambda + 1 - \gamma)$ is greater or less than 1 depending on whether λ is greater or less than 1. Since $\bar{\lambda}_D < 1$, it is clear from the phase diagram (fig. 10.5) that if $k_0 < \bar{k}_D$, then after a finite time $\lambda < 1$, whilst if $k_0 > \bar{k}_D$, λ always exceeds unity. Thus, the relation

$$\lambda/(\gamma\lambda + 1 - \gamma) < 1 \tag{82}$$

holds for all except a finite time interval along the dynamic path of the communist economy and hence, comparing with (30), we find that

$$x(k)_{\text{communism}} < x(k)_{\text{competitive capitalism}}, \tag{83}$$

for all except a finite time interval. So, with the same capital stock the communist economy generally will call forth less labor than the competitive capitalist economy and, because of relation (66), will pay a lower wage.

4.2. Cooperative labor management

Following DS we assume that the workers all have the same preferences (now including time preferences) and enter production symmetrically. Our approach parallels that of DS in that we analyze the consequences when each worker assumes that his fellows will contribute as much work on the average as he himself does.

The workers elect a council whose task is to determine the capital accumulation program which maximizes the utility of a typical worker, given the time path of the labor participation ratio, $x(t)$, of a typical worker. The typical worker, acting as a von Stackelberg leader, thus knows what share in output, i.e. income (or imputed wage), he can expect from a given $x(t)$, and will determine and then supply the $x(t)$ which maximizes his own utility.

Thus, taking $x(t)$ as given the council seeks $y(t)$, the share in output going to a typical worker, so as to maximize

$$\int_0^\infty e^{-\rho t}\log(y-x^\gamma)\,dt, \tag{84}$$

the typical worker's utility integral, subject to the accumulation equation

$$\dot{k}=k^\alpha x^\beta - y, \tag{85}$$

showing output/worker $(k^\alpha x^\beta)$ being divided between output share/worker (y) and investment $(\dot{k})$. Here ρ is the discount factor common to all workers. In the utility integral (84) we have chosen a logarithmic utility function so as to avoid the technical complications involved in dealing with a singular arc optimal control problem.

Once the council has solved its optimal control problem the workers are in a position to know how the output share per worker varies as the $x(t)$ time varies. The typical worker then chooses $x(t)$ so as to maximize the utility integral (84).

The dynamic path which results from this optimization procedure is the same as that obtained if the utility integral (84) were simultaneously maximized with respect to y and x, subject to (85). The solution so obtained is precisely the neoclassical solution of section 2. So the cooperatively labor-managed economy that we postulate here mimicks entirely the neoclassical world of section 2.

If we define the imputed wage as $w_{\mathrm{i}} = y/x$, we find that the equilibrium imputed wage, $\bar{w}_{\mathrm{i}}$, is given by

$$\bar{w}_{\mathrm{i}} = \bar{w}_{\mathrm{A}}/\beta. \tag{86}$$

Now this result is at variance with the corresponding static one of DS who found that under cooperative labor management the imputed wage agreed with that under competitive capitalism.

Appendix

Defining

$$f(k) = \left(\frac{\beta}{\gamma}\right)^{\beta e} k^{\alpha\gamma e} \tag{A1}$$

and

$$g(k) = \alpha\left(\frac{\beta}{\gamma}\right)^{\beta e} k^{-\delta e}, \tag{A2}$$

we have from (11)–(12) that the slope of nn', the path followed by the neoclassical economy, is given by

$$\left(\frac{\mathrm{d}k}{\mathrm{d}\lambda}\right)_{\mathrm{n}} = \frac{(1-\beta/\gamma)f(k) - 1/\lambda}{\lambda(\rho - g(k))}. \tag{A3}$$

While from (31)–(32) the slope of AA', the dynamic path of competitive capitalism, is given by

$$\left(\frac{\mathrm{d}k}{\mathrm{d}\lambda}\right)_{\mathrm{A}} = \frac{(1-\beta)f(k) - 1/\lambda}{\lambda(\rho - g(k))}. \tag{A4}$$

Now

$$(1-\beta/\gamma)f(k) - 1/\lambda > (1-\beta)f(k) - \lambda \tag{A5}$$

for all k, and so

$$\left(\frac{\mathrm{d}k}{\mathrm{d}\lambda}\right)_{\mathrm{n}} > \left(\frac{\mathrm{d}k}{\mathrm{d}\lambda}\right)_{\mathrm{A}} \tag{A6}$$

for all k such that $\dot{\lambda} > 0$, i.e. for $k < \bar{k}_{\mathrm{A}}$ in fig. 10.2. On the other hand,

$$\left(\frac{\mathrm{d}k}{\mathrm{d}\lambda}\right)_{\mathrm{n}} < \left(\frac{\mathrm{d}k}{\mathrm{d}\lambda}\right)_{\mathrm{A}} \tag{A7}$$

for all k such that $\dot{\lambda}<0$, i.e. for $k>\bar{k}_A$ in fig. 10.2. Hence, at any point of intersection the curve nn' is steeper than AA' for $k<\bar{k}_A$, and AA' is steeper than nn' for $k>\bar{k}_A$. Given this information and the fact that $\bar{\lambda}_A>\bar{\lambda}_n$ (eq. (38)) it is clear that the curves nn' and AA' can never cross, as shown in fig. 10.2.

The slope of BB', the path followed by capitalism with monopsony capital, is found from (42)–(43) to be

$$\left(\frac{dk}{d\lambda}\right)_B=\frac{\gamma^{-\beta e}(1-\beta/\gamma)f(k)-1/\lambda}{\lambda(\rho-\gamma^{-\beta e}g(k))}. \tag{A8}$$

As γ increases from 1 to ∞, the function

$$Z(\gamma)=\gamma^{-\beta e}(1-\beta/\gamma)/(1-\beta) \tag{A9}$$

increases monotonically from 1 to asymptotically approach $1/(1-\beta)$, so it follows that

$$(1-\beta)f(k)<\gamma^{-\beta e}(1-\beta/\gamma)f(k). \tag{A10}$$

Furthermore,

$$\rho-\gamma^{-\beta e}g(k)>\rho-g(k). \tag{A11}$$

All of our subsequent remarks are made for the case $\gamma>\gamma^*$. In the case $\gamma<\gamma^*$ it does not seem possible to make any definite assertion about the relative slopes of AA' and BB'.

Setting

$$F_A=(1-\beta)f(k)-1/\lambda,$$

$$F_B=\gamma^{-\beta e}(1-\beta/\gamma)f(k)-1/\lambda,$$

$$G_A=\lambda(\rho-g(k))$$

and

$$G_B=\lambda(\rho-\gamma^{-\beta e}g(k)),$$

we have shown that

$$F_A<F_B \quad \text{and} \quad G_A<G_B.$$

For $k<\bar{k}_B$, when $\dot{k}>0$ and $\dot{\lambda}<0$ and therefore F_A, $F_B>0$ and $G_A, G_B<0$, it follows that at an intersection point of AA' and BB'

$$\left(\frac{dk}{d\lambda}\right)_B<\left(\frac{dk}{d\lambda}\right)_A.$$

For $k > \bar{k}_{A}$, when $\dot{k} < 0$ and $\dot{\lambda} > 0$ and therefore F_{A}, $F_{B} < 0$ and G_{A}, $G_{B} > 0$, it follows that at an intersection point of AA' and BB'

$$\left(\frac{\mathrm{d}k}{\mathrm{d}\lambda}\right)_{A} < \left(\frac{\mathrm{d}k}{\mathrm{d}\lambda}\right)_{B}.$$

These facts, together with the fact (under the assumption $\gamma > \gamma^{*}$) that $\bar{\lambda}_{A} > \bar{\lambda}_{B}$, indicate that AA' and BB' do not cross.

References

Chase, E.S. (1967) "Leisure and Consumption", in: K. Shell, ed., *Essays on the Theory of Optimal Economic Growth* (M.I.T. Press).

Chiarella, C. (1980) Internal Report, New South Wales Institute of Technology.

Dirickx, Y.M.I. and M.R. Sertel (1978) "Capitalism, Communism and Labor Management in a Nutshell under Constant Returns to Scale", European Institute for Advanced Studies in Management, Working Paper 78-1.

Rockafellar, R.T. (1976) "Saddle Points of Hamiltonian Systems in Convex Lagrange Problems Having a Nonzero Discount Rate", *Journal of Economic Theory*.

APPENDIX

Characterizing cooperative solutions to enterprise design problems*

PAUL R. KLEINDORFER and MURAT R. SERTEL

The purpose of this appendix is to provide a simple characterization of the solutions to a class of vector maximization problems which arise in applying cooperative game theory to organizational design problems.

We assume (as in most of the chapters in this volume) a group of agents $N=\{0,1,\ldots,n\}$, equipped with real-valued utility functions $u_i: X\times\mathfrak{R}\to\mathfrak{R}$ $(i\in N)$, defined on some (behavior) space X and the real line $\mathfrak{R}$. Critical to the result below is our assumption that each u_i is of the separable form:

$$u_i(x,r)=w_i(x)+r \qquad (i\in N, (x,r)\in X\times\mathfrak{R}), \tag{1}$$

where $w_i: X\to\mathfrak{R}$ is a real-valued function.

Denote by Δ a non-empty set of "designs" and let $\underline{x}:\Delta\to X$ and $\underline{r}_i:\Delta\to\mathfrak{R}$ $(i\in N)$ be mappings, from which we define the functions $\underline{u}_i:\Delta\to\mathfrak{R}$ through

$$\underline{u}_i(\delta)=u_i(\underline{x}(\delta),\underline{r}_i(\delta))=w_i(\underline{x}(\delta))+\underline{r}_i(\delta) \qquad (i\in N, \delta\in\Delta). \tag{2}$$

A typical interpretation of the above constructs would be that of the enterprise design problem as defined in, for example, Kleindorfer and Sertel (1976b), with participants N, collective behavior space X and equilibrium behavior $\underline{x}(\delta)$, where δ is the enterprise design (e.g. the particular incentive scheme implemented). In this framework, $\underline{u}_i(\delta)$ would represent the utility level achieved at equilibrium by agent $i\in N$.

Our interest here is to characterize the design $\delta_M\in\Delta$ which would be chosen by any given coalition $M\subset N$ if this coalition acts cooperatively in

*This is extracted in large measure from Kleindorfer and Sertel (1978), which is itself a revision of Kleindorfer and Sertel (1976a).

choosing the design and if lump-sum transfers of income are allowed among all agents $i \in N$. We show that, for every design coalition $M \subset N$, the additively separable form of the utility functions $u_i(x, r)$ leads members of M to select a design $\delta \in \Delta$ which maximizes the sum $\Sigma_N \underline{u}_i(\delta)$. Thus, when lump-sum transfers of income are possible, a simple scalar maximization problem characterizes the cooperative solution to the problem of finding a Pareto-efficient design $\delta \in \Delta$ maximizing the benefits accruing to any given coalition. (A similar result is proved in Groves, 1978.)

A1. Notation. Given any design $\delta \in \Delta$, denote $T(\delta) = \{t \in \mathfrak{R}^{n+1} \mid \Sigma_{i=0}^{n} t_i = 0,\ u_i(\underline{x}_i(\delta), \underline{r}_i(\delta) + t_i) \geqslant W_i$, for all $i \in N\}$, i.e. using (2),

$$T(\delta) = \left\{ t \in \mathfrak{R}^{n+1} \,\middle|\, \sum_{i=0}^{n} t_i = 0,\ \underline{u}_i(\delta) + t_i \geqslant W_i, \text{ for all } i \in N \right\}, \tag{3}$$

where $\{W_i \mid i \in N\}$ are given real numbers. An element $t \in T(\delta)$ will be called a feasible lump-sum *transfer* of income at δ among the agent of Ω.

A typical coordinate t_i of a transfer $t \in \mathfrak{R}^{n+1}$ is to be interpreted as a net payment of income *to* agent i in lump-sum fashion, i.e. independently of x. The feasibility of such a transfer for an agent $i \in N$ amounts to its making the agent no worse off than he would be in alternative employment, which is assumed to yield the reservation utility level $\underline{u}_i = W_i$. Although we need not formally constrain W_i in any way for the results that follow, it would be natural to expect $W_i \geqslant \sup\{w_i(x) \mid x \in X\}$, which represents the maximum utility level attainable by an agent when he receives no compensation ($r_i = 0$). When $X \subset \mathfrak{R}^{n+1}$ and w_i depends on $x = (x_0, x_1, \ldots, x_n)$ only through x_i (which could then be viewed as agent i's behavior) then $\sup\{w_i(x) \mid x \in X\}$ represents the utility level achievable by agent i if he quits the personnel N and maximizes w_i independently. We may note that $\underline{u}_i + t_i \geqslant \sup w_i$ also implies the desirable feasibility condition that, at equilibrium, $r_i + t_i \geqslant 0$, i.e. that the net lump-sum payment $-t_i$ by the agent at equilibrium not exceed the agent's income r_i from the enterprise [$w_i + r_i + t_i = \underline{u}_i + t_i \geqslant \sup w_i$ gives $r_i + t_i \geqslant \sup w_i - w_i \geqslant 0$]. For example, if agent 0 bears the costs $-w_0$, the feasibility of t is a matter of $-t_0$ not exceeding the agent's net income $u_0 = w_0 + r_0$ after deducting $-w_0$ from the agent's gross income r_0 from the enterprise.

A2. Definition. Let $\{\underline{u}_i \mid i \in N\}$ and Δ be as defined above and let $M \subset N$. The design problem with lump-sum transfers for M w.r.t. Δ is the vector maximization problem:

$$\underset{\delta \in \Delta,\, t \in T(\delta)}{\text{maximize}} \; \{u_i(\underline{x}(\delta), \underline{r}_i(\delta) + t_i)\}_{i \in M}. \tag{4}$$

In the chapters in this volume the design set typically represents a set of feasible incentive solutions and the enterprise design takes two typical points of view: that of the capitalist (the case $M = \{0\}$) and that of the workers (the case $M = N \setminus \{0\}$). The first corresponds to profit maximization while the latter case corresponds to the design of labor-managed enterprises.

The next theorem reformulates the vector maximization problem with transfers defined in definition A2 in terms of a technically more tractable scalar maximization problem.

A3. Lemma (characterization). Let $M \subset N$ and Δ be nonempty. Then the design problem with lump-sum transfers from M w.r.t. Δ is solved precisely by the pairs (δ^*, t^*) in which δ^* solves the problem

$$\underset{\delta \in \Delta}{\text{maximize}} \; \sum_{i=0}^{n} u_i(\underline{x}(\delta), \underline{r}_i(\delta)) \tag{5}$$

and t^* belongs to the set $T_M(\delta^*)$, defined for any $\delta \in \underline{\Delta}(\Omega)$ by

$$T_M(\delta) = \{t \in T(\delta) \mid \underline{u}_i + t_i = W_i, \text{ for all } i \in N \setminus M\}, \tag{6}$$

where

$$\underline{u}_i = u_i(\underline{x}(\delta), \underline{r}_i(\delta)) \qquad (i \in N). \tag{7}$$

N.B. Thus, $T_M(\delta)$ consists of the transfers in $T(\delta)$ giving the minimal lump-sum amounts to agents in $N \setminus M$, exhaustively distributing the remaining feasible sum $\Sigma_M t_i$ amongst the agents $i \in M$ in one or another way.

Proof. Supposing $\delta^* = (r^*, x^*)$ solves (5), we first show that (δ^*, t^*) solves the Ω-enterprise design problem with transfers for M w.r.t. Δ, so long as $t^* \in T_M(\delta^*)$. Take any $t^* \in T_M(\delta^*)$ and any (δ, t) with $\delta \in \Delta$ and $t \in T(\Delta)$, and suppose

$$\underline{u}_i + t_i \geqslant \underline{u}_i^* + t_i^* \qquad (i \in M) \tag{8}$$

with

$$\underline{u}_j + t_j > \underline{u}_j^* + t_j^* \tag{9}$$

for some $j \in M$, where

$$\underline{u}_i^* = u_i(\underline{x}(\delta^*), \underline{r}_i(\delta)) \qquad (i \in N). \tag{10}$$

Then, by definition of T and T_M (see notation A1 and (6), respectively)

$$\underline{u}_i + t_i \geqslant \underline{u}_i^* + t_i^* \qquad (i \in N \setminus M), \tag{11}$$

so that, from (8)–(10) we have directly

$$\sum_{i=0}^{n} \underline{u}_i + \sum_{i=0}^{n} t_i > \sum_{i=0}^{n} \underline{u}_i^* + \sum_{i=0}^{n} t_i^*. \tag{12}$$

As $\Sigma t_i = \Sigma t_i^* = 0$, we then have

$$\sum_{i=0}^{n} \underline{u}_i > \sum_{i=0}^{n} \underline{u}_i^*, \tag{13}$$

contradicting that δ^* solves (5). Thus, no (δ, t) with $\delta \in \Delta$ and $t \in T(\delta)$ satisfies (8) and (9), showing that, for every δ^* solving (5) and any $t^* \in T_M(\delta^*)$, (δ^*, t^*) solves the design problem with transfers for M w.r.t. Δ.

Now suppose $(\delta, \bar{t})$ solves the design problem with transfers for M w.r.t. Δ. Then, clearly, $t \in T_M(\delta)$, leaving us to show only that δ solves (5). To that end, suppose δ does not solve (5), i.e. that using the abbreviations (7) and (11),

$$\sum_{i=0}^{n} \underline{u}_i^* > \sum_{i=0}^{n} \underline{u}_i \tag{14}$$

for some $\delta^* \in \underline{\Delta}$. Defining the transfer $t \in T(\delta^*)$ by

$$\hat{t}_i = \underline{u}_i + t_i - \underline{u}_i^* \qquad (i \in M \setminus \{0\}), \tag{15}$$

$$\hat{t}_i = W_i - \underline{u}_i^* \qquad (i \in N \setminus (M \cup \{0\}) \tag{16}$$

and

$$\hat{t}_0 = -\sum_{i=1}^{n} \hat{t}_i, \tag{17}$$

we first note that, since $t \in T(\delta)$, $u_i + t_i \geqslant W_i$, so (15) and (16) directly give $u_i^* + \hat{t}_i \geqslant W_i$ $(i \in N \setminus \{0\})$. Thus, to see that $t \in T(\delta^*)$, it remains only to see that $u_0^* + \hat{t}_0 \geqslant W_0$. For notational convenience, denote $M_0 = M \setminus \{0\}$ and $M^0 = N \setminus (M \cup \{0\})$. Now from (15) and (17) we observe that

$$\begin{aligned} \underline{u}_0^* + \hat{t}_0 &= \underline{u}_0^* - \sum_{i=1}^{n} t_i \\ &= \underline{u}_0^* + \sum_{M_0} (\underline{u}_i^* - \underline{u}_i) - \sum_{M_0} t_i - \sum_{M^0} \hat{t}_i, \end{aligned} \tag{18}$$

and (16) together with the fact that $t \in T(\delta)$ yields

$$\underline{u}_i^* + \hat{t}_i = W_i \leqslant \underline{u}_i + t_i \qquad (i \in M^0), \tag{19}$$

which, together with (18), then gives

$$\underline{u}_0^* + \hat{t}_0 \geqslant \underline{u}_0^* + \sum_{i=1}^{n} (\underline{u}_i^* - \underline{u}_i) - \sum_{i=1}^{n} t_i, \tag{20}$$

while, from $t \in T(\delta)$, we have

$$-\sum_{i=1}^{n} t_i = t_0 \geqslant -\underline{u}_0 + W_0, \tag{21}$$

combining with (20) to yield

$$\underline{u}_0^* + \hat{t}_0 - W_0 \geqslant \sum_{i=0}^{n} (\underline{u}_i^* - \underline{u}_i), \tag{22}$$

the r.h.s. of which is positive in view of (14), showing that

$$u_0^* + \hat{t}_0 - W_0 > 0 \tag{23}$$

and, thus, that $\hat{t} \in T(\delta^*)$.

We now consider two cases: $0 \in N \setminus M$ and $0 \in M$. If $0 \in N \setminus M$, define the transfer t^* by

$$t_i^* = \begin{cases} -\underline{u}_0^* + W_0, & \text{if } i = 0, \\ \hat{t}_i + (u_0^* + \hat{t}_0 - W_0)/m, & \text{if } i \in M, \\ \hat{t}_i, & \text{if } i \in M^0, \end{cases} \tag{24}$$

where m is the cardinality of M. Then $t^* \in T(\delta^*)$.

[$\Sigma_{i=0}^{n} t_i^* = \Sigma_{i=0}^{n} \hat{t}_i = 0$ is immediate; $\underline{u}_0^* + t_0^* \geqslant W_0$ holds by (24); $u_i^* + t_i^* \geqslant W_i$ $(i \in N)$ follows from $t \in T(\delta^*)$ and the fact (see (23)) that $t_i^* \geqslant \hat{t}_i$ $(i \in N)$.] Moreover, (23) and (24) imply $t_i^* \geqslant \hat{t}_i$ for all $i \in M$; so, from (15) we have

$$\underline{u}_i^* + t_i^* > \underline{u}_i + t_i \qquad (i \in M) \tag{25}$$

when $0 \in N \setminus M$, contradicting the fact that (δ, t) is a Pareto solution to the design problem with transfers for M w.r.t. Δ. Similarly, if $0 \in M$, we let $t_i^* = \hat{t}_i$, $i \in N \setminus \{0\}$, and use (20) and (21) to obtain

$$(\underline{u}_0^* + \underline{t}_0^*) - (\underline{u}_0 + \underline{t}_0) \geqslant \sum_{i=0}^{n} (\underline{u}_i^* - \underline{u}_i), \tag{26}$$

the r.h.s. of which is positive by (14). From this and (15) we see again that

(δ, t) cannot be a solution to the indicated design problem. In any case, (14) then leads to a contradiction, and so for every solution (δ, t) to the design problem, δ solves (5). This completes the proof. □

The above result characterizes the cooperative solution to the game $\{\underline{u}_i, i \in N; \Delta\}$ when lump-sum transfers can be effected among all agents $i \in N$ and when the size of these transfers is determined by the design coalition M. Subject to achieving reservation utility levels for all $i \in N$, the question naturally arises as to how this result might change if only members of M can transfer income with one another, while agents in $N \setminus M$ cannot. Following the above arguments, it is readily established that the optimal design δ_M corresponding to this is the solution to the constrained optimization problem:

$$\max_{\delta \in \Delta} \sum_{i \in M} \underline{u}_i(\delta) \tag{27}$$

subject to

$$\underline{u}_i(\delta) \geqslant W_i \qquad (i \in N \setminus M). \tag{28}$$

Thus, the additively separable utility functions assumed here lead to quite simple characterizations of cooperative design problems for arbitrary coalitions and under various assumptions on the nature of the ex post income transfers allowed.

References

Groves, T. (1978) "Efficient Collective Choice with Compensation", Technical Report No. 258, The Institute for Mathematical Studies in the Social Sciences, Stanford.

Kleindorfer, P.R. and M.R. Sertel (1976a) "Optimal Design of Enterprises Through Incentives", Mimeo, International Institute of Management, West Berlin.

Kleindorfer, P.R. and M.R. Sertel (1976b) "Equilibrium Analysis of Sharecropping", IIM-Preprint Series I-76-33, International Institute of Management, West Berlin. (See Chapter 6 of this book.)

Kleindorfer, P.R. and M.R. Sertel (1978) "Pre-enterprises and Enterprises", IIM-Preprint Series DP-78-38, International Institute of Management, West Berlin.

Index